THE SPATIAL MARKET PROCESS

ADVANCES IN AUSTRIAN ECONOMICS

Series Editors: Roger Koppl and Steve Horwitz

Recent Volumes:

Volume 6: Austrian Economics and Entrepreneurial Studies – Edited by Roger Koppl

Volume 7: Evolutionary Psychology and Economic Theory – Edited by Roger Koppl

Volume 8: The Dynamics of Intervention: Regulation and Redistribution in the Mixed Economy – Edited by P. Kurrild-Klitgaard

Volume 9: The Cognitive Revolution in Economic Science – Edited by Elisabeth Krecké, Carine Krecké and Roger Koppl

Volume 10: The Evolution of Consumption: Theories and Policy – Edited by Marina Bianchi

Volume 11: Explorations in Austrian Economics – Edited by Roger Koppl

Volume 12: Unexplored Dimensions: Karl Menger on Economics and Philosophy (1923–1938) – Edited by Giandomenica Becchio

Volume 13: The Social Science of Hayek's 'The Sensory Order' – Edited by William N. Butos

Volume 14: What is so Austrian About Austrian Economics? – Edited by Roger Koppl, Steven Horwitz and Pierre Desrochers

Volume 15: Hayek in Mind: Hayek's Philosophical Psychology – Edited by Leslie Marsh

ADVANCES IN AUSTRIAN ECONOMICS VOLUME 16

THE SPATIAL MARKET PROCESS

EDITED BY

DAVID EMANUEL ANDERSSON
Institute of Public Affairs Management, National Sun Yat-sen University, Taiwan

Emerald

United Kingdom – North America – Japan
India – Malaysia – China

Emerald Group Publishing Limited
Howard House, Wagon Lane, Bingley BD16 1WA, UK

First edition 2012

British Library Cataloguing in Publication Data
A catalogue record for this book is available from the British Library

ISBN: 978-1-78190-006-2
ISSN: 1529-2134 (Series)

CONTENTS

PART III: INSTITUTIONS AND SPATIAL ORDER

PART IV: MARKETS, INVESTMENTS, AND SPACE

LIST OF CONTRIBUTORS

Åke E. Andersson	Department of Economics, Finance and Statistics, Jönköping International Business School, Jönköping, Sweden
David Emanuel Andersson	Institute of Public Affairs Management, National Sun Yat-sen University, Kaohsiung, Taiwan
Pierre Desrochers	Department of Geography, University of Toronto Mississauga, Mississauga, ON, Canada
Johan E. Eklund	Department of Economics, Finance and Statistics, Jönköping International Business School, Jönköping, Sweden
Fred E. Foldvary	Leavey School of Business, Santa Clara University, Santa Clara, CA, USA
Peter Gordon	Sol Price School of Public Policy, University of Southern California, Los Angeles, CA, USA
Randall G. Holcombe	Department of Economics, Florida State University, Tallahassee, FL, USA
Sanford Ikeda	Purchase College, State University of New York, Purchase, New York, NY, USA
Lawrence W. C. Lai	Department of Real Estate and Construction, University of Hong Kong, Hong Kong S.A.R., China
Jan Lambooy	Section of Economic Geography, Faculty of Geosciences, Utrecht University, Utrecht, The Netherlands

Johan P. Larsson — Department of Economics, Finance and Statistics, Jönköping International Business School, Jönköping, Sweden

Samuli Leppälä — Department of Economics, University of Turku, Turku, Finland

Frank T. Lorne — School of Management, New York Institute of Technology, Vancouver, British Columbia, Canada

Stefano Moroni — Department of Architecture and Planning, Politecnico di Milano, Milan, Italy

Johanna Palmberg — Department of Economics, Finance and Statistics, Jönköping International Business School, Jönköping, Sweden and The Ratio Institute Stockholm, Sweden

Jason Potts — School of Economics & Finance, Royal Melbourne Institute of Technology, Melbourne, Australia and CCI, Queensland University of Technology, Brisbane, Australia

Erik Stam — Utrecht University School of Economics, Utrecht, The Netherlands

James A. Taylor — Jones Lang LaSalle, Beijing, China

THE SPATIAL MARKET PROCESS

> There is beyond question a body of very important but unorganized knowledge which cannot possibly be called scientific in the sense of knowledge of general rules: the knowledge of the particular circumstances of time and place. (Friedrich Hayek)

In what is perhaps the best-known article in the history of the Austrian school, Friedrich Hayek (1945) asserts that market prices distill and thus reflect the unique local knowledge of a multitude of individuals, each of whom resides and works in a particular place. Because only an autonomously acting individual can take advantage of her unique creativity, skills, and personal connections to others, centralization of economic decision-making guarantees that much useful local knowledge is irretrievably lost. It is *impossible* to communicate the totality of all local entrepreneurial ideas and tacit knowledge to a small group of top-down planners; their cognitive limitations guarantee substandard economic performance (Hayek, 1952). We should therefore not be surprised that it is valuable to possess "knowledge of people, of local conditions, and special circumstances" (Hayek, 1945, p. 522).

Given the great number of citations to Hayek (1945) in the general economics literature, it would require no great stretch of the imagination to imagine that Hayek – and by extension the Austrian school – had set in motion a way of theorizing about economic phenomena that later gave rise to theories about knowledge spillovers, urbanization economies, and local social networks. But this was not to be. There are virtually no references to Hayek or any other Austrian economist in the spatial economics literature prior to the year 2000. The lack of interest in Austrian economics among spatial economists was reciprocated by a similar lack of interest in spatial economics among self-professed Austrians. To my knowledge, Pierre Desrochers (1998) wrote the first explicitly Austrian contribution that deals exclusively with spatial economic phenomena.

In spite of this historical disconnect, Austrian ideas have entered the spatial economics, economic geography, and urban planning literatures because of the close parallels between the influential ideas of the urbanist Jane Jacobs and Austrian market process theory. While Jacobs (1961) does not refer to

Hayek or any other Austrian, her *Death and Life of Great American Cities* at times reads like an Austrian theory of urban planning:

> [N]obody, including the planning commission, is capable of comprehending places within the city other than in either generalized or fragmented fashion. ... They do not even have the means of gathering and comprehending the intimate, many-sided information required, partly because of their own unsuitable structural inadequacies in other departments. Here is an interesting thing about coordination both of information and of action in cities, and it is the crux of the matter: The principal coordination needed comes down to coordination among different services within localized places. This is at once the most difficult kind of coordination, and the most necessary. (Jacobs, 1961, quoted in Ikeda, 2006, p. 22)

With her emphases on (implicit) methodological individualism, the importance of local knowledge, and complex evolving orders, Jacobs provides a rich source of insights for those who wish to combine Austrian economic theory with a dynamic approach to agglomeration economies. Such a dynamic approach focuses on entrepreneurial processes rather than on idealized equilibrium states.

Unsurprisingly, both Hayek and Jacobs figure prominently in this volume. But they are far from the only influences. This book is a collection of 13 essays that address spatial aspects of the market process from refreshingly diverse approaches. They range from the extension of Austrian theory to spatial phenomena over hybrid combinations of ideas from distinct traditions to state-of-the-art spatial models that integrate Austrian concepts such as "roundaboutness" or entrepreneurial innovation.

Apart from Hayek and Jacobs, other seminal (Austrian and non-Austrian) thinkers that are invoked repeatedly by the chapter authors include Eugen von Böhm-Bawerk, Ronald Coase, Richard Florida, Israel Kirzner, Fritz Machlup, Joseph Schumpeter, and Knut Wicksell. In the following four sections of this introduction, I will give a brief guide to the most intriguing features of each chapter.

FOUNDATIONS

In "An Austrian Theory of Spatial Land," Fred E. Foldvary addresses the disregard of spatial issues in basic Austrian economic theory as formulated by Carl Menger (1871) and elaborated upon by Ludwig von Mises (1940). Foldvary shows that Johann Heinrich von Thünen (1826) and Henry George (1879/1884), in particular, serve to fill these gaps in the classical Austrian theory of the market process. Moreover, a theory that incorporates spatial land leads to the conclusion that Austrian business cycle theory is incomplete: The "malspeculation" that accompanies urbanization whenever capital and labor rather than land are the main sources of tax revenue will have to be added to the malinvestment that is caused by expansionary monetary policies.

Samuli Leppälä and Pierre Desrochers ("Regional Economic Analysis: The Case for Methodological Individualism") contend that the problem with mainstream spatial analysis is that it relies on theories and empirical studies that treat regions as if they were actors with holistic comparative advantages. Such methodological collectivism, they argue, lead to misleading analyses and erroneous conclusions. Consequently, the Austrian insistence on treating the individual as the analytical starting point would improve spatial theories, while empirical analyses would benefit from relying on observations of individual or household behavior rather than on regional aggregates that imitate nation-based macroeconomics.

In "Time, Space, and Capital," Åke E. Andersson presents an analysis that is much more grounded in the methodological apparatus of contemporary mainstream economics than most of the other chapters. He sees Vienna not as the source of a heterodox postwar paradigm, but rather as the source of most theoretical developments that have stood the test of time. In particular, the Austrian emphasis on the long run, the importance of the time dimension, and the insight that all goods are capital goods provide guidelines that help resolve otherwise intractable economic problems. These range from nonspatial problems such as the long-run sustainability of monetary policies (which according to Åke E. Andersson leads to "Wicksellian" recommendations) to ones at the core of spatial economics. His most important conclusion is that the durability of goods, transaction costs, and transport costs jointly determine the spatial allocation of resources as well as the total number of market competitors. While Åke E. Andersson shares the early Austrians' skepticism about the usefulness of general equilibrium models, he contends that modern "synergetic modeling" does not suffer from the same limitations.

ENTREPRENEURSHIP AND SPACE

The new field of evolutionary economic geography promises fertile ground for the application of Austrian economic theory, according to Erik Stam and Jan Lambooy ("Entrepreneurship, Knowledge, Space, and Place: Evolutionary Economic Geography Meets Austrian Economics"). Evolutionary economic geographers analyze regional economies as localized processes of innovation, feedback, and selection, rather than as local equilibria. Regions differ in their ability to foster innovation, since they host different industrial structures, cultures, and institutions. Distinct regional selection environments create localized path-dependent processes, since the price signals that reward or penalize firms may differ greatly among regions.

Stam and Lambooy argue that since evolutionary economic geography tends to disregard the role of the individual in economic development, Austrian theory serves as a complement. It does this by focusing on the prior personal knowledge of entrepreneurs, the dissemination of their local knowledge through the price system, and the role of institutions in shaping individuals' alertness to profit opportunities. At the same time, evolutionary economic geography may provide the most promising venue for extending Austrian theories in spatial directions, since both Austrian and evolutionary theories view human behavior as intrinsically creative and boundedly rational.

In "Entrepreneurship in Action Space," Sanford Ikeda proposes a novel connection between Austrian entrepreneurship theory and social network theory. He also links both theories to how the design of public spaces influences the creation and maintenance of social networks (cf. Jacobs, 1961). For entrepreneurship, "weak ties" to other people are the ones that really matter (Granovetter, 1973), since it is only through such ties that individuals are likely to make the kind of surprising discoveries that occasionally cause entrepreneurial profits. When ties are strong, it usually means that the individuals involved know all the same people and therefore have a great deal of knowledge and information in common. One of the main conclusions of Ikeda's chapter is that spatial locations with high Jacobs Density (Gordon & Ikeda, 2011) are more conducive to network creation and entrepreneurship, since such locations are particularly likely to generate serendipitous discoveries.

Lawrence W. C. Lai and Frank T. Lorne ("Schumpeterian Innovations, the Coase Theorem, and Sustainable Development: A Hong Kong Case Study of Bus Innovations") reach what is perhaps the most controversial conclusion in this volume. They contend that two privately run but price-regulated duopolistic firms that provide public transport services can have sufficient incentives to engage in substantial amounts of profit-seeking innovation, whereby they improve service quality and cut costs. While the ban on price competition and regulatory barriers to entry would seem to impede such innovation to lower-than-necessary levels, Lai and Lorne contend that such regulation may still be desirable if various sustainability issues – such as air quality standards – impose tight constraints on acceptable economic behavior.

INSTITUTIONS AND SPATIAL ORDER

One of Hayek's most influential contentions was that the market is best understood as a "spontaneous order." Thus, Hayek (1973) claims that the market exhibits orderly structural features, in spite of not being designed by anyone in particular. Peter Gordon ("Spontaneous Cities") extends the notion of spontaneous order by arguing that the city is in itself the most important manifestation of a *spatial* spontaneous order.

While urban planners have been responsible for numerous monuments and infrastructural investments in cities around the world, the effects of spontaneous urban markets have been far greater. Gordon notes that North America, Western Europe, Australia, and Japan have all experienced similar suburbanization processes after World War II, despite widespread hostility to urban sprawl among urban planners. This is indicative of the way that bottom-up "spontaneous fill-in" trumps top-down development plans whenever individuals retain sufficient autonomy in their location choices.

In "The Rise and Fall of Agglomeration Economies," Randall G. Holcombe addresses urban development with the help of a theoretical apparatus that combines Austrian entrepreneurship theory and the public-choice notion of rent seeking. As city regions expand, the increasing concentration of people and economic activities give rise to agglomeration economies such as better accessibility to consumers, suppliers, and tacit knowledge. A big-city location engenders static and dynamic productivity benefits for big-city firms and households. But these same benefits enable interest groups to lobby politicians with the aim of redistributing a portion of the location-specific benefits with the help of political legislation. Sometimes they extract more than is actually available, as the rise and fall of Detroit and the Big Three illustrate.

James A. Taylor and I test Holcombe's prediction on domestic interstate migration flows in the United States after 2000. We use three indices of economic or overall freedom as our proxies for the overall political redistribution of private property rights at the state level. In addition, we use Richard Florida's (2002) State Creativity Index to address the average presence of agglomeration economies in each state. One key finding is that states that score high on freedom attract net inflows in all demographics. Another key finding is that agglomeration economies are attractive to the young and the highly educated rather than migrants in general. While our results are consistent with Holcombe's description of events, we additionally claim that competition between spatially delimited jurisdictions constitutes yet another spontaneous order; inter-jurisdictional flows of people and capital perform the same kind of function that revenue and cost flows perform in ordinary markets.

Stefano Moroni addresses two different types of unintended consequences in his chapter on land-use planning ("Land-Use Planning and the Question of Unintended Consequences"). The first type refers to all those consequences that are undesired or perverse from the planner's standpoint, while the second type refers to beneficial or virtuous consequences that the responsible individuals did not foresee. What is most important is that unintended perverse consequences are mostly associated with detailed top-down plans that aim at specific quantifiable patterns of outcomes, whereas the unintended beneficial consequences are mostly associated with general rules that regulate relationships among autonomous actors. Moroni's proposal is that urban planners give up traditional planning practice in favor of an "urban code of rules" that supports the spontaneous order of the urban market system.

MARKETS, INVESTMENTS, AND SPACE

Jason Potts ("Novelty-Bundling Markets") discusses the role of novelty-bundling markets in organizing the consumption of new experience goods of which consumers have little knowledge. His argument is that there is a type of producer that specializes in filtering and organizing choice in a way that helps consumers orient themselves in the face of a multitude of possible new experiences. In addition, this type of producer offers a choice environment that is in itself an experience good. Conventional neoclassical models treat the presence of bundlers of experience goods as a sign of market failure, whereas Potts argues that such models miss the point. Combining Austrian, evolutionary, and sociological approaches, he shows that "novelty-bundlers" provide valuable services for buyers who learn from their consumption. Such services, for example arts or music festivals, also benefit disproportionately from the knowledge externalities that typify urban environments.

Few industries are as spatially concentrated as the financial industry. This should come as no surprise, according to Johanna Palmberg ("Spatial

Concentration in the Financial Industry"). Rather than focusing on distribution costs or other traditional explanations, Palmberg pinpoints two factors as decisive for the relative spatial concentration of an industry. First, industries that make use of knowledge that is unusually private, specialized, and tacit tend to benefit disproportionately from agglomerations of human knowledge. Second, a fluid coordination environment makes it especially important to have access to up-to-the-minute specialized information, which also favors spatial concentration. Advanced financial services combine highly specialized tacit knowledge with a fluid coordination environment, which explains the extraordinary willingness to pay for locations in places such as Wall Street, the Square Mile, and Hong Kong Central.

Johan E. Eklund and Johan P. Larsson ("The Use of Knowledge in Investment Theory") argue that it is only through an Austrian understanding of knowledge as opposed to information (cf. Boettke, 2002) that one can explain the location choices of specialized investors. Using the concept of "knowledge conveyors" as elaborated by Fritz Machlup (1962), they distinguish between six different types of knowledge conveyors with different levels of creativity and tacit knowledge. Crucially, spatial proximity to higher-level knowledge conveyors is more valuable than proximity to lower-level ones. This makes investors in knowledge-intensive firms especially prone to locate near the recipients of their funding.

LOOKING AHEAD

The 13 chapters in this volume show both the depth and the diversity that result when one applies Austrian concepts and theories to spatial economic phenomena. And it is not only one or two Austrian contributions that help illuminate the spatial aspects of the market process. The chapters in this volume apply and develop Austrian notions as diverse as entrepreneurial alertness, methodological individualism, roundaboutness, spontaneous order, and tacit knowledge in ways that explicate spatial processes in novel ways. Austrian-influenced analyses give rise to several insights that are almost entirely overlooked in the established spatial economics, economic geography, and urban planning literatures. But unlike the Austrian analysis of time, the Austrian analysis of space is still in its early stages. It is my hope that this book will provide a starting point for a whole new field; one that sees the market as a process in both time *and* space.

ACKNOWLEDGMENTS

A number of people provided helpful comments and suggestions that influenced the contents of this book. In particular, I would like to thank Gus diZerega (Studies in Emergent Order), Laurent Dobuzinskis (Simon Fraser University), Daniel Halvarsson (Royal Institute of Technology), Steve Horwitz (St. Lawrence University), Dan Johansson (Ratio Institute), Roger Koppl (Farleigh Dickinson University), Peter Lewin (University of Texas at Dallas), Leslie Marsh (University of British Columbia), Charlotta Mellander (Jönköping International Business School), Gloria Zúñiga y Postigo (University of Texas at Arlington), and Daniel J. Smith (Troy University). I would also like to thank all the contributors for their varied insights, especially those who contributed anonymous referee reports as well as book chapters.

David Emanuel Andersson
Editor

REFERENCES

Boettke, P. J. (2002). Information and knowledge: Austrian economics in search of its uniqueness. *Review of Austrian Economics*, *15*(4), 263–274.

Desrochers, P. (1998). A geographical perspective on Austrian economics. *Quarterly Journal of Austrian Economics*, *1*(2), 63–83.

Florida, R. (2002). *The rise of the creative class*. New York, NY: Basic Books.

George, H. (1884). *Progress and poverty*. London: William Reeves.

Gordon, P., & Ikeda, S. (2011). Does density matter? In: D.E. Andersson, Å.E. Andersson & C. Mellander (Eds), *Handbook of creative cities*. Cheltenham, UK: Edward Elgar.

Granovetter, M. S. (1973). The strength of weak ties. *American Journal of Sociology*, *78*(6), 1360–1380.

Hayek, F. A. (1945). The use of knowledge in society. *American Economic Review*, *35*(4), 519–530.

Hayek, F. A. (1952). *The sensory order*. Chicago, IL: University of Chicago Press.

Hayek, F. A. (1973). *Law, legislation and liberty* (Vol. 1). Rules and Order. Chicago, IL: University of Chicago Press.

Ikeda, S. (2006). Jane Jacobs. *The Freeman*, *56*, 20–22.

Jacobs, J. (1961). *The death and life of great American cities*. New York, NY: Random House.

Machlup, F. (1962). *The production and distribution of knowledge in the United States*. Princeton, NJ: Princeton University Press.

Menger, C. (1871). *Grundsätze der Volkswirtschaftslehre*. Wien: Wilhelm Braumüller.

Mises, L. von (1940). *Nationalökonomie*. Genève: Editions Union.

Thünen, J. H. von (1826). *Der Isolierte Staat in Beziehung auf Landwirtschaft und Nationalökonomie*. Hamburg: Perthes.

PART I
FOUNDATIONS

AN AUSTRIAN THEORY OF SPATIAL LAND

Fred E. Foldvary

The Austrian school of economic thought has emphasized the role of capital goods, the interest rate, and market dynamics. Land and its rent have previously played a minor role. The Austrian business cycle theory has had a gap in its omission of the important role performed by land values in the economic boom and bust. The prevailing theory has emphasized "malinvestment" in capital goods, but has overlooked the related concept of "malspeculation" in site values. The omission of spatial land in Austrian economics has also resulted in a deficient discussion of public finance, including the implicit subsidies of land rent and land value, and the prevention of such subsidy by the use of land rent for public revenue, both in the private and government sectors.

The key questions addressed here are how Austrian theory applies to space, and in turn, how that application enhances both Austrian microeconomics and macroeconomics. The recognition of the importance of spatial land in market dynamics constitutes a significant advance. This chapter presents a general Austrian theory of economic space, incorporating also some theory from other schools, to include land as a vital element of Austrian theory.

The first section defines key terms and analyzes land as a factor of production. The second section discusses material land, including tangible natural resources such as water, minerals, and forests. The third section

The Spatial Market Process
Advances in Austrian Economics, Volume 16, 3–23

ISSN: 1529-2134/doi:10.1108/S1529-2134(2012)0000016004

applies the Austrian concept of praxeology to the rent of land. The fourth section analyzes location theory. The fifth section focuses on public revenue from land rent. The sixth section integrates the role of spatial land in the Austrian business cycle. The seventh section analyzes the general role of space in Austrian macroeconomics. The eighth section summarizes and concludes.

LAND AS A FACTOR OF PRODUCTION

Definitions

Classical economics recognizes three categories of inputs into production: land, labor, and capital goods. The three factors are also germane to Austrian economics.

"Economic nature" consists of everything apart from human action. After human beings alter a natural resource, it is no longer a part of economic nature. For example, oil in the ground is natural, but after it is extracted, it is no longer in economic nature. The molecules of oil remain the same, but the location and access to the oil are now altered, which makes the oil no longer economically natural.

"Economic land" is a complete synonym for economic nature. Thus, when water is drained from a site and replaced with soil and rocks, the improvements are made by human action, and are therefore not economic land. Economic land cannot be improved, since improvements are produced by human action.

"Economic land rent" is the economic yield of land, usually expressed as an annual amount. It is also called "ground rent" or "geo-rent" (Foldvary, 2005). The economic land rent can differ from the rental payment of a particular tenant to the landlord, since the economic rent is the maximum rent that a plot of land would generally obtain in a market.

A "good" is "an item that impacts a person" (Foldvary, 1998, p. 155). "Final goods" are those which directly provide utility, in contrast to intermediate goods that are used to produce other goods. Goods include services, "goods simultaneously produced and consumed" (Foldvary, 1998, p. 156). Economic texts often contain the term "goods and services" to emphasize that services are included, but by definition, goods include services. "Economic wealth" consists of produced goods with a positive market value. (When referring to "natural," "land," "rent," and "wealth" in this chapter, the "economic" qualifier is here included implicitly.)

Labor is human exertion engaged in the production of wealth. Labor includes human capital – the skills, knowledge, and training of workers that increases their productivity (Machlup, 1962). Labor also includes entrepreneurial exertion. Carl Menger (1871/1976, p. 172), founder of Austrian economics, stated that "[e]ntrepreneurial activity must definitely be counted as a category of labor services." The yield of labor is "wages," which for employee labor is generally a payment based on the marginal product of the labor, while for owners of firms and many entrepreneurs, it is a portion of the profit of the firm.

A "capital good" is wealth that has been produced but not yet consumed. Land is therefore distinct from capital goods. Capital goods can also be referred to as tools, such as machines, buildings, and inventory, but land is also a tool. Capital goods include intangible items such as written knowledge as well as reputation. Capital goods are generally subject to depreciation, a loss of value due to wearing out and obsolescence, although it is possible for a capital good to retain its value.

Knowledge is part of both human capital (hence labor) and of capital goods. While human capital is tangible at the molecular level of brain structures, for economics, human knowledge is treatable as intangible, while the knowledge embedded in capital goods is usually tangible. Software, for example, exists in tangible form in codes that are written on media such as paper or computer disks. (Godin, 2008, has a classification of knowledge into tangible and intangible divisions.)

The yield of capital goods can be designated a "capital yield." The yield consists of depreciation and the implicit interest on the non-depreciated portion of value.

"Consumer goods" are those that are typically bought by households, in contrast to producer goods. As a factor of production, there is no economic distinction between producer and consumer goods. An automobile owned by a household for its own use is just as much a capital good as a car owned by a rental firm. All goods are capital goods until depreciated by consumption.

The term "capital" can mean capital goods, financial assets, and human capital. To avoid ambiguity, the term "capital" will not be used by itself in this chapter; instead, the text uses the specific terms "capital goods," "financial capital," and "human capital."

Types of Land

Land can be divided among several categories. The land that has been most relevant to economics is the three-dimensional space surrounding the earth.

Within some given boundary, the amount of spatial land is fixed. The alterations of the materials in space are capital goods, so no new land can be produced.

The "supply of spatial land" has two meanings. One is the amount of spatial land that exists within some boundary. The second meaning is the amount of space that is offered for sale at some moment in time. The first meaning will be implied in the term "supply of land" unless "offer supply" is used.

Material land consists of water, minerals, soil, and fuel sources in the ground as provided by nature. Material land becomes depleted when extracted, and converted to capital goods. Material land can be a fixed resource, whose supply cannot increase, or a renewable resource such as water in lakes and streams. Wildlife is a material natural resource that is renewable unless a species or ecosystem is driven toward extinction.

The electromagnetic spectrum is also a natural resource. Frequencies used for communication are fixed and scarce. Solar radiation enters the earth as a free good but becomes a scarce good in populated locations as it makes locations inhabitable and productive. Spatial land also obtains value from the plant growth and climate provided by the sun, as was recognized by Faustmann (1849) for forests.

Land versus Other Factors

Land is distinct from capital goods in that it is not produced by human action. Carl Menger (1871/1976, pp. 165–166) recognized this distinction: "A widespread school of economists has recognized correctly that the value of land cannot validly be traced back to labor or to the services of capital." This widespread school was evidently the classical school of Adam Smith and David Ricardo as well as of the German land economist Johann Heinrich von Thünen (cf. the fourth section).

Menger added (*ibid.*, p. 169) that while the laws of economics apply to land just as they do to labor and capital goods, the "existence of the special characteristics that land and the services of land, as well as many other kinds of goods, exhibit is by no means denied. In any country, land is usually available only in quantities that cannot be easily increased; it is fixed as to situation; and it has an extraordinary variety of grades. All the peculiarities of value phenomena we are able to observe in the case of land and the services of land can be traced back to these three factors."

Since capital goods are in turn produced by land, labor, and capital goods, the ultimate and original factors are land and labor. In one sense, human beings are "natural" when born, but people are the subject of social sciences as the acting beings, and although in a sense human beings are produced, they are self-determining actors in contrast to land and capital goods being the objects to which human action is applied.

Subjective Values

While neoclassical economics acknowledges that values are subjective, the Austrian school places greater centrality on subjectivity. The value of spatial land is subjective; land such as a backyard can be of direct use, in which case its market rent or purchase price is based on the importance that people place on such use. Land can also be what Austrian theory calls a "higher-order good," which is used as a factor in the production of final goods, in which case its value derives from its contribution to the final output. Since the value of that output is subjective, ultimately the value of all land derives from subjective values. There is no inherent or intrinsic value in land.

Derived Demand

The value of the factors of production derives from the value of the products, or in the case of spatial land, either the value of the direct use of the site or the value of the final goods. The value of labor is likewise derived, as is the value of the capital goods used to produce the final goods.

The Marginal Utility and Marginal Product of Land

"Utility" is the importance people place on goods, and the satisfaction derived from their use. Marginal utility is the gain in utility from one more item, holding all other items constant. In neoclassical theory, marginal utility is treated mathematically (such as with derivatives). Austrian theory treats utility as equivalent to ordinal preferences. In either theory, the market price of goods is based on the marginal rather than the total utility. The classic case is water, which has many uses, for which the marginal utility is for the least important use, the more important uses having been fulfilled. The total utility of water is high, but the marginal utility, such as a gallon used to wash a car, is relatively low, and the price people are willing to pay for another gallon for car wash – water is thus low.

For land used in production, the marginal product is the contribution of extra land to the value of the output, holding other factors constant. For example, suppose a farmer obtain one more hectare of land and uses the same amount of labor and capital goods to produce crops. If the added land would raise the value of the output by $1,000 per year, that sum sets the rent of that site, if that is its best use.

After some amount, the marginal products of factors decline, extra amounts contributing ever less to output. In general, the factors are hired until their marginal products equal the price (including wages and rent). Therefore the average product value (the total value of the output divided by the number of input units) can be higher than the marginal product, creating a surplus beyond the costs of labor and capital goods. In competitive industries, the owners only make normal returns on investment, as competition will bring entry if there are profits greater than normal. So with neither the firm owners nor labor getting the surplus, it goes to the only factor left, which is land. Much of the surplus from production is thus absorbed as spatial rent.

THE RENT OF MATERIAL NATURAL RESOURCES

Economic rent being the remaining revenue after subtracting all normal costs of production, there is economic rent in the presence of underground material resources such as water, oil, and substances that are mined (hence, minerals). The economic rent can be observed ex ante as the payment made to lease a location to extract the resources, and in principle by the monopoly profit of an operation – the economic profit left after subtracting the explicit and implicit costs from revenue, and after subtracting the profits due to entrepreneurship.

The theory of the rent of forestland, in conjunction with the timing of tree harvesting, was developed by the German economist Martin Faustmann (1849, 1968), who derived the formula for the present value of income from forest rotation. The rotation problem is the decision of when to harvest the forest. The present value formula (Brazee, 2007, p. 259) is

$$P = \frac{e^{(-rT)} v f(T) - C}{1 - e^{(-rT)}} \tag{1}$$

where P is the present value; T is the harvest age; v is the stumpage value, $f(T)$ is the amount of timber (stumpage) at T; r is the discount rate; and C is the stand regeneration cost. The theorem states that the optimal time to cut the forest is when the time rate of change of its value is equal to the interest rate on the value of the trees and site rent. As Gaffney (2010, p. 3) put it, "his answer was, when it stops growing fast enough to earn interest on its own embodied capital, plus rent on the land underneath it". Bertil Ohlin (1921/1995) derived the solution much later, but, as stated by Gaffney (p. 4), "never consulted the forestry literature to discover Faustmann had scooped him by 70 years."

This model assumes that all the variables are known and constant, and that there are no credit constraints. Dynamic optimization models can enhance the Faustmann concept, although the uncertainty of the future gives scope to entrepreneurial speculations, decisions, and profits.

THE PRAXEOLOGICAL ORIGIN OF LAND RENT

Both Carl Menger (1871/1976) and Ludwig von Mises (1949/1963), along with others in the Austrian school, derived pure or universal theory using the axiomatic deductive method. The method begins with premises that are based on inductive logic and generalizations that have wide – even universal – agreement (see Foldvary (2011, pp. 5–6) for a listing of the axioms of economic theory). Mises called the deductive theory of social science "praxeology," of which pure economic theory is a subset.

The pure theory of space and its rent is thus derived from axioms and concludes with prepositions that apply universally, regardless of culture, time, or place. The premises of the pure theory of economic space include scarcity, the existence of lands of various quality, diminishing returns from the expansion of a variable when other variables are fixed, unlimited human desires, subjective values, diminishing marginal utility, economizing (maximizing benefits or minimizing costs), time preference (present day goods are generally preferred to those in the future), and the uncertainty of the future. Mises used as a foundational premise "human action," by which persons economize in the use of means in their purposeful pursuit of ends, which are subjectively ranked by degrees of importance.

Scarce resources generate market prices, and so the scarcity of land in some locations generates the rent of land. Time preference generates a rate of interest which becomes the rate at which streams of income become capitalized into asset values; hence the price of land is a function of the rent and the rate of interest. The tapping of the rent for public revenue capitalizes land value down just as does a higher rate of interest.

Because land of a particular quality is fixed in supply, then when it is scarce, the positive externalities of the neighborhood generate land rent, while negative externalities reduce land rent. Unlike the economic profits of labor and capital goods, the supply cannot expand, and so the rent is an economic profit and a surplus that remains.

The Classical Margin of Production

In classical theory – as developed by Adam Smith and David Ricardo (1817/1963) – land can be divided into areas of various qualities, and the least productive land in use is called "the margin of production." Von Thünen extended this analysis to include differences in locations having differing transport costs, thus causing differences in rent.

Labor being mobile, the general wage level for an economy is set by the wage at the margin. The value of output minus the costs of labor and capital goods constitutes the land rent surplus. Economic progress (i.e., better technology and investment in capital goods and human capital) can generate not only higher wages but also greater rent, and rent tends to absorb much of the gains from economic progress. As production moves to less productive margins, wages fall and rent rises.

Public works and civic services that make locations more productive and attractive generate greater rent, which is capitalized into higher land value. If landowners do not pay back this value received, in effect they get subsidized. Since most of current taxation falls on labor and capital goods, the land value subsidy is the greatest of all subsidies. In the United States, land ownership receives special tax reductions, including income tax deductions for mortgage interest and property taxes, tax exemptions from capital gains, tax-free property exchanges, and depreciation on buildings.

If such works and services were provided by private enterprise, landowners would have to pay for them out of their explicit or implicit rental income. The provision by government at the expense of those other than landowners provides a subsidy that increases inequality, shifts taxation to sources with deadweight losses, and results in land value booms and busts.

The subsidy to land value creates incentives for malspeculation, a counterpart to the Austrian concept of malinvestment. Malspeculation occurs when there is excessive speculation due to subsidies, which ends in a collapse of asset values. Malspeculation is discussed below in the context of business cycles.

Rent in the Evenly Rotating Economy

In *Human Action* (1949), Ludwig von Mises introduces the model of the evenly rotating economy (ERE) (Schumpeter (1912/1934) had also analyzed a static circular flow that lacked entrepreneurial profit). Imagine an economy in which the exact same patterns repeat themselves continuously. There is no population growth, innovation, or other deviation from the cycle of eternal recurrence. The future is known with certainty, and so in this cyclical equilibrium, there is no entrepreneurship. Indeed, the purpose of the model is to explain the origin of entrepreneurship.

In the ERE, factor incomes are constant: wages, rents, and capital yields do not change. There is no change in land use, interest rates, or expectations; hence there is no speculation, and thus no malspeculation. There are therefore no booms and busts. Land rent captures the surplus, and the price of land equals the rent divided by the sum of the interest and tax rates.

Change and entrepreneurship dislodge the ERE equilibrium. This would not be the equilibrating arbitrage entrepreneurship described by Israel Kirzner (1992), but the creative destruction, actually creative reconstruction, analyzed by Joseph Schumpeter (1942/1975). New goods and marketing and changes in preferences and natural turbulence (drought, storms) would also affect the spatial rent. The fruits of entrepreneurship go to the entrepreneur and his investors, but the general neighborhood and economy-wide surpluses go to land rent.

Entrepreneurship and Rent with Uncertainty

Entrepreneurial profit arises from uncertainty, the possibility of gain or loss with unknowable probabilities. The uncertainty of the future is central to Austrian thought, and as the demand for innovative products is uncertain, and future supplies and government policies are uncertain, talent and skill in entrepreneurial economic calculation get rewarded with economic profit.

The developer–entrepreneur seeks to profit from all factors – his entrepreneurial labor, the sales of the capital goods (buildings), and the rise in the site value. To the extent that the development raises the value of the neighborhood site rentals and prices, this is a return on labor and capital goods rather than land as a natural resource. Thus the gains from successfully confronting uncertainty are the economic profits of entrepreneurship and also capital yields rather than land rent.

The buyer–owner of real estate also faces an uncertain future, but changes in rent are to some extent hedgeable and insurable. The Case–Shiller real-estate index and associated future markets now provide a way to hedge against an unfavorable change in price. Real-estate index funds offer a way to hedge generally for economy-wide trends, and if there were significant public revenue from land rent, most likely, insurance would arise against an unexpected increase in the site rent. Diverse local fluctuations in land values could have calculable probabilities.

Market Dynamics and Rent

Austrian economics emphasizes disequilibrium. What is often called "market mechanisms" and the "market process" can also aptly be labeled "market dynamics." Technological progress as well as wider trade generates what can be called specific and general gains. The specific gains go to higher wages, the economic profits of successful firms, and profits from works protected from competition such as from patents and copyrights. The general gains in an industry, which neoclassical economics calls a "producer surplus," goes to land rent, as discussed above.

For competitively produced goods, competition induces entry into industries with economic profits. But the only way one can enter into the land business is if a previous owner exits, with an exchange of titles. The economic profit remains as land rent.

In a pure market economy, entrepreneurs will seek out the best use of land, but where land values are subsidized by government policies, the rising land values will induce malspeculation. Some locations will be developed too quickly as builders hope to gain from the rising site value, while other locations will be held idle, since the rise in land value creates an implicit return that may match that of other rising assets.

LOCATION THEORY

An Austrian theory of economic space integrates the theories of other schools of thought into its paradigm. The theory of location pricing was developed by Johann Heinrich von Thünen. In *The Isolated State* (1826/2009), he explained land rent as a function of transportation costs. In a city shaped like a circle, the location with the least transportation cost is the center, and rent rises to equalize the firms' costs of business there with the costs at the periphery of the market area. Even with modern communications, urban commercial and financial centers still have economies of scope, density, and scale, as evidenced by tall buildings.

Cities exist because of economies of density and because of transportation costs. If there were no economies of density, then the population could be spread out evenly. If transportation costs were zero, then people could live anywhere and get zapped into locations with economies of density. As stated by Batt (2009), "site rent is the price of accessibility."

In von Thünen's location theory, the rent of land is based on its marginal productivity. The basic equation (Krumme, 2010) is

$$R = Y(p - c) - YFm; \tag{2}$$

where $R =$ land rent; $Y =$ yield (output) per unit area of land; $p =$ the market price per unit of output; $c =$ production cost per unit of output; $F =$ freight rate; and $m =$ distance to market. In that model, the site value is the capitalized transportation cost. As the city radius becomes larger, the rent at the center will rise as the area served by the center expands by the square of the radius.

Empirical evidence is consistent with location theory. A study for the Urban Land Institute found that in Portland, Oregon, a 10-mile difference in location, relative to the city center, generates about $56,000 in land value. The 10-mile difference amounts to 4,600 miles annually for 230 days of commuting, plus nonwork trips to the central area (Dunphy, 1998).

If the highways leading to marginal land at the edge of a city were improved by the government (e.g., by increasing speed), the reduction in transport costs results in a higher income and higher rental payments. Much of the productivity due to useful infrastructure generates greater site rentals. If the public works are financed from sources other than locational rent, the landowners receive an implicit subsidy, and entrepreneurship gets misdirected into speculative rent seeking. Speculators will guess (or obtain from insider knowledge) which locations will benefit from development, and they will bid up land values ahead of time. In some cases, the high anticipatory land values will shift development elsewhere, into locations that will not be as productive.

The greater productivity and rent in city centers can be offset by negative aspects such as crime, noise, and pollution. Rent control can reduce maintenance and eventually create blight and slums. Development then shifts to edge cities. These negative aspects are preventable, as they stem from both governmental subsidies and imposed costs. Congestion and pollution are negative externalities caused by polluters' trespass, which is preventable by internalizing the costs. The portion of property taxes that fall on improvements imposes a higher marginal cost on maintenance and features such as beauty, penalizing vertical construction.

The implicit subsidy to land rentals, of public works financed from taxes on labor and capital goods, generates excessive horizontal development. The tax system thus penalizes vertical development at the center and rewards urban sprawl. If public revenue were derived from land rentals, it would result in more efficient market-generated vertical and horizontal development. Moreover, since the tapping of economic land rent for public revenue is based on the potential rental – of land put to its highest and best use – tapping the site rent for public revenues pushes landowners to maintain their real estate to maximize their rental incomes.

PUBLIC REVENUE AND PUBLIC POLICY

In a pure free-market economy with all resources held privately, communities would be consensually contractual (Foldvary, 1994). The civic services would generate greater site rental and value, and if the assessments or dues were based on the rent or site value, then the payments would not change the rental but would capitalize the price back down. If the payments are based on other criteria, such as equal amounts or on total property value, then there would be a partial capitalization down of the site values. At any rate, there would not be a significant subsidy to the site values, nor any deadweight loss on economic action.

In current government public finances, taxes are mostly on labor, enterprise, and goods. Tenant workers are double-billed for the territorial collective goods, paying both higher rents and taxes. Landowners receive the implicit subsidy of higher rentals and site values. Both the taxes and subsidies are interventions that create deadweight losses and distort the market signals of prices and profits. Thus, the optimal public policy is to either privatize governance and collective goods, or else use the site rentals for public revenue.

Governmental regulation of space also distorts the market. Zoning restricts the use of land, often to prevent higher densities and mixed land uses. City mercantilism also typically prohibits people from legally working in their homes, and required permits reduce competition and add to costs. Mises (1949/1963) analyzed that intervention creates waste, and Hayek

(1945, 1991) analyzed the decentralized nature of knowledge that makes zoning and other such governmental planning a "fatal conceit."

SPATIAL LAND IN THE BUSINESS CYCLE

The prevailing Austrian theory of the business cycle is based on the money supply, interest rates, and the structure of capital goods. As first theorized by Menger (1871/1976), there is a time structure of capital goods that depend on their period of production – the time from the initial investment to the final profit provided. Goods with a quick turnover, such as inventory, are "lower-order" capital goods, while those with a long period are "higher order." As capital goods range from lowest to highest order, the structure is affected by the rate of interest. Since capital yields (the rate of return on capital goods) compete with interest from bonds, when the return on investment is lower than the prevailing interest rate, the investment is not made.

Lower rates of interest make the structure of capital goods steeper, as the higher-order investments are profitable, their returns being greater than from bonds. High interest rates flatten the structure, since now many of the long-term investment pay less than bonds. In a pure free market, the rate of interest makes investment equal to net savings, and also allocates income between investment and consumption spending. Greater savings implies less consumption, and the lower rate of interest induces more investment, so the reduction in consumption is offset by an increase in economic investment in capital goods and human capital.

The central planning of the money supply and interest rates skews the transaction rate of interest away from its natural free-market rate, as first analyzed by the Swedish Austrian economist Knut Wicksell (1901/1938, 1936/1965). The expansion of money by a central bank lowers the interest rate. This lower interventionist rate has the effect of greater savings, although intended consumption has not changed. The lower rate induces greater investment in higher-order capital goods, but this spending competes with consumption, and prices rise. The central bank later reduces the growth of the money supply, to stop the rise of price inflation, and then the higher interest rates reduce these investments. Workers in these industries get laid off, reducing the demand for goods, which then causes a recession.

Empirically, the most important highest-order capital good is real estate. Construction is a major industry, and involves complementary durable goods such as furniture and appliances. Construction creates a demand for materials such as copper, lumber, and cement. Real estate also employs people in services such as finance, brokerage, and appraisals. Every recession has been preceded by peaks in construction (Foldvary, 1997, 2007).

The Austrian business cycle theory has been incomplete in not including the land factor in its analysis. The cyclical theory of Henry George (1879/1975) complements and completes Austrian theory by integrating space with capital goods. In the geo-Austrian synthesis, the expansion of cheap credit by the monetary authority induces the purchase of the space along with the capital goods attached to the site.

Spatial land is not an investment, as it is not produced. The purchase transfers the title along with the property rights. The excessive purchase induced by artificially low rates of interest results in malspeculation. Developers and speculators expect the rent and the price of land to rise, and the early buyers get large profits from leverage, putting down a small fraction of the price as a down payment. During the boom, the speculative demand adds to the demand for the use of space, and prices rise more rapidly, as they did, for example, prior to the 2006 peak of real-estate values in the United States. But the rise in the price of land creates a distortion, as the ratio of purchase prices to rentals rises.

As interest rates rise back up and real-estate prices escalate, real estate becomes unaffordable to households, and the high prices also deter businesses from obtaining more space. The same phenomenon happened in Japan during the 1980s, which illustrates the statement by the German philosopher Georg Hegel (1822/1991, p. 6), "what experience and history teach is this – that peoples and governments never have learned anything from history, or acted on principles deduced from it."

After peaking out, real-estate prices then fall, and the malspeculators who bought near the top of the peak suffer the winners' curse. The crash of real-estate prices, as occurred in 2008, is really a crash of land values – a fall in the market price of space. The fall in land values brings down the banking system, as much of the bank lending, and associated derivatives such as mortgage-backed securities, was made to finance the purchase of spatial land.

In a pure free market, the land boom malspeculation would be prevented. With free-market banking (free banking), the interest rate would be the natural rate, which is based on the supply and demand for loanable funds (investable resources), without being distorted by central bank money creation (Selgin, 1988). There would be no credit subsidy, no government-sponsored and subsidized enterprises such as Fannie Mae, and also, there would be no public-goods subsidy. Landowners would pay the cost for public works and civic services that apply to their sites, such as streets, security, and fire protection. The basic cause of the boom-bust cycle – monetary and fiscal subsidies to land value – would not exist, and thus the real-estate cycle would not exist, and neither would the resultant business cycle.

LAND IN AUSTRIAN MACROECONOMICS

An Austrian theory of macroeconomics was pioneered by Friedrich Hayek, who integrated the Austrian theory of capital goods into a theory of the macro-economy. Roger Garrison (2001, p. 6) points out that the title of Keynes's (1936) epic book, *The General Theory of Employment, Interest, and Money*, left out capital goods. One could also point out that the title omits land.

Building on Hayek's (1935/1967) thought, Roger Garrison in 2001 established Austrian macroeconomics in his book *Time and Money: The Macroeconomics of Capital Structure*. Of course Mises, Rothbard, Yeager, and others had written on economy-wide phenomena, but perhaps the most comprehensive treatment is that of Garrison, who also relates the Austrian theory to that of the prevailing Keynesian doctrines.

Economists divide spending into two categories, consumption and investment. The payment of rent for the personal use of land for leisure fits into the category of consumption. The space itself is not consumed, but space is consumed as a flow of site services over time that generates a market rent. Suppose the rental of a house includes a backyard. The yard offers a continuous flow of service as a place to enjoy the outdoors. The user consumes that flow over time. Though the space remains, every hour of yard service is an hour of spatial service that is gone as soon as that time passes. As a flow, the spatial service is simultaneously generated and consumed.

Now, suppose an enterprise is renting real estate that contains a factory. The property has a capital good (the building) and land – the three-dimensional space. The rental payment for the use of the building is the equivalent of borrowing funds to buy the building, and then paying a mortgage interest on the loan; the rental is the equivalent of the loan payment.

Capital goods depreciate, and that loss of value is called "capital consumption." Thus, ownership of capital goods constitutes in part an investment in the enduring value and in part the consumption of the capital good. The consumption of the capital good is a cost of the enterprise, as is the payment of wages. The land that the building sits on provides the services of location and spatial extension. The cost to the user is the payment of rent that continuously flows from the site. Thus the rent of land is consumption, regardless of its use.

The purchase of land is neither consumption nor investment. The purchase is a transfer at some moment of the title to the land in exchange for another asset, usually money. Money is not an investment either, but only a liquid claim on goods.

The ratio of pure land rent to land value is a capitalization rate on land. If the rent is free of risk, this capitalization rate should be equal to the natural rate of interest. Indeed, one way to calculate the "true" rate of interest – when there are central bank interventions that skew the transaction rates for borrowing – is to observe the rent/price ratios. Austrian theory regards the pure rate of interest as the discounting of future values due to time preference, which corresponds to the tendency to value present goods higher than future goods (i.e., goods for which one has to wait to buy them in the future).

Relative to income, time preference affects both the amount of savings and the amount of borrowing. In the market for loanable funds, higher interest rates induce greater savings, creating an upward-sloping supply of loanable funds, while the demand to borrow slopes down as more funds are borrowed at lower rates of interest. Thus, while savings and borrowing appear to be functions of the interest rate, in actuality, the market rate – graphically the intersection of these curves – reflects the general time preference of the population. In a pure market, the supply and demand for loanable funds are themselves shaped from time preference, and so the long-run causation is from time preference to the pure interest rate.

When one borrows to buy land, the interest is paid from the rent of that land. Thus, the interest payment is really rent that is transferred to the lender. If there is a 100 percent tax on the rent, then the price of the land is zero, and one obtains the land essentially free. The tax then replaces the interest that would have been paid. In general, after the transition, a shift to land value taxation does not impose a burden even on the landowner, because the tax payment replaces what would have been an interest payment, whether explicit or implicit.

As noted by Garrison (2001, p. 8), labor and natural resources (land) are the ultimate and original factors of production. Household goods are the ultimate end to which production is directed; hence producer capital goods are temporally intermediate between the original factors and the ultimate ends.

Land is one of the original factors, but the intermediate capital goods also sit within space. As noted above, the production process involves the consumption of space, just as it involves capital consumption and the consumption of labor services.

The intertemporal structure of capital goods has counterparts in the intertemporal structure of space and the intertemporal structure of labor. The rate of interest affects the production of higher or lower capital goods, and also the hiring of the land and labor associated with those capital goods.

Consider as an example the planting of trees. Suppose the rate of interest paid by bonds is 6 percent. There will not be investment in trees with a long period of production, such as mahogany trees that grow at a rate of 3 percent and require 30 years to mature for harvesting. Suppose there is then a quantum leap in savings, resulting in a large reduction in the rate of interest on bonds, such as from 6 to 2 percent. Land is switched from growing Christmas trees with a rapid turnover to growing the mahogany trees that grow in value by 3 percent per year (cf. Faustmann, 1968; Ohlin, 1921/1995).

The rent of the Christmas-tree land is based on the profit from the trees, and if there is only a normal accounting profit for the firms, thus zero economic profit, then the rent will be based on the relative productivity of the tree-farming land, such as is due to the climate and proximity to markets. When the site is switched to growing mahogany, it is because the 3 percent growth rate of the trees is now better than the 2 percent from bonds. Land rent is capitalized into site value at the prevailing two percent bond interest rate, and the extra percent that mahogany yields would at first result in a higher price for the mahogany seeds or seedlings. The higher price for the seeds brings the yield from growing mahogany down to the 2 percent bond rate.

The shift in production has increased the price of the capital-good inputs (seeds), providing the sellers with a temporary economic profit, until the increased competitive production of seeds brings the profit down to normal. Meanwhile, the generally greater productivity of the economy due to the greater investment in the higher-order capital goods will be absorbed by a greater ground rent. Thus, in the end, the shift in production raises rent while profit goes back to normal. Land rent captures the eventual gains from greater savings and investment and the reduction in the rate of interest and the shift in production towards higher-order capital goods.

Labor could take some of the gains from greater productivity. If better technology requires more human capital, wages would stay higher as a return to human capital. But if human capital stays the same, the wage would not change, as the marginal product of labor would be unchanged. The macroeconomic result is that ground rent captures the gains from the greater productivity.

Note that these Austrian macroeconomic conclusions have been derived using methodological individualism, in contrast to the holistic aggregates of demand-side doctrines. The responses of entrepreneurs to changes in interest rates are those of individuals, which then have an economy-wide effect. Moreover, there are no unexplained systemic "animal spirits," but only entrepreneurs reacting to changes in real costs and expected gains. Of course speculative fever and panics can become economy-wide, but these too have an economic cause rather than themselves being instigators.

Traditional Austrian macroeconomics uses the stages of production over time, such as from mining to manufacturing and then to retailing. Thus, production that goes through many stages can take a great deal of time from mining to the final sale. But for a particular firm, what matters is the period of production for its own product. When a firm uses funds, what matters is how long the funds will be locked up until finally used up and then repaid by profit. It does not matter to the entrepreneur where the firm is in the structure of production. For example, a mine that can extract materials and sell it in a few days will have a short period of production and be little affected by the transaction rate of interest. Since the impact of the rate of interest is on the period of production faced by individual firms and entrepreneurs, the interest rate does not affect the total production time as stages. The fact that mining is far removed from the ultimate household goods is irrelevant. As stated by Garrison (2001, p. 49), "the time dimension measures the extent to which valuable resources are tied up over time."

In Garrison's (2001, p. 50) graphic depiction of Austrian macroeconomics, the supply and demand for loanable or investable funds determines the rate of interest and amount of net savings, which equals investment. The investment involves more and better capital goods, greater human capital, and shifts in land use.

There can be quantum leaps of land use which result in much greater productivity and thus also of land rent, and quantum leaps to lower production and employment from taxes and restrictions, especially from taxes on enterprises that are unable to pass the tax burden to customers and shut down when taxes on their revenue result in a negative economic profit (Gaffney, 2006).

The amount of investment then sets the point on the production possibilities curve, which has the two categories of investment and consumption. Consumption determines the height of the Hayekian triangle with time-stages of production on the horizontal line. The slope of the hypotenuse is the rate of interest, although as analyzed above, the time structure is based on the period of production regardless of the stage of production.

Due to the high land value that is induced by government subsidy, much of bank lending goes to pay for land, constituting an unproductive use of loanable funds. As pointed out by Mason Gaffney (1982), both artificially low interest rates and artificially high land prices result in an excessive conversion of circulating capital goods to fixed capital goods. Overpriced land also misguides investing by leading it into forms of capital goods that substitute for land.

In a pure free market, more loanable funds would go to pay for capital goods and human capital, and with labor and enterprise free of taxes and arbitrary restrictions, the economy would grow as fast as is warranted by the preference for savings and thus for future consumption.

SUMMARY

Austrian economics has heretofore mostly ignored the role of land in an economy, a gap that made its theory incomplete, and especially left a gap in its explanation of business cycles and in policy prescriptions to prevent their occurrence.

The concepts of Austrian economics that apply to land include the propositions that value is subjective, that the rent is equal to the marginal product, and that the rent is derived from the marginal utility and the value of the goods produced on the site.

Land is the factor that is provided by nature, apart from human action, although its rent and value also derives from the territory's population and commerce. Spatial land is fixed, and its rent – reflecting differentials in the output of various locations – is a surplus. Land values capitalize the locational externalities, including public works and civic services, and capture much of the gains from economic expansion. When collective goods are paid for by taxing labor and enterprise, this amounts to an implicit subsidy. In a pure market, the landowners would pay for such services.

Land values play a key role in the business cycle, as the transaction rate of interest that gets pushed below the natural rate due to monetary expansion induces both malinvestment in capital goods and malspeculation in land value. Fiscal subsidies also generate the real-estate booms that precede recessions and depressions. The integration of spatial theory into Austrian economics provides the second essential remedy to the intervention-caused boom-bust cycle. Besides the elimination of the financial side of the cycle with free banking, the complete elimination of the boom-bust cycle requires also the abolition of subsidies to land value.

ACKNOWLEDGMENT

I extend thanks to two anonymous referees who provided excellent enhancement suggestions.

REFERENCES

Batt, H. W. (2009). Land value maps are not new, but their utility needs to be re-discovered. *International Journal of Transdisciplinary Research, 4*(1), 108–158.

Brazee, R. J. (2007). The Faustmann face of optimal forest harvesting. In *The international yearbook of environmental and resource economics 2006/2007* (pp. 255–288). Cheltenham, UK: Edward Elgar Publishing.

Dunphy, R. T. (1998, October). *The cost of being close: land values and housing prices in Portland's High Tech Corridor*. ULI Working Paper No. 660. Urban Land Institute, Washington, DC.

Faustmann, M. (1849). Berechnung des Werthes, welchen Waldboden sowie nachnichthaubare Holzbestandefür die Weldwirtschaftbesitze. *Allegemeime Forst und Jagd Zeitung, 25*, 441.

Faustmann, M. (1968). Calculation of the value which forest land and immature stands possess for forestry (English translation). In W. Lennard & M. Gane (Eds.), *Martin Faustmann and the evolution of discounted cash flow*. Oxford, UK: Commonwealth Forestry Institute (Institute Paper No. 42).

Foldvary, F. (1994). *Public goods and private communities*. Aldershot, UK: Edward Elgar.

Foldvary, F. (1997). The business cycle: A Georgist-Austrian synthesis. *American Journal of Economics and Sociology, 56*(4), 521–541.

Foldvary, F. (1998). *Dictionary of free-market economics*. Cheltenham, UK: Edward Elgar.

Foldvary, F. E. (2005). Geo-rent: A plea to public economists. *Econ Journal Watch, 2*(1), 1–12.

Foldvary, F. (2007). *The depression of 2008*. Berkeley, CA: The Gutenberg Press.

Foldvary, F. (2011). *The science of economics*. San Diego, CA: Cognella.

Gaffney, M. (1982). *Causes of downturns: An Austro-Georgist synthesis*. Working Paper. Retrieved from http://www.masongaffney.org/workpapers/Causes_of_downturn–Austro-Georgist_synthesis_1982.pdf. Accessed on March 22, 2012.

Gaffney, M. (2006). *The quantum leap effect*. Working Paper. Retrieved from http://www.foldvary.net/works/gafquant.html. Accessed on March 22, 2012.

Gaffney, M. (2010, July). Turgot and Faustmann: Death, rebirth, and second death. Manuscript for the *annual meetings of HES*, Syracuse, NY.

Garrison, R. W. (2001). *Time and money*. London, UK: Routledge.

George, H. (1879/1975). *Progress and poverty*. New York, NY: Robert Schalkenbach Foundation.

Godin, B. (2008). The knowledge economy: Fritz Machlup's construction of a synthetic concept. Project on the History and Sociology of S&T Statistics: Working Paper No. 37, Quebec, Canada. Retrieved from http://www.csiic.ca/PDF/Godin_37.pdf. Accessed on March 22, 2012.

Hayek, F. A. (1935/1967). *Prices and production* (2nd ed.). New York, NY: Augustus M. Kelley.

Hayek, F. A. (1945). The use of knowledge in society. *American Economic Review*, *35*(4), 519–530.

Hayek, F. A. (1991). *The fatal conceit*. Chicago, IL: University of Chicago Press.

Hegel, G. W. F. (1822/1991). *The philosophy of history* (J. Sibree, Trans.). Amherst, NY: Prometheus Books.

Keynes, J. M. (1936). *The general theory of employment, interest, and money*. New York, NY: Harcourt, Brace, and Company.

Kirzner, I. M. (1992). *The meaning of market process*. London, UK: Routledge.

Krumme, G. (2010). *Thünen's rent functions*. Retrieved from http://faculty.washington.edu/krumme/450/rent.html. Accessed on November 26, 2011.

Machlup, F. (1962). *The production and distribution of knowledge in the United States*. Princeton, NJ: Princeton University Press.

Menger, C. (1871/1976). *Principles of economics*. (J. Dingwall & B. Hoselitz, Trans.). New York, NY: New York University Press.

Mises, L. von. (1949/1963). *Human action*. New Haven, CT: Yale University Press.

Ohlin, B. (1921/1995). Till frågan om skogarnas omloppstid. In *Ekonomisk Tidskrift: Festschrift to Knut Wicksell*. [Concerning the Question of the Rotation Period in Forestry.] *Journal of Forest Economics*, *1*, 89–114.

Ricardo, D. (1817/1963). *Principles of political economy and taxation*. Homewood, IL: Richard D. Irwin.

Schumpeter, J. A. (1912/1934). *The theory of economic development: An inquiry into profits, capital, credit, interest, and the business cycle* (R. Opie, Trans.). Cambridge, MA: Harvard University Press.

Schumpeter, J. A. (1942/1975). *Capitalism, socialism and democracy*. New York, NY: Harper Colophon Books Edition.

Selgin, G. (1988). *The theory of free banking*. Totowa: Rowman & Littlefield.

Thünen, J. H. von. (1826/2009). *The isolated state in relation to agriculture and political economy*. Hampshire, UK: Palgrave Macmillan.

Wicksell, K. (1901/1938). *Lectures on political economy* (E. Classen, Trans.). New York, NY: The Macmillan Company, 3d Impression.

Wicksell, K. (1936/1965). *Interest and prices* (R. F. Kahn, Trans.). New York, NY: Augustus M. Kelly.

REGIONAL ECONOMIC ANALYSIS: THE CASE FOR METHODOLOGICAL INDIVIDUALISM

Samuli Leppälä and Pierre Desrochers

Urban and regional economics has made some inroads among Austrian economists (Desrochers, 1998, 2001; Ikeda & Staley's, 2004 introduction to the June 2004 special issue of *The Review of Austrian Economics*). That regional economies would seem a natural context for Austrian analysis has long been a given in light of Hayek (1949/1976, p. 80) emphasis on "the particular circumstances of time and place." As Ikeda (2007) notes, however, Austrians have traditionally put much emphasis on the former and neglected the latter.

Besides a "push" effect from Austrian economists toward regional analysis, one can also notice some "pull" already at work among some economic geographers and regional scientists (Heijman & Leen, 2004; Hite, 1995; Rees, 1992, 1999). In addition, while economic geographers' relation to (mainstream) geographical economics has been somewhat tense, the field has a long tradition of welcoming and absorbing ideas, concepts, and perspectives from different schools of economics, especially heterodox ones (Martin & Sunley, 1996). While mutual interests and affinities are strong, however, there is a risk that radically divergent methodological stances might hinder a fruitful interdisciplinary exchange.

The Spatial Market Process
Advances in Austrian Economics, Volume 16, 25–56

ISSN: 1529-2134/doi:10.1108/S1529-2134(2012)0000016005

In our opinion, the primary tension concerns methodological individualism. For Austrian economists, methodological individualism is a foundational and indispensable building block of scientific inquiry, whereas most economic geographers eschew the notion entirely. For example, while for David Emanuel Andersson (2005), studying the spatial nature of entrepreneurship, requires a commitment to methodological individualism, economic geographers typically build their analysis on "regionally based" concepts such as "innovative milieu," "learning regions," "regional innovation networks," "industrial districts," and "clusters" (Rutten & Boekema, 2007). The main problem is that regional economic analysis often takes aggregates as the unit of analysis, but arbitrarily defined geographic areas do not engage in production and exchange, nor do they enter and exit markets. Conversely, methodological individualism suggests that regional economic activity should be explained in terms of individuals and their interactions.

The remainder of the chapter is structured into two major sections. The first considers the meaning of methodological individualism from the perspective of the philosophy of science and briefly notes its prominent role in Austrian economics. We then review the opposition to the concept as laid out in the regional science and economic geography literatures and discuss the origins of these (mis)perceptions. We conclude by elaborating on the implications of a consistent application of methodological individualism for regional economic analysis.

Building on the previous discussion, the third section elaborates on three major topics and issues in regional economic analysis. We attempt not only to demonstrate that methodological individualism is applicable to this field of inquiry but also that its coherent application can move the field forward in the form of both theoretical developments, such as by improving our understanding of traditional concepts, for example, regional comparative advantage and agglomeration economies, and empirical research, as in the case of localized knowledge spillovers. We conclude by providing further thoughts on an emerging Austro-regional synthesis and of the role of methodological individualism as a crucial foundation in this respect.

METHODOLOGICAL INDIVIDUALISM: WHAT IS IT GOOD FOR?

Methodological Individualism and Austrian Economics

Besides subjectivism (in terms of value and cost) and the market process approach (as opposed to mainstream economics' equilibrium analysis), methodological individualism is a foundational methodological principle of Austrian economics. While being (arguably) more consistently and consciously practiced within Austrian economics, methodological individualism is far from unique to this tradition and is a well-recognized principle of inquiry in the social sciences (Watkins, 1952a, 1952b). Needless to say though, methodological individualism remains controversial and discussions of its true meaning and adequateness periodically resurface in the philosophy of science literature (Hodgson, 2007; Udehn, 2002).

Although there are many versions of methodological individualism, its central tenets can be summarized in the following way: (1) in terms of their structure and change, "all social phenomena ... are in principle explicable only in terms of individuals – their properties, goals, and beliefs" (Elster, 1982, p. 453); (2) there is no mysterious social entity beyond individual interactions, for "a collection of individuals is a society if there is strong interaction between them; this interaction is due to the fact that when any one individual acts (rationally) on the basis of his own aims and interests, he takes into account the existence of other individuals with aims and interests" (Agassi, 1960, p. 244). In other words, the ontological or metaphysical principle behind methodological individualism is that all social phenomena result from individual beliefs, purposes, and actions. All social phenomena should therefore be explained in terms of individuals and their interactions. While ontological individualism is less disputed, the question of whether methodological individualism necessarily follows from it is more controversial (Udehn, 2001, p. 2).

Among the social sciences, the status of methodological individualism is particularly strong in economics, and each subfield within the discipline builds its analysis upon rationally acting individuals within the framework of microeconomic theory. True, in the aftermath of the Keynesian revolution, macroeconomics moved beyond any micro theory (Leijonhufvud, 1973), but after the Lucas (1976) critique the idea that all macroeconomic theories should be derived from assumptions about individual behavior became the professional standard. Thus even if DSGE-macro models came under heavy criticism after the 2008 financial crisis, their particular failures were not attributed to their overall adherence to methodological individualism, but to the particular additional assumptions made on micro behavior, such as the exclusion of interaction between the agents and the assumptions of the representative individual, rational expectations, and unbounded rationality (Colander, Howitt, Kirman, Leijonhufvud, & Mehrling, 2008; Colander et al., 2009; De Grauwe, 2010). While methodologically individualistic, Austrian economists have always been critical of this line of mainstream economics. As such, methodological individualism is but a starting point for social inquiry that comes in many forms, and whose ultimate success also depends on other assumptions made by social scientists.

In Austrian economics, methodological individualism has been explicitly advocated since Carl Menger and the *Methodenstreit* with the German Historical School (although the specific term only came into use later) (Yeager, 1954b). While one can always identify fine distinctions between specific exponents' views on the issue, methodological individualism has been advocated by all prominent Austrian scholars from Ludwig von Mises and Friedrich Hayek to Israel Kirzner, Ludwig Lachmann, and Murray Rothbard. As such, there is a largely unified Austrian view on methodological individualism which differs from mainstream methodological individualism in certain respects. For example, methodological individualism as it is applied in mainstream economics is better described as methodological atomism, as the possibility of interaction between individuals is often, while not always, excluded. This is a restrictive assumption that is typically rejected by Austrian economists (Zwirn, 2007).

Much of the resistance toward methodological individualism seems to arise from viewing it as a particular type of monolithic – and thus objectionable – position, whereas the commitment to methodological individualism as such is after all a moderately flexible approach to scientific inquiry. While some may feel that this amounts to unacceptable imprecision (e.g., Hodgson, 2007), we merely see it as a reasonable starting point for a process in which ultimately the results should speak for themselves. After all, a method is not merely what you say it to be but how you apply it.

Methodological Individualism and Regional Economic Analysis

If one accepts the basic tenets of methodological individualism, then it follows that it should be a foundational methodological principle in regional economic analysis (i.e., economic geography, urban economics, and regional science) as well. Even though economic geographers and regional scientists may study the impact of nonsocial factors on human activities, their foremost task is ultimately to understand social phenomena such as the spatial concentration of production or innovative activities.

Methodological individualism is no stranger to regional economic scholars. While the term is rarely used in any theoretical or empirical contribution, it surfaces from time to time in methodological commentary. The context in which methodological individualism appears is, however, usually negative. For example, the socio-spatial ontology historically favored by most economic geographers eschews a strict adherence to methodological individualism (Miller, 1992; Plummer & Sheppard, 2006). To understand the negative connotation of methodological individualism, it is worthwhile to briefly consider the history of economic geography (in certain aspects, the history of regional science has been less volatile [Rees, 1999]).

As Scott (2000, p. 484) writes, "[t]he history of economic geography over the second half of twentieth century is characterised by a complex series of twists and turns of substantive focus and sudden changes of theoretical mood." By the late 1950s, emerging quantitative methods began to lead the way in economic geography, and in the early 1960s they had fully secured their position in the profession (Scott, 2000). The early practitioners of quantitative methods largely subscribed to methodological individualism, while for practical reasons their analysis was often restricted to statistical aggregates (Poon, 2004).

Because spatial analysis and regional science grew on the theoretical roots of neoclassical economics, beginning in the 1960s some economic geographers began to search for a "more nuanced conception of human motivation and the behavioural environment" (Scott, 2000, p. 488). Along with economic problems in North America and Western Europe, the ideological and methodological tide began to turn in the 1970s:

> The insistent methodological individualism of then dominant forms of economic geography was clearly inadequate to the task of dealing with the grand structural forces that seemed to lie behind these developments, and the perception of its inadequacy was reinforced by the critique of capitalism which had now suddenly appeared on the agenda in various branches of social sciences. (Scott, 2000, p. 489)

The Marxist turn in the 1970s, followed by the post-modernism of the 1980s (Rees, 1999), is still very much affecting economic geography today, for

> the majority of geographers have rejected the neoclassical tradition, in their minds associated with spatial analysis and mainstream economics, in favor of neo-Marxian and post-Keynesian political economy – which in turn has diversified into feminist and post-structural approaches. For many geographers engaged in this cultural turn, quantitative approaches have come to be rejected as positivist, pro-market and neoliberal. (Plummer & Sheppard, 2006, p. 619)

As such, one problem with methodological individualism is that in the minds of economic geographers it has become associated with both political individualism and methodological atomism. Austrian scholars should hence be careful to acknowledge these misunderstandings when communicating with economic geographers and contributing to the literature. Misunderstandings is in our opinion the right word, since the term was first coined by Joseph Schumpeter (1908) to clarify the difference between methodological individualism and political individualism. Methodological individualism as an approach to scientific inquiry has no need for political commitments that favor the free market. Indeed, according to Jon Elster (1982, 1993), it is fully compatible with Marxian analysis.

Regarding atomism, however, the criticism is more warranted. Methodological individualism, as practiced by mainstream economics, has conventionally included other restrictive assumptions, such as the lack of interaction between economic agents. This is a point the critics among economic geographers repeatedly seize upon (e.g., Barnes & Sheppard, 1992; Miller, 1992). To some extent this view is outdated, as it mainly applies to traditional microeconomic theory and to the model of perfect competition, and hence ignores more recent developments in mainstream economics. However, the recent studies that explicitly include, for example, cultural and institutional factors have not yet made a substantial impact on the core of the economics profession. Furthermore, the now frequent use of game theory – while enabling economists to study strategic interaction – still precludes the inclusion of the (innovating) entrepreneur, which is incompatible with models based on optimizing behavior (Baumol, 1968, 1993, 2002). As such, most mainstream economists are likely ontological individualists, and yet they practice methodological atomism, arguably due its relative convenience.

Furthermore, for economic geographers, methodological individualism is associated with strong rational choice assumptions allowing for the "rigorous modeling of exclusively self-interested individuals who are unaffected by place-specific social relations" (Miller, 1992). Therefore, "[r]elation geographers do not resort to methodological individualism by viewing actors as atomistic units" (Boggs & Rantisi, 2003). Instead, they emphasize that "individual action is grounded in social relations rather than methodological individualism" (Barnes & Sheppard, 1992, p. 8). As argued above, however, for Austrian and other heterodox scholars, methodological individualism does not imply atomism (see also Rothbard, 1976). When and what type of interactions should be accounted for does, however, depend on the research context.

An underlying worry in these methodological proclamations seems to be that with methodological individualism, geography itself ceases to matter. But a methodological individualist perspective on regional growth and development does not imply that local attributes have no effect on individual activities, only that they do not unilaterally determine what individuals in a region are capable of doing and what they actually do. As the economist Ludwig von Mises pointed out in his discussion of "environmentalism" (now more commonly referred to as "geographical determinism"):

> The inherent misconception of this interpretation is that it looks upon geography as an active and upon human action as a passive factor. However, the geographical environment is only one of the components of the situation in which man is placed by his birth, that makes him feel uneasy and causes him to employ his reason and his bodily forces to get rid of this uneasiness as best he may. Geography (nature) provides on the one hand a provocation to act and on the other hand both means that can be utilized in acting and insurmountable limits imposed upon the human striving for betterment. It provides a stimulus but not the response. Geography sets a task, but man has to solve it. Man lives in a definite geographical environment and is forced to adjust his action to the conditions of this environment. But the way in which he adjusts himself, the methods of his social, technological, and moral adaptation, are not determined by the external physical factors. The North American continent produced neither the civilization of the Indian aborigines nor that of the Americans of European extraction. (Mises, 1957/1985, pp. 324–325)

It seems that for economic geographers, methodological individualism implies a whole bag of additional, restrictive, and unwanted assumptions. Plummer and Sheppard (2006, p. 622) thus reject methodological individualism because "[e]conomic actors are neither fully rational nor autonomous. Their interests and preferences are shaped by their socio-spatial position, their knowledge is imperfect, and they engage in collective action." Their conclusion is that mathematical and statistical modeling in economic geography should be kept and endorsed, but refocused away from microfoundations *à la* mainstream economics. A methodological stance that treats individuals as the basic agents of change, however, does not necessarily imply any specific assumptions about their beliefs, preferences, and interactions, nor about how to incorporate these into mathematically defined economic models (Arrow, 1994, p. 4).

The recent intrusion of geographical economics into the traditional domain of economic geographers has resurrected some past disagreements and led to a heated debate (see Mäki & Marchionni, 2011; Marchionni, 2004, for an overview). It is telling that the term "geographical economics" was coined by economic geographers, who were resentful of Paul Krugman's "new economic geography." By now many economists (e.g., Overman, 2004) have willingly adopted the term proposed by geographers, but the tension between the professions continues. On the one hand, for economic geographers, the new economic geography or geographical economics seems more or less a reworking of the sort of approaches they discarded years ago (Martin, 1999). On the other , mainstream geographical economists claim that their models give economic geography the long-needed internal consistency that is required when moving from micro to macro behavior (Overman, 2004). No doubt, the aftermath of the 2008 Financial Crisis will create criticism toward this latter logic. For this reason, it will be important for Austrian economists to point out that that the mainstream economic models are not the only game in town when it comes to microfoundations and methodological individualism.

Furthermore, according to Martin (1999), geographical economics neglect a host of important factors that influence regional economic activity, such as the role of local infrastructures, local institutions, state spending and intervention, regulatory arrangements, foreign investment and disinvestment, and global competition. He sees mathematical representation and modeling as incompatible with the key social, cultural, and institutional factors that are involved in spatial economic development. Many Austrian could not agree more, and Austrian economics itself is a prime example that methodological individualism need not imply mathematical modeling.

Despite the common resistance against mainstream economics, some economic geographers recognize the need for microfoundations (e.g., Boggs & Rantisi, 2003; Maskell & Malmberg, 2007) and advice others to look into nonorthodox or heterodox forms of economics (Martin, 1999). This is, of course, exactly what Austrian economics could clearly offer, as Rees (1992, 1999) and Hite (1995) noted long ago.

Methodological Individualism in Action

Having said that Austrian economists are explicit in their commitment to methodological individualism does not imply that they say much about how to employ it in practice. In fact, even among Austrians it is common to concentrate on the ontological side of individualism, at the expense of methodology (Hodgson, 2007). Among Austrians, perhaps only Hayek was truly concerned with methodological issues. Hayek (1952/1979, p. 64) contends that a methodologically individualistic social scientist "consistently refrains from treating these pseudo-entities [such as society, the economic system, capitalism or imperialism] as facts, and [instead] systematically starts from the concepts which guide individuals in their actions and not from the results of their theorizing about their actions." Hayek

(1952/1979, p. 65, emphasis in the original) adds that "it is the attitudes of individuals which are the familiar elements and by combination of which we try to reproduce the complex phenomena, the results of individual actions, which are much less known – a procedure which often leads to the *discovery* of principles of structural coherence of the complex phenomena which had not been (and perhaps could not be) established by direct observation."

As such, for theoretical research, which for Austrians is also the starting point for empirical research, the setup is such that in every case the *explanandum* is the macro phenomenon and its *explanans* is micro behavior. By starting with individual actions and those factors which guide them, we attempt to reproduce the complex phenomenon at the macro level.

The *explanandum* in our context is clear and unlikely to be contested by any economic geographer or regional scientist; it is regional economic activity. Unfortunately for the *explanans*, which is here the critical issue from the methodologically individualistic point of view, the case is less clear in the literature on regional economies. For example, a significant problem with the interregional competition literature is that it is not always even clear what a competing agent is (Lagendijk & Oinas, 2005, p. 12) and a long-standing "shortcoming of urban growth models is that they take spatial entities as the unit of analysis," even though such entities are not agents of change (Frenken & Boschma, 2007, p. 636).

One reason for this intellectual stance could be that the *explananda* of regional studies is at a somewhat indeterminate "mesolevel" situated between the micro and macro levels. Hence, many studies seem to attempt to explain regional economic development and growth on the basis of regional attributes, whereas the methodologically individualistic approach would be to reproduce these complex phenomena from individual actions. The result of methodological holism is that individual actions, if they have any explicit role, merely respond to the exogenous constraints, which then have all the explanatory power. To help overcome this mechanistic world-view is what is requested from Austrian economists: "The patterns of regional activity that we can observe empirically are also the product of purposeful and complex human imagination and creativity. The domain of science emphasized by Austrian economists is a necessary complement to the mechanistic models of regional phenomena" (Hite, 1995, p. 178).

Of course, abstraction is often necessary, and acting collective units – such as regions or countries – can be helpful metaphors or examples (Behrens & Thisse, 2007). This is also true of the firm, since it is not truly one individual unless it is completely operated by one entrepreneur (as such, the Austrian theory of entrepreneurship is less problematic).

While a firm is composed of individuals possessing different but complementary skills, it is nonetheless a goal-oriented organization that has, at least in theory, a command structure that directs the whole entity (even if internal relations and the need to decentralize operations obviously complicate this picture) and well-defined boundaries. As such, it is an acceptable unit of analysis from a methodological individualistic perspective (see also Udehn, 2001, pp. 265–272). Furthermore, despite the multiproduct nature of most firms of any significance, a firm is typically built around one or a few core competencies.

Outside the context of a centrally planned system, however, geographical units do not share these fundamental characteristics. Thus, apart from the fact that too often regional analysts "use interchangeably different, yet equally unclear, words such as locations, regions or places without being aware that they often correspond to different spatial units" (Behrens & Thisse, 2007, p. 458), a consistent application of methodological individualism implies that only individuals and not "learning regions," "regional networks," or "regional systems of innovation" have skills, capabilities, and tastes. Besides, unlike firms, geographical units whose boundaries are arbitrarily defined do not enter and exit markets, nor do they produce or trade goods and services. In short regions do not act like individuals or even organizations do (Boschma, 2004). We therefore suggest that methodologically individualistic theorizing becomes necessary when causal explanations are sought in the context of regional growth and development. This, however, does not imply that any theory formulated at the macro level should be considered false. Rather, the decision should be based on whether the theory is reducible to its individual parts and, if it is, whether the reproduced phenomenon remains unchanged (see Nozick, 1977).

Regarding empirical research, Austrian views – such as the impossibility of verifying or falsifying economic theory (if derived from true premises) and the distaste for econometrics (e.g., Rothbard, 1976; Heijman & Leen, 2004) – might strike many empirically oriented economic geographers and regional scientists as extreme. We will resist discussing these issues here as they are not fully agreed upon among Austrian economists and because methodological individualism as such has no implications for them. It is, however, useful to note that the Austrian criticism of empirical economics has its roots in the early debate with the German Historical School. As Steve Horwitz (2011) notes, the issue is mostly that from the Austrian perspective empirical research (or history) is necessarily based on a theory and, hence, such research would benefit from being based on explicit theorizing. That is, the claim is not that empirical research is irrelevant or useless, but that it should be grounded on a methodologically individualistic theory, which tells the researcher what the relevant facts are and how they are connected.

Regarding the particular choice of empirical method, methodological individualism makes no demands. As always, the choice of method depends on the research question. Hence, both quantitative and qualitative methods are in principle fully compatible with methodological individualism. What matters is that it is micro behavior which is supposed to explain macro phenomena.

The main challenge for quantitative approaches is to find suitable data on the explanatory individual factors that would perfectly correspond to the individual actions that the theoretical framework posits as the causal factors. The continuous emergence of micro-level data on firms and individuals can help to overcome these difficulties, and hence methodological individualism can be considered as a further rationale for shifting away from aggregate econometrics toward micro-econometric approaches. Any micro-level data is likely to be far from ideal, however. Hence, some challenges for quantitative methods are certain to persist.

One challenge for empirical research grounded in Austrian theory comes from identifying entrepreneurial discovery *processes* in empirical data. As such it is not surprising that econometric studies on agglomeration economies, even those utilizing micro-level data, many times run into endogeneity problems (Rosenthal & Strange, 2004). As Austrian theory would suggest (e.g., Hayek, 1978; Kirzner, 1997), there are various loop causalities among firm-level decisions and regional economic outcomes. Other complementary methods for analyzing the underlying mechanisms, such as the role of institutions, are likely to be needed in many cases.

Qualitative methods are more readily compatible with methodological individualism as the focus is usually already on individual actions and perceptions. As such they provide deeper knowledge of the contributing factors at the individual level. However, establishing the causal chains from the individual level to the complex regional level is more challenging in this context. First, the chosen sample and the study method should be guided by theory, meaning that the individual actions studied are deemed relevant causal factors by the underlying theory. Second, as always with qualitative methods, one should make sure that the chosen sample, which is necessarily small in size, is representative of these actions. Therefore, quantitative methods retain their usefulness when one wishes to address the universality of a phenomenon or the relative importance of a particular factor as compared with others.

To conclude, the main thrust of methodological individualism for empirical research is the commitment to studying the causal chains from individuals and their interaction to complex regional phenomena. That is, it is a methodological position on what is supposed to explain what, but it is reasonably flexible as to any particular method of inquiry. Of course, the usual issues of "the right method for the right question" and good practices considering the chosen research method always hold.

HOW METHODOLOGICAL INDIVIDUALISM CAN ENRICH AND CONTRIBUTE TO REGIONAL ECONOMIC ANALYSIS: THREE EXAMPLES

Our purpose so far has been to convince the reader that methodological individualism is a reasonable approach for regional economic analysis. Regarding its application, we wanted to highlight some potential misunderstanding and discuss the requirements that it poses for both theoretical and empirical research in this field. This second half of the chapter builds upon our previous work (Leppälä & Desrochers, 2010) in order to illustrate through three chosen cases that methodological individualism is indeed a fruitful approach for regional economic analysis and can yield important insights on topics much discussed by economic geographers and regional scientists. The first two cases are theoretical while the last one is mostly empirical.

Regional Comparative Advantage

Although Robert Torrents shares the credit for its discovery, the classical economist David Ricardo is best known for formulating the law of comparative advantage. The greatness of his contribution was to fully explain for the first time the mutually beneficial character of trade when there are differences in the comparative costs of production. Despite this fundamental discovery, the law of comparative advantage has created confusion in the hands of economic geographers and regional scientists. While applying the law to the regional economic level and ignoring methodological individualism, some of them have mistakenly understood the law as a proper public policy guide in the form of a justification for regional specialization. Before demonstrating where the problem lies through the use of methodological individualism, we first briefly review the law of comparative advantage and the rationale for specialization.

Many economists, most prominently Adam Smith, had long considered trading activities mutually beneficial. The most notable difference between Smith and Ricardo, however, was that the former had couched the rationale for trade in terms of absolute advantage while Ricardo (1817) illustrated that it would not matter if one of the trading parties had an absolute advantage in producing every commodity as long as their opportunity costs were different. With different opportunity costs, both parties would have a comparative advantage in producing the good in which they were relatively better at or least disadvantaged. After specializing according to their comparative advantage and by trading the surplus with each other, both would be better off than in autarky. This law of comparative advantage was chosen by Paul Samuelson as one of the greatest in economics, and it was the answer that Samuelson (1969, p. 9) gave to the mathematician Stanislaw Ulam's challenge to name "one proposition in all of the social sciences which is both true and non-trivial."

Ricardo's contribution is typically considered a direct improvement upon Smith's idea, but there are important differences between Smithean and Ricardian logic and analysis (Buchanan & Yoon, 2002). In the first place, for Smith the division of labor (or specialization) created increasing returns and, subsequently, opportunities for trade, whereas for Ricardo the differences in opportunity costs between the potential trading partners provided a reason to specialize. In other words, Ricardo considered these differences in productive capabilities to be inherent, but for Smith they were the consequence, not the cause, of the division of labor. Cannan (1893/1967, p. 39) explains that while Smith noticed natural advantages, he "despised that advantage as compared with the advantage which results from each kind of labor being performed solely by the individuals who, in consequence of the division of labor, have the largest amount of acquired skill and dexterity." This egalitarian outlook can probably be explained by Smith's historical circumstances.

A second difference between Smith and Ricardo is the level of analysis. Smith explained his idea in terms of individuals. As such, he might not have viewed foreign trade as any different from trade between individuals in the same country (Maneschi, 1998, p. 41). For Ricardo the context was trade between countries; specifically the Anglo-Portuguese cloth and wine trade. Later textbook examples, however, often present the law of comparative advantage in the context of two individuals, perhaps because the idea becomes more intuitively compelling in this context. For example, Samuelson

(1948, p. 669) gave the example of the best lawyer/typist in town, who nevertheless specializes in legal practices and hires someone else as his secretary, resulting in a better allocation of scarce resources than would have otherwise been the case.

While Ricardo's and later economists' theoretical contributions to the law of comparative advantage was done in the context of international trade, economic geographers and regional scientists transferred the idea to the regional level. This is a general feature of regional economic analysis, where many models and techniques are mere extensions of those used at the national level (Behrens & Thisse, 2007). As such, it became widely believed that regional specialization is the normal and desirable outcome of market processes. For example, the economist Leland Yeager (1954a, non-paginated) argues that, like improved transportation, free trade "promotes interregional specialization and increases through trade the results that a country gets from its productive powers." The geographer G. T. Renner probably expressed this idea as strongly as anyone when he stated the following:

> As commercial competition increases, any region will, unless prevented from doing so by political controls, tend to specialize in the production of those commodities for which it possesses a natural or technological advantage. [...] Wherever there are several alternative uses for land and other resources, that use which is most advantageous will be selected. (1955/1958, p. 511)

While the above quotations reflect the view that regional specialization is the optimal division of labor and the outcome of the free market rather than government intervention, later commentators have turned it upside down. Reflecting the widespread influence of Michael Porter's (1990) "cluster" framework, Karlsson and Stough (2002, p. 1) write that economic development "is no longer a question of national specialization and competitive power but of regional specialization often based on clusters and geographical competitive advantages." More or less implicit in this argument is that the market may fail in developing optimum regional specializations, in which case public intervention is needed.

This stance, however, begs the question as to why the division of labor should not proceed further down to the individual level, where it would seem equally valid. In other words, the argument for regional specialization typically proceeds from the macro to the meso level, while disregarding microfoundations altogether. As will now be argued, taking the principle of comparative advantage to the individual level actually undermines the case on behalf of national or regional specialization, or territorial division of labor to use Torrens's term (Blaug, 1962/1996).

To illustrate the failing of the collective specialization argument with a numerical example, let us revisit the textbook version of Ricardo's comparative advantage (from Blaug, 1962/1996).

As these numbers in Table 1 illustrate, here Portugal has an absolute advantage in producing both cloth and wine as less hours of labor are required. For example, if everyone in England were to produce cloth only, it would take a total of 100 hours of labor to produce one unit of it. As the law of comparative advantage tells us, instead of costs we should compare the cost ratios, as illustrated by the last column. Portugal has a comparative cost advantage in wine, in which case England, even though being less efficient in absolute terms, has by necessity a comparative advantage in cloth. If England specializes in cloth production and trades its surplus with Portugal for wine at a price ratio less than 1.2, and Portugal specializes in making wine and trades the surplus with England at more than a 0.88 ratio, both countries will be better off. Without knowing the pattern of demand, we are not able to establish the actual price ratio, but can say that it will be between 0.88 and 1.2. Through territorial division of labor, less labor is required for the same output or, equivalently, the same labor input yields a higher output. Before trade, it took $100+90+120+80=390$ hours of labor for England and Portugal each to produce one unit of cloth and wine. After trade these four units require only $100+100+80+80=360$ hours of labor.

A critical assumption in the textbook model is that the production costs are constant within each geographical area. To be fair to Ricardo, however, he never believed that one could specialize without undergoing diminishing returns and he never suggested complete specialization, and the textbook version does not do full justice to Ricardo's insights on the dynamic aspects of trade (Maneschi, 1998).

Constant marginal cost is indeed a very peculiar assumption, since aggregate production within any country or region is done by multiple firms and individuals. The only case when the aggregate marginal cost would be

Table 1. Labor Hours Required to Produce a Unit of Cloth and Wine.

	Cloth	Wine	P_w/P_c
England	100	120	1.2
Portugal	90	80	0.88

constant holds when each producer has the same constant marginal cost. Note, however, that this implies that in autarky there is neither trade nor specialization within these countries.

For convenience, suppose that in the previous example there are two individuals in both England (let's call them Alice and Thomas) and Portugal (Ana and Tiago). Furthermore, assume that in the previous table the hours of work were split equally, that is, each individual works for half of the total hours in Table 1.

To be consistent with the previous values for the countries, the individuals in these countries could have labor hour requirements as in Table 2 above. For example, if both Alice and Thomas in England concentrate on cloth production, 100 hours of labor will yield $50/112.5 + 50/90 = 1$ unit of cloth, as before. While these number are otherwise fully arbitrary, the same holds for all the aggregate values. As such, while England still has a comparative advantage in cloth production, the individual comparative advantages can be very different.

Thus, if instead of national specialization, each of these individuals specializes in production of the good in which they have an individual comparative advantage, the outcome is improved. Among the four individuals, Alice and Ana have a comparative cost advantage in wine production and Thomas and Tiago in making cloth. If each of them were to specialize according to these comparative advantages it would take only $108 + 90 + 72 + 82.5 = 352.5$ hours of labor to produce two units of each good.

Regional specialization is the outcome of specialization according to individual comparative advantages only in the specific case in which individuals within the same geographical regional have their comparatives advantages in the same good (see also, Leppälä & Desrochers, 2010).

Table 2. Labor Hours Required to Produce a Unit of Cloth and Wine after Disaggregation.

	Cloth	Wine	P_w/P_c
England	100.0	120.0	1.2
Alice	112.5	108.0	0.96
Thomas	90.0	135.0	1.5
Portugal	90.0	80.0	0.88
Ana	99.0	72.0	0.73
Tiago	82.5	90.0	1.09

Hence, the law of comparative advantage – in the sense of specialization as the efficient outcome – holds only at the individual level where actual production takes place. Furthermore, efficient regional or national specialization is the outcome of individual specialization and not the other way around.

A central policy implication of this theoretical result is that the lack of – or imperfect – regional specialization cannot be justifiably considered as a sign of market failure. This issue connects to the "knowledge problem," which Hayek (1949/1976) argues that any central planning authority faces. Even if the central planner knows the regional comparative advantages, a heroic assumption in itself, it is not enough to guarantee an efficient division of labor. Instead, the central planner would have to know the comparative costs that everyone in the regional economy faces. Regional specialization is efficient only when it is derivative of individual comparative advantages, but in that case there is likewise no reason not to expect it to emerge through natural market processes. Consistent application of methodological individualism demonstrates that bottom-up market processes outperform top-down publicly planned regional specialization.

One could consider individual comparatives advantages to be typically the same, as they are partly affected by their local or regional circumstances. Ricardo attributed a country's relative superiority to "its situation, its climate, and its other natural or artificial advantages" (quoted in Maneschi, 1998, p. 3). The later Heckscher–Ohlin model is an extension to national or regional factor endowments, and the emphasis on natural attributes is still predominant in geographical economics (e.g., Fujita, Krugman, & Venables, 1999). Indeed, Börje Johansson (2002, p. 506) has even suggested a shift in terminology from comparative advantage to location advantage.

Despite natural attributes, heterogeneity among individuals and within regions can be highly significant. While this is fundamentally an empirical issue, individual skills affect the relative productivity of the factors of production just as much (and perhaps typically much more) than regional or natural conditions. Arguably, this is even more the case in a modern service or knowledge-intensive economy, where relative productivity is more dependent on human capital. The strong emphasis on creative and knowledge-intensive industries in related current debates seems to further support this point.

As can be expected, the law of comparative advantage has been criticized in many quarters. For example, Unger (2007, Ch. 2) argues that the "doctrine" of comparative advantage is incomplete since the model choice allows for multiple solutions and does not account for dynamic properties or different institutional settings. As a result, no top-down blueprint is possible and no answer can be given as to what production a given country or region should specialize in. As Viner noted long ago, the "doctrine of comparative costs is, indeed, but a statement of some implications of this rule, and adds nothing to it as a guide for policy" (quoted in Maneschi, 1998, p. 35). In addition to this remark, however, we would further emphasize that the law of comparative advantage, while useless as a specific policy guide, nonetheless retains its value in terms of conveying the mutually beneficial character of trade and as a useful pedagogical device.

To summarize, the treatment of regions as the basic units of production hides the true source of economic prosperity: specialization according to individual comparative advantage. Furthermore, it can lead to false policy conclusions if one regards regional specialization as an optimal state that is dictated by the law of comparative advantage. Rather than providing a top-down blueprint for regional policy, the law describes how the gains of trade are achieved through a bottom-up process based on individual specialization. This is a prime example of the case where methodological individualism has both theoretical and policy relevance.

Agglomeration Economies

Ricardo's writings on international trade were driven by the view that natural shifts in production should not be prevented; he opposed agricultural protectionism in particular. Other nineteenth-century economists, most notably Alexander Hamilton, John Rae, and Friedrich List, took a more interventionist stance. In their view, comparative advantages, though they did not use the term, can be created with the assistance of public policy (Maneschi, 1998, p. 75). A similar view can be found in Krugman's (1987) dynamic model of comparative advantage. Krugman's argument can be summarized as follows: "It is not the case that nations [or regions] specialize in what they are good at so much as they are good at what they specialize in" (Pinch & Henry, 1999, p. 816). This view is based on Adam Smith's increasing returns from the division of labor, but takes the argument from the individual to the regional and national levels. If it is true that regional specialization creates increasing returns, then despite the demonstrated inefficiencies in the previous static setting, it could still be the case that publicly planned regional specialization is efficient in a dynamic sense. We will now assess this argument from the perspective of methodological individualism.

Since Alfred Weber, agglomeration economies have had a central place in regional economic analysis, even though the exact meaning of the term has varied (Parr, 2002a). Broadly speaking, the concept refers to the wide range of benefits that households and firms acquire by locating close to each other. As such, it is a central explanation as to why most people and economic activity are concentrated in city-regions, despite higher rents and other nuisances. The benefits can take the form of reduced costs of transportation or infrastructure, better availability of skilled labor, intermediate inputs and financial and marketing services, improved communication or greater local demand for produced goods. At this level, agglomeration tells us nothing about the type of co-located firms other than that more is better. More detailed approaches to analyzing localized economies of scale and scope are clearly needed.

Finer types of agglomeration economies, such as localization economies and urbanization economies, were identified by Bertil Ohlin (1933). On the one hand, localization economies are external to a single firm and derive from the co-location of independent firms in the same industry (see Parr, 2002b). As such they can be considered localized economies of scale specific to a single industry. Urbanization economies, on the other hand, are localized economies of scope. They derive from the overall diversity of local economic activity, are external to a single firm, but gained by all firms in the local economy.

Localization economies draw from three sources, most memorably discussed by Alfred Marshall (1892) in the context of industrial districts: pools of skilled labor, the availability of intermediate inputs and production-related services, and knowledge spillovers between competing firms. As the last of these will be discussed in the next section, we shall now concentrate on the first two.

Economies of scale that are internal to a firm are straightforward. When means of production are characterized by decreasing marginal costs, an expansion in the scale of production implies increasing returns. The mere existence of decreasing costs is, however, insufficient for localization economies. As Maskell (2001) has noted, an agglomeration theory of localized economies of scale should be able to explain why there is a cluster of N co-localized firms of size S undertaking related activities, rather than a single firm of size $N \times S$ producing the same goods or services. In other words, these economies of scale need to be external to a firm, but internal to a region, for otherwise any firm could achieve identical results simply by expanding its output, in which case there would be nothing regional about these economies (Parr, 2002b).

Naturally, the co-location of firms in an industry implies a larger labor pool and more firms providing intermediate inputs in the local economy. The mere higher availability of the means of production, however, does not directly imply lower costs as there are now also more rival firms demanding these. One could argue, perhaps, that the co-location of firms in an industry creates dis-coordination among the labor force and input providers, resulting in excess local supply. While this would benefit downstream firms, at the regional level this is largely a zero-sum game as it involves a shift of bargaining power from the suppliers to the buyers. Furthermore, in the longer run such dis-coordination is unlikely to persist.

Another assumption that lies behind the argument for localization economies is that the means of production are specialized to the extent that they can service only one or a set of related industries. While some capacities are specific to one industry or type of production, our contention is that most are not. Many functions in firms are performed by specialists such as sales and marketing people, accountants, R&D personnel, machinists, and so on. These occupations show a deep division of labor at the individual level, but their basic skills can be used in a wide variety of businesses. Indeed, as Alfred Marshall observed several decades ago in the context of industrial machinery:

> Modern work is more narrowly specialized, in so far as the number and variety of the operations performed by a modern worker are on the average less than those of elementary skilled handicraftsman; but it is less narrowly specialized, in the sense than an operative, who has mastered the accurate, delicate and prompt control of machinery of any kind in one industry, can now often pass, without great loss of efficiency, to the control of similar machinery in an industry of a wholly different kind, and perhaps working on different material. (Marshall, 1923, p. 10)

On a related point, one unquestionable benefit of a large local labor pool is that it facilitates matching between jobs and skills (Helsley & Strange, 1990). If workers' skills are industry-specific, however, matching is naturally less of a problem. Conversely, if workers are deeply specialized but their skills are not industry-specific, the diversity – and not only the size – of the local economic base facilitates matching.

The driving force in the growth of the modern industrial enterprise and of industrial capitalism is to exploit organizationally based competitive advantages such as economies of scope (Chandler, 1990/1994, p. 39). In other words, firm managers continually and actively look for such economies and opportunities to work with or expand in different industries. In addition to cost advantages, firms and individuals might adopt this strategy for "portfolio" reasons, as they do not want to become too dependent on one product line because of changing demand conditions, new competition, or potential offshoring. The search for economies of scope at the firm level implies that firms are constantly looking for new ways to put their specific capabilities to new uses, thereby resisting the tendency to become too dependent on the parent industry. Therefore, and in addition to the labor force, few input providers desire to base their businesses and productive capabilities on a specific industry. In order to reduce risk, they instead diversify their range of services whenever possible.

Moreover, the argument for localization economies assumes that the means of production cannot be provided beyond the local economy. Particularly for intermediate inputs, however, this is increasingly less true due to improvements in transportation and communication. Hence the actual externalities, if any, would not be limited to the local economy when it is not the only relevant market area. To sum up, transferring the idea of scale economies from the organizational level to the level of regional economies is unsound: its core assumption is that a regional economy is a coherent acting unit without any interesting microfoundations.

While localization economies are theoretically suspect and hence do not provide a sound justification for publicly planned regional specialization, we argue that theoretically, and from the perspective of methodological individualism, urbanization economies seem a more defensible concept. Possible sources of urbanization economies stem from the availability of a range of municipal services, public utilities, transportation and communication facilities, the existence of wide variety of business and commercial services, and complementarity in the labor supply (Parr, 2002b). These are economies of scope external to the individual firm but internal to the urban concentration, the distinguishing feature being that they are not specific to firms within a particular industry.

Similar to localization economies, it is important to distinguish urbanization economies from economies of scope internal to the individual firm. Economies of scope are gained when the production of several lines of products or services within the same firm or plant is less costly than producing them separately. In some cases these economies are internal to the firm, in which case it results in a multiproduct company (Panzar & Willig, 1981). As the capabilities and comparative costs of firms differ, however, it is usually more advantageous to specialize in a narrower set of output. Yet as several industries are able to use related intermediate inputs, the economies of scope are external to the individual firm but internal to the (local) market. Firms themselves have cost disadvantages in using the inputs in other lines of production, but the presence of different firms using similar inputs increases their availability.

An extreme case of where firms are able to exploit their orthogonal cost advantages is so-called industrial symbiosis. The concept refers to localized inter-firm linkages, in which costly waste (in terms of its disposal) to one firm is a valuable input to another (Chertow, 2000). While the present-day literature on industrial symbiosis is mostly ahistorical, industrial waste recycling linkages have a long history (Desrochers & Leppälä, 2010). Indeed, none other than Karl Marx (1894, Vol. 3, part 1, Ch. 5, non-paginated) observed that the capitalist mode of production extends "the utilisation of the excretions of production and consumption" and that the "so-called waste plays an important role in almost every industry." The historic cases of industrial symbiosis have, however, spontaneously emerged through bilateral deals, while the typical failures of "eco-industrial parks" (Deutz & Gibbs, 2004) highlight the challenges in creating these inter-firm linkages through government planning.

Besides the means of production, the local infrastructure that facilitates production is a relevant source of urbanization economies, as infrastructure is often characterized by decreasing marginal costs, but is not specific – unless so designed – to any particular industry. How the local infrastructure should be provided and funded for is, of course, another question, which we do not attempt to address here (see, e.g., Oates, Howrey, & Baumol, 1971).

Finally, Adam Smith argued that there is a crucial limit to the division of labor, namely the extent of the market. As the local economy grows or as connections to external markets improve, ever finer degrees of specialization become profitable. This, however, does not imply co-specialization; the implication is the opposite. Regional specialization implies, by definition, similarity between co-located firms. Similarity is, again by definition, quite distinct from complementarity. For this reason, growing cities, just like growing mature ecosystems, tend to get more diversified over time (Jacobs, 1969). An attempt to prevent this change is folly, as it goes against a major source of prosperity.

Localized economies of scope are arguably harder to detect, especially for outsiders, than localized economies of scale. This feature is even stronger when these economies are built on know-how that is not easily observable to outsiders. Therefore, a region with a diverse portfolio of different industries might appear inefficient when the linkages between firms are not obviously seen or understood. While a sound theoretical perspective, neither does the existence of urbanization economies provide any top-down blueprint for regional policy. As localized economies of scope can come in a variety of forms, it is more likely that alert entrepreneurs rather than regional policy makers will discover them.

To summarize, one should, once again, be careful when making analogies from firm-level activities to regional economies. If there are economies of scale (or scope) associated with the particular technologies that the firms are using, it does not imply that there are similar localized economies of scale (or scope) at the regional level, where we have multiple firms. Rather, the case should be the opposite. Both localization and urbanization economies imply that they are internal only at the regional level and external otherwise. Taking a methodologically individualistic perspective on agglomeration economies, it becomes more plausible to expect that most agglomeration economies are based on urbanization economies. That is, the co-location of dissimilar firms with different capabilities and outputs creates opportunities for nearby firms that each firm in itself is unable to utilize. Neither type of agglomeration economies is, however, likely to offer much of a detailed guide for a sound regional policy.

Localized Knowledge Spillovers

Malmberg and Maskell (2002) consider knowledge-creating mechanisms a more valid explanation for agglomeration than cost savings. Variation between different firms, both at the horizontal and vertical levels, creates knowledge which spills over to other users. Building on the influential contribution of Glaeser, Kallal, Scheinkman, and Shleifer (1992), a growing number of economists, geographers, and regional scientists have attempted to study localized knowledge spillovers by classifying them into three categories. The first is known as MAR spillovers because it refers to the insights of the economists Alfred Marshall (1890/1953), Kenneth Arrow (1962), and Paul Romer (1986), who suggest that spillovers between firms in the same industry are the most important kind and that they occur more abundantly in the absence of competition between firms. Porter spillovers, named for management scholar Michael Porter (1990), similarly emphasize spillovers within an industry, but view intense competition between rival firms as the best way to foster them.

The last type of localized knowledge spillovers, Jacobs spillovers, are based on the urban theorist Jane Jacobs' idea that innovations result from the interaction of people possessing different skill sets and know-how. In Jacobs' (1969, p. 47) own words, innovation is about "new work being added to old," which is similar to Weitzman's (1998) idea of recombinant growth.

In contrast to MAR and Porter spillovers, Jacobs spillovers are thus inter-industrial in nature and more abundant in diverse local economic environments. Like Porter spillovers, Jacobs spillovers are positively associated with the degree of competition (Audretsch, 1998), even though little is said about that by Jacobs herself.

All these spillover theories are based on the idea that they are uncompensated benefits (positive externalities) that are also limited to the local economy. Due to limited theoretical reflection, little more is said about them and, as such, they are not mutually exclusive explanations. They have, however, provided a vast and still growing number of empirical researchers with multiple hypotheses to test. Therefore, our commentary concentrates on the empirical research on localized knowledge spillovers, which has so far largely focused on the relative strengths of these spillovers and on whether specialized or diverse regions are better incubators of growth and employment. Despite much work, it seems that once again the great expectations placed on empirical research to arrive at unambiguous answers have failed to materialize due to limitations in data and methodology (for a broader discussion of this type of problem, see Teixeira, 2007). That is, support for all spillover theories have been found in different contexts (Beaudry & Schiffauerova, 2009; de Groot, Poot, & Smit, 2009; Döring & Schnellenbach, 2006).

Current research on knowledge spillovers is caught in a circular causality bind as knowledge spillovers are supposed to explain the existence of agglomeration, but the geographical agglomeration of economic activities is now taken as evidence of the existence of such spillovers. Since there are many sources of agglomeration economies, finding evidence for their existence is not the same as identifying their source (Hanson, 2001). The researchers explicitly regard individuals as the agents behind knowledge spillovers and are therefore ontological individualists, but studying the effect of some regional aggregates on others they practice methodological holism. These empirical tests are based on finding correlations between unrelated inputs (greater or lesser regional diversity or specialization of large or small firms) and outputs (such as R&D expenditures, patents, job creation, economic growth per capita, and innovation counts) (Beaudry & Schiffauerova, 2009). However, fundamental explanations of large-scale phenomena cannot be found in terms of other large-scale phenomena, but rather need to be deduced from statements about the dispositions, beliefs, resources, and inter-relations of individuals (Watkins, 1957). While some studies have made use of more disaggregated data, such as patent citations, it is questionable whether they are representative and relevant in uncovering the causal mechanisms in this case.

In a review of 67 such studies, Beaudry and Schiffauerova (2009, p. 320) not only observe that the "exact spillover mechanism is not yet fully understood and documented," but also that there is "no direct proof of the existence of knowledge spillovers." Indeed, "virtually no contribution has explored the ways in which knowledge is actually transferred among people located in the same geographic area" and knowledge spillovers are a convenient "black box' providing researchers "with an escape route to avoid studying the specific mechanisms through which [geography and innovation] are linked" (Breschi & Lissoni, 2001, pp. 994 and 976). Niles Hansen (2002, p. 261) thus concludes that regions, networks, and information technologies are innate entities that cannot learn or innovate and that "more meaningful analyses ... would require disaggregated empirical studies of how knowledge in fact passes among persons." Similarly, Breschi and Lissoni (2001, p. 1001) call for "additional evidence on the identity and the activities of individual firms and inventors."

Judging by these comments, the underlying problem seems to be the dismissal of methodological individualism. Empirical research based on methodological individualism would proceed from the individual and firm level to explain aggregate phenomena. Thus, we need more disaggregated data and clearer hypotheses on how knowledge in fact passes among individuals, the effect of regional factors on these processes, and how these processes ultimately result in greater innovativeness. Both qualitative methods (see Desrochers & Leppälä, 2011) and micro-econometrics can be a way forward. But Oxley, Walker, Thorns, and Wang (2008) note that the problems of empirical research regarding the knowledge economy cannot be solved solely by better data, since such research requires a robust theoretical foundation as well.

To conclude, our contention here is that empirical research can also benefit from a methodological individualistic approach. In the empirical knowledge-spillover literature, the actual knowledge spillovers have been largely left out of the equation. Some aggregate variables are regressed against others, while the knowledge spillovers are simply assumed to be the causal intermediating factor. It is no wonder that direct evidence on knowledge spillovers or the actual spillover mechanisms are yet to be found. Methodological individualism – taking the choices, beliefs, and actions of the individuals as the explaining variables – seems yet again to be the way forward.

CONCLUDING THOUGHTS

The starting point of this chapter was that while there are mutual gains of trade between Austrian economics and regional economic analysis, fundamental disagreements over methodological stances are in danger of obstructing potential collaboration. While methodological individualism is foundational to the way Austrians approach economic analysis, contributors to the subdisciplines of economic geography and regional science largely eschew it. This tension can be largely attributed to the intellectual history of economic geography in particular. Hence it is important to articulate, once again, that methodological individualism as practiced by Austrians does not imply normative individualism or methodological atomism.

Methodological individualism is, after all, a reasonably flexible and suitable approach for regional economic analysis. It does not impose any particular theoretical approach or specific empirical methods. Rather, it merely guides researchers in analyzing individuals and their actions in order to better grasp more complex and aggregate economic phenomena. In the case of regional economies, this implies that the *explanans* for regional economic activity are the individuals and firms which operate in that particular location.

While we hope to have succeeded in convincing Austrians and non-Austrians alike that, when clearly articulated, methodological individualism is fully compatible with regional economic analysis, we also wanted to demonstrate that it is in fact a very promising methodological approach, as illustrated by our discussion of three active debates in the economic geography and regional science research communities. In the case of regional comparative advantage, we demonstrated that while specialization according to individual comparative advantage is always efficient, this in no way implies that the concept is suitable at the regional scale nor that it logically demonstrates the inherent benefits of regional specialization. Furthermore, the law of comparative advantage demonstrates the mutual benefits of trade but adds nothing as a policy guide. A microfoundational look at agglomeration economies further revealed that localization economies, or localized economies of scale, are theoretically suspect and hence provide no sound justification for regional specialization policy. While urbanization economies, or localized economies of scope, amount to a theoretically sound description of the beneficial linkages that arise in regional economies, it does not provide any policy prescription and is more likely to occur spontaneously through market processes. Finally, we illustrated how empirical research on localized knowledge spillovers that are not grounded in methodological individualism can only deliver mixed and confusing results.

During the last 20 years, some economic geographers and regional scientists have suggested that Austrian economics could provide a valuable alternative framework to move their subfields forward. At the same time a few Austrian economists have moved toward applying their tradition to analyze issues in regional economics, especially in terms of drawing lessons from national planning policies at the regional level (e.g., Desrochers & Sautet, 2004; Glăvan, 2008; Holcombe, 2004; Ikeda, 2004). Beside the multiple policy issues concerning regional economies, such as bidding for creative resources (Cowen, 2007), we see a large potential for Austrian economics in advancing both theoretical and empirical research on regional economies more widely. As Sanford Ikeda (2004) notes, echoing the methodological individualism of Austrian economics, Jane Jacobs argued that the life and economic prosperity of a city results from the interactions of its residents. That is, the city is a prime example of a spontaneous order.

REFERENCES

Agassi, J. (1960). Methodological individualism. *The British Journal of Sociology*, *11*(3), 244–270.

Andersson, D. E. (2005). The spatial nature of entrepreneurship. *Quarterly Journal of Austrian Economics*, *8*(2), 21–34.

Arrow, K. (1962). The economic implications of learning by doing. *The Review of Economic Studies*, *29*(3), 155–173.

Arrow, K. (1994). Methodological individualism and social knowledge. *American Economic Review*, *84*(2), 1–9.

Audretsch, D. B. (1998). Agglomeration and the location of innovative activity. *Oxford Review of Economic Policy*, *14*(2), 18–29.

Barnes, T. J., & Sheppard, E. (1992). Is there a place for the rational actor? A geographical critique of the rational choice paradigm. *Economic Geography*, *68*(1), 1–21.

Baumol, W. J. (1968). Entrepreneurship in economic theory. *American Economic Review*, *58*(2), 64–71.

Baumol, W. J. (1993). Formal entrepreneurship theory in economics: Existence and bounds. *Journal of Business Venturing*, *8*(3), 197–210.

Baumol, W. J. (2002). Towards microeconomics of innovation: Growth engine hallmark of market economics. *Atlantic Economic Journal*, *30*(1), 1–12.

Beaudry, C., & Schiffauerova, A. (2009). Who's right, Marshall or Jacobs? The localization versus urbanization debate. *Research Policy*, *38*(2), 318–337.

Behrens, K., & Thisse, J.-F. (2007). Regional economics: A new economic geography perspective. *Regional Science and Urban Economics*, *35*(4), 457–465.

Blaug, M. (1962/1996). *Economic theory in retrospect* (5th ed). Cambridge, UK: Cambridge University Press.

Boggs, J. S., & Rantisi, N. M. (2003). The "relational turn" in economic geography. *Journal of Economic Geography*, *3*(2), 109–116.

Boschma, R. (2004). Competitiveness of regions from an evolutionary perspective. *Regional Studies*, *38*(9), 1001–1014.

Breschi, S., & Lissoni, F. (2001). Knowledge spillovers and local innovation systems: A critical survey. *Industrial and Corporate Change*, *10*(4), 975–1005.

Buchanan, J. M., & Yoon, Y. J. (2002). Globalization as framed by the two logics of trade. *The Independent Review*, *6*(3), 399–405.

Cannan, E. (1893/1967). *A history of the theories of production and distribution in English political economy from 1776 to 1848*. New York, NY: Augustus M. Kelley Publishers.

Chandler, A. D., Jr. (1990/1994). *Scale and scope: The dynamics of industrial capitalism*. Cambridge, MA: Harvard University Press.

Chertow, M. (2000). Industrial symbiosis: Literature and taxonomy. *Annual Review of Energy and the Environment*, *25*, 313–337.

Colander, D., Goldberg, M., Haas, A., Juselius, K., Kirman, A., Lux, T., & Sloth, B. (2009). The financial crisis and the systemic failure of the economics profession. *Critical Review*, *21*(2–3), 249–267.

Colander, D., Howitt, P., Kirman, A., Leijonhufvud, A., & Mehrling, P. (2008). Beyond DSGE models: Toward an empirically based macroeconomics. *American Economic Review*, *98*(2), 236–240.

Cowen, T. (2007). When should regions bid for artistic resources? *Review of Austrian Economics*, *20*(1), 1–10.

De Grauwe, P. (2010). The scientific foundation of dynamic stochastic general equilibrium (DSGE) models. *Public Choice*, *144*(3), 413–443.

de Groot, H. L. F., Poot, J., & Smit, M. J. (2009). Agglomeration externalities, innovation and regional growth: Theoretical perspectives and meta-analysis. In R. Capello & P. Nijkamp (Eds.), *Handbook of regional growth and development theories* (pp. 256–281). Cheltenham, UK: Edward Elgar.

Desrochers, P. (1998). A geographical perspective on Austrian economics. *Quarterly Journal of Austrian Economics*, *1*(2), 63–83.

Desrochers, P. (2001). Geographical proximity and the transmission of tacit knowledge. *Review of Austrian Economics*, *14*(1), 25–46.

Desrochers, P., & Leppälä, S. (2010). Industrial symbiosis: Old wine in recycled bottles? Some perspective from the history of economic and geographical thought. *International Regional Science Review*, *33*(3), 338–361.

Desrochers, P., & Leppälä, S. (2011). Opening up the 'Jacobs Spillovers' black box: Local diversity, creativity and the processes underlying new combinations. *Journal of Economic Geography*, *11*(5), 843–863.

Desrochers, P., & Sautet, F. (2004). Cluster-based economic strategy, facilitation policy and the market process. *Review of Austrian Economics*, *17*(2/3), 233–245.

Deutz, P., & Gibbs, D. (2004). Eco-industrial development and economic development: Industrial ecology or place promotion? *Business Strategy and the Environment*, *13*(5), 346–362.

Döring, T., & Schnellenbach, J. (2006). What do we know about geographical knowledge spillovers and regional growth? A survey of the literature. *Regional Studies*, *40*(3), 375–395.

Elster, J. (1982). The case for methodological individualism. *Theory and Society, 11*(4), 453–482.
Elster, J. (1993). *Political psychology*. Cambridge, UK: Cambridge University Press.
Frenken, K., & Boschma, R. (2007). A theoretical framework for evolutionary economic geography: Industrial dynamics and urban growth as a branching process. *Journal of Economic Geography, 7*(5), 635–649.
Fujita, M., Krugman, P., & Venables, A. J. (1999). *The spatial economy: Cities, regions, and international trade*. Cambridge, MA: MIT Press.
Glaeser, E. L., Kallal, H. D., Scheinkman, J. A., & Shleifer, A. (1992). Growth in cities. *The Journal of Political Economy, 100*(6), 1126–1152.
Glăvan, B. (2008). Coordination failures, cluster theory, and entrepreneurship: A critical view. *Quarterly Journal of Austrian Economics, 11*(1), 43–59.
Hansen, N. (2002). Dynamic externalities and spatial innovation diffusion: Implications for peripheral regions. *International Journal of Technology, Policy and Management, 2*(3), 260–271.
Hanson, G. H. (2001). Scale economies and the geographic concentration of industry. *Journal of Economic Geography, 1*(3), 255–276.
Hayek, F. A. (1949/1976). *Individualism and economic order*. London, UK: Routledge & Kegan Paul.
Hayek, F. A. (1952/1979). *The counter-revolution of science: Studies on the abuse of reason*. Indianapolis, IN: Liberty Fund.
Hayek, F. A. (1978). Competition as a discovery procedure. In *New studies in philosophy, politics, economics and the history of ideas* (pp. 179–190). Chicago, IL: University of Chicago Press.
Heijman, W. J. M., & Leen, A. R. (2004). On Austrian regional economics. *Papers in Regional Science, 83*(2), 487–493.
Helsley, R. W., & Strange, W. C. (1990). Matching and agglomeration economies in a system of cities. *Regional Science and Urban Economics, 20*(2), 189–212.
Hite, J. (1995). We are not rats: Seeking a regional version of Austrian economics. *International Regional Science Review, 18*(2), 177–183.
Hodgson, G. (2007). Meanings of methodological individualism. *Journal of Economic Methodology, 14*(2), 211–226.
Holcombe, R. G. (2004). The new urbanism versus the market process. *Review of Austrian Economics, 17*(2/3), 285–300.
Horwitz, S. (2011). Theory, history, and the great recession. *Review of Austrian Economics, 24*(2), 171–184.
Ikeda, S. (2004). Urban interventionism and local knowledge. *Review of Austrian Economics, 17*(2/3), 247–264.
Ikeda, S. (2007). Urbanizing economics. *Review of Austrian Economics, 20*(4), 213–220.
Ikeda, S., & Staley, S. (2004). Introductory essay for a symposium on "urban interventionism". *Review of Austrian Economics, 17*(2/3), 151–154.
Jacobs, J. (1969). *The economy of cities*. New York, NY: Random House.
Johansson, B. (2002). How can regional policies influence the location advantages of a region? In B. Johansson, C. Karlsson & R. R. Stough (Eds.), *Regional policies and comparative advantage* (pp. 503–514). Cheltenham, UK: Edward Elgar.
Karlsson, C., & Stough, R. R. (2002). Introduction: Regional policy evaluation in the new economic geography. In B. Johansson, C. Karlsson & R. R. Stough (Eds.), *Regional policies and comparative advantage* (pp. 1–21). Cheltenham, UK: Edward Elgar.

Kirzner, I. M. (1997). Entrepreneurial discovery and the competitive market process: An Austrian approach. *Journal of Economic Literature*, *35*(1), 60–85.

Krugman, P. (1987). The narrow moving band, the Dutch disease, and the competitive consequences of Ms Thatcher: Notes on trade in the presence of dynamic scale economies. *Journal of Development Economics*, *27*(1/2), 41–55.

Lagendijk, A., & Oinas, P. (2005). Proximity, external relations, and local economic development. In A. Langendijk & P. Oinas (Eds.), *Proximity, distance, and diversity: Issues on economic interaction and local development* (pp. 3–22). Aldershot, UK: Ashgate.

Leijonhufvud, A. (1973). Life among the econ. *Western Economic Journal*, *11*(3), 327–337.

Leppälä, S., & Desrochers, P. (2010). The division of labor need not imply regional specialization. *Journal of Economic Behavior and Organization*, *74*, 137–147.

Lucas, R. (1976). Econometric policy evaluation: A critique. *Carnegie-Rochester Conference Series on Public Policy*, *1*, 19–46.

Mäki, U., & Marchionni, C. (2011). Is geographical economics imperializing economic geography? *Journal of Economic Geography*, *11*(4), 645–665.

Malmberg, A., & Maskell, P. (2002). The elusive concept of localization economies: Towards a knowledge-based theory of spatial clustering. *Environment and Planning A*, *34*(3), 429–449.

Maneschi, A. (1998). *Comparative advantage in international trade: A historical perspective*. Cheltenham, UK: Edward Elgar.

Marchionni, C. (2004). Geographical economics versus economic geography: Towards a clarification of the dispute. *Environment and Planning A*, *36*(10), 1737–1753.

Marshall, A. (1890/1953). *Principles of economics* (8th ed). London, UK: Macmillan.

Marshall, A. (1892). *Economics of industry*. London, UK: Macmillan.

Marshall, A. (1923). *Industry and trade*. London, UK: Macmillan.

Martin, R. (1999). The new "geographical turn" in economics: Some critical reflections. *Cambridge Journal of Economics*, *23*(1), 65–91.

Martin, R., & Sunley, P. (1996). Paul Krugman's geographical economics and its implications for regional development theory: A critical assessment. *Economic Geography*, *72*(3), 259–292.

Marx, K. (1894). *Capital, volume III: The process of capitalist production as a whole*. Retrieved from http://www.econlib.org/library/YPDBooks/Marx/mrxCpC5.html#Part%20I,%20Chapter%205. Accessed on July 1, 2011.

Maskell, P. (2001). Towards a knowledge-based theory of the geographical cluster. *Industrial and Corporate Change*, *10*(4), 921–943.

Maskell, P., & Malmberg, A. (2007). Myopia, knowledge development and cluster evolution. *Journal of Economic Geography*, *7*(5), 603–618.

Miller, B. (1992). Collective action and rational choice: Place, community, and the limits to individual self-interest. *Economic Geography*, *68*(1), 22–42.

Mises, L. von. (1957/1985). *Theory and history: An interpretation of social and economic evolution*. Auburn, AL: Ludwig von Mises Institute.

Nozick, R. (1977). On Austrian methodology. *Synthese*, *36*(3), 353–392.

Oates, W. E., Howrey, E. P., & Baumol, W. J. (1971). The analysis of public policy in dynamic urban models. *Journal of Political Economy*, *79*(1), 142–153.

Ohlin, B. (1933). *Interregional and internal trade*. Cambridge, MA: Harvard University Press.

Overman, H. G. (2004). Can we learn anything from the economic geography proper? *Journal of Economic Geography*, *4*(5), 501–516.

Oxley, L., Walker, P., Thorns, D., & Wang, H. (2008). The knowledge economy/society: The latest example of "measurement without theory"? *Journal of Philosophical Economics*, *2*(1), 20–54.

Panzar, J. C., & Willig, R. D. (1981). Economies of scope. *American Economic Review*, *71*(2), 268–272.

Parr, J. B. (2002a). Agglomeration economies: Ambiguities and confusions. *Environment and Planning A*, *34*(4), 717–731.

Parr, J. B. (2002b). Missing elements in the analysis of agglomeration economies. *International Regional Science Review*, *25*(2), 151–168.

Pinch, S., & Henry, N. (1999). Paul Krugman's geographical economics, industrial clustering and the British motor sport industry. *Regional Studies*, *33*(9), 815–827.

Plummer, P., & Sheppard, E. (2006). Geography matters: Agency, structures and dynamics at the intersection of economics and geography. *Journal of Economic Geography*, *6*(5), 619–637.

Poon, J. P. H. (2004). Quantitative methods: Past and present. *Progress in Human Geography*, *28*(6), 807–814.

Porter, M. (1990). *The competitive advantage of nations*. London, UK: Macmillan.

Rees, J. (1992). Regional development and policy under turbulence. *Progress in Human Geography*, *16*(2), 223–231.

Rees, J. (1999). Regional science: From crisis to opportunity. *Papers in Regional Science*, *78*(1), 101–110.

Renner, G. T. (1955/1958). Principles and laws of economic geography. In F. E. Dohrs (Ed.), *Outside readings in geography* (pp. 506–514). New York, NY: Thomas Y. Crowell.

Ricardo, D. (1817). *On the principles of political economy and taxation*. Retrieved from http://www.econlib.org/library/Ricardo/ricP.html. Accessed July 1, 2011.

Romer, P. M. (1986). Increasing returns and long-run growth. *Journal of Political Economy*, *94*(5), 1002–1037.

Rosenthal, S. S., & Strange, W. C. (2004). Evidence on the nature and sources of agglomeration economies. In J. V. Henderson & J.-F. Thisse (Eds.), *Handbook of regional and urban economics* (Vol. 4, pp. 2119–2171). Amsterdam: Elsevier.

Rothbard, M. N. (1976). Praxeology: The methodology of Austrian economics. In E. Dolan (Ed.), *The foundations of modern Austrian economics* (pp. 19–39). Kansas City, MO: Sheed and Ward.

Rutten, R., & Boekema, F. (2007). *The learning region, foundations, state of the art and future*. Cheltenham, UK: Edward Elgar.

Samuelson, P. A. (1948/1976). *Economics* (10th ed). Tokyo: McGraw-Hill Kogakusha.

Samuelson, P. A. (1969). The way of an economist. In P. A. Samuelson (Ed.), *International economic relations: Proceedings of the third congress of the international economic association* (pp. 1–11). London, UK: Macmillan.

Schumpeter, J. A. (1908). *Das Wesen und der Hauptinhalt der theoretischen Nationalökonomie*. Leipzig: Duncker and Humblot.

Scott, A. J. (2000). Economic geography: The great half-century. *Cambridge Journal of Economics*, *24*(4), 483–504.

Teixeira, P. N. (2007). Great expectations, mixed results and resilient beliefs: The troubles of empirical research in economic controversies. *Journal of Economic Methodology*, *14*(3), 291–309.

Udehn, L. (2001). *Methodological individualism: Background, history, and meaning*. London, UK: Routledge.

Udehn, L. (2002). The changing face of methodological individualism. *Annual Review of Sociology*, *28*, 479–507.

Unger, R. M. (2007). *Free trade reimagined: The world division of labor and the method of economics*. Princeton, NJ: Princeton University Press.

Watkins, J. W. N. (1952a). Ideal types and historical explanation. *The British Journal for the Philosophy of Science*, *3*(9), 22–43.

Watkins, J. W. N. (1952b). The principle of methodological individualism. *The British Journal for the Philosophy of Science*, *3*(10), 186–189.

Watkins, J. W. N. (1957). Historical explanation in the social sciences. *The British Journal for the Philosophy of Science*, *8*(30), 104–117.

Weitzman, M. L. (1998). Recombinant growth. *The Quarterly Journal of Economics*, *113*(2), 331–360.

Yeager, L. B. (1954a). *Free trade: America's opportunity*. New York, NY: Robert Schalkenbach Foundation. Retrieved from http://oll.libertyfund.org/?option=com_staticxt&staticfile=show.php%3Ftitle=2038. Accessed on March 22, 2012.

Yeager, L. B. (1954b). The methodology of Henry George and Carl Menger. *American Journal of Economics and Sociology*, *13*(3), 233–238.

Zwirn, G. (2007). Methodological individualism or methodological atomism: The case of Friedrich Hayek. *History of Political Economy*, *39*(1), 47–80.

TIME, SPACE, AND CAPITAL

Åke E. Andersson

VIENNA AS A GLOBAL CENTER OF ECONOMICS

The three Austrian or Viennese economic "schools" all focused on the role of time and capital in the development of economies. However, they had almost no analysis of the spatial dimension of the economy. The major analysts within each school – according to my classification scheme – were:

I. Carl Menger, Eugen von Böhm-Bawerk, Knut Wicksell, Ludwig von Mises, and Gottfried Haberler
II. Joseph Schumpeter, Fritz Machlup, and Friedrich Hayek
III. Abraham Wald, John von Neumann, and Oskar Morgenstern

The first Austrian school was preoccupied with the nature of capital, its time dimension, and the necessity of interest. The second school also focused on economic dynamics, but with an orientation toward issues related to entrepreneurial activity as well as the use of information and knowledge in economic evolution. The third Austrian school, which was organized around Karl Menger's mathematical colloquium in Vienna, clarified the necessary and sufficient conditions for static and dynamic economic equilibriums. In addition, it created the foundations of economic game and negotiation theories.

The Spatial Market Process
Advances in Austrian Economics, Volume 16, 57–77

ISSN: 1529-2134/doi:10.1108/S1529-2134(2012)0000016006

My main claim is that the three Austrian schools of economics provided the foundations for almost all of economic analysis that was further developed after World War II.

In this chapter I attempt to show that a proper refocusing on the *time dimension* can shed light on the *dynamics of economies in space*. Three approaches are necessary for such a synthesis:

1. Subdividing products and production systems according to their different and always positive durabilities, implying that everything that is produced is capital.
2. Subdividing goods into private and public goods, while allowing for nonlinearity.
3. Allowing for differences in the time scales of economic processes.

With these distinctions it can be shown that economic development in time *and* space is determined by the impact of scale economies and the durability of goods.

AUSTRIA AND THE CREATIVE CITY OF VIENNA, 1870–1936

Why did Austria and more specifically its capital, Vienna, develop into a global center of scientific creativity at the end of the nineteenth century? More profoundly, how could this city become the focal point of most social and economic analysis, which was later to influence political movements throughout the twentieth century?

A number of books describe Vienna in the late nineteenth and early twentieth century. The most important ones are arguably Carl Schorske's *Fin de Siècle Vienna* (1981) and Allan Janik's and Stephen Toulmin's *Wittgenstein's Vienna* (1973).

A recurrent theme in *Wittgenstein's Vienna* is the question of how it was possible that the seemingly unrelated fields of philosophy, economics, medicine, psychology, mathematics, literature, music, painting, architecture, theater, and journalism could be in such a rapid creative flux at the same time and in the same city. *Fin de Siècle Vienna*, on the other hand, delves more deeply into the cross-fertilization of ideas from music, literature, painting, design, and architecture, with a special emphasis on the impact of the Freudian psychological revolution on these different art forms.

One of the causes that can be detected in all these examples is the disequilibrium and structural instability that characterized the social, institutional, and political structures of Vienna. The Vienna of the last decades of the Habsburg monarchy could be compared to a pressure cooker on a hot stove. A rather authoritarian political regime that was combined with the rigid values of the Viennese *bourgeoisie* increasingly constrained the cultural, social, and economic experiments that were demanded by the intellectual – liberal or socialist – elites.

The conflicts between different creative groups and between the intellectuals and the obsolete institutional structure became increasingly antagonistic from the 1870s onward. One well-known example is the conflict concerning legitimate scientific problems and methods between Sigmund Freud and the medical establishment. A second example is the increasing intensity of the conflict between liberal and socialist economists, having a focal point in the anti-Marxian economic analyses of Eugen von Böhm-Bawerk, Joseph Schumpeter, and Friedrich Hayek. Another overtly political example is the recurring conflict between the journalist Karl Kraus and Vienna's conservative politicians, with Karl Lueger as the most prominent personality.

The growing structural instability that set the stage for the wide range of scientific, social, and cultural creativity in Vienna was for the most part due to the inability of the declining monarchy to control the dynamic processes of economic and political change. The old-fashioned rules and regulations were entirely inappropriate for dealing with the ethnically diverse and cosmopolitan urban populations of the Austro-Hungarian double monarchy.

Vienna had experienced unprecedented economic growth during the second half of the nineteenth century. It was in this period that Vienna had become an industrially advanced city with modern boulevards and monumental architecture. Intellectuals as well as industrial workers from all parts of the Austro-Hungarian Empire were attracted by the economically dynamic city with its expanding economy. In the first decade of the twentieth century, the population of Vienna increased by almost 20,000 *per year*, without corresponding increases in the supply of new housing.

Knowledge and skills are necessary conditions for creativity in both the sciences and the arts. Vienna had an impressive number of highly skilled scientists and artists at the onset of its creative "take-off" in the late nineteenth century, as is indicated in Table 1.

The creative expansion of Vienna was built on an impressive infrastructure of knowledge. In the arts and sciences creative processes extended and transformed established knowledge. I have analyzed the creativity of Vienna

Table 1. Vienna's Infrastructural Creators, 1870s to 1930s.

Discipline	Individuals
Philosophy	Ludwig Wittgenstein; members of the *Wiener Kreis*
Mathematics and physics	Ernst Mach; Ludwig Boltzmann
Psychology	Sigmund Freud
Economics	Carl Menger; Eugenvon Böhm-Bawerk; Ludwig von Mises; Joseph Schumpeter; Fritz Machlup; Gottfried Haberler; Friedrich Hayek; Friedrichvon Wieser; Abraham Wald; Oskar Morgenstern; John von Neumann
Political journalism	Karl Kraus; Theodor Herzl
Fine arts	Gustav Klimt; Oskar Kokoschka; Egon Schiele
Architecture	Otto Wagner; Adolf Loos; Josef Hoffmann
Music	Gustav Mahler; Arnold Schönberg; Alexander Zemlinsky

more extensively in Andersson (2011). That analysis can be summarized as follows:

1. Vienna was the major node of transport and trade in the Habsburg Empire and central Europe.
2. The city experienced a massive growth of its population that was driven by migration from the different parts of the empire.
3. Many of the most creative individuals had migrated from other cities in Austria-Hungary.
4. New political movements reinforced the disequilibrium and structural instability of the political system.
5. The city had a population consisting of many ethnic groups; a disproportionate share of the creative scientists and artists were Jews.
6. The growing population and the resulting housing shortage sparked an increase in the demand and supply of public meeting places, such as the coffee houses within the *Ringstraße* that surrounded the city center.

Vienna was probably the creative capital of the world during the period 1870–1936, when it all came to an abrupt end as a result of Europe's rapidly growing totalitarianism.

TIME IN ECONOMICS

How is time to be represented in economic theory and models? The first and most obvious way is to represent time as a continuous variable that represents the accumulation of capital and other dynamic economic processes. This implies that the processes are modeled as differential equations.[1] The second way is to represent the dynamic economic processes as a discrete set of periods (e.g., weeks, months, quarters, or years). The third way is to allow for many different continuous and interactive *time scales* of the dynamic economic processes. The final important aspect in this context is to represent the dynamic characteristic of each good as its technologically and economically determined *durability*.

Building on Böhm-Bawerk's (1889) concept of "roundaboutness" in production, Knut Wicksell (1906/1966) shows how the duration of production can be economically optimized, subject to physical, biological, or technological process constraints. But the durability of the goods is also determined by the duration and the resource accumulation of the production process.

In the following section I shall show how the durability of goods (seen as capital objects) will influence not only the dynamics of economies but also the spatial structure of production.

TIME AS THE ESSENTIAL ELEMENT OF CAPITAL

The labor theory of value had been taken for granted by most of the classical economists. In Karl Marx's *Das Kapital* it had been formulated as *the* fundamental proposition of economics, having repercussions not only for most contemporaneous economic theorizing but also for the political interpretations of economic theory. Marx had assumed that capital was simply an accumulation of labor during the period of its creation. Eugen von Böhm-Bawerk (1889) sets out to show the errors of the labor theory of value in its application to the theory of capital. Böhm-Bawerk (*ibid.*) introduces the idea of roundabout production and comes to the provisional conclusion that the *time structure* of inputs is of essential importance in determining the value of capital. Formulating a numerical example as in the table below, he concludes that the decision of timing and the prevailing rate of interest are essential for determining the optimal value of capital:

> In an earlier chapter I called attention to the well-attested fact that the lengthening of the capitalist process always leads to extra returns, but that, beyond a certain point, these extra returns are of decreasing amount. Take again the case of fishing. If what we might call the one month's production process of making of a boat and net leads to the return of the day's labour being increased from 3 to 30, – i.e. by 27 fish, – it is scarcely likely that the lengthening of the process to two or three months will double or treble the

> return: Certainly the lengthening it to 100 months will not increase the surplus by a hundredfold. The surplus return – for there will always be a surplus return – will increase by a slower progression than the production period. We may, therefore, with approximate correctness represent the increasing productivity of extending production periods by the following typical scheme.

Without capital	£15	**Increases**
With capital/1 year	35	£20
2 years	45	10
3	53	8
4	58	5
5	62	4
6	65	3
7	67	2
8	68:10s	1:10s
9	69:10s	1
10	70	0:10s

His conclusion is:

> The rate of interest under the foregoing assumptions is limited and determined by the productivity of the last prolongation of the production period which is still economically permissible and that of the next prolongation which is not so permissible. (Böhm-Bawerk, 1889, book VIII, section VII.I.9)

The Swedish young economist Knut Wicksell was deeply influenced by Böhm-Bawerk's analysis of capital and time: "I remember it as if it had happened yesterday, a day 25 years ago, when I, in a bookstore window in Berlin – where I was living on a Gustaf Lorén scholarship – for the first time, read the book title *Positive Theorie des Kapitales* by Eugen von Böhm-Bawerk ... this work was to me a revelation." (Wicksell, 1914, p. 322, translated from Swedish).

Wicksell, who was a mathematician, understood that Böhm-Bawerk's tables could be generalized into a mathematical optimization problem. This became the famous wine maturation problem, in which he set out to determine the economically optimal duration of storing a wine. He then assumed that the value of the wine would be continuously growing if the wine was stored. During the process of storage there is of course a biological process, during which solar energy and the activity of yeast and other components of the wine contribute to the growing value, which is finally determined by the utility to the consumer as expressed by the willingness to pay for the matured wine. The constraining factor was the opportunity cost of storage, determined by the cost of labor, the human capital of the wine producer, the price of the storage facility, and the market rate of interest. The necessary condition of the optimal economic duration of storage states that the storage of the wine should cease when *the rate of the growth of value equals the rate of interest*.

A number of theorists have claimed that this is a special dynamic case, only relevant for point-input, point-output decision problems. This conclusion is incorrect. It can easily be shown that the condition also holds for continuous sequences of harvesting of a growing biological resource over time (e.g., trees in a natural forest or fish in the sea).[1]

The debate about the Marxian labor theory of value had come to an end. Not only would land (natural resources) be an indispensable fundamental factor of production besides labor, as had already been shown by Johann Heinrich von Thünen (1826/1875). Capital could not be reduced to labor by any procedure. Time had been shown to be the crucial variable in the determination of capital and its value.

DURABILITY, CAPITAL, PRODUCTION, AND ECONOMIC GROWTH

The average durability of goods (or capital) in the macro-economy can be determined by observing that the value of capital is a stock concept, which is observable at any instant in continuous time. The value of production is however a flow concept, which requires measurement over some time period. The value of the stock divided by the value of the flow thus has the dimension of time (Hawkins, 1948; Hawkins and Simon, 1949).

This implies that the average durability of the good (i.e., capital) is determined by the ratio of the value of capital to the value of production. This, in its turn, implies that the average durability of capital is determined by quantities of capital and production as well as their prices. The durability of capital is closely related to depreciation. If the durability is known with certainty to be T years, then the optimal depreciation per year is $1/T$. If the durability is uncertain but has a known mean value, the depreciation can be determined with the aid of entropy theory; in that case, the depreciation rate is a constant fraction of the net asset value (Lev and Theil, 1978).

Assume that total production is subdivided into currently used production and production for future use (i.e., investment). Current production requires inputs at the rate ay, where a gives the necessary input per unit of output y. Investments are determined by bgy, where g signifies the rate of growth of y and b is the capital requirement per unit of increase of production. As b divided by a equals the durability of the product and $b = \tau a$, τ is the durability of the product (y). Thus:

$$y = ay + g\tau ay \tag{1}$$

Furthermore, it is a long-run equilibrium condition that the price equals the cost of current inputs as well as the capital cost:

$$p = pa + rp\tau a \quad \text{or} \quad (1 - a)/\tau a = r \tag{2}$$

This implies that $g = r$ or that *the rate of interest must in an economically sustainable equilibrium equal the rate of growth of this simplified economy.*

However, it can be shown that this result is also valid for an economy with any number of sectors and a technology that is represented by the input–output and capital–output matrices **A** and **B** where **B** = **TA**, with **T** being a diagonal matrix of durabilities.

The greater the durability is, the lower the rate of interest and growth would have to be. The only way of extending overall durability without a decline in the rate of interest and growth would be through a sufficiently large reduction in the use of current inputs.

CASSEL, WALD, VON NEUMANN, AND THE BIRTH OF GENERAL EQUILIBRIUM THEORY IN VIENNA

Although Carl Menger's, Böhm Bawerk's, Wicksell's, and Schumpeter's books and articles played a great role in the formation of economic theory in Austria and Germany, the most widely used *textbook* in economics in the German-speaking world from 1917 onward was Gustav Cassel's *Theoretische Sozialökonomie* (1917/1927). Karl Menger, the son of the economist Carl Menger, assembled some of the greatest mathematicians of the time in his *Mathematische Kolloquium* in Vienna in the early 1930s. This was no random event. Menger's efforts aimed at bringing to fruition his father's (Carl Menger), Böhm-Bawerk's, Wicksell's, and Cassel's theories by transforming them into a consistent mathematical economic theory. His focus was on the axiomatization of the fundamental ideas of Austrian economics. Karl Menger's *Kolloquium* became the birthplace for a formalized static and dynamic general economic equilibrium as laid out by

Cassel in his textbook. Cassel, of course, had accepted the idea that utility is essential for determining economic decisions by the individual consumer. But he was against the idea that there is an absolute need for a deduction of aggregate demand from the theory of individual consumer utility. It was, according to Cassel, sufficient to have knowledge of all demand and supply functions (which were dependent on a complete set of prices) in order to generate a general static equilibrium. Wald (1936) proved that this was indeed the case.

If aggregation of individual utility or demand functions could be shown to be possible, this would also cover the general equilibrium problem as formulated by Menger (1871) and Walras (1874).

John von Neumann proceeded along the route that had been opened up by Wald in order to show that a dynamic model based on the same approach could be combined with the growth model as formulated in Cassel's textbook. That growth model saw the equilibrium rate of growth as being determined by the willingness to abstain from current use of resources through savings and the technologically determined capital–output ratio. This is in its essence the same growth model as formulated above. Von Neumann proceeded to generalize this model into a theory of an economically sustainable dynamic general equilibrium, based on the use of the saddle point theorem that he had proved in the 1920s.

He introduced time into his theory in two ways. First, he formulated the basic model as discrete period dynamics. Second, the durabilities of all goods were treated as rates of depreciation between periods. Von Neumann further assumed joint production in order to treat depreciation efficiently.

For example, the process of making paper involves wood, electricity, and machines as inputs at the start of the process. At the end of the process a *joint product*, consisting of paper and machines (older and thus smaller in capacity) make up the vector of outputs.

The sustainable equilibrium is a saddle-point solution that determines the equilibrium price and quantity vectors. At that same point the minimum rate of interest and the maximum sustainable rate of growth are equalized. This is consistent with Wicksell's and Böhm-Bawerk's results for microeconomic growth processes. The weakness from a classical Austrian point of view is that von Neumann's theory lacks a foundation that represents the utility of the decision-makers in the model.

The work of the *Kolloquium* came to an end in 1936. The participants had by then created a foundation for the development of modern mathematical economics, including game theory as later developed by John von Neumann and Oscar Morgenstern (1944) and general static equilibrium theory with the assumption of utility-maximizing consumers, as reformulated by Gerard Debreu (1959). It is furthermore reasonable to regard von Neumann's introduction of saddle point theory as one of the preconditions for linear and nonlinear programming and modeling.

DETERMINATION OF THE RATE OF INTEREST

Böhm-Bawerk gave three reasons why the interest rate has to be positive. First, people's marginal utility of future income is lower than the same present income if they expect economic growth. Second, psychologically most people are impatient and simply prefer a given income now, instead of waiting for it. These two reasons imply a willingness to pay a positive interest rate to get access to loans in the present, and a corresponding requirement to be paid interest when extending credit to someone. The third reason is according to Böhm-Bawerk the technological advantages of a roundabout production process as described above. Wicksell accepted these microeconomic reasons, but insisted on treating the interest rate as a macroeconomic variable, which is exogenous to individual households and firms. According to Wicksell, one must distinguish between the *natural* (or normal) rate of interest, and the rate of interest that is determined by the supply and demand for credit in the money market. A steady state macroeconomic equilibrium with a constant level of prices requires a money-market rate of interest that is equal to the natural rate of interest. A desirable monetary policy would then imply a policy of adjusting the interest rate of the central bank to the rate of inflation.

If the general price level would start increasing, the proper response of the central bank would be to increase the rate of interest. Conversely, it should cut the interest rate in a deflationary situation (Wicksell, 1906/1966). Wicksell's analysis is essentially dynamic: A monetary rate of interest that is reduced to a level below the natural rate of interest would trigger an increase in investments. This would imply an increase in total demand beyond the supply capacity. The market response would then initially be an increase in the price of machinery, building material and other investment goods as well as an increase in the wages of construction labor. The increase in the income of this type of labor would imply increasing demand for consumer goods and a corresponding reduction of real savings. The prices of consumer goods and the wages of other workers would thus also have to be increased, and this cumulative inflationary process would continue for as long as the monetary rate of interest is kept lower than the natural rate of interest. The only way of halting this inflationary process is by increasing the monetary rate of interest to the level of the natural rate, at which time the willingness to save would again correspond to the marginal productivity of capital.

Recent decades have shown a return from Keynesian and naïve monetary economic policies to Wicksellian central bank strategies in many countries. (The Federal Reserve is the most conspicuous exception to this Wicksellian trend in the developed world.)

Hayek accepted Wicksell's analysis of the relation between the natural and the monetary rate of interest, but tried to extend its importance considerably. He agreed with Wicksell in viewing an artificially low central-bank rate of interest as the cause of a cumulatively rising price level. But Hayek went much further than Wicksell, viewing monetary policy as the key mechanism to be used to combat inflation as well as unemployment. In other words, monetary policy would also regulate the business cycle.

Wicksell thought of his contribution as a theory of the general price level and its control. Monetary effects on relative prices – as assumed by Hayek – and on resource allocation as well as on business cycle fluctuations were to Wicksell of secondary importance. Wicksell therefore disapproved of the use of his theory by Mises (1912) and Hayek, who had adapted his basic analytical idea to business cycle theory.

Schumpeter, who in many respects admired Böhm-Bawerk and Wicksell, had a dramatically different view of the rate of interest. In the static and no-growth equilibrium of an economy, the interest rate would automatically fall to zero, because he saw a positive rate of interest as relevant only to a developing economy (Schumpeter, 1912; Haberler, 1937). This view is consistent with the equilibrium theory of economic growth, as formulated by von Neumann. But a closer scrutiny of that model also reveals why duality requires the interest rate to be equal to the growth rate on the equilibrium trajectory. The model is based on two important and simplified assumptions. First, there is no uncertainty in the modeled economic system. Second, households are treated as any other sector of production. There is no room for trade-offs between future and current consumption, and thus no consideration of Böhm-Bawerk's first and second reason for a positive rate of interest.

If decision-makers are uncertain about the future, for example as a consequence of variations in the weather, in the health of workers or in other natural conditions that influence production or consumption, there would be a need for a positive rate of interest in order to bridge the gap between lenders and borrowers. We can thus conclude that a general economic equilibrium with uncertainty requires that *the rate of interest is kept above the rate of economic growth.*

CAPITAL CONTROVERSIES

Böhm-Bawerk (1889, 1921/1959) as well as Hayek (1941) had been struggling with the creation of a complete theory of capital, including a disaggregation of all capital goods and a consistent method of aggregation into a macroeconomically consistent capital stock. The essence of their problem was the heterogeneity of the capital goods. This was later followed up by the Marx-influenced capital controversy of the Cambridge/Italy school (Pasinetti, 1969).

I am convinced that the problem of capital aggregation can be resolved, as soon as we accept the necessary uncertainty of capital investments and the determination of capital prices in the markets for financial capital, especially in the stock market. It is reasonable to assume that macroeconomic capital equals the value of capital at the prices that are expected by financial investors. A firm that is traded on the stock market is – as is discussed below – essentially an aggregated value of different capital goods, including knowledge capital in different forms. The modern theory of financial markets claims that the total equilibrium value of capital of any traded firm is determined (as an average over some period of observation) in the markets for securities and bonds, taking expected prices, perceived risks, and the real rate of interest into consideration.

The theory of financial markets was initially formulated by Markowitz (1952) and further developed by Modigliani and Miller (M-M) (1958), Sharpe (1964), Lintner (1965), and Mossin (1966). Their claim is that the capital market is "M-M-efficient," implying that the totality of all capital allocation opportunities can be captured by the expected return ($r(m)$) and the risk or standard deviation ($\beta(m)$) for the market portfolio of all traded instruments. The value of a firm (seen as an aggregate of material and nonmaterial capital) can be determined in an analogous way. The risk-free or deterministic capital allocation would give $\beta(0)=0$ and $r(0)\geq g$.

From this the conclusion follows that the heterogeneous capital value – as aggregated by the firm and valued in the stock market – generates the average durability of the capital that has been invested in the firm when it is divided by the firm's scale of production.

THE FIRM AS AN EMERGENT ORDER OF CAPITAL

The theory of the firm as formulated by Oliver Williamson (1981) and others – being based on Ronald Coase's (1937) transaction cost assumptions – is a useful starting point for an analysis of the formation of firms, but it is only a starting point. It tells us nothing about the best organization of material and human capital in the organization of the firm.

A haphazard arrangement of the carriers of human capital and the machinery and other material capital will not give the same high level of output as a better arrangement that generates greater profits to the entrepreneur. However, it can be shown that maximizing the profitability of interactions between large numbers of such discrete objects can often not be found, even with the aid of powerful computers.[2] For a firm with only 10 groups of employees to be allocated to 10 different tasks, there are in fact 3.6 million possible assignment patterns, and the number of possible patterns increases with the factorial of the number of tasks and employee groups. Already with a size of 20 tasks and employee groups the total number has risen to 2,432,902,008,176,640,000 possible assignment patterns. With numerous advantageous interaction combinations, there will be a great number of local profit maxima in this class of problems. The search for the global maximum is thus a challenging one.

However, the probability of finding solutions close to the global maximum is vastly increased if different firms in the same product market are experimenting with their organization of production. Competition will then reveal best-practice firms with superior organizations in terms of their profitability.

An evolutionary procedure called the "Patch Procedure," where a patch can be a predetermined team of employees, has been developed by Stuart Kaufmann and his associates:

> The results hint at something deep and simple about why flatter, decentralized organizations may function well: contrary to intuition, breaking an organization into "patches" where each patch attempts to optimize for its own selfish benefit, even if that is harmful to the whole, can lead, as if by an invisible hand, to the welfare of the whole organization. The trick, as we shall see, lies in how the patches are chosen. We will find an ordered regime where poor compromises for the entire organization are found, a chaotic regime where no solution is ever agreed on, and a phase transition between order and chaos where excellent solutions are found rapidly... Therefore, as a general summary, it appears that the invisible hand finds the best solution if the coevolving system of patches is in the ordered regime rather near to the transition to chaos. (Kauffman, 1995, p. 147, p. 264)

At the end of such an evolutionary process the superior firms with their structure of teams will have a capital value far above what would be indicated by their book-value of purchased machines and human capital.

In accounting practice, the part of the capital value that cannot be easily accounted for is often called "goodwill value":

> Business goodwill is a key intangible asset that represents the portion of the business value that cannot be attributed to other business assets. Put differently, business goodwill reflects the synergy among the various assets used by the business to produce income: in a well-run business the whole is greater than the sum of the parts. (Haleo Corporation, 2012)

The only way to value tangible and intangible organizational capital properly is through the valuation of the firm in the stock market or through the sale of the firm as an organized entity.

THE DURABILITY OF GOODS AND PRODUCTION LOCATION PATTERNS

The problem of the spatial structure of production is related to the sustainable scale of each firm as well as to the total demand for their products. The sustainable scale of a firm is determined by the minimum long-term total average cost, including interest on capital, transaction, and transport costs. The long-term equilibrium of the firm requires the output price to correspond to this minimal long-run average cost.

In order to determine the impact of product durability on the spatial structure of production, we need to specify the long-run average production cost function (APC) and its dependence on the scale of production, x. A simple but mostly realistic assumption is to subdivide the total production cost into fixed cost (F) and variable cost ($V(x)$). The fixed cost is the cost of all the capital of the production unit and is independent of the scale of operation as soon as the production unit has been established. For simplicity we assume that the production unit is identical to the firm.

This analysis provides a convenient connection to Austrian economics and specifically to the theories of Böhm-Bawerk and Wicksell. Their analysis of the importance of roundabout production and the duration of the production process addresses the amount of capital needed and thus the fixed cost of production. Large fixed costs are especially pronounced in knowledge-intensive production, which requires a long period of research and development before actual production can occur. Typical examples are the pharmaceutical and advanced electronics industries, which regularly invest more than twenty percent of their sales value in the creation and innovation of new products and associated production equipment.

The variable cost is normally monotonously increasing with the scale of operation up to the capacity limit of the firm's capital. We consequently assume that the optimal scale of operation is smaller than or equal to that upper limit. The simplest variable cost is the linear case $V(x) = vx$. The total production cost function would then be $\mathrm{TPC} = F + vx$; and the average production cost function is consequently $\mathrm{APC} = F/x + v$.

Transport and transaction costs are caused by the contacts between the firm and its customers. If customers are more or less evenly spread around the firm, the total cost of such contacts would increase progressively with increases in the scale of production and sales. This implies that the average cost of transactions and transport would also be increasing with the scale of operations. A simple, yet reasonable, approximation is an average transport and transaction cost function $\mathrm{ATC} = kx$. The term k can be decomposed into cost per unit of shipment, a, and the frequency of contacts, which depends inversely on the durability, t, of the product. The average transport and transaction cost is thus $\mathrm{ATC} = (a/t)\ x$. Greater durability thus implies smaller average transport and transaction cost.

The total average cost A equals the sum of the average production cost APC and the average transport and transaction cost ATC: $A = F/x + c + (a/t)\ x$. The minimum average cost requires that the derivative of A with respect to the scale of production is set equal to zero. This implies that the optimal scale of production is:

$$x(opt) = \sqrt{\frac{Ft}{a}}$$

The optimal scale of production of the firm is thus increasing with increasing fixed cost of production (primarily of capital and land in the roundabout production process) and with increasing durability of the product. To reiterate, the fixed cost is an increasing function of the duration or roundabout degree of production.

The optimal number of firms is determined by the total scale of the market. The maximal total market scale is today the world market, as it is integrated by information and transport networks. The existence of an accessible world market is a precondition for free competition for most tradable goods.

The total number of firms in the world market, N, for a good is then determined as $N = \text{Total demand}/x(\text{opt})$, which implies that the total number of firms is a decreasing function of the fixed cost of the representative firm and is also a decreasing function of the durability of the good being produced.

Increasing the fixed cost – as influenced by the duration of the production process – and the durability of the good being produced reinforce each other by reducing the number of firms, if the demand of the world market is given. In some cases the number of firms is so severely constrained that assumptions of near-perfect or free competition cannot be upheld even if the product is globally traded. Examples are trains, ships, airplanes, and nuclear reactors, all of which are produced in a handful of locations that serve a global market.

The number of firms is thus determined by this procedure, but not the locations in geographical space. For that a connection with the theory of location and trade is needed. A theory of location and trade that summarizes the contributions by David Ricardo, Johann Heinrich von Thünen, Eli Heckscher, Bertil Ohlin, and Martin Beckmann is the recent variational inequality model as formulated by Anna Nagurney (1999). In her model, the demand and supply in each location are represented by the prices that are announced in the various locations. An increased flow of a good from one location to another one requires the price difference to be greater than the sum of transport and transaction costs associated with a one-unit trade flow between the two locations.

The pattern of production locations and trade flows reaches equilibrium when each good-price difference is equal to (or smaller than) the sum of transaction and transport costs. As we have seen above, the durability of each good determines their transaction and transport cost. The greater the durability of the good is, the smaller this cost will be. Trade will increase until there are no price differences between different locations for the limiting case of extremely durable goods. For goods with extreme durability and low transportation and transaction costs, the law of one price will prevail.

INFRASTRUCTURE – CAPITAL THAT IS DURABLE AND PUBLIC

The static and dynamic equilibrium theories and models that were developed by the different Austrian schools have provided the foundations for modern economics. But they are all inadequate in one important respect. They cannot handle the dynamics of durable public goods or infrastructure, for example, constitutions, scientific knowledge, or communication networks. In most Austrian theories, the infrastructure is an exogenously determined stable stage on which the economic games are played. The economic and social consequences of different infrastructural stages are discussed, for instance in the analysis of socialism versus the market economy in writings from Böhm-Bawerk and Wicksell to Mises and Hayek. But a dynamic analysis of the interdependent evolution of the infrastructure and the economic games is essentially lacking, even if traces of such an analysis can be found in Schumpeter's *Capitalism, Socialism, and Democracy* (1942/1950).

The reason for this omission is quite clear. The necessary mathematical foundation for such an analysis of interdependencies did not exist before the 1960s. The first attempt to analyze catalytic and other collective phenomena was by the Field Medalist Reneé Thom in his *Structural Stability and Morphogenesis: An Outline of a General Theory of Models* (1972/1989). In this book, Thom shows how collective phenomena can be modeled with singularity theory and applied to biological phenomena, such as the simultaneous blooming of a certain species when influenced by the slowly rising temperature.

In the 1950s and 1960s, physicists developed the theory of the laser. The German physicist Hermann Haken was one of the key theorists behind that theory. A central part of this work was what later came to be known as *Synergetics*. Synergetic theory was to be published in the 1970s (Haken, 1977). Haken showed that predictability can often be achieved by subdividing dynamic processes into widely separated time scales. A general equilibrium of the combined dynamic system is a possibility, if the slowly changing variables are causally impacting a large number of rapidly changing variables.

The institutional and material infrastructure is by definition such a collective (or public) variable, which moves on a qualitatively slower time scale than the private goods that are allocated by markets. The infrastructure has the following two defining traits:

1. It is simultaneously used by many firms or households
2. It is extremely durable, compared with other types of capital

The following dynamic model of a market economy illustrates the power of subdividing the economic system into widely different time scales.

The dynamics of the markets for ordinary goods is determined by differential equations that determine the price trajectories of all goods:

$$\begin{aligned} dp/dt &= f(p,k,A^*); \\ s(k)dk/dt &= g(p,k,A^*); \end{aligned} \tag{3}$$

where p is a vector of prices of ordinary market goods (including factor services), k is a vector of capital or investment goods, A^* is the infrastructure as represented by accessibility of knowledge over networks and $s(k)$ is a parameter representing the large durability and thus slow speed of capital growth.

The development of the infrastructure (as represented by accessibility to fundamental knowledge) can be represented by the equation:

$$s(A)dA/dt = m(p, k, A); \tag{4}$$

where $s(A) = t/T(A)$. $T(A)$ indicates the extreme durability of infrastructure, implying that $s(A)$ is a very small, positive number, possibly on the order of .01 or smaller.

This implies that in the time frame of the other variables of this system, dA/dt can be set approximately equal to zero, *most of the time*, but not always. Very rarely, the fast and slow processes will be synchronized and the whole system will go into a period of creative destruction, eventually transforming itself into a new economic structure.

We thus have a dynamic system:

$$\begin{aligned} dp/dt &= f(p, k, A^*), \\ s(k)dk/dt &= g(p, k, A^*); \end{aligned} \tag{5}$$

which is to be solved subject to the *temporary constraint*:

$$m(p, k, A^*) = 0 \tag{6}$$

For systems of this kind we can apply Tikhonov's theorem (Sugakov, 1998): Assume a dynamic system of N ordinary differential equations, which can be divided into two groups of equations. The first group consists of m fast equations, the second group consists of $m + 1, \ldots, N$ slow equations.

Tikhonov's theorem states that the system:

$$\begin{aligned} dx(i)/dt &= f(i)(x, g); \quad i = 1, \ldots, m, \quad \text{(fast equations)} \\ f(j)(x, g) &= 0; \quad j = m + 1, \ldots, N, \quad \text{(slow equations)} \end{aligned} \tag{7}$$

has a solution under certain economically reasonable conditions.

For each position of the slow subsystem, representing the dynamics of the infrastructure, the fast market subsystems have plenty of time to stabilize. Such an approximation is called adiabatic (Sugakov, 1998).

In the very long run dA/dt cannot be assumed to be zero, and the system as a whole would then cease to be as well behaved as in the short and medium terms.

The system would in the *very long run* have all the bifurcation properties that are typical of nonlinear, interactive dynamic systems. Between periods of changes to the economic structure, there would be periods of stable market-growth equilibrium.

The Austrian economists from Schumpeter to Hayek were skeptical about the possibility to model a dynamic economic system mathematically. The modern mathematical theory of dynamic systems supports this view. General equilibrium theory, as conventionally formulated by Arrow, Debreu, and others, is not general enough to be expandable into dynamic systems (or combined spatial and dynamic systems).

However, I have shown above that this impossibility can be resolved if the dynamic models of the economy make proper distinctions between the time scales of markets, capital accumulation, and the slow changes to the infrastructural stage on which the markets operate.

CONCLUSIONS

The theories and observations of the role of the time dimension by the early Austrians, including the Swedish economist Knut Wicksell, are fundamental to our understanding of dynamic economic processes. The economic importance of the choice of the duration of a roundabout process was proposed by Böhm-Bawerk and Wicksell. With the increasing importance of scientific research, industrial research, and technological development this issue has become increasingly important.

But the duration of the production process must be complemented by the durability of the goods that are produced. The durability of the goods – and all goods are also capital – is a determinant of many aspects of the economy as a growing system.

The durability of the goods and the duration of production processes influence the determination of the following factors:

- the macroeconomic capital–output ratio,
- the maximal rate of economic growth,
- the minimal real rate of interest,
- the optimal number of firms, and thus
- the spatial extent of the competitive market and
- the pattern of location and trade.

The extreme durability of institutions, networks, and other infrastructure is especially important as it provides a theory for modeling complex dynamic systems. We thus have the methodology needed to avoid the limitations of standard general equilibrium theory in favor of a more complete and yet formal dynamic general theory of the evolving market economy.

NOTES

1. Maximize harvesting income $= \int pux(exp(-rt))dt$;
subject to growth $= dx/dt = ax - bx^2 - ux$;

where $u =$ the rate of harvesting (assumptions: infinite time horizon and constant price). Maximize the Hamiltonian:

$$H = pux(\exp(-rt)) - \lambda(ax - bx - ux)$$

This leads to an optimal rate of harvesting at each instance of time. Optimality furthermore requires that $\lambda'/\lambda = r$. This means that the rate of growth of value should equal the rate of interest at the optimal rate of harvesting.

2. If we assume indivisible units of machines and humans and that the productivity of a machine or a human (x_i) depends on interaction with (x_j), and if these interaction net benefits can be captured by the quadratic form $\mathbf{x'Cx}$, then there is no simple incentive mechanism or computerized search algorithm that can provide the route to a global maximum for most interaction matrices $\mathbf{C}$ (Koopmans and Beckmann, 1957).

REFERENCES

Andersson, Å. E. (2011). Creative people need creative cities. In D. E. Andersson, Å. E. Andersson & C. Mellander (Eds.), *Handbook of creative cities*. Cheltenham, UK: Edward Elgar.

Böhm-Bawerk, E. von (1889). The positive theory of capital. 1923 reprint of 1891 smart translation. New York: Stechert. 1959 Huncke translation printed as *Capital and Interest: Volume II – Positive Theory of Capital*. South Holland, IL: Libertarian Press.

Böhm-Bawerk, E. von (1921/1959). *History and critique of interest theories* (First published as *Kapital und Kapitalzins*). South Holland, IL: Libertarian Press.

Cassel, G. (1917/1927). *Theoretische Sozialökonomie*, *4*, verb. und wesentlich erw. Aufl. Leipzig: Deichertsche Verlagsbuchhandlung.

Coase, R. (1937). The nature of the firm. *Economica*, *4*(16), 386–405.

Debreu, G. (1959). *Theory of value: An axiomatic analysis of economic equilibrium*. New Haven, CT: Yale University Press.

Haberler, G. von (1937). *Prosperity and depression: A theoretical analysis of cyclical movements*. Geneva: League of Nations.

Haken, H. (1977). *Synergetics: An introduction – Nonequilibrium phase-transitions and self-organization in physics, chemistry and biology*. Berlin: Springer.

Haleo Corporation. (2012). Retrieved from http://www.haleo-corporation.software.informer.com/

Hawkins, D. (1948). Some conditions of macroeconomic stability. *Econometrica*, *16*(4), 309–322.

Hawkins, D., & Simon, H. A. (1949). Note: Some conditions of macroeconomic stability. *Econometrica*, *17*, 245–248.

Hayek, F. A. (1941). *The pure theory of capital*. London: Routledge and Kegan Paul.

Janik, A., & Toulmin, S. (1973). *Wittgenstein's Vienna*. Chicago, IL: Ivan R. Dee Publishers.

Kauffman, S. (1995). *At home in the universe: The search for laws of self-organization and complexity*. London: Penguin Books.

Koopmans, T., & Beckmann, M. (1957). Assignment problems and the location of economic activities. *Econometrica*, *25*, 53–76.

Lev, B., & Theil, H. (1978). A maximum entropy approach to the choice of asset depreciation. *Journal of Accounting Research*, *16*(2), 286–293.

Lintner, J. (1965). The valuation of risk assets and the selection of risky investments in stock portfolios and capital budgets. *Review of Economics and Statistics*, *73*, 13–37.

Markowitz, H. (1952). Portfolio selection. *Journal of Finance*, *12*, 71–91.

Menger, C. (1871/1981). *Grundsätze der Volkswirtschaftslehre* [*Principles of economics*] (J. Dingwall & B. Hoselitz, Trans.). New York, NY: New York University Press.

Mises, L. von (1912). *Theorie des Geldes und der Umlaufsmittel*. Leipzig: Duncker und Humblot.

Modigliani, F., & Miller, M. (1958). The cost of capital, corporation finance, and the theory of investment. *American Economic Review*, *48*(3), 261–297.

Mossin, J. (1966). Equilibrium in a capital asset market. *Econometrica*, *34*(4), 768–783.

Nagurney, A. (1999). *Network economics: A variational inequality approach*. Amsterdam: Kluwer Academic Publishers.

Pasinetti, L. (1969). Switches of techniques and the "rate of return" in capital theory. *The Economic Journal*, *79*, 508–531.

Schorske, C. E. (1981). *Fin de Siècle Vienna*. New York, NY: Knopf.

Schumpeter, J. A. (1912). *Theorie der wirtschaftlichen Entwicklung*. Leipzig: Duncker und Humblot.

Schumpeter, J. A. (1942/1950). *Capitalism, socialism, and democracy*. New York, NY: Harper and Row.

Sharpe, W. F. (1964). Capital asset prices: A theory of market equilibrium under conditions of risk. *Journal of Finance*, *19*(3), 425–442.

Sugakov V. I. (1998). *Lectures in synergetics*. World Scientific Series on Nonlinear Science, Series A, Vol. 33, Singapore.

Thom, R. (1972/1989). *Structural stability and morphogenesis: An outline of a general theory of models*. Reading, MA: Addison-Wesley.

von Neumann, J., & Morgenstern, O. (1944). *Theory of games and economic behavior*. Princeton, NJ: Princeton University Press.

von Thünen, J. H. (1826/1875). *Der isolierte Staat in Beziehung auf Landwirtschaft und Nationalökonomie* (Vols. 1–3, 3rd ed.). Berlin.

Wald, A. (1936/1951). On some systems of equations of mathematical economics. *Econometrica*, *19*(4), 368–403 (translated from *Zeitschriftfür Nationalökonomie*).

Walras, L. (1874/1954). *Éléments d'économie politique pure, ou théorie de la riches se sociale* [*Elements of pure economics, or the theory of social wealth*] (W. Jaffé, Trans.). London: Allen and Unwin.

Wicksell, K. (1906/1966). *Föreläsningar i nationalekonomi*. Lund: Gleerups.

Wicksell, K. (1914). Lexis och Böhm-Bawerk. *Ekonomisk Tidskrift*, *16*(11), 322–334.

Williamson, O. E. (1981). The economics of organization: The transaction cost approach. *The American Journal of Sociology*, *87*, 548–577.

PART II
ENTREPRENEURSHIP AND SPACE

ENTREPRENEURSHIP, KNOWLEDGE, SPACE, AND PLACE: EVOLUTIONARY ECONOMIC GEOGRAPHY MEETS AUSTRIAN ECONOMICS

Erik Stam and Jan Lambooy

What would we learn from bringing together Austrian economics and evolutionary economic geography? In this chapter, we argue that these approaches are very complementary and commensurable. We will investigate the spatial aspects of the conditions of entrepreneurship on the one hand, and the consequences of entrepreneurship on the other hand. The consequences are the effects of individual interactions that may lead to the emergence of complex systems that are largely the "result of human action, but not of human design" (Hayek, 1967). These emergent systems have spatial coordinates and localized effects on the growth of knowledge and economic activity. The emergent systems – new organizations, institutions, industrial clusters, cities, and regions – in turn form the context for subsequent entrepreneurial actions.

In this chapter, we will show the strengths and opportunities of Austrian economics for the indeterminate dynamic analysis of entrepreneurship and evolving selection environments, and the spatial aspects of these processes and structures. We will explicitly investigate the bridge between

The Spatial Market Process
Advances in Austrian Economics, Volume 16, 81–103

ISSN: 1529-2134/doi:10.1108/S1529-2134(2012)0000016007

evolutionary economic geography (Boschma & Frenken, 2006; Boschma & Lambooy, 1999; Boschma & Martin, 2010) and Austrian economics. The chapter is structured as follows: first, we introduce Austrian as well as evolutionary geographic treatments of entrepreneurship. In the second section, we investigate entrepreneurship and its conditions of space and place. In the third section, we elaborate on the urban aspects of the conditions of entrepreneurship as it is approached in evolutionary theories. The fourth section centers on the spatial aspects of the consequences of entrepreneurship, with a particular focus on its impact on urban and regional development.

AUSTRIAN ECONOMICS AND EVOLUTIONARY ECONOMIC GEOGRAPHY

Entrepreneurship and Geography in Austrian Economics

In a society with dispersed knowledge, entrepreneurs have to identify opportunities, recognize them as relevant, and match them with (demand) preferences, technological feasibilities, and their own skills. According to Austrian theory, this is done on a subjective basis: different people not only have different preferences but also different perceptions, interpretations, and understandings of values and feasibilities, which they adapt in mutual interaction and communication in specific contexts over their unique life courses (Nooteboom, 2000). Different minds think different things (Lachmann, 1978), and the entrepreneurial opportunities people perceive very much depend on their prior knowledge (Shane, 2000).

Hayek (1945) teaches us that there is no "God-like view" of society from which any single individual could fully know the preferences and available means of others. This knowledge is dispersed among all the individual members of a society. Hayek (1945) makes a distinction between scientific knowledge – knowledge of general rules by experts – and local (or practical) knowledge, with the latter being knowledge of particular circumstances of time and place. This implicitly brings geography – that is, places – into the Austrian framework.

Practically every individual has some advantage over all others. Each individual has this advantage since she possesses unique information that she might use in beneficial ways. However, the beneficial use of the information requires either that the decisions are left to the individual with the unique information or that the decisions are made with her cooperation (cf. Shane, 2000, on prior knowledge). The knowledge of the particular circumstances of time and place is a key input in the entrepreneurial process, and provides the bridge from general scientific knowledge to useful applications in particular contexts. Hayek (1945) shows that the success of the market comes from its effectiveness in bringing private and local knowledge into use, as opposed to scientific knowledge. Hayek's argument resembles the more recent knowledge-spillover theory of entrepreneurship (Audretsch, Keilbach, & Lehmann, 2006), in which entrepreneurs are seen as the agents that turn scientific knowledge into knowledge that can be used in daily practice (and introduced in and diffused through the market).

This knowledge of particular circumstances of time and place is even more important because of the continuous changes that affect the stock of scientific knowledge; knowledge about its practical applications; and local circumstances – that is, the restless nature of capitalism (Metcalfe, 2002). In the 1930s, Hayek emphasized information as a basic element in the price system as well as for understanding economic development. Later, he developed this concept further into the wider one of knowledge (Hayek, 1945).

The entrepreneurial discovery approach is central to the Austrian tradition (Kirzner, 1997). Key elements are the role of knowledge and entrepreneurial discovery in the process of market equilibration: "the systemic process in which market participants acquire more and more accurate and complete *mutual knowledge* of potential demand and supply attitudes" (Kirzner, 1997, p. 62), which reduces the sheer (i.e., unknown) ignorance of market participants. Entrepreneurial discovery[1] involves a type of alert entrepreneurial choice in which imagination and boldness play central roles. Entrepreneurs thus discover – by surprise – innovations in an open-ended uncertain world (Knight, 1921).[2]

This process is not without preconditions: rivalrous competition is needed. This competition serves the twin purpose of offering the best possible deals to consumers (the traditional interpretation of market competition), and of revealing information to market participants. The information is such that no one had previously been aware that they lacked it (see Hayek, 1978, p. 179 on competition as a discovery procedure). In this information-revealing sense, entrepreneurial discovery can be compared with the Popperian approach to scientific progress. Entrepreneurship, like science, is a problem-solving activity in which competing solutions to a problem are generated. Each solution is a guess; a conjecture: experiments and trial-and-error processes will reveal which of the proposed solutions solves the problem best. In this process, it is also possible that the problem should be redefined, or that underlying problems are revealed. Harper (1996, 1998) suggests that the entrepreneurial process is similar to the scientific process of conjecture and refutation: alert entrepreneurs discover an opportunity to create value in the market; however, this conjecture needs to be tested in the market. Through the market test the entrepreneur will learn whether the opportunity is really valuable, and the entrepreneur might amend his conjecture. This process of trial-and-error may be repeated many times, and delivers knowledge not only to the entrepreneur but also other market actors, including emulators and new competitors.

Austrians also focus on the importance of institutions in economic life. Two aspects stand out regarding institutions and entrepreneurship. First, the role of institutions in securing social order by providing certainty and shared expectations in social interactions, which thereby enable the individual to concentrate on innovative actions that are inherently full of uncertainty. Examples of key institutions in this respect are the rule of law and property-right regimes. The second aspect concerns the role of institutions in the allocation of talent in general (cf. Acemoglu, 1995; Murphy, Shleifer, & Vishny, 1991), and entrepreneurial efforts in particular (Baumol, 1990). Austrian economic theory includes the assumption that entrepreneurship is an omnipresent aspect of human action. If every context for action is to some degree novel, people have to improvise – if ever so slightly – in all of their behavior (Koppl, 2007). To improvise is to do something in a new and different way – in other words, innovators are improvisers. This omnipresent "innovation" makes entrepreneurship an aspect of all human action.[3]

If one assumes that entrepreneurship is an omnipresent aspect of human action, it cannot be the "cause" of economic development as such (Boettke & Coyne, 2003): the rules of the game determine the payoffs of different types of entrepreneurship, and in that way guide entrepreneurial action in more or less productive directions.[4] Institutions are thus seen both as a fundamental precondition for entrepreneurial action to take place, and as the rules that affect the allocation of entrepreneurial talent (see Table 1). These institutions are often created in particular places, and their effects are often limited to certain – spatially confined – groups.

Entrepreneurship in Evolutionary Economic Geography

Entrepreneurship is a fundamental driver of economic evolution. Evolutionary approaches emphasize differentiation, unexpected situations, and

Table 1. Entrepreneurship and Geography in Austrian Economics.

Key Concept	Source	Effect
Prior knowledge	Individual biographies (spatiotemporally specific)	Directs entrepreneurship; transforms scientific knowledge into practical knowledge
Entrepreneurial discovery	Rivalrous competition of potential solutions	Creates novel knowledge/ reduces ignorance
Institutions	Unintended effect of human action	Provides certainty that enables focused innovation; allocates entrepreneurship

continuous change in external conditions and in the composition of elements. Entrepreneurs can be seen as the key actors to optimally benefit from new unexpected opportunities. Entrepreneurship is also a distinctly spatially uneven process, and thus an important explanation of the uneven economic development of regions and nations. Not surprisingly, entrepreneurship is a key element in evolutionary economics (Grebel, Pyka, & Hanusch, 2003; Metcalfe, 2004; Schumpeter, 1934; Witt, 1998) and has been recognized as an important factor in explanations of (regional) economic development (Acs & Armington, 2004; Audretsch et al., 2006; Fritsch, 2008).

This means that the explanation of regional variations in entrepreneurship has become an important issue, which is not surprising since there are pronounced differences within and between nations in rates of entrepreneurship and in their determinants (Bosma & Schutjens, 2008; Reynolds, Storey, & Westhead, 1994; Stam, 2005). These differences tend to be persistent over time, reflecting path dependence in industry structure (Brenner & Fornahl, 2008), formal institutions (Casper, 2007), and culture (Beugelsdijk, 2007; Giannetti & Simonov, 2009; Saxenian, 1994). Such regional attributes vary widely across regions, but are relatively inert over time. Next to path dependence, cumulative causation also magnifies spatial differences in entrepreneurship: the pursuit of entrepreneurial opportunities feeds further opportunities (Holcombe, 2007). First, any change by one entrepreneur alters the economic environment and provides opportunities for additional adjustments by other entrepreneurs. Second, entrepreneurial activity is likely to create wealth and in that way increases demand and the extent of the market. Third, the creation of market niches that did not previously exist provides opportunities for new entrepreneurs to enter and expand this market niche. Entrepreneurial opportunities thus come into being because of prior acts of entrepreneurship (cf. Metcalfe, 2002 on the growth of knowledge). Holcombe (2007, p. 61) writes that "Bill Gates could not have made his fortune had not Steve Jobs seen the opportunity to build and sell computers, and Steve Jobs could not have built a personal computer had not Gordon Moore invented the microprocessor." Historical processes produce uneven spatial economic patterns of both the characteristics of individuals and the "availability" of opportunities that taken together condition but do not determine economic behavior (Boschma & Frenken, 2006; Lambooy, 2010b), of which entrepreneurship is a special class.

Next to the creation and diffusion of entrepreneurial opportunities, selection plays an important role in entrepreneurship, reflected in the fact that most new firms do not survive for very long, as well as in the fact that few firms (often less than one out of 10 start-ups) attain substantial growth (Reynolds & White, 1997; Stam & Wennberg, 2009). Selection is generated by the decisions of external resource holders to allocate their resources among these firms (Aldrich, 1999; Baum & Silverman, 2004).

New firm formation is affected by different selection environments. Most directly there is competition in product markets: a lack of competition may either indicate an opportunity (a gap to be filled) or a constraint (high entry barriers). Fierce competition forces firms to produce and sell efficiently, if they are to survive. For new firms that need to reach a substantial size, selection in the capital, and labor markets are also important. Such firms need to attract financial and human resources in competition with other organizations that also need these resources in the face of limited supply. Competition is often a very local process: more distant firms are less likely to compete for the same pool of human resources or product markets than firms in spatial proximity (Baum & Mezias, 1992; Cattani, Pennings, & Wezel, 2003; Sorenson & Audia, 2000). Another aspect of the selection environment is the size and the nature of local demand; however, entrepreneurs can also extend external trade relations and gain increasing returns in the value chain (Chandra & Sandilands, 2005; Young, 1928). Table 2 gives a summary of the treatment of entrepreneurship in evolutionary economic geography.

Austrian economic theories provide useful theories that deal with entrepreneurship and the market process that implicitly take into account the spatial aspects of (practical) knowledge and institutions. Evolutionary economic geography, on the other hand, provides useful insights into the causes of uneven economic development over space and time, while only

Table 2. Entrepreneurship in Evolutionary Economic Geography.

Key Concept	Source	Effect
Spatiotemporal heterogeneity	Regional variety in entrepreneurial action and path dependence in structures	Causes diverging rates of entrepreneurship and of economic growth
Regional path dependence	Stickiness of industry-specific investments (in tangible and intangible resources), institutions, and culture	Generates continuity in entrepreneurship rates and direction (industrial structure) over time
Selection environment	Markets (resource munificence and competition); institutions	Productivity of firms; choice of particular governance form

implicitly taking account of the role of entrepreneurs and markets as agents and outcomes of evolutionary processes.

THE BIOGRAPHY OF ENTREPRENEURS IN SPACE

Different people not only have different preferences but also different perceptions, interpretations, and understandings of values and feasibilities, which they adapt in mutual interaction and communication in specific contexts over their unique life histories. Different minds think different things (Lachmann, 1978), and the entrepreneurial opportunities people perceive very much depend on their prior knowledge (Shane, 2000). The biography of an entrepreneur provides her with accumulated knowledge about particular circumstances, especially knowledge about the spatial distribution of particular means and preferences. On the one hand entrepreneurs connect different "worlds," either literally (see Saxenian, 2006 on the "new Argonauts") or in a cognitive sense (see Nooteboom, 2000), and in this way make novel combinations. On the other hand, empirical studies have shown that entrepreneurs, just like other human beings, are relatively inert in a spatial sense: it is a stylized fact that entrepreneurs are most likely to start their firm in the region where they live and work (Stam, 2010).

For nascent entrepreneurs, the focal choice concerns what kind of firm to start, given their location; the choice rarely concerns choosing a location for a given firm (Stam, 2007). The social ties of the potential entrepreneurs are likely to be localized, and induce entrepreneurs to start their firm in close spatial proximity to their homes and to their current employers (Cooper & Folta, 2000; Parwada, 2008; Sorenson, 2003; Stam, 2007). The fraction of entrepreneurs working in the region where they were born is significantly higher than the corresponding fraction for dependent workers (Michelacci & Silva, 2007).[5] A study of Portuguese manufacturing firms found that entrepreneurs were willing to accept labor costs three times higher than in alternative locations to locate the new business in their current region (Figueiredo, Guimaraes, & Woodward, 2002). A British study found that individuals are more likely to be self-employed if they have not moved regions recently (in the previous seven years; Blanchflower & Oswald, 1990). A recent Danish study (Dahl & Sorenson, 2011) found that firms perform better – they survive longer and generate greater annual profits and cash flows – when they are located in regions in which their founders have lived longer. This effect appears substantial, similar in size to the value of prior experience in the industry (i.e., the value of being a spin-off).

This locational stickiness is quite a sharp contrast to the modern-day phenomenon of entrepreneurs leaving their country of origin (especially India and China), and, like "argonauts," roaming the world in search of opportunities (Saxenian, 2006). This kind of mobility of (migrant) entrepreneurs has been documented for centuries (see, e.g., Swedberg, 2000), but is unlikely to represent a substantial part of the total population of entrepreneurs (yet?).

The Growth of Knowledge

New knowledge created at universities and research centers generates opportunities for entrepreneurship, especially in high-technology industries. Often such organizations are not able to fully recognize and appropriate the ensuing opportunities to commercialize their knowledge. Knowledge workers in such organizations respond to the opportunities that this type of new knowledge generates by starting new firms. In this way, they can appropriate the expected value of their endowment of knowledge (Acs, Braunerhjelm, Audretsch, & Carlsson, 2009; Audretsch et al., 2006; Kirchhoff, Newbert, Hasan, & Armington, 2007; Zucker, Darby, & Brewer, 1998).[6] Spatial proximity to these sources of new knowledge is an asset, if not a prerequisite, to entrepreneurial firms seeking to access and absorb spillovers from universities and research centers (Audretsch & Feldman, 1996; Audretsch & Lehmann, 2005a, 2005b; Audretsch, Lehmann, & Warning,

2005; Audretsch & Stephan, 1996; Lambooy, 2010a). But spatial proximity is neither a sufficient nor a necessary condition. Having the ability to absorb knowledge is instead a necessary condition for using new knowledge that has been created by others (cf. Cohen & Levinthal, 1990), often in rather unexpected (to the inventor) ways (Shane, 2000). The creation of embodied knowledge, via education and learning-by-doing, takes several years (possibly at several locations).

The degree to which technological change promotes new firm formation (in high-technology industries) depends on various factors, with the institutional environment as a dominant condition. The institutional setting affects the nature of high-technology labor markets, venture capital markets, and the structure of buyer–supplier ties. These markets and ties are highly relevant for the incentive and appropriability constraints that affect incumbent and start-up firms, respectively (Casper, 2007; Chesbrough, 1999). For example, institutions that support a fluid labor market, a well-developed venture capital market, and loose buyer–supplier ties allow new firms to rapidly assemble and deploy experienced engineering talent, and to move quickly to commercialize advanced technology. Cross-country research has shown that this situation is common in the United States, in contrast to Japan (Chesbrough, 1999). As another example, cross-regional research found that Silicon Valley was much more conducive to new technology-based firms than Route 128 (Massachusetts) for similar reasons (Kenney & Von Burg, 1999; Saxenian, 1994).

The institutional environment also affects the opportunity costs of leaving a (relatively secure) job at a university or research center for independent entrepreneurship (cf. Feldman, 2001). The institutional environment thus acts as a mediating factor between investments in the knowledge base of a society and the knowledge spillovers that entrepreneurs exploit.

Spin-Offs

Although some individuals become successful entrepreneurs without related prior experience, they are the exception rather than the rule. Entrepreneurs are often organizational products, that is, they spin off a firm from their previous employer (Audia & Rider, 2005, 2006; Klepper, 2001). Far from being the universal choice, entrepreneurial action is relatively constrained: instead of looking around to seek the most profitable opportunity, the potential entrepreneur focuses his attention on a familiar industry. A person working in an industry is more likely to identify a market gap than a person without any industry experience (O'Farrell & Crouchley, 1984), irrespective of the degree of industry competition and growth prospects (Storey, 1982). Prior experience (Shane, 2000) and personal networks are likely to be acquired during the entrepreneur's career in existing organizations (Agarwal, Echambadi, Franco, & Sarkar, 2004; Gompers, Lerner, & Scharfstein, 2005; Klepper, 2001). The importance of this type of prior knowledge for the nature and performance of the new firm, in combination with the spatial inertia of firm founders, explain why the nature and number of organizations in a region are important determinants of entrepreneurship in a region.

Klepper and colleagues (see Klepper, 2009, 2011) present a model in which spin-offs exploit knowledge from their parents. Firms are assumed to differ in terms of their initial competence at the time of entry, which shapes long-term performance. This competence is acquired from firms in related industries and from prior entrants in the same industry. The stock of incumbents and firms in related industries in a region determine the entry rate and postentry performance of firms in a particular industry. Inter-regional differences in entry are not necessarily determined by localization economies – the presence of specialized suppliers, thick labor markets, or spillovers between firms. Spillovers are instead more likely to be within firms, with employees spinning out afterwards. The model is tested by using detailed data on entrants in multiple industries, varying from automobiles (Boschma & Wenting, 2007; Klepper, 2002, 2007), to semiconductors (Klepper, 2010; Moore & Davis, 2004), and fashion design (Wenting, 2008). Their findings support the basic premise of the model that spin offs inherit knowledge from their parents, shaping their nature at birth, and their survival chances.

URBANIZATION AND ENTREPRENEURSHIP

Cities have long been known to be society's predominant sites of innovation[7] and wealth creation (see Hall, 1998), yet they are also its main source of negative externalities, such as crime, pollution, and disease (Bettencourt, Lobo, Helbing, Kuhnert, & West, 2007b). That urban areas are important for economic growth, because of agglomeration economies, is generally accepted. Labor productivity is higher in large agglomerations than elsewhere, but the explanations for this advantage are far from complete (Storper, 2011). Marshall (1890) and Jacobs (1961, 1969) emphasize that the colocation of similar (Marshall) or differentiated and related (Jacobs) activities enable entrepreneurs to successfully start firms that benefit from the specific urban environment.

Urban regions are riddled with externalities, both negative and positive. Although externalities are considered to be "market failures" in neoclassical approaches, positive externalities can also be seen as opportunities for entrepreneurs to meet the "hidden demand." Agglomeration economies enable all kinds of entrepreneurs to start firms, who thereby benefit from externalities and increasing returns. On balance, urban areas are favorable places for entrepreneurship: population density has been found to positively affect entrepreneurship (Reynolds et al., 1994; Wagner & Sternberg, 2004). Some authors have argued that this positive effect of population density (most obvious in big cities) might be a temporary phenomenon: the resurgence of big cities in the 1990s is connected both to a reduction in negative social interactions such as crime and to an increase in positive social interaction (Glaeser & Gottlieb, 2006).

However, urbanization and its most straightforward indicators – population size and density – cover many mechanisms, which may have different weights and values in different contexts. This is for example reflected in the large differences in entrepreneurship rates between world cities (Acs, Bosma, & Sternberg, 2011). Advantages stemming from high population density include the relative ease of access to customers as well as to the inputs required (capital, labor, suppliers) to produce various goods and services. The classical "incubation hypothesis" in urban economics states that individuals aspiring to start small-scale production find themselves less obviously barred by a high cost structure at the center of an urban area than on the periphery (Chinitz, 1961; Dumais, Ellison, & Glaeser, 1997; Hoover & Vernon, 1959, p. 47). In addition, cities provide contexts in which serendipitous meetings are more likely to occur than in less densely populated areas (Jacobs 1969); these serendipitous meetings increase the likelihood of new opportunities and collaborations that might trigger the emergence of a new firm.

Urban density also improves the likelihood of getting into contact with high-skilled individuals in the same or related knowledge domains: learning from higher-skilled peers stimulates human capital accumulation in urban environments (Glaeser, 1999) and may lead to the creation and recognition of better-quality entrepreneurial opportunities. This human capital effect influences entrepreneurial opportunities and is strengthened by the relatively high concentration of universities and research centers in urban areas. Organizations that produce new scientific and technological knowledge have also been recognized as an important additional source of entrepreneurial opportunities (Audretsch et al., 2006; see also the sub-section headed "the growth of knowledge" above). The risks attached to starting a business in urban areas are also relatively low, due to relatively abundant employment opportunities that function as an occupational buffer for the entrepreneur if her firm fails.

Urban areas are often concentrations of educated individuals with business experience in their early and middle adult years, and in that way they constitute a source of entrepreneurs (Glaeser, 2007). Such areas also have important advantages regarding the demand that specialist entrepreneurs serve, as they contain sufficient demand for a rich variety of services and consumer goods (cf. Glaeser, 2007; Glaeser, Kolko, & Saiz, 2000). Urbanization also positively affects diversification of consumer demand. This latter phenomenon is central in flexible specialization theory (Piore & Sabel, 1984), which explains such trends in terms of the breakup of the mass market for standardized goods and services and the consequent emergence of a variety of smaller niche markets that new or small firms may exploit. This diversification is, next to urbanization, also directly driven by the growth in overall demand.

URBAN AND REGIONAL DEVELOPMENT

In evolutionary approaches, differentiation and the emergence of new products and of new constellations of structural relations among agents, such as firms and end-users, are important elements. Novelty in economic and social structures and processes is related to heterogeneity and chance. The changes in quality that are associated with structural development make it necessary to investigate the process of selection. The role of agency and interactions with (evolving) selection environments are therefore emphasized. This agency is affected by and affects several ontological layers, ranging from the cognitive abilities of entrepreneurs to macro-economic and environmental shocks (see Fuller & Moran, 2001). Entrepreneurs are agents who are conditioned by, and sometimes change or even initiate, complex adaptive systems. These systems are situated in particular geographic contexts, and emerge, grow, and decline over time (cf. Fuller & Moran, 2001; Martin & Sunley, 2007).

Complex systems that are currently well-known because of their high levels of entrepreneurship, for example the high-technology clusters in Silicon Valley and around the University of Cambridge, are located in regions that were dominated by agriculture and exhibited low levels of entrepreneurship some decades ago. The supply of venture capital is created by coevolutionary processes in which the emergence of entrepreneurial communities is strengthened (e.g., due to serial entrepreneurs who have sold their businesses and reinvest their money in new ventures as business angels or venture capitalists) by the development of a venture capital community. The latter community tends to follow the emergence of a cluster rather than the other way around (Feldman & Francis, 2003; Orsenigo, 2006; cf. Kreft & Sobel, 2005). In addition, the institutional infrastructure that supports entrepreneurship also often emerges as a product of a critical mass of entrepreneurship in a particular industry or set of related industries. The growth of these industries – by both the indigenous creation of new firms and the attraction of subsidiaries – is then reinforced by the institutional structure (Garnsey & Heffernan, 2005; Keeble, Lawson, Moore, & Wilkinson, 1999).

These virtuous cycles of development can turn into vicious circles once congestion effects become stronger – to the extent that they are not offset by new agglomeration economies (Maggioni, 2006). The location patterns of "technological hotspots" (the main centers of dynamic technological developments) can shift over time. Many regions have tended to cling to their old established industries. Evolutionary economists call this "lock-in." The path dependency then reflects an old and formerly successful development path, even though the associated technologies, markets, and organizational structures have become obsolete. Completely deteriorated regions lack new technologies and new organizational structures and are thus technological "cold spots." Examples include the Ruhr area in Germany and Detroit in the United States.

This does not mean that it is impossible for lagging regions to regenerate and gradually build a new base with new technologies and production. One important barrier tends to be the lack of new entrepreneurs, since attitudes in lagging regions are often dominated by large corporations in cahoots with labor unions and regional governments. The old textile region of Manchester and the Ruhr area have shown that – although it takes time – new developments can evolve successfully, by the development of a new generation of entrepreneurs (Boschma & Lambooy, 2000). In such a dynamic approach a focus on industry structure is turned into a focus on industrial dynamics. The spatial concentration (or its absence) of an industry is not only an outcome of a process of industrial evolution, but also affects an industry's further evolution (Boschma & Frenken, 2006). This recursive relationship has, at the very least, three dimensions (Boschma & Wenting, 2007; Hannan, Carroll, Dundon, & Torres, 1995; Stuart & Sorenson, 2003; Van Wissen, 2004). First, the spatial concentration of industrial activities can generate agglomeration economies that foster start-ups and innovation and, possibly, the birth of a related industry in the region. Second, geographic concentration of firms increases the level of competition and the exit of under-performing firms raises the average fitness of routines. Third, colocated firms can also facilitate successful collective action; initiatives are more likely to emerge among proximate agents that can more effectively control opportunistic behavior.

The location of both new and already existing firms is crucial for the development of regional and urban economies. The nature of their relations to one another and to consumers in regional markets is decisive for further developments, unless new technologies and new external conditions, for instance new export markets, can open new windows for development. To investigate urban and regional development it is necessary to investigate the nature of dynamic forces, such as knowledge, technology, and institutional structures (Boschma & Frenken, 2009; Boschma & Lambooy, 1999; Lambooy & Boschma, 2001). However, location can in its turn be a strong conditioning factor for the development of dynamic forces and growth, as is evident from the impact of region-specific institutional arrangements, distance costs, the advantages of proximity, and agglomeration advantages (Klepper, 2010; Krugman, 1995; Lambooy, 1998). Evolutionary economic geography emphasizes five groups of dynamic factors that affect the process of development and economic growth:

1. *(technological) knowledge* (or more broadly, formation of human capital, based on education, research, and experience from learning-by-doing); for instance, technologies leading to much lower transport costs and improved communication;
2. *impacts of technological developments on production and consumption systems;*
3. the often *unexpected results of creative economic actors* (entrepreneurship and innovation);
4. the wide array of *effects of agglomerations on human relations (networks), and on creativity and productivity,* and;
5. in the longer run attention is also given to *changing institutions* (values, habits, laws, and rules).

Regional and urban development from this perspective of complexity and dynamism cannot be investigated as just quantitative development (economic growth). Instead, we need to study continuous changes in economic structure, production technologies, firms, organizations, governance, and behavior. Such an approach needs a different theory of growth than the neoclassical one. This can be based on Austrian and Neo-Schumpeterian evolutionary theory. Although evolutionary approaches also focus on types of inputs and the structure of prices, their principal interest is in the interaction between technology, institutions, and heterogeneous organizations in the process of economic development.

Evolutionary economic geography focuses on innovation, increasing variety, and increasing returns to scale, mostly with the firm as the unit of analysis. It supports the thesis of Jane Jacobs (1969, 1984) and Alfred Marshall (1890) that increasing variation is the source of economic growth: "The tendency to variation is the chief cause of progress"(Marshall, 1890, p. 355; see also Cohen & Malerba, 2001). Although this view is too narrow to explain growth, it is still a good way to explain *interregional* differences in growth (Frenken & Boschma, 2007; Hidalgo & Hausmann, 2009). Another key issue in evolutionary economic geography is that if a certain level of human capital is concentrated in one place, it will generate more positive externalities (this kind of diffusion is also called "spillover benefits") than does the same level of human capital spread over different locations (Martin & Sunley, 1998).

In regions with diversified information fields, access to appropriate information and knowledge enhances the growth prospects of innovative firms. Many cumulative processes and feedback mechanisms explain the success of such regions. Spatial concentration results from an economic process that depends on the entrepreneurial function, which exploits (new) technologies (such as steam engines) and new kinds of organization (such as the headquarters of business services). This process can, of course, take many years to evolve into its eventual form (Hirooka, 2006).

CONCLUSION

In this chapter, we have argued that Austrian economics and evolutionary economic geography are both complementary and commensurable. They are complementary since key elements in Austrian economics – such as entrepreneurial discovery, the market process, and institutions – have not received sufficient attention in evolutionary economic geography. Austrian economics leaves implicit the role of space and place, while spatially uneven economic activity, changing technological and spatial patterns, and economic development are all central in evolutionary economic geography. Evolutionary economic geography is commensurable with Austrian economics since it focuses on dynamics (Knightian) uncertainty, bounded rationality, and rule-following (routines), and it is complementary to Austrian theories with its explicit analysis of the role of space and place.

In this chapter we have investigated the spatial aspects of the conditions of entrepreneurship on the one hand, and the consequences of entrepreneurship on the other hand. These consequences are the effects of individual interactions that may lead to the emergence of complex systems, which have spatial coordinates and localized effects on the growth of knowledge and economic activity. These emergent systems – new organizations, institutions, cities, and regions – in turn form the context for subsequent entrepreneurial actions.

Evolutionary economic geography and Austrian economics provide key inputs for a new orthodoxy in economics, in which bounded rationality, rule-following, institutions, cognition, and evolution have moved to center stage (cf. Koppl, 2006). Together they provide a framework for understanding economic development as a bottom-up process, resulting in particular meso-structures that subsequently shape microbehavior.

One of the key insights that results from a combination of Austrian economics and evolutionary economic geography is how entrepreneurship leads to the emergence of new industries. It is a process of entrepreneurial discovery, where the knowledge of one entrepreneur is combined with the knowledge of other actors. The knowledge is different enough to lead to a novel combination, but at the same time it involves actors that are not so different that they do not understand each other – we may call this "knowledge combination with an optimal cognitive distance" (cf. Nooteboom, 2000). Such combining of knowledge is more likely to occur among actors in spatial proximity than among distant actors, and it is especially likely to occur in places in which there is an abundance of actors with different prior knowledge (e.g., in cosmopolitan urban areas, or in highly diversified regional clusters; see Huber, forthcoming).

Such knowledge combinations take place before they trigger prices and market exchanges (the context of discovery), for example, in entrepreneurial teams or through alliances of organizations. But markets play a key role in discovering the usefulness of these novel knowledge combinations (the context of justification), diffusing them beyond the initial locations of the respective combinations. Markets are thus instrumental in the rise of new industries (and the potential destruction of old ones). This will result in the growth of useful knowledge, with local origins and local applications, which entrepreneurial discovery connects to the market process.

NOTES

1. According to Kirzner (1997, p. 72), "[t]he notion of discovery, midway between that of deliberately produced information in standard search theory, and that of sheer windfall gain generated by pure chance, is central to the Austrian approach." In contrast, evolutionary economics focuses more heavily on chance, including chance events (see Boschma & Lambooy, 1999). However, even chance "favors the prepared mind," and discovery is more likely to take place by actors with related knowledge (Nooteboom, 2000), so prior (localized) knowledge plays a role here as well (cf. Feldman & Francis, 2003).

2. This refers to uncertainty in the radical, Knightian sense (Knight, 1921), where no probability calculations with known expected outcomes apply.

3. On this abstract level, all people can be entrepreneurs; entrepreneurial behavior is a human universal; and the theory of entrepreneurship is a way of looking at all types of human action (Koppl, 2007; cf. Van Gelderen, 2000). However, one could argue that this perspective is more relevant in situations of uncertainty than in "mechanistic" predictable settings, and that certain psychological traits, for example, an internal locus of control (see Harper, 1998), tend to make individuals more entrepreneurial (i.e., alert to entrepreneurial opportunities).

4. See Nooteboom (2000, pp. 96-99). Nooteboom argues that incentives for entrepreneurship constitute the ultimate cause of economic action.

5. In general, individuals respond to opportunities for higher pay elsewhere, but their sensitivity to this factor pales in comparison to their preference for living near family and friends, in Europe as well as in the United States (Dahl & Sorenson, 2010).

6. A strong science base is not a sufficient condition for an entrepreneurial region to arise. There are multiple regions where a strong scientific base has failed to spawn entrepreneurship (e.g., Ithaca (Cornell) and New Haven (Yale)). A study on new firm formation in the Netherlands (Bosma, Van Stel, & Suddle, 2007) was also unable to find a relationship between the presence of a university and high levels of new firm formation. The authors explain this with a general lack of knowledge transfer from universities in the Netherlands.

7. Bettencourt, Lobo, and Strumsky (2007a) show that larger metropolitan areas contain relatively many inventors (a super-linear relationship of inventors to population), while the productivity of individual inventors stays essentially constant across metropolitan areas. They also show that research and development establishments and employment in other creative professions follow super-linear scaling relations to metropolitan population size.

REFERENCES

Acemoglu, D. (1995). Reward structures and the allocation of talent. *European Economic Review*, *39*(1), 17–33.

Acs, Z. J., & Armington, C. (2004). Employment growth and entrepreneurial activity in cities. *Regional Studies*, *38*, 911–927.

Acs, Z. J., Bosma, N. S., & Sternberg, R. (2011). Entrepreneurship in world cities. In M. Minniti (Ed.), *The dynamics of entrepreneurship*. Oxford, UK: Oxford University Press.

Acs, Z. J., Braunerhjelm, P., Audretsch, D. B., & Carlsson, B. (2009). The knowledge spillover theory of entrepreneurship. *Small Business Economics*, *32*(1), 15–30.

Agarwal, R., Echambadi, R., Franco, A. M., & Sarkar, M. B. (2004). Knowledge transfer through inheritance: Spin-out generation, development and survival. *Academy of Management Journal*, *47*(4), 501–522.

Aldrich, H. (1999). *Organizations evolving*. London, UK: Sage.

Audia, P. G., & Rider, C. I. (2005). A garage and an idea: What more does an entrepreneur need? *California Management Review*, *48*, 6–28.

Audia, P. G., & Rider, C. I. (2006). Entrepreneurs as organizational products revisited. In R. Baum, M. Frese & R. Baron (Eds.), *The psychology of entrepreneurship* (pp. 113–130). Mahwah, NJ: Lawrence Erlbaum Associates.

Audretsch, D. B., & Feldman, M. P. (1996). R&D spillovers and the geography of innovation and production. *American Economic Review*, *86*, 630–640.

Audretsch, D. B., Keilbach, M. C., & Lehmann, E. (2006). *Entrepreneurship and economic growth*. Oxford, UK: Oxford University Press.

Audretsch, D. B., & Lehmann, E. (2005a). Do university policies make a difference? *Research Policy*, *34*, 343–347.

Audretsch, D. B., & Lehmann, E. (2005b). Does the knowledge spillover theory of entrepreneurship hold for regions? *Research Policy*, *34*, 1191–1202.

Audretsch, D. B., Lehmann, E., & Warning, S. (2005). University spillovers and new firm location. *Research Policy*, *34*, 1113–1122.

Audretsch, D. B., & Stephan, P. E. (1996). Company-scientist locational links: The case of biotechnology. *American Economic Review*, *86*(3), 641–652.

Baum, J. A. C., & Mezias, S. J. (1992). Localized competition and organizational failure: The Manhattan hotel industry 1898-1990. *Administrative Science Quarterly*, *37*, 580–604.

Baum, J. A. C., & Silverman, B. S. (2004). Picking winners or making them? Alliances, patents, and human capital as selection criteria in venture financing and performance of biotechnology startups. *Journal of Business Venturing*, *19*, 411–436.

Baumol, W. J. (1990). Entrepreneurship: Productive, unproductive and destructive. *Journal of Political Economy*, *98*, 893–921.

Bettencourt, L. M. A., Lobo, J., & Strumsky, D. (2007a). Invention in the city: Increasing returns to patenting as a scaling function of metropolitan size. *Research Policy*, *36*, 107–120.

Bettencourt, L. M. A., Lobo, J., Helbing, D., Kuhnert, C., & West, G. B. (2007b). Growth, innovation, scaling, and the pace of life in cities. *Proceedings of the National Academy of Sciences*, *104*(17), 7301–7306.

Beugelsdijk, S. (2007). Entrepreneurial culture, regional innovativeness and economic growth. *Journal of Evolutionary Economics*, *17*(2), 187–210.

Blanchflower, D. G., & Oswald, A. J. (1990). *What makes a young entrepreneur?* NBER Working Paper No. 3252. National Bureau of Economic Research, Cambridge, MA.

Boettke, P., & Coyne, C. (2003). Entrepreneurship and development: Cause or consequence? *Advances in Austrian Economics*, *6*, 67–88.

Boschma, R. A., & Frenken, K. (2006). Why is economic geography not an evolutionary science? *Journal of Economic Geography*, *6*, 273–302.

Boschma, R., & Frenken, K. (2009). Some notes on institutions in evolutionary economic geography. *Economic Geography*, *85*(2), 151–158.

Boschma, R. A., & Lambooy, J. G. (1999). Evolutionary economics and economic geography. *Journal of Evolutionary Economics*, *9*(4), 411–429.

Boschma, R. A., & Lambooy, J. G. (2000). The prospects of an adjustment policy based on collective learning in old industrial regions. *GeoJournal*, *49*, 391–399.

Boschma, R. A., & Martin, R. L. (Eds.). (2010). *The handbook of evolutionary economic geography*. Cheltenham, UK: Edward Elgar.

Boschma, R. A., & Wenting, R. (2007). The spatial evolution of the British automobile industry. Does location matter? *Industrial and Corporate Change*, *16*(2), 213–238.

Bosma, N., & Schutjens, V. (2008). Mapping entrepreneurial activity and entrepreneurial attitudes in European regions. *International Journal of Entrepreneurship and Small Business*, *7*(2), 191–213.

Bosma, N. S., Van Stel, A. J., & Suddle, K. (2007). The geography of new firm formation: Evidence from independent start-ups and new subsidiaries in the Netherlands. *International Entrepreneurship and Management Journal*, *4*(2), 129–146.

Brenner, T., & Fornahl, D. (2008). *Regional path dependence in start-up activity*. PEEG Paper No. 08.12, Urban and Regional Research Centre, Utrecht University, Utrecht.

Casper, S. (2007). *Creating Silicon Valley in Europe: Public policy towards new technology industries*. Oxford, UK: Oxford University Press.

Cattani, G., Pennings, J. M., & Wezel, F. C. (2003). Spatial and temporal heterogeneity in founding patterns. *Organization Science*, *14*(6), 670–685.

Chandra, R., & Sandilands, R. J. (2005). Does modern endogenous growth theory adequately represent Allyn Young? *Cambridge Journal of Economics*, *29*, 463–473.

Chesbrough, H. (1999). The differing organizational impact of technological change: A comparative theory of national institutional factors. *Industrial and Corporate Change*, *8*(3), 447–485.

Chinitz, B. (1961). Contrasts in agglomeration: New York and Pittsburgh. *American Economic Review*, *51*(2), 279–289.

Cohen, W. M., & Levinthal, D. A. (1990). Absorptive capacity. *Administrative Quarterly*, *35*, 128–153.

Cohen, W. M., & Malerba, F. (2001). Is the tendency to variation a chief cause of progress? *Industrial and Corporate Change*, *10*(3), 587–607.

Cooper, A. C., & Folta, T. B. (2000). Entrepreneurship and high technology clusters. In D. L. Sexton & H. Landstrom (Eds.), *Handbook of entrepreneurship* (pp. 348–367). Oxford, UK: Blackwell.

Dahl, M. S., & Sorenson, O. (2010). The social attachment to place. *Social Forces*, *89*, 633–658.

Dahl, M. S., & Sorenson, O. (2011). *Home sweet home: Entrepreneurs' location choices and the performance of their ventures*. Retrieved from http://ssrn.com/abstract=1596810. Accessed on March 23, 2012.

Dumais, G., Ellison, G., & Glaeser, E. L. (1997). *Geographic concentration as a dynamic process*. NBER Working Paper No. 6270. National Bureau of Economic Research, Cambridge, MA.

Feldman, M. P. (2001). The entrepreneurial event revisited: Firm formation in a regional context. *Industrial and Corporate Change*, *10*, 861–891.

Feldman, M. P., & Francis, J. (2003). Fortune favors the prepared region: The case of entrepreneurship and the capitol region biotechnology cluster. *European Planning Studies*, *11*, 765–788.

Figueiredo, O., Guimaraes, P., & Woodward, D. (2002). Home-field advantage: Location decisions of Portuguese entrepreneurs. *Journal of Urban Economics*, *52*, 341–361.
Frenken, K., & Boschma, R. A. (2007). A theoretical framework for evolutionary economic geography industrial dynamics and urban growth as branching processes. *Journal of Economic Geography*, *7*(5), 635–649.
Fritsch, M. (2008). How does new business formation affect regional development? Introduction to the special issue. *Small Business Economics*, *30*(1), 1–14.
Fuller, T., & Moran, P. (2001). Small enterprises as complex adaptive systems: A methodological question? *Entrepreneurship and Regional Development*, *13*(1), 47–63.
Garnsey, E., & Heffernan, P. (2005). High tech clustering through spin out and attraction; the Cambridge case. *Regional Studies*, *39*(8), 1127–1144.
Giannetti, M., & Simonov, A. (2009). Social interactions and entrepreneurial activity. *Journal of Economics & Management Strategy*, *18*(3), 665–709.
Glaeser, E. L. (1999). Learning in cities. *Journal of Urban Economics*, *46*, 254–277.
Glaeser, E. L. (2007). *Entrepreneurship and the city*. NBER Working Paper No. W13551. National Bureau of Economic Research, Cambridge, MA.
Glaeser, E. L., & Gottlieb, J. D. (2006). Urban resurgence and the consumer city. *Urban Studies*, *43*(8), 1275–1299.
Glaeser, E. L., Kolko, J., & Saiz, A. (2000). Consumer city. *Journal of Economic Geography*, *1*(1), 27–50.
Gompers, P., Lerner, J., & Scharfstein, D. (2005). Entrepreneurial spawning: Public corporations and the formation of new ventures, 1986–1999. *Journal of Finance*, *60*, 577–614.
Grebel, T., Pyka, A., & Hanusch, H. (2003). An evolutionary approach to the theory of the entrepreneur. *Industry and Innovation*, *10*, 493–514.
Hall, P. (1998). *Cities in civilization*. New York, NY: Pantheon Books.
Hannan, M. T., Carroll, G. R., Dundon, E. A., & Torres, J. C. (1995). Organizational evolution in multinational context: Entries of automobile manufacturers in Belgium, Britain, France, Germany and Italy. *American Sociological Review*, *60*(4), 509–528.
Harper, D. (1996). *Entrepreneurship and the market process: An inquiry into the growth of knowledge*. London, UK: Routledge.
Harper, D. (1998). Institutional conditions for entrepreneurship. *Advances in Austrian Economics*, *5*, 241–275.
Hayek, F. A. (1945). The use of knowledge in society. *American Economic Review*, *35*(4), 1–11.
Hayek, F. A. (1967). *Studies in philosophy, politics, and economics*. Chicago, IL: University of Chicago Press.
Hayek, F. A. (1978). *New studies in philosophy, politics, economics, and the history of ideas*. London, UK: Routledge and Kegan Paul.
Hidalgo, C., & Hausmann, R. (2009). The building blocks of economic complexity. *Proceedings of the National Academy of Sciences*, *106*, 10570–10575.
Hirooka, M. (2006). *Innovation dynamism and economic growth*. Cheltenham, UK: Edward Elgar.
Holcombe, R. G. (2007). Entrepreneurship and economic growth. In B. Powell (Ed.), *Making poor nations rich: Entrepreneurship and the process of economic development*. Stanford, CA: Stanford University Press.
Hoover, E. M., & Vernon, R. (1959). *Anatomy of a metropolis*. Cambridge, MA: Harvard University Press.

Huber, F. (forthcoming). On the role and interrelationship of spatial, social and cognitive proximity: Personal knowledge relationships of R&D workers in the Cambridge information technology cluster. *Regional Studies*.

Jacobs, J. (1961). *The death and life of great American cities*. New York, NY: Vintage Books.

Jacobs, J. (1969). *The economy of cities*. New York, NY: Vintage Books.

Jacobs, J. (1984). *Cities and the wealth of nations*. New York, NY: Vintage Books.

Keeble, D., Lawson, C., Moore, B., & Wilkinson, F. (1999). Collective learning processes, networking and 'institutional thickness' in the Cambridge region. *Regional Studies*, *33*(4), 319–332.

Kenney, M., & Von Burg, U. (1999). Technology and path dependence: The divergence between Silicon Valley and Route 128. *Industrial and Corporate Change*, *8*(1), 67–103.

Kirchhoff, B. A., Newbert, S. L., Hasan, I., & Armington, C. (2007). The influence of university R&D expenditures on new business formations and employment growth. *Entrepreneurship Theory and Practice*, *31*(4), 543–559.

Kirzner, I. M. (1997). Entrepreneurial discovery and the competitive market process: An Austrian approach. *Journal of Economic Literature*, *35*, 60–85.

Klepper, S. (2001). Employee startups in high-tech industries. *Industrial and Corporate Change*, *10*(3), 639–674.

Klepper, S. (2002). The capabilities of new firms and the evolution of the US automobile industry. *Industrial and Corporate Change*, *11*(4), 645–666.

Klepper, S. (2007). Disagreements, spinoffs, and the evolution of Detroit as the capital of the U.S. automobile industry. *Management Science*, *53*, 616–631.

Klepper, S. (2009). Spinoffs: A review and synthesis. *European Management Review*, *6*, 159–171.

Klepper, S. (2010). The origin and growth of industry clusters: The making of Silicon Valley and Detroit. *Journal of Urban Economics*, *67*(1), 15–32.

Klepper, S. (2011). Nano-economics, spinoffs, and the wealth of regions. *Small Business Economics*, *37*, 141–154.

Knight, F. H. (1921). *Risk, uncertainty and profit*. Boston, MA: Hart, Schaffner & Marx.

Koppl, R. (2006). Austrian economics at the cutting edge. *Review of Austrian Economics*, *19*(4), 231–241.

Koppl, R. (2007). Entrepreneurial behavior as a human universal. In A. Zacharakis, M. Minniti, S. Spinelli, M. P. Rice & T. G. Habbershon (Eds.), *Entrepreneurship: The engine of growth* (Vol. 1, pp. 1–20). Westport, CT: Greenwood Publishing Group.

Kreft, S. F., & Sobel, R. S. (2005). Public policy, entrepreneurship, and economic growth. *Cato Journal*, *25*(3), 595–616.

Krugman, P. (1995). *Geography, trade and development*. Cambridge, MA: MIT Press.

Lachmann, L. (1978). An Austrian stocktaking: Unsettled questions and tentative answers. In L. Spadaro (Ed.), *New directions in Austrian economics* (pp. 1–18). Kansas City, MO: Sheed, Andrews & McMeel.

Lambooy, J. G. (1998). *Agglomeration economies: Cities in the knowledge economy*. Utrecht: Utrecht University.

Lambooy, J. G. (2010a). Knowledge transfers, spillovers and actors. *European Planning Studies*, *18*(6), 873–891.

Lambooy, J. G. (2010b). The evolution of spatial patterns over long time-horizons. In R. A. Boschma & R. Martin (Eds.), *The handbook of evolutionary economic geography* (pp. 471–486). Cheltenham, UK: Edward Elgar.

Lambooy, J. G., & Boschma, R. A. (2001). Evolutionary economics and regional policy. *Annals of Regional Science*, *35*(1), 113–133.

Maggioni, M. A. (2006). Mors tua, vita mea? The rise and fall of innovative industrial clusters. In P. Braunerhjelm & M. Feldman (Eds.), *Cluster genesis* (pp. 219–242). Oxford, UK: Oxford University Press.

Marshall, A. (1890). *Principles of economics*. London, UK: Macmillan.

Martin, R., & Sunley, P. (1998). Slow convergence? The new endogenous growth theory and regional development. *Economic Geography*, *74*, 201–227.

Martin, R., & Sunley, P. (2007). Complexity thinking and evolutionary economic geography. *Journal of Economic Geography*, *7*(5), 573–601.

Metcalfe, J. S. (2002). Knowledge of growth and the growth of knowledge. *Journal of Evolutionary Economics*, *12*(1-2), 3–15.

Metcalfe, J. S. (2004). The entrepreneur and the style of modern economics. *Journal of Evolutionary Economics*, *14*(2), 157–175.

Michelacci, C., & Silva, O. (2007). Why so many local entrepreneurs? *Review of Economics and Statistics*, *89*(4), 615–633.

Moore, G., & Davis, K. (2004). Learning the Silicon Valley way. In T. Bresnahan & A. Gambardella (Eds.), *Building high-tech clusters: Silicon Valley and beyond* (pp. 7–39). Cambridge University Press, UK: Cambridge.

Murphy, K. M., Shleifer, A., & Vishny, R. W. (1991). The allocation of talent: Implications for growth. *Quarterly Journal of Economics*, *106*, 503–530.

Nooteboom, B. (2000). *Learning and innovation in organizations and economics*. Oxford, UK: Oxford University Press.

O'Farrell, P. N., & Crouchley, R. (1984). An industrial and spatial analysis of new firm formation in Ireland. *Regional Studies*, *18*, 221–236.

Orsenigo, L. (2006). Clusters and clustering: Stylized facts, issues, and theories. In P. Braunerhjelm & M. Feldman (Eds.), *Cluster genesis: Technology-based industrial development* (pp. 195–218). Oxford, UK: Oxford University Press.

Parwada, J. T. (2008). The genesis of home bias? The location and portfolio choices of investment company start-ups. *Journal of Financial and Quantitative Analysis*, *43*, 245–266.

Piore, M. J., & Sabel, C. F. (1984). *Second industrial divide: Possibilities for prosperity*. New York, NY: Basic Books.

Reynolds, P., Storey, D. J., & Westhead, P. (1994). Cross-national comparisons of the variation in new firm formation rates. *Regional Studies*, *28*, 443–456.

Reynolds, P. D., & White, S. B. (1997). *The entrepreneurial process: Economic growth, men, women, and minorities*. Westport, CT: Quorum Books.

Saxenian, A. (1994). *Regional advantage: Culture and competition in Silicon Valley and route 128*. Cambridge, MA: Harvard University Press.

Saxenian, A. (2006). *The new argonauts: Regional advantage in a global economy*. Cambridge, MA: Harvard University Press.

Schumpeter, J. A. (1934). *The theory of economic development*. Cambridge, MA: Harvard University Press.

Shane, S. (2000). Prior knowledge and the discovery of entrepreneurial opportunities. *Organization Science*, *11*, 448–469.

Sorenson, O. (2003). Social networks and industrial geography. *Journal of Evolutionary Economics*, *13*, 513–527.

Sorenson, O., & Audia, P. G. (2000). The social structure of entrepreneurial activity: Geographic production of footwear in the United States, 1940-1989. *American Journal of Sociology*, *106*, 1546–1588.
Stam, E. (2005). The geography of gazelles in the Netherlands. *Tijdschrift voor Economische en Sociale Geografie*, *96*(1), 121–127.
Stam, E. (2007). Why butterflies don't leave. *Economic Geography*, *83*, 27–50.
Stam, E. (2010). Entrepreneurship, evolution and geography. In R. Boschma & R. L. Martin (Eds.), *The handbook of evolutionary economic geography* (pp. 307–348). Cheltenham, UK: Edward Elgar.
Stam, E., & Wennberg, K. (2009). The roles of R&D in new firm growth. *Small Business Economics*, *33*(1), 77–89.
Storey, D. J. (1982). *Entrepreneurship and the New Firm*. London, UK: Croom Helm.
Storper, M. (2011). Why do regions develop and change? The challenge for geography and economics. *Journal of Economic Geography*, *11*, 333–346.
Stuart, T. E., & Sorenson, O. (2003). The geography of opportunity: Spatial heterogeneity in founding rates and the performance of biotechnology firms. *Research Policy*, *32*, 229–253.
Swedberg, R. (2000). *Entrepreneurship – The social science view*. Oxford, UK: Oxford University Press.
Van Gelderen, M. (2000). Enterprising behaviour of ordinary people. *European Journal of Work and Organizational Psychology*, *9*(1), 81–88.
Van Wissen, L. (2004). A spatial interpretation of the density dependence model in industrial demography. *Small Business Economics*, *22*(3-4), 253–264.
Wagner, J., & Sternberg, R. (2004). Start-up activities, individual characteristics, and the regional milieu: Lessons for entrepreneurship support policies from German micro data. *Annals of Regional Science*, *38*, 219–240.
Wenting, R. (2008). Spinoff dynamics and the spatial formation of the fashion design industry, 1858-2005. *Journal of Economic Geography*, *8*, 593–614.
Witt, U. (1998). Imagination and leadership – The neglected dimension of an evolutionary theory of the firm. *Journal of Economic Behavior and Organization*, *35*(2), 161–177.
Young, A. (1928). Increasing returns and economic progress. *Economic Journal*, *38*, 527–542.
Zucker, L. G., Darby, M. R., & Brewer, M. B. (1998). Intellectual human capital and the birth of U.S. biotechnology enterprises. *American Economic Review*, *88*, 290–306.

ENTREPRENEURSHIP IN ACTION SPACE

Sanford Ikeda

Don't you know that I heard it through the grapevine? – Marvin Gaye

If price signals guide and reflects decisions in the market process,[1] how does that information actually make its way to individual decision makers? If entrepreneurship is the discovery of a profit opportunity that can trigger competitive rivalry, how does a person actually acquire the information from which she draws her discovery and how do her rivals then become aware of it?

I believe social-network theory can help to answer these questions. In particular, concepts such as social distance, density, and structure can shed light on how information relevant for entrepreneurial discovery is acquired and diffused. Moreover, the approach I develop here can advance Jane Jacobs's (1961) analysis of how the design and location of public spaces influence economic development.

The first section explains the nature and significance of action space in relation to social networks. The second section discusses the concept of "Jacobs Density" and explains how action space interacts with entrepreneurship in the market process. The third section examines the relationship between action space and urban design. The fourth section offers some concluding thoughts.

The Spatial Market Process
Advances in Austrian Economics, Volume 16, 105–139

ISSN: 1529-2134/doi:10.1108/S1529-2134(2012)0000016008

THE NATURE AND SIGNIFICANCE OF ACTION SPACE

According to Ludwig Von Mises (1949/1963), economics studies the causes and consequences of goal-directed action. Each of us seeks to improve our situations as we see it. But just how each of us perceives our situation, and what alternative ends and means we believe are available to us, depends crucially on the context.[2] Action is never without context but is instead undertaken by someone for something at a certain time and a certain place (Hayek, 1945).

While O'Driscoll and Rizzo (1985), for example, show the importance of recognizing that action takes place in real time, it is at least as important to recognize that action is never placeless. Moreover, that place is not arbitrary, especially when it comes to the actions and social interactions that constitute a complex social order. You cannot do anything just anywhere. There are more or less appropriate times and places to do business (over lunch rather than at a funeral), smile at a stranger (in a small town rather than a big city), or argue about baseball (in a bar rather than a library). So complex interactions do not happen randomly across space; we observe them more in some places than in others, whether we are talking about small groups of people as they gather in public spaces (Whyte, 1980, pp. 247–68) or large agglomerations of people in a city (Lewis, 2003, p. 19). Sometimes such gatherings are the result of deliberate design, but the more important interactions are spontaneous orders – the unplanned orders that are the result of human action but not of human design (Hayek, 1967; Jacobs, 1961, p. 433).

Now actions that constitute a complex social order can take place in *private space* where you would not expect to encounter strangers (such as your living room), as well as in *public space* where you would expect to encounter strangers (such as a city sidewalk). When I use the terms "private" and "public" here, I hope it is clear that I am not referring to the form of ownership: a privately owned coffeehouse is a public space in this sense, while CIA Headquarters, though held by the United States government, is a private space.[3] Because encounters among strangers are central to the "impersonal market," with its extensive and complex divisions of labor and knowledge among countless strangers, the action space most relevant here – and the principal venue for entrepreneurship – is public space. A person's action space then is a particular place: an office or workplace, a concert hall or coffeehouse, a shopping mall or sidewalk.

Action Space and Social Networks

Kirzner (1973) characterizes entrepreneurship as alertness to pure profit opportunities and essentially an act of arbitrage, of buying low and selling high. But as I have pointed out, that level of abstraction does not tell us how someone first acquires the information that leads to the discovery of those opportunities. Where does that information come from? How reliable is it? Suppose someone tells me that I can buy apples around the corner for one dollar apiece and then sell them across the street for two dollars. Who is this person to me and how reliable is she and the information she is giving me? The first question is about the nature of interpersonal contacts, the second is about trust. I believe the answer to both questions lies in an understanding of social networks.

Drawing a discovery from a given set of information and discovering reliable sources of information, which might later be used to carry information to others, are both creative acts. In the first case, the entrepreneur is able to recognize and interpret information in a way others have not; and in the second case, she is able to make a valuable personal connection that others have not. It is true that sometimes information may be broadcast indiscriminately to a large number people, as in a television program or an Internet website, but the most critical information for entrepreneurship tends to come through personal contacts, often from people you do not know very well. These creative acts – forming and dissolving social ties and discovering profit opportunities – take place in action space.

Being creative, both acts are unpredictable: you cannot say with certainty where ties will be made or unmade, otherwise someone would already have made or unmade them; and even if an agent is exposed to information that contains a profit opportunity, there is no guarantee that she will recognize it. Both can be understood in relation to "the particular circumstances of time and place" (Hayek, 1945).[4] The "who, what, and how" of a discovery depends on the spatiotemporal context – the "where and when."

In addition, you cannot predict how a tie, having been established between agent A and agent B for one purpose, might later serve other purposes that neither A nor B could have foreseen. For example, a regular customer might tell you of a new competitor who has moved into your neighborhood, a teacher might introduce you to a future business partner, or a colleague might give you a tip about someone working on a project related to your own (Desrochers, 2001). It is also possible that other uses for a particular connection could arise unexpectedly, as when your new sister-in-law turns out to be an excellent tax attorney. Ties that serve multiple uses at the same time are termed *multiplex* (see below).

Again, some sources of information, about stock prices for example, that may be broadcast over a wide range of the population are impersonal and may have a high degree of reliability. Usually, however, the most important entrepreneurial information comes through interpersonal channels, often by accident. Important business decisions, for businesses big and small, rely on information conveyed by flesh-and-blood people who are connected to the decision maker in ways that are not arbitrary. From choosing a plumber to choosing the site of a new factory, making a decision in the "impersonal market" depends a great deal on how much you know about the people whom you plan to work with or from whom you plan to buy or sell, even though you may never know those slightly upstream or downstream from you in the production process.

Hayek (1945) argued long ago that the price system is a marvel at coordinating the decisions of a myriad of anonymous decision makers and at economizing the amount of information any given person has to know. Nevertheless each decision maker has an enormous amount of contextual knowledge about the local situation, gained from face-to-face contact (Ikeda, 2002). Here indispensable contextual knowledge includes knowledge about personal connections, as well as their reliability or relevance for acquiring or passing along particular kinds of information. Who you would ask for advice about where to find potential investors is probably a different person from the one whom you would ask about what to invest in. Being able to tell the difference is vital, even though you may not be able to explain how you do it, even to yourself. So Hayek is right about the price system economizing considerably on the technical knowledge ("knowing that") you would need to, say, build a house; but the amount of contextual knowledge required ("knowing how") to decide, say, whom to ask about where to find the best price for a house should not be underestimated. *My focus here is not on the knowledge transmitted through personal connections such as price signals, but on an agent's knowledge of the connections themselves.*

Now, if information were perfect, there would be no need to make or break social connections, because the problem of acquiring relevant information from others would not exist. Social networks form as a way of coping with less-than-perfect information. Like price signals, they enable us to utilize local knowledge, skills, and tastes that would otherwise be inaccessible. As Ronald Burt has remarked: "Through relations with colleagues, friends, and clients come the opportunities to transform financial and human capital into profit" (Burt, 1995, l. 155). Action space, then, because it is where an agent acts entrepreneurially, seeking arbitrage opportunities and profitably making and breaking connections that others have overlooked, consists of the points of contact between the agent and the networks relevant to her particular purposes.

Before saying more about the relationship between entrepreneurship and action space, I would like to elaborate on a few concepts from social network theory that will be important to that discussion.

Density, Distance, and Structure

A *social network* is a set of people (or nodes) who are tied to one another through personal connections (or arcs or edges) (Degenne & Forsé, 1999, p. 28). "In a very basic sense, then, a social network is an organized set of people that consists of two kinds of elements: human beings and the connections between them" (Christakis & Fowler, 2009, p. 13).

The network can be planned or unplanned. Because the network connections relevant to the market process are unpredictable, my focus will be on unplanned social networks.

Less formally, we can speak of a *network community*, which "can be defined as a group of people who are much more connected to one another than they are to other groups of connected people found in other parts of the network" (Christakis & Fowler, 2009, p. 11). As this suggests, social networks have no sharp boundaries. However, despite the claim of Degenne and Forsé (1999, p. 22) that "no network has 'natural' frontiers; researchers impose them," I believe it is possible in practice to identify a number of nonarbitrary social networks – such as your family, close friends, or colleagues – even though their frontiers are somewhat fuzzy.

The connections or interpersonal ties between any two people may be weak or strong in Granovetter's (1973) sense. The *strength of a tie* between persons is an increasing function of the following:

1. Its duration
2. Its emotional intensity
3. The level of intimacy
4. Frequency of exchange of services

To this list Degenne and Forsé (1999, p. 109) add a fifth criterion, *multiplexity*, by which they mean the ability to transact several kinds of exchange, for different purposes, concurrently within the same network; or

$$m = \frac{n}{p} \tag{1}$$

where n is the total number of exchanges and p is the number of agent-pairs effecting at least one exchange (*ibid.*, p. 46).

It is sometimes useful to talk about the *ego network*, which is simply a social network considered from the viewpoint of a particular person (ego) in that network.

If z_{jq} is a variable that indicates a relationship from agent j to agent q, and if N_i is the size or the number of agents in ego's (i's) network, then you can derive a simple measure of the density of ego's network by dividing the sum of all actual relationships between all of the agents in a network ($z_{jq} = 0$, if there is no relationship between j and q, $z_{jq} = 1$ if there is) by the maximum possible number of relations among all of the agents in the network, or $N_i\,(N_i - 1)/2$.[5]

$$\text{Density} = \frac{(\sum_j \sum_q z_{jq})}{[N_i(N_i - 1)/2]}, \quad j \neq q \tag{2}$$

Density is then the ratio of actual to all possible connections. For example,[6] the network in Fig. 1 has 9 connections out a possible maximum of 28 (e.g., agent 1 is directly connected to agents 2 and 3 but only indirectly connected to agents 4 through 8).

Its density is therefore

$$D = \frac{9}{28} = 0.32$$

The *distance* between two particular agents, i and j, is the shortest path (minimum number of arcs or degrees) between them.

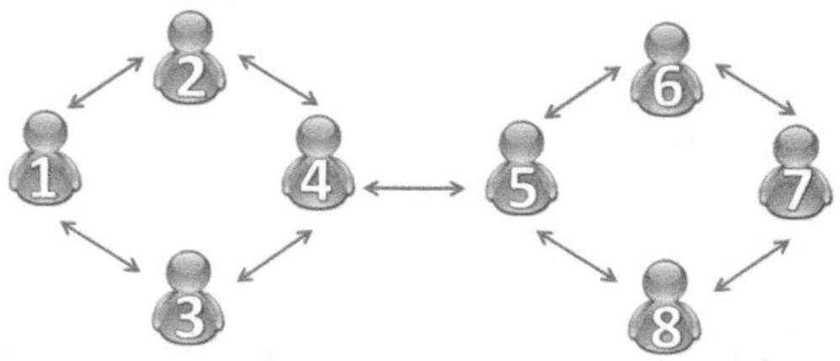

Fig. 1. Network A.

You can calculate the *average distance* that a person would expect to travel to reach any other person in a network, as follows: For a given person, find the total distance she would have to travel to reach each and every other person in the network on separate journeys, then sum these distances over all N persons and divide that result by $N_i\ (N_i - 1)/2$.

For Network A, then, the average distance is (64/28 =) 2.29 degrees. In other words, agent 1 (or any other agent in the network) would have to travel over on average 2.29 arcs to get to anyone else in the network (see the appendix for calculations for the average distance for Networks A and B).

The *structure* of a network refers to the way in which the nodes are connected (or not) to one another. Network B in Fig. 2 has the same number of nodes and ties as Network A, but because they are connected differently the structure is different.

Agents i and j are said to be *structurally equivalent* to the extent that they have the same contacts with every other agent in the network (Burt, 1995, l. 276). In Network C in Fig. 3, agents 1 and 2 are structurally equivalent.

Because agents 1 and 2 are structurally equivalent, the tie connecting them does not help either one to reach any other agent in the network (other than each other), that is, it does not reduce average distance. From that strategic point of view, such a tie is said to be *redundant*.

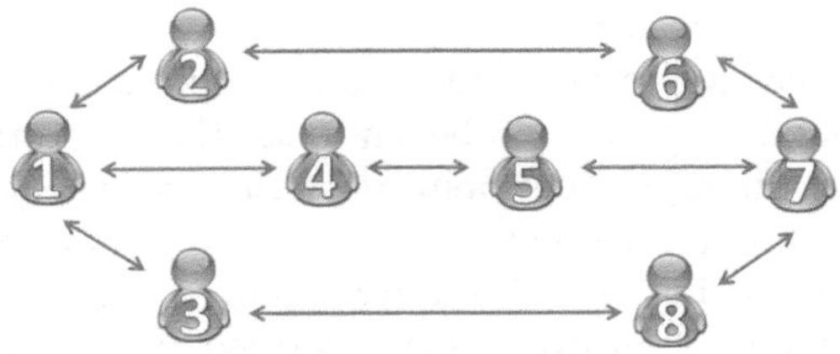

Fig. 2. Network B.

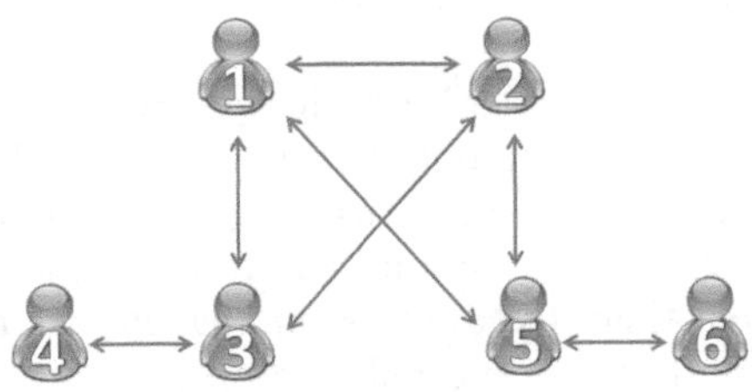

Fig. 3. Network C.

Burt (1995, l. 270) discusses another form of redundancy that is not based on structural equivalence but on cohesion. *Cohesion* means having a strong tie with another agent who has access to and possesses the same information that you do, so that knowing her gives you no strategic advantage. "Cohesion concerns direct connection; structural equivalence concerns indirect connection by mutual contact" (*ibid.*, l. 277). So redundancy is an increasing function of both structural equivalence and cohesion.

Population Density Versus Network Density

In the real world, people do not randomly distribute themselves across space. Instead, they choose to occupy particular locations for specific reasons. Some places are more conducive than others for certain kinds of action. William Whyte (1980), for instance, explains why people may choose to sit or stand in certain spots in a public plaza according to how comfortable, convenient, safe, and interesting it is. Larger agglomerations, such as cities,[7] attract people for similar reasons with the added draw of economic opportunity, cultural diversity, and privacy (Jacobs, 1961, pp. 56 and 143). Of course, terrain and natural resources strongly influence the site and situation of large settlements. But rivers, harbors, and lumber are valuable only because people find them useful for particular purposes – trade and defense, for example.

Beginning in the late nineteenth century, public authorities and the nascent urban-planning profession began to see the congestion and squalor that accompanied the rapid development of cities as a major public-policy problem. Their solution, broadly speaking, was either to bring open space to urban residents (le Corbusier) or to move urbanites out to the suburbs and countryside (Ebenezer Howard). They regarded population density as a source of social ills if not a vice in itself. The tide began to turn in the latter third of the twentieth century, in no small part because of writings and activism of the urbanist Jane Jacobs.[8] Planners began to see density as a virtue.

Among those today who attribute the productivity, or at least the liveliness, of cities in large part to population density are New Urbanists and advocates of Smart Growth policies.[9] *Given* a population rich in diversity of skills and tastes, the closer to one another these people live (reside, work, play) and the greater their freedom of movement is, the greater is the likelihood that formal and especially informal contacts will happen. Informal contacts in turn form the basis for mutually beneficial trades and other forms of voluntary association that result when urbanites discover valuable complementarities in knowledge and tastes.

But skeptics point to continuing advances in communication and transport technology, which seemingly obliterate physical distances among people, as challenges to the raison d'être of the traditional city. Each wave of technical change – telephony, radio, television, the Internet; the railroad, the car, the airplane – has indeed increased the possibility – and perhaps the appeal – of living in greater physical isolation while remaining socially connected. Ebenezer Howard's "Garden City" or Frank Lloyd Wright's "Broadacre," each predicated on low-density and relatively autonomous residential development (the former transit based, the latter based on the car), are today more achievable than ever.

While the density of the traditional city center has generally fallen throughout the developed world, urbanized areas anchored to one or more central cities have at the same time grown apace and will by the mid-twenty-first century attract 75 percent of the global population (Burdett & Sudjic, 2008). Population gradients have risen upward even as they have flattened (Bruegmann, 2006). Technical advances in communication and transport have certainly perturbed the evolution of the city, but not killed it.

There is no denying, however, that technical change, especially the rise of the Internet and mobile communication, has had a huge impact on the way people interact. Despite the persistent human propensity to agglomerate, it may yet be helpful to retool the standard concept of population density in the face of these changes with the aid of social network theory.

The Importance of Network Structure

Economic development, by which I mean economic growth that is driven by innovation and the increasing division of knowledge (Hayek, 1945), is the result of entrepreneurship (Kirzner, 1973). To address the two questions posed at the beginning of this chapter – regarding how agents acquire and then diffuse entrepreneurially relevant information – it is important to appreciate how relatively small differences in network structure can dramatically influence social distance. I can clarify this point by comparing the two networks presented in Figs. 1 and 2.

We already know that Network A has a density of 0.32. Network B, using the same algorithm, has the same density. However, while the average distance in Network A is 2.29, the average distance for Network B is 1.93. To reach anyone else in the network, the distance any given agent has to travel would be about 16 percent shorter in Network B than in Network A. The networks have the same number of connections but they have different structures. Other things being equal, if the goal is to facilitate the movement of entrepreneurially relevant knowledge, Network B seems to have a structural advantage over Network A. The structural change shortens the average distance among the agents within the network.

This simple example is meant to suggest that a social network's density and especially its structure can affect the level of entrepreneurship, by bringing information sources closer and more "densely" together. The next section looks at how entrepreneurship itself changes the structure of a social network.

ENTREPRENEURSHIP AND ACTION SPACE

The previous discussion suggests that a change in structure that reduces average distance between agents in a network can shorten the "social distance" between them. And by closing this distance, structural changes – by which I mean here the adding or subtraction of ties to different agents – can increase the flow of entrepreneurially relevant knowledge and thereby increase the likelihood of discovery. It also suggests that you can do this without a net increase in ties, or by adding ties indiscriminately, which is something I discuss later in this chapter.

Social Distance, Tie Strength, and Diversity

What exactly is social distance? I have been treating *social distance* as the minimum number of ties or "degrees of separation" between two agents. In Fig. 2, for example, agent 7 is the most socially distant from agent 1 (at three degrees of separation) compared with anyone else. The maximum social distance between any two agents in Network B is three degrees and the minimum is one degree (so earlier I calculated "average distance" by taking the weighted average of those distances).

But social distance seems to have at least two other meanings in the literature. The first has to do with the level and kind of interaction between two agents. This is essentially Granovetter's concept of a weak versus strong tie. The weaker the tie between two agents – the shorter the duration and the less intimate, emotionally intense, frequently used, and multiplex the contact – the more socially distant they are said to be. Therefore, I will subsume this aspect of social distance into the *strength of the tie*.

The second meaning relates to what are called "affective" and "normative" social distances. *Affective* social distance varies inversely with the level of sympathy one feels for another (Bogardus, 1947). I will not use this concept in this chapter. *Normative* social distance relates to whether an agent is regarded as an insider or outsider to the group or social network (Karakayali, 2009). (The latter seems to underlie Robert Putnam's distinction between *bonding social capital* and *bridging social capital*, see Putnam, 2000, pp. 22–23.) While both are important, the more relevant for my purpose is the idea of normative distance, which would include cultural differences – such as Christians versus Muslims, urbanites versus rural dwellers, and Americans versus Japanese. Somewhat related to the normative concept of social distance, and highly relevant to the question at hand, are differences in an agent's knowledge and skills (which together constitute her *human capital*) and differences in tastes. While the latter are not always normative differences, it will be convenient for my purposes to treat them as if they were. I will thus fold "normative social distance" into the concept of *diversity*.

In sum, in this chapter I treat the level and kind of personal interaction between agents as factors in the strength of a tie, and normative social distance as a source of diversity. Doing so will help me to clearly distinguish "social distance," qua degrees of separation, from both the "strength" of a particular tie and how "diverse" two agents are from each other.

While conceptually separate, these factors do interact. Most importantly, closing social distance can (though it need not) result over time in the strengthening of ties, which as a result of more frequent and intimate contact can reduce the diversity among more-strongly tied agents. This is a matter of the dynamics of action space, to which I will return later.

Jacobs Density

Recall that the simple definitions of *population* density and *network* density are, respectively, the number of individuals per unit area and the ratio of actual to potential ties within a given network. In some respects, network density is secondary to the diversity of knowledge of the agents in a network in terms of its importance in promoting entrepreneurial discoveries, in the same way that population density is only secondary to the diversity of land use.

That is, population density fails to do the heavy lifting some urbanists expect it to do. For example, the New Urbanists rely on population density in their recommendations, and Smart Growth policies impose "green belts" and other interventions to increase the number of people per square mile, hoping it will produce a host of benefits, from community building to environmental responsibility to reducing income inequality and sprawl (Leccese & McCormick, 2000, pp. v–vi). And in the case of social networks, I have shown that sometimes network density has little to do with closing social distance.

Moreover, the measured correlation between population density and economic vitality is tenuous at best. Gordon and Ikeda (2011) used Public Use Microdata to show that when you look at densities for areas below the standard metro level, the correlation between human capital – a common measure of potential economic development – and measured density tends to disappear. That is "because the areas that form the denominator of the density ratio are typically far too large and fail to capture important differences at the neighborhood level, especially where … cities have multiple 'employment sub-centers'" (Gordon & Ikeda, 2011, p. 442).

Instead, diversity – in land use, knowledge, skills, and tastes – rather than density per se is the key to economic development.[10]

It is true that sometimes New Urbanists and supporters of Smart Growth policies trace their ideas to Jane Jacobs, who argued that population density is an important factor in economic development. But Jacobs (1961, pp. 143–221) had something beyond mere population density in mind when emphasizing "high concentrations of people at different times during the day." The main value she attached to density derived from its ability to both harness and stimulate diverse land uses in a city. In her analysis it does so in two ways. First, large concentrations are necessary to have a steady stream of people using public space around the clock – what Jacobs calls "eyes on the street" (*ibid.*, p. 35) – which promotes safety. Second, "people attract people" (*ibid.*, p. 37). If people feel safe and comfortable using public space, either to consume or produce goods and services, more and more will feel inclined to use it, and that in turn will increase the chances of agents having the kind of frequent and informal contacts from which trust and what Jacobs termed "social capital" can arise. Personal proximity via density is also valuable to an agent to the extent that it increases the likelihood that she will have informal contact in public space with agents who possess knowledge, skill, or tastes complementary to, and therefore different from, her. Desrochers (2001, p. 34) shows that such contacts often result in unexpected benefits.

So the intuition is I think a strong one that density in some sense is an important factor in fostering greater (informal) contact among agents, thereby facilitating information flows that enable greater entrepreneurial discovery. The following is my attempt to align that intuition with a view of economic development as an entrepreneurial competitive process by means of a concept of density that is applicable to both abstract social networks and to actual urban environments.

Peter Gordon and I recently proposed an alternative to conventional density called "Jacobs Density," that we intended to capture the interdependence among proximity, population size, and diversity. We defined Jacobs Density as "the level of potential informal contacts of the average person in a given public space at any given time" (Gordon & Ikeda, 2011, p. 448). I believe an even better way to conceptualize Jacobs Density draws from social network theory. The *Jacobs Density* of an action space relates the number of direct contacts Ego has in her action space to the total number of contacts (direct and indirect) she can access through them. Jacobs Density is the ratio of the latter to the former.

Jacobs Density differs then from the measure of network density I discussed earlier, which was the ratio of actual to all possible connections in a given network. The following is a simple illustration of increasing Jacobs Density.

Ego in the first case forms a triangle with John and Mary in her action space, which indirectly connects her to Juan, Jamal, Marcie, and Mariko outside of that particular space (Fig. 4).

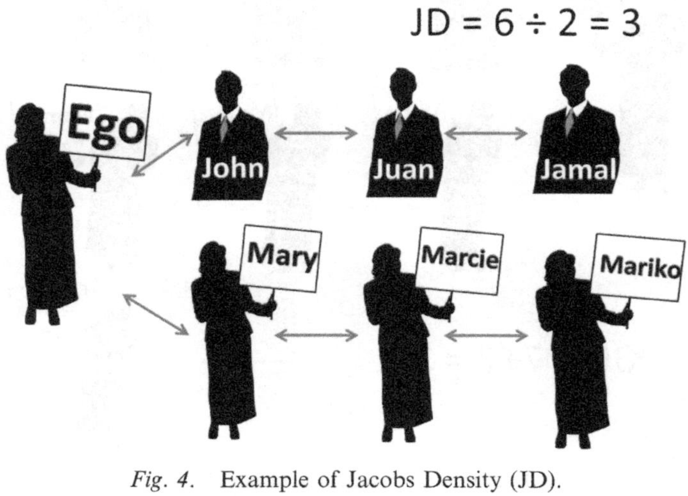

Fig. 4. Example of Jacobs Density (JD).

If later Marcie creates a new link with Moritica, with whom Ego had previously no or only very distant social contact, Ego's Jacobs Density increases by .5, as is shown in Fig. 5.

Since Moritica was previously socially distant from Ego, the new contact has shortened the distance between them.

Ego can also herself strategically break an old tie and form a new one if she discovers the opportunity to do so. In the third case, Ego believes that – although cutting ties with John would lose her three connections – she can thereby increase her Jacobs Density by forming a tie directly with Frank in her action space and indirectly link with Fergie, Fernando, Alice, Alina, and Kalim (Fig. 6).

The point I made earlier is that it is possible to make changes in the structure of a social network that leaves standard network density unchanged (by keeping the number of connections constant) but reduces average social distance and that this can promote entrepreneurial discovery.

Also, in each of three cases here I have limited the distance between Ego and the farthest contact to three degrees, following Christakis and Fowler's (2009, l. 485) finding that influence and information typically degrades significantly beyond three degrees of separation. If influence and

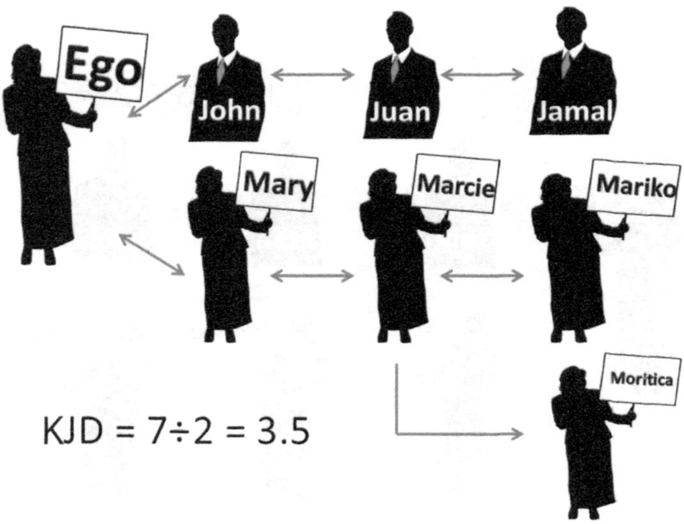

Fig. 5. Example of Increasing Jacobs Density (JD).

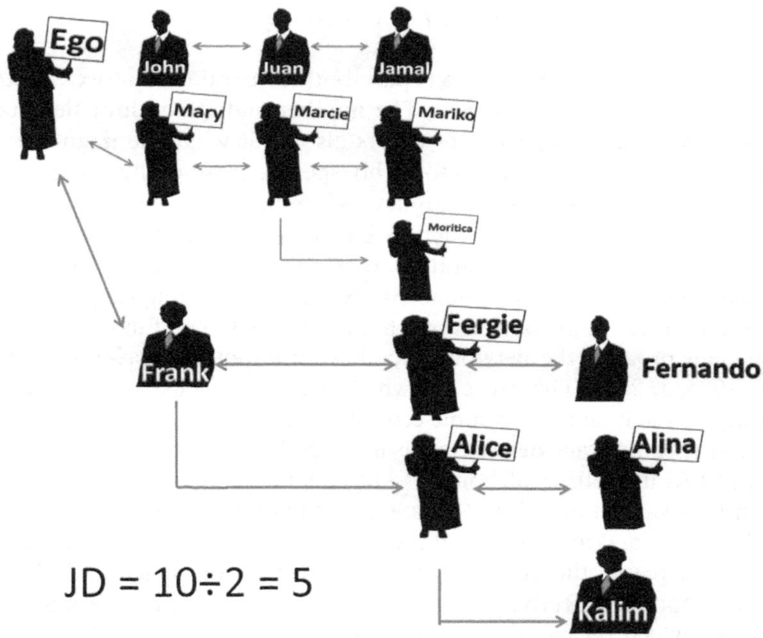

Fig. 6. Example of Strategic Ties to Increase Jacobs Density (JD).

information did not degrade significantly before six degrees of separation, and if indeed any two people on earth are separated by about six degrees as Barabasi (2003, pp. 25–40) reports, then everyone's Jacobs Density would be the same: it would equal the world's population.

So we have discussed two independent factors that can promote entrepreneurial discovery. The first is an increase in Jacobs Density, which increases the number and diversity of information that a person can access through a given set of contacts in her action space. The second (as discussed earlier) is a reduction in average social distance, which because of the three-degrees-of-separation rule means there is less information lost among people in that particular network. If Ego were to link directly to Marcie, or indeed anyone in the network beyond John and Mary, the average distance in the network would fall.

I believe Jacobs Density and average distance taken together capture the intuitive sense of "density" as it relates to entrepreneurship and economic development. But it is now possible to say more.

Trapped or Connected?

At a given moment in time, action space both constrains what we can know and liberates our creative powers. The number and strength of ties that at any moment connect a person to others also limit what she might become aware of – for example, a doctor who spends most of her time among patients and professional colleagues is unlikely to discover a profit opportunity in, say, the construction business. But those very limits may prevent the information generated in a dynamic economy from overwhelming her, allowing her to focus on recognizing meaningful patterns in a more tractable set of areas. "Given a limit to the volume of information that anyone can process, the network becomes an important screening device" (Burt, 1995, l. 212). The areas on which a person focuses may indeed be changing all the time in a dynamic economy – the doctor might notice that a technique used to brace delicate walls in a building renovation project could be applied to the setting of bones[11] – but cognitive limits keep the number she can be aware of at a fairly constant and manageable level. At the same time, however, making direct and indirect connections with socially distant networks increases the Jacobs Density of her action space and shortens average distances, effectively increasing within those limits the number of areas from which she can draw diverse and useful information. It allows her in a sense to be smarter and more creative.

Besides Jacobs Density and shorter average distances, there are two other factors to consider in evaluating the entrepreneurial effectiveness of an action space: the prevailing norms and the levels of trust.

Norms

Again, a person's action space is a particular place: a home, workplace, coffeehouse, or sidewalk. The kind of information she may become aware of or pass along, which might then become the basis for an entrepreneurial discovery, depends not only on who else is there and her relationship to them (i.e., the strength of the social tie) but also on the norms and conventions prevailing at that moment in that space. As mentioned earlier, a restaurant on a weekday is a more socially acceptable time and place to conduct business than a funeral. Other things being equal, the greater the freedom with which you are able to observe or mingle with others, especially those who are relative strangers to you and who therefore are more likely to be different from you, the better the chances will be that you will encounter diverse and perhaps novel information that you might then interpret in profitable ways.[12]

So, one person might tell another about a possible profit opportunity, or pass on information that could be valuable in some other way, because a tie exists between them. And the strength of that tie depends on the reliability of the informant and the information, which goes to the question of trust.

Trust

If we understand trust as purely a function of how well A knows B, then the stronger the tie,[13] the more likely A will trust B, *if* indeed B is trustworthy. Hardin (2002, p. 58) refers to this kind of trust as *cognitive trust*, or trust based on how much you know about someone else.[14] Again, in the context of a given network structure, in which ties are neither forming nor dissolving, stronger ties correlate with greater cognitive trust. The downside of this is that over time strong ties are likely to grow redundant – you know all the same people. In a completely static world, novelty and diversity would eventually disappear owing to "redundancy by cohesion."

There is, however, another phenomenon that also goes by the name of "trust" that while relevant in the static context is even more important in the dynamic context.

The Dynamics of Action Space

As I suggested earlier, simply multiplying weak ties willy-nilly, while it may raise simple network density and shorten average distance, does not necessarily increase Jacobs Density. A person would do better to focus on nonredundant ties.[15] In Fig. 1, for example, the tie between agents 4 and 5 is nonredundant. It is also a *bridge*.[16] The entrepreneurial discovery of a new nonredundant tie will be profitable if it yields greater benefits than the cost of establishing the new tie (which might also entail the cost of breaking an old tie).According to Burt (1995), ties with lower redundancy, perhaps even bridges, can be found in "structural holes."

Structural holes are "are disconnections or nonequivalencies between players in the arena" according to Burt (1995, l. 47), but as such they are also unexploited "entrepreneurial opportunities for information access, timing, referrals, and control" (*ibid.*). In the context of social networks, therefore, entrepreneurship manifests itself in the discovery of strategically valuable ties that span structural holes. Structural holes shorten average distances.

There is no certain indicator that a structural hole is present. The hole itself is an "invisible scam of nonredundancy waiting to be discovered by the able entrepreneur" (Burt, 1995, l. 648).

Note the similarity to Kirzner (1973). As it is for Kirzner, for Burt "competition is a process, not just a result," whereas "most theories of competition concern what is left when competition is over" (Burt, 1995, l. 102). Moreover, "the structural hole argument is a theory of competition made imperfect by the freedom of individuals to be entrepreneurs" (*ibid.*, l. 111). These imperfections represent profit opportunities to alert entrepreneurs, who establish the weak ties that span structural holes, shorten social distances, and increase Jacobs Density.[17]

When an entrepreneur E buys from A and sells to B, she not only engages in an act of arbitrage but also establishes a *relationship* among herself, A, and B. That relationship may not last beyond the exchange, but when it does it represents a tie – a weak one, if the agents have had little or no contact before. The three form a *transitive* relation, a triangle (Christakis & Fowler, 2009, l. 339). If it persists it can later transmit novel information from more distant network groups, with A or B rather than E acting entrepreneurially; or in time it can serve multiplex uses beyond the original trade function (e.g., A and B might become kinsmen as well as business partners). Not only is entrepreneurship critical in forming these weak ties, but over time competitive rivalry tends to fill structural holes.

Although structural holes may exist in networks near ego's own, they are, as we have seen, most likely to be found between socially distant networks or cliques. That is because, owing to homophily,[18] strong ties tend to bind agents in a network that is fairly homogenous and of low average distance from an ego or agent. And it is likely that the new connection constituting the nonredundant tie will be a weak tie: "weak ties are essential to the flow of information that integrates otherwise disconnected social clusters into a broader society" (Burt, 1995, l. 364).

Now, Christakis and Fowler argue that

> [p]eople with high transitivity live in densely clustered cliques where everyone knows everyone else. People with low transitivity, in contrast, tend to have friends in several different groups. Such people often act as bridges between completely different groups of people. (Christakis & Fowler, 2009, l. 3694)

In a social network that has been around a very long time, it may be extraordinarily difficult to discover structural holes because so many ties would already have been formed among the members, approaching maximal (non-Jacobs) density. In other words, because of structural equivalence or cohesion, over time ties will become more and more redundant. So in long-established and static networks we should expect transitivity to be very high, but there will also be little room for entrepreneurship and weak-tie formation. Again, low transitivity and structural holes are more likely to be found in socially distant, especially unconnected and therefore highly diverse, networks:

> As you expand your inventory from your closest, most frequent contacts to your more distant, contacts tend to be people like yourself before you reach a sufficiently low level of relationship to include people from completely separate social worlds. (Burt, 1995, l. 387)

But this raises a paradox.

If by "trust" we mean "cognitive trust" – A's propensity to rely on another agent because she knows him well – and if agents in diverse and socially distant networks are most likely to be strangers to her, how do weak ties form in the first place? From whence comes the trust that enables her to connect to another agent, about whom she knows little or nothing? Cognitive trust is the basis of the strong ties to agents in networks closer to A's own. Now, it is true that an agent C, who may be acquainted with both A and B, may serve as a bridge. This, however, simply pushes the question one step back: how did C become acquainted with A and B? It stands to reason that at some point in the past C was not strongly tied to both of them – perhaps to neither.

I believe the paradox can be resolved by pointing out a completely different kind of trust that is often conflated with cognitive trust.

Behavioral Trust

That concept is *behavioral trust*, which is "an act of choice that overcomes a lack of knowledge or uncertainty" (Ikeda, 2007, p. 219).[19]

Let us say that complete knowledge of another agent's trustworthiness, in a subjective-probability sense, is 100-percent certainty and complete ignorance is zero-percent certainty. Suppose that A needs 85-percent certainty before she can cognitively trust B enough to trade with him – say, the point at which gain x0.85> loss x (1–0.85). At that level of certainty or higher A will then cognitively trust B. Suppose, however, that in A's opinion she can trust B only up to 60 percent, but that for her to engage in trade still requires 85 percent certainty. Here A does not cognitively trust B and will not trade. Behavioral trust, therefore, is what could enable A to trade with B by overcoming the 25-percentage-point gap if she *chooses* to. Her trust in this case would be a kind of leap of faith.

In other words, while cognitive trust is a psychological propensity (Hardin, 2002, p. 58) – that is, you either have it or you don't – behavioral trust is an act of choice, a choice that is taken in the presence of radical uncertainty, in contrast to calculable risk (Coleman, 1990, pp. 97–108). An agent who cognitively trusts says: "I know you very well, so I can trust you." An agent who behaviorally trusts says: "I don't know you very well, but I'm going to trust you, anyway."

Cognitive trust is associated with strong ties; our familiarity with another person. Now, strengthening a tie does not necessarily mean that A will place greater reliance on B. After all, A's repeated contact with B may simply confirm her opinion that he is indeed a scoundrel who should not be trusted at all (in any sense). There may be members of your family that you would never rely on, and so forth. But A can place greater reliance on *her* evaluation of his trustworthiness or lack of it.

Behavioral trust on the other hand is the basis for the formation of a new tie. Because by definition you form a weak tie with someone you do not know very well, especially with someone with a very different background from yourself, the level of cognitive trust may be very low. In order to form a tie, to have contact and establish a relation with such a person, assuming you believe the expected benefit will be high, will require to a greater or lesser extent a leap of faith.[20]

Cutting a tie also involves both kinds of trust.[21] Should A leave her small town for the big city, or vice versa? Letting go of a relationship or a familiar clique or network may be based purely on calculation of given estimated benefits and costs, and when the former exceeds the latter a rational agent automatically severs the tie. Typically, however, the agent lacks the amount of information needed to make the "decision" that easily, in which case she will have to choose based on behavioral trust. Such choices also involve a leap of faith.

Freedom and Competition

The ability to form weak ties and to dissolve strong ties depends on the level of freedom allowed among the various networks. In the limit it is the freedom to enter or exit at any time any social network one chooses, subject to conditions that anyone could satisfy in principle, and to allow others to do the same. Freedom in this sense goes beyond the legal rights triumvirate of private property, freedom of contract, and the rule of law that is associated with *economic* freedom, although it would probably include them. I believe it would also have to include the absence of "social pressure," issuing perhaps from a set of traditional norms and conventions that could, despite the presence of formal grants of free association, stifle the movement of persons across either geographic or social space. The law may give same-sex couples the right to marry, for example, but strong disapprobation from family members may discourage many from doing so. And it would also entail a measure of *political* freedom insofar as coercion hinders social and geographic mobility.

When either social pressure or coercion prevents contact with outsiders, at least some agents will feel trapped as the thickness of ties encroaches ever further into their personal autonomy. You could say that in the extreme all private space becomes public space; but from the point of view of entrepreneurial competition and economic development, it may be closer to the truth to say that all public space becomes private space, in which there are no strangers. Ties would be interchangeable and redundant through both cohesion and structural equivalence – that is, everybody knows everybody else really, really well[22] – and structural holes would not exist. Novelty in such an "island network" cut off from the greater world of diverse ideas, tastes, and skills, must arise locally, with the practical result that it would rarely arise at all.

So, improving your situation as you see it entails not only forming new ties but also, crucially, breaking old ones; adding new friends, colleagues, suppliers, customers, and competitors as well as leaving old ones behind. That freedom permits us to loosen or end relationships we consider bad or unprofitable and to then add new ones (that may or may not turn out to be better than the old ones). Tolerance is obviously key to free entry and exit. But equally important is the freedom to criticize – the ability to openly evaluate your past, present, and future relationships – and to do so passionately, short of violence. Radical tolerance and radical criticism are complements. Tolerance without criticism is insipid; criticism without tolerance is intolerable.

That kind of freedom, which we might call *social* freedom, creates both the opportunity and the necessity to enter and exit. That it creates the opportunity is clear enough. It is competition, however, that makes it necessary. That is, the fact that entry and exit into social networks are free (although actually forming or dissolving ties may involve costs) makes the process of discovering structural holes in action space a competitive one. The agent who fails to effectively and profitably make and break ties will be at a competitive disadvantage.

Note, however, that competition takes place along two different dimensions. Entrepreneurial agents compete over already-established networks, and they also compete to make and break ties. Competition thus refers not only to the activities of rivals who are using already-established networks, through which they acquire information about prices and quantities, but also to attempts to profitably change the very structure of their networks.

To summarize: Social networks are a way of coping with incomplete knowledge in action space. Free entry and exit minimizes conflict and promotes trade, but it also offers a way to escape any remaining personal conflicts (or undesirable associations generally). Free entry and exit among the networks that come into contact with an agent's action space enable her to discover profitable opportunities to alter the structure of her networks. Behavioral trust is essential in that dynamic; without it she could neither form few weak ties nor cut strong ones. Trade is typically the catalyst, with an agent's contacts as the source of the information about trades – price signals, tips, assurances, and so on. Assuming that there is a potential profit opportunity, she evaluates the information and its sources and then decides whether or not to form a trade relationship with a new partner. Whether the particular trade is successful or not, the relationship formed may persist and later serve other, possibly multiplex, functions.

Of course, she can also make valuable connections by means other than trade. Casual or informal contact often sets the stage for important trading opportunities in the future.

Unintended Consequences

While an entrepreneur intentionally changes the structure of her social networks in order to generate profit opportunities for herself, doing business with a new client, for example, may not in itself prove profitable. If the client is relatively nonredundant, however, he may in the future have important strategic value to her. But because there are limits to her cognitive capabilities, changing the structure of her network will have consequences she will not be able to predict. Here are some of them.

As we have seen, the new tie may turn out to have other uses, or other people whom she may not currently know may later use the tie in ways she may or may not like.

I have also pointed out that the same connections that bring information to a person may help to diffuse the knowledge that she generates back to the rest of her ego network and beyond. Sometimes she may want this to happen (even if she does not intend it), as when she earns a reputation for trustworthiness. Other times she may not, as when she gains a reputation for untrustworthiness, or when knowledge of her discovery of a profit opportunity becomes known to rivals.

Another important unintended consequence of the competitive restructuring of social networks occurs when ties grow stronger over time.[23] As trade increases the frequency and intimacy of contact between A, who represents the values and norms of her network, and B, who represents the values and norms of his, over time differences between the knowledge and norms in their respective networks may decrease. So while a higher degree of homogeneity and homophily may reduce some kinds of conflict, on the downside diversity – which inspires novelty and innovation in commerce and culture – will tend to decrease. Relations become more substitutable and less complementary. Sufficiently high social freedom may counteract this homogenizing tendency by spurring experimentation and trial and error, both within an existing network community and across the greater global network. In this way it may be possible in an ever-changing environment to maintain Jacobs Density at levels high enough that cultural and economic development will continue to flourish.

Also, making and breaking ties have external effects. If someone severs an old tie by leaving a network it may create a kind of positive externality for those "left behind," as they become marginally less redundant than they were before the old network was changed. If A severs ties with B, and the shortest way for C to reach A had been through B, it opens a structural hole between C and A that someone – A, C, or some other agent D – might profitably fill. At the same time, if A connects to a new network by bridging a structural hole, this raises to some degree the level of redundancy in the latter, which is a kind of negative externality.

Finally, when A connects with nonredundant agent B, she not only increases the Jacobs Density for her own clique but also the Jacobs Density of anyone indirectly (i.e., more than one-degree distant) connected to her. Moreover, if B then entrepreneurially forms a connection with a diverse, socially distant agent with an entirely new set of connections, that would in turn increase A's Jacobs Density. This corresponds to case (2) above. B could also, of course, sever a tie that might reduce A's Jacobs Density. In general, however, I believe A would find it in her interest to secure social freedom for as many other agents as she can in order to maximize her own Jacobs Density, which may promote greater overall economic development.

SOME THOUGHTS ON URBAN DESIGN: FOSTERING SOCIAL CAPITAL IN ACTION SPACE

Jane Jacobs long ago explained how the design of public space can profoundly influence economic development. One of the key factors in her analysis is social capital. According to Burt (1995, l. 194): "Social capital is at once the resources contacts hold and the structure of contacts in a network."[24] Jacobs (1961, p. 138) coined the term "social capital" to refer to social networks of trust and reciprocity[25] that are particularly relevant to economic development and the market process. Granovetter (1973) later elaborated on the concept and used it in his work on social networks, and mathematicians such as Barabasi (2003) then formalized aspects of Granovetter's work. Finally, as we have seen Burt (1995) applies social-network theory to the study of entrepreneurship in the context of imperfect competition. Here we may bring the circle back to Jacobs.

I have argued elsewhere (Ikeda, 2007, 2008) that the difference between weak and strong ties is the basis for the difference between what Robert Putnam (2000) calls "bridging social capital" and "bonding social capital." The terminological parallel between bridging social capital and a network "bridge" is not coincidental. I have argued here that weak ties are indispensable in an entrepreneurially competitive process. The same kind of meaningful tolerance and criticism that are the foundation for free entry and exit among social networks also underlies bridging social capital. Bridging social capital, as the name suggests, promotes weak connections between socially distant and diverse agents. It rests on norms and beliefs that promote inclusivity as well as change. Bonding social capital, on the other hand, serves to increase homogeneity, homophily, and strong ties among agents in a given network. It promotes exclusivity, stability, and stasis. As a result, bonding social capital, while present in and necessary to all kinds of social settings, is more prevalent in less dynamic and less socially free systems. In creative market processes, then, bridging social capital is at least as important as bonding social capital.

Jacobs on the Death and Life of Social Capital

Jacobs described some of the mechanisms by which social capital is either nurtured or undermined by the physical environment. Jacobs, tutored by the sociologist William Whyte (Flint, 2009, p. 26), pioneered the analysis of how the design of public spaces affects economic development. The discussion in the previous section sheds light on the process.

Whyte offered specific recommendations at the micro level based on his classic time-lapse studies of public spaces. He recorded the effects of location, seating, light, accessibility, and other factors on how people use public plazas in New York City. His research emphasized the importance of location, comfort, and safety in the design of those spaces, and it has been applied by city planners – perhaps nowhere more successfully than in Bryant Park in Midtown Manhattan (Gratz, 2010, p. 123; Whyte, 1980).

Jacobs created an analytical framework that explains how safety, trust, and land-use diversity emerge spontaneously in successful urban environments (Jacobs, 1961, 1969). Based on her careful observations of urban street life, she recommended a built environment that minimizes visual dullness (short blocks), includes buildings of different ages (old buildings) that lower the cost of experimentation, encompasses multiple attractors that bring people into public areas (mixed primary uses), and provides for a population density high enough to supply those concentrations of people (population density). Again, the principle that people attract people provides what she called the "eyes on the street" that informally police public spaces. And if that happens during most of the day and night people will regard public spaces as places of safety and security, the "bedrock attribute" of all successful cities (Jacobs, 1961, p. 30 and pp. 143–221).

Although mindful that those conditions would manifest themselves differently depending on the time and place, she argued that they would encourage the prime ingredient for economic development: informal, typically unplanned, contact on streets and sidewalks, or whatever the particular form of the public space is. Those contacts, she said, are the "small change from which city's wealth of public life may grow" (*ibid.*, p. 72). On the other hand, for Jacobs border vacuums, cataclysmic money, and visual homogeneity undermine or destroy social capital in the same way that the erosion of social freedom would do so.

Border vacuums are massive, single-purpose land uses that may attract people for short periods of time (such as a civic center, football stadium, or railroad yard) but leave the area dull, deserted, and dangerous at other times. *Cataclysmic money* refers to the sudden and massive influx (though occasionally withdrawal) of investment into a neighborhood or district that – because everything is built relatively quickly – creates a large collection of new structures that offer little cheap space, requires repair at the same time, and presents a stifling homogeneity. This last factor, *visual homogeneity*, contributes to long-term economic stagnation because it implies a kind of visual border vacuum that lacks visual and tactile intricacy and interest (Sasaki, 1998). Indeed, each of these factors run counter to spontaneous economic development, because they create what Jacobs aptly calls a "great blight of dullness" (*ibid*., p. 41). People generally avoid dullness, unless they wish to be unseen, and fewer people means fewer "eyes on the street" and higher levels of perceived, and eventually actual, danger (*ibid*., pp. 257–317). Jacobs Densities would fall and the action spaces for many would shrink or disappear altogether.

Norms that discourage informal contact with strangers, and thus the formation of bonding social capital would, like a border vacuum, block the discovery of serendipitous complementarities among socially distant persons with diverse knowledge, skills, and tastes. Indeed cataclysmic money, border vacuums, and visual homogeneity – by thwarting informal contact – might themselves over time engender norms and beliefs that are more exclusive than inclusive, thereby reinforcing a degenerative process that Jacobs calls a "dynamic of decline."

Implications for Urban Design and Policy

Urban development projects that are very large in relation to the built environment in which they are placed are problematic. Large, purely private developments usually get that way by growing incrementally over time, whereas government-supported projects tend to be built much faster and tend to be much larger and more costly to change when conditions change. Enormous "giga-projects" are rarely the result of private investment unaided by government intervention in the form of protection against competition, eminent domain, and soft budget constraints. The virtue of slower development is that it provides more opportunities for entrepreneurial adjustments to the uncertainty of future demand and supply conditions, and it better enables open social networks to evolve over time. A market-based approach also tends to promote an architecture of the organic that avoids gigantism (Ikeda, 2010, 2011).

Here are a few general recommendations:

1. As much as possible, avoid developments, especially giga-projects, that depend for their success on soft budget constraints and extra-market mechanisms. And whatever the construction of massive government-funded highways, airports, municipal centers, and the like may have in their favor, the negative impact on action spaces that these cataclysmic expenditures will have is unambiguous: visual homogeneity; typically closed architectural design; massive border vacuums; and the absence of the intricacy, human scale, and social fine-structure that foster and maintain robust social networks. These problems may be unavoidable, but planners may also be able to minimize them if they are aware of them.
2. Where they are indeed unavoidable, such government projects should to the extent possible leave future development open-ended. That means slow, incremental development of civic centers, business districts, sports complexes, and the like. Furthermore, as Jacobs (1961, p. 252) recommends, civic projects should not be clustered together where they will constitute massive border vacuums, but rather be strategically decentralized and placed in districts where nine-to-five land use is uncommon.
3. Because politics encourages rapid, large-scale development, economic development should rely as much as possible on private enterprise and less on government intervention.
4. While private–public hybrids have problems of their own, where private investment alone is not likely to generate the kind of economic development deemed necessary, or where it is expected to take place too slowly for political purposes, hybrids may work best when the bulk of the planning and financial responsibility lies with the private entity.[26] Corruption, however, will be hard to avoid.

In general, design (public or private) should advance diversity along the dimensions of land use, knowledge, skills, and lifestyles – ideally creating the sort of safe, trust-promoting environments in which action-space-rich networks can emerge. This is obviously a political challenge, given the typical interventionist mindset of urban politics. Left to its own resources, however, local politics can be more responsive to genuine local needs or at least do less damage than federally financed, initiated, and directed policies that are imposed from above at the local level.

CONCLUDING THOUGHTS

Agents in a dynamic market process operate in action space through real time. A given agent's action spaces will change according to her purposes, but each is an entry point into its own complex web of social networks. The ever-changing nodes and strong and weak ties that constitute those networks are the conduits through which relevant (and irrelevant) information is conveyed to the agent and from her to others.

Under free entry and exit, the structure of those networks will change as a result of entrepreneurial discovery, by the agent herself and by those within her networks. By finding structural holes, either in the process of engaging in trade or through informal social contact, she will be able to alter her action space (as well as find new ones), perhaps not being aware of all of the consequences of her actions, in a way that can increase Jacobs Density, shorten average distance, and facilitate information transmission. How structures in public space are planned and located can impinge on the action spaces of the multitude of people who live in the cities that are central to the modern market process. The design and placement of public spaces can in this way promote or retard the dynamics of economic development.

Nonequilibrium prices are important objects of entrepreneurial discovery in the market process, but they are not the only one. Outside of equilibrium, social networks are also indispensable for, among other things, conveying the meaning of those prices to the people who make decisions. In that sense, social networks, and changes to their structure, are as important to the market process as the market prices themselves. What then is the theoretical status of the action spaces that enable people to plug into those networks?

Purposeful action and entrepreneurship are, of course, foundational to market-process theory in a way that action space may not be. But while action space is not necessary for understanding the *nature* of entrepreneurship, I believe it is essential for understanding how entrepreneurship actually operates in the market process. Trying to grasp the significance of entrepreneurship in that context without considering action space is a little like trying to appreciate the advantages of driving over walking without considering roads. And just as thinking seriously about how you actually drive a car reveals much about the conditions necessary to do it successfully and safely, thinking seriously about how people in the market process actually acquire and convey information makes clear how important the spatial environment is to their decision making.

NOTES

1. Equilibrium prices do this differently from nonequilibrium prices. The equilibrium price of apples relative to the equilibrium price of oranges accurately reflects the relative scarcity of apples to oranges, enabling rational agents to make efficient choices. If the apple market is not in equilibrium, the spread of disequilibrium apple prices offers arbitrage-profit opportunities for entrepreneurially alert agents, whose actions may then help to order the system. My focus here will be on agents and markets outside of equilibrium.

2. Andersson (2005) makes a similar point: "Moreover, the spatiotemporal setting influences both the knowledge stocks that individuals embody and the flows that they receive. In other words, individual skills, cognitive capacities, and knowledge of specific external stimuli (e.g., facts, people, and prices) depend on the spatiotemporal location, even if we accept that some skills and capacities are innate". Andersson's essay addresses a problem and raises points very similar to mine, although his solution does not use social-network theory. I would also link this chapter with Virgil Storr's work (2008) on Austrian economics and social space.

3. These terms are loosely related to what Jacobs (1961, p. 262) calls "special land" and "general land."

4. In addition to Ikeda (2007) on this, see the discussion in Ikeda (2002) on the tendency to interpret "local knowledge" too narrowly as relating to production activity.

5. For the moment, I will ignore the strength of these relations. Also, the value of the ties is not relevant here and I will assume that they are bidirectional and positive.

6. Figs. 1 and 2, and some of the accompanying analysis, are based on Degenne and Forsé (1999, p. 4).

7. While it is not crucial for this chapter, I will follow Jacobs (1969, p. 262) and define a *city* as a "settlement that consistently generates is economic growth from its own local economy."

8. This is because of her emphasis on "high concentrations of people at different times of the day," but she is very clear that that is important only insofar as density is a "generator of diversity" (Jacobs, 1961, p. 143).

9. See, for example, this website dedicated to the New Urbanism: http://www.newurbanism.org/ (see also Leccese & McCormick, 2000).

10. Jacobs (1961, pp. 200–221) lists density as only one of four "generators of diversity" in urban neighborhoods; the others being short blocks, plenty of old worn-down buildings sprinkled among the new, and multiple primary uses that attract outsiders. Short blocks encourage walking, contribute to the visual interest of public space, and create more intersections that serve as landmarks. Old buildings offer entrepreneurs and artists cheap working space to incubate new ideas. And mixed primary uses draw people into a neighborhood at different times of the day. Density then provides people in large numbers who serve as the "eyes on the street" that help make the neighborhood safe and who demand and supply all that diversity. Without diversity, density is a nonstarter.

11. This example comes from a recent conversation I had with a well-known orthopedic surgeon.

12. "Everything else constant, a large, diverse network is the best guarantee of having a contact present where useful information is aired. This is not to say that benefits must increase linearly with size and diversity ... but only that, other things held constant, the information benefits of a large, diverse network are more than the information benefits of a small, homogenous network" (Burt, 1995, l. 247).

13. Christakis and Fowler (2009) report on other factors such as homophily that also increase the level of this kind of trust.

14. Ikeda (2007, p. 218) discusses this concept of trust and compares it to "behavioral trust" at greater length.

15. "But increasing network size without considering diversity can cripple a network in significant ways. What matters is the number of nonredundant contacts" (Burt, 1995, l. 255).

16. "An edge is a bridge between two parts in a graph when it is the only link that spans the two parts, that is, every node in one part can only reach a node in another part via that link ... An edge can be considered a local bridge if it is the shortest path between two parts of a graph, that is, where all other chain lengths are > 2" (Degenne and Forsé, 1999, p. 110).

17. This has been essential historically for urban development. Pirenne (1952) is the authority on the social impact of trade in the Late Middle Ages; Algaze (2008, l. 166) has found evidence of the role of trade in the southern Mesopotamian delta in the late Uruk period, circa 3400 to 3100 BC.

18. Homophily is the tendency to form stronger ties with those with whom you share more characteristics (Christakis & Fowler, 2009, l. 308).

19. I make this distinction also in Ikeda (2008, p. 173), which is in the tradition of Niklas Luhmann (see Seligman, 1997, for a discussion). Like "cognitive trust," the term "behavioral" derives from Hardin (2002, pp. 58–69), although he does not necessarily endorse the concept.

20. Some have argued that behavioral trust simply amounts to a "risk-loving" propensity. I deal with this objection elsewhere (Ikeda, 2006) and cannot address it here, except to point out that even a rational risk-loving person, when faced will two gambles involving identical risk, would never "choose" the one about which she is less informed than the other. Behavioral trust, however, would grant the possibility that she would indeed choose a gamble about which she is ill-informed.

21. Adding new ties may actually necessitate the cutting of old ones, according to Dunbar's Law, especially when the ties are strong (see Christakis and Fowler, 2009, l. 3914).

22. The so-called "three-degree of influence rule" and "Dunbar's number" will ensure that the actual size of ego's local network is relatively small (see Christakis & Fowler, 2009, l. 485 and l. 3914). Even if binding, however, Dunbar's number would not seem to limit the number of *weak* ties that one could have.

23. Again, weak ties need not always grow into strong ties. Indeed, as Jacobs (1961, pp. 62–65) points out, there are good reasons, both for herself and for the community in which she operates, for an agent not to let too much of her personal information become public. Great cities enable anonymity and privacy; if losing one's privacy is the price of public contacts, people may have an incentive to avoid making those kinds of contacts at all, resulting in insularity, population homogeneity, and shrinking action space.

24. "More accurately, social capital is as important as competition is imperfect and investment capital is abundant" (Burt, 1995, l. 158).

25. I have written elsewhere that from the perspective of the market process, social capital consists of "norms of generalized reciprocity and networks of trust that emerge unplanned over time, that operate in public space among members of an open-ended community, and that help to promote entrepreneurial discovery" (Ikeda, 2008, p. 181).

26. In 2006, the city governments of Tempe and Chandler, Arizona, partnered with a private firm to install $4 million-worth of transmitters to provide city-wide WiFi service to anyone anywhere with a computer and modem (Jensen, 2011). With the rise in the next two years of so-called smartphones, tablets, and 4G networks that circumvented WiFi technology, this cutting-edge infrastructural idea became largely obsolete. The devices today hang uselessly from light poles, because the private companies that bore the brunt of the investment and operating costs pulled out very quickly. This private–public venture was a failure, but because the private investors had the knowledge and incentive to cut their losses, a good one.

ACKNOWLEDGMENTS

I wish to thank Simon Bilo, Gene Callahan, Peter Gordon, David Harper, Chidem Kurdas, Shruti Rajagopalan, Mario Rizzo, Virgil Storr, and Ed Stringham for their comments. Arthur Chou transformed my primitive diagrams into useful graphics. Any remaining errors or omissions are mine alone. I also thank the Earhart Foundation for supporting my earlier research on trust and social capital.

REFERENCES

Algaze, G. (2008).*Ancient mesopotamia at the dawn of civilization: The evolution of an urban landscape*. Chicago, IL: University of Chicago Press (Kindle Edition location indicators "l." rather than page numbers).

Andersson, D. E. (2005). The spatial nature of entrepreneurship. *Quarterly Journal of Austrian Economics*, *8*(2), 21–34.

Barabasi, A.-L. (2003). *Linked: How everything is connected to everything else and what it means for business, science, and everyday life*. New York, NY: Plume.

Bogardus, E. S. (1947). Measurement of personal-group relations. *Sociometry*, *10*(4), 306–311.

Bruegmann, R. (2006). *Sprawl: A compact history*. Chicago, IL: University of Chicago Press.

Burdett, R., & Sudjic, D. (Eds.). (2008). *The endless city*. New York, NY: Phaidon Press.

Burt, R. (1995). *Structural holes: The social structure of competition*. Cambridge, MA: Harvard University Press (Kindle Edition location "l." indicators rather than page numbers).

Christakis, N. A., & Fowler, J. H. (2009). *Connected the surprising power of our social networks and how they shape our lives*. New York, NY: Little, Brown (Kindle Edition location indicators "l." rather than page numbers).

Coleman, J. S. (1990). *Foundations of social theory*. Cambridge, MA: The Belknap Press.
Degenne, A., & Forsé, M. (1999). *Introducing social networks*. London, UK: Sage.
Desrochers, P. (2001). Geographical proximity and the transmission of tacit knowledge. *Review of Austrian Economics*, *14*(1), 25–46.
Flint, A. (2009). *Wrestling with Moses: How Jane Jacobs took on New York's master builder and transformed the American city*. New York, NY: Random House.
Gordon, P., & Ikeda, S. (2011). Does density matter? In D. E. Andersson, Å. E. Andersson & C. Mellander (Eds.), *Handbook of creative cities*. Cheltenham, UK: Edward Elgar.
Granovetter, M. S. (1973). The strength of weak ties. *American Journal of Sociology*, *78*(6), 1360–1380.
Gratz, R. B. (2010). *The battle for Gotham: New York in the shadow of Robert Moses and Jane Jacobs*. New York, NY: Nation Books.
Hardin, R. (2002). *Trust & trustworthiness*. New York, NY: Russell Sage Foundation.
Hayek, F. A. (1945). The use of knowledge in society. In F. A. Hayek (Ed.), *Individualism and economic order*. Chicago, IL: Gateway.
Hayek, F. A. (1967). The results of human action but not of human design. In F. A. Hayek (Ed.), *Essays in philosophy, politics, and economics*. Chicago, IL: University of Chicago Press.
Ikeda, S. (2002). The role of "social capital" in the market process. *Journal des Economistes et des Etudes Humaines*, *12*(2/3), 229–240.
Ikeda, S. (2006). *Is it rational to trust?* Unpublished working paper.
Ikeda, S. (2007). Urbanizing economics. *Review of Austrian Economics*, *20*(4), 213–220.
Ikeda, S. (2008). The meaning of "social capital" as it relates to the market process. *Review of Austrian Economics*, *21*, 167–182.
Ikeda, S. (2010). Is there a "libertarian architecture"? *The Freeman Online*, March 23.
Ikeda, S. (2011). The breezes of creative destruction. *The Freeman Online*, July 26.
Jacobs, J. (1961). *The death and life of Great American cities*. New York, NY: Vintage.
Jacobs, J. (1969). *The economy of cities*. New York, NY: Vintage.
Jensen, E. (2011). Tempe, Chandler's bold Wi-Fi project fizzled fast. *The Arizona Republic*, August 13.
Karakayali, N. (2009). Social distance and affective orientations. *Sociological Forum*, *23*(3), 538–562.
Kirzner, I. M. (1973). *Competition and entrepreneurship*. Chicago, IL: University of Chicago Press.
Leccese, M., & McCormick, K. (Eds.). (2000). *Charter of the new urbanism*. New York, NY: McGraw Hill.
Lewis, P. F. (2003). *New Orleans: The making of an urban landscape*. Santa Fe, NM: Center for American Places.
O'Driscoll, G. P., & Rizzo, M. J. (1985). *The economics of time and ignorance*. New York, NY: Blackwell.
Pirenne, H. (1952). *Medieval cities: Their origin and the rival of trade*. Princeton, NJ: Princeton University Press.
Putnam, R. D. (2000). *Bowling Alone: The collapse and revival of American community*. New York, NY: Simon & Schuster.
Sasaki, K.-I. (1998). For whom is city design? Tactility versus visuality. In M. Miles, T. Hall & I. Borden (Eds.), *The urban cultures reader*. New York, NY: Routledge.
Seligman, A. B. (1997). *The problem of trust*. Princeton, NJ: Princeton University Press.

Storr, V. H. (2008). The market as a social space: On the meaningful extra economic conversations that can occur in markets. *Review of Austrian Economics*, *21*(2/3), 135–150.

Von Mises, L. (1963). *Human action: A treatise on economics*. Chicago, IL: Regnery.

Whyte, W. H. (1980). Small urban spaces. In A. LaFarge (Ed.) (2000), *The essential William H. Whyte*. New York, NY: Fordham University Press.

APPENDIX

Network A

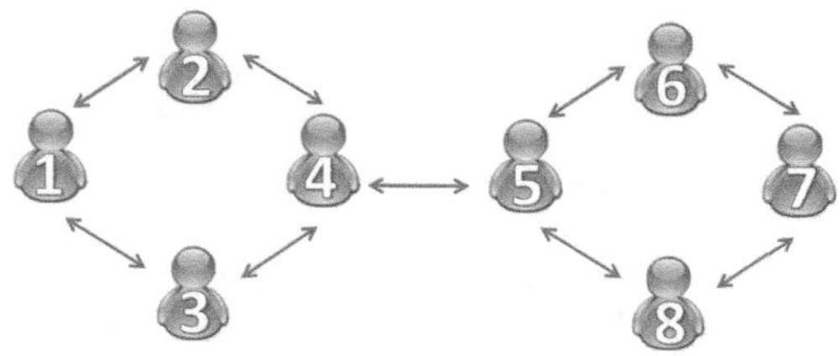

1–2: 1

1–3: 1 2–3: 2

1–4: 2 2–4: 1 3–4: 1

1–5: 3 2–5: 2 3–5: 2 4–5: 1

1–6: 4 2–6: 3 3–6: 3 4–6: 2 5–6: 1

1–7: 5 2–7: 4 3–7: 4 4–7: 3 5–7: 2 6–7: 1

1–8: 4 2–8: 3 3–8: 3 4–8: 2 5–8: 1 6–8: 2 7–8: 1

Total 20 + 15 + 13 + 8 + 4 + 3 + 1 = 64

$64 \div 28 = 2.29$

Network B

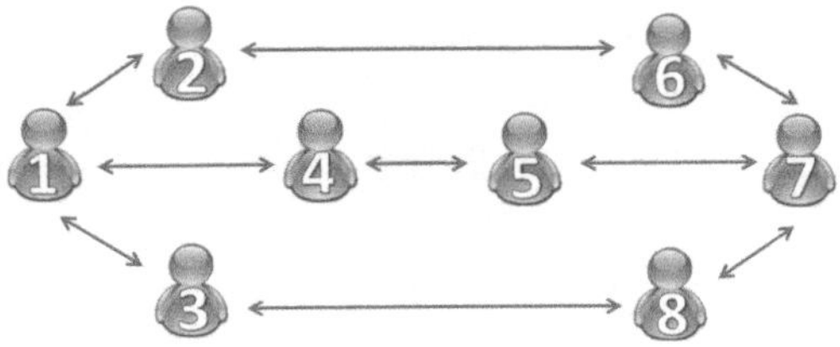

1–2: 1

1–3: 1 2–3: 2

1–4: 1 2–4: 2 3–4: 2

1–5: 2 2–5: 3 3–5: 3 4–5: 1

1–6: 2 2–6: 1 3–6: 3 4–6: 3 5–6: 2

1–7: 3 2–7: 2 3–7: 2 4–7: 2 5–7: 1 6–7: 1

1–8: 2 2–8: 3 3–8: 1 4–8: 3 5–8: 2 6–8: 2 7–8: 1

Total 12 + 13 + 11 + 9 + 5 + 3 + 1 = 54

$54 \div 28 = 1.93$

SCHUMPETERIAN INNOVATIONS, THE COASE THEOREM, AND SUSTAINABLE DEVELOPMENT: A HONG KONG CASE STUDY OF BUS INNOVATIONS

Lawrence W. C. Lai and Frank T. Lorne

The diversity of interest in Joseph Schumpeter's work has been prolific, as is revealed in the chapters in this book. One prominent line of research is to investigate Schumpeter's concept of *entrepreneurial innovations* (cf. Holcombe, 2003) as a driving force in economic development, with one branch of study synthesizing his ideas and those of Israel Kirzner (see, for instance, Yu, 2001). Another line of research deals with the broader relationship between Austrian economics and new institutional economics (see Kim & Mahoney, 2006; Witt, 1999).

This chapter seeks to combine both lines of endeavor in an attempt to demonstrate that Schumpeter's concept of innovations and Coasean thinking are useful for building a model of sustainable development, taking the concept a step further than in our previous work (Lai & Lorne, 2006) by including a *spatial* dimension (Andersson, 2005; Desrochers, 1998, 2001, 2004). Our methodology conforms to the empirical tradition of new

The Spatial Market Process
Advances in Austrian Economics, Volume 16, 141–178

ISSN: 1529-2134/doi:10.1108/S1529-2134(2012)0000016009

institutional economic research as adopted by Ronald Coase (1959, 1974, 2000) and Steven Cheung (1968, 1973, 1975). It is a case study of a real firm – a price-regulated natural monopoly – that has been making profits in the absence of government subsidies.

Prior to specifying our research problem, we need to clarify a number of fundamental definitional issues. First, we need to define what Schumpeterian innovations actually are and how they differ from inventions. Second, we need to position Coasean economics vis-à-vis Schumpeterian economics in terms of sustainable development.

SCHUMPETERIAN INNOVATIONS DEFINED

The types of innovation considered to be Schumpeterian can be very broad. What is an innovation? According to *The Advanced Learner's Dictionary* (Hornby, Gatenby, & Wakefield, 1973, p. 545), an innovation is "something *new* that is *introduced*." This covers both inventions and their introduction. Thus, introducing methods to a new market can certainly be a form of Schumpeterian innovation. Schumpeter, however, distinguished *innovations* (innovators) from *inventions* (inventors) (Swedberg, 1991, p. 173). He considered innovations as the prime movers in the capitalist process. Johannessen, Olsen, and Lumpkin (2001) dwell on six measures of the "newness" of an innovation based on his interpretation of Schumpeter and others, but glossed over the distinction between innovations and inventions. What, then, was Schumpeter's original formulation?

Innovations, in Schumpeter (1934), refer to five distinct categories of "new combinations" that are put together by the entrepreneur, who may be an individual or a whole team or company (Swedberg, 1991, p. 173), namely:

(a) "The *introduction* of a new good ... or of a new quality of a good";
(b) "The *introduction* of a new method of production";
(c) "The opening of a new market";
(d) "The conquest of a new source of supply of raw materials or half-manufactured goods";
(e) "The carrying of the new organization of any industry, like the creation of a monopoly position ... or the breaking up of a monopoly position" (Schumpeter, 1934, quoted in Swedberg, 1991, p. 34).

Obviously, Schumpeter made no distinction between what Giersch (1984) calls "advanced" and "less advanced" areas and did not insist that innovations are inventions. Indeed, as Ruttan (1959) notes, Schumpeter did not only reject the idea that innovation is dependent on invention in a direct manner, he also asserted that the social process that produces innovations is different from that which produces inventions.

More importantly, Schumpeter argued – in what has become known as "the Schumpeterian hypothesis" – that monopolistic or larger firms are more conducive to innovation than competitive or smaller firms (Swedberg, 1991, p. 157). Interestingly, this important hypothesis, which stresses the importance of a monopoly *firm*, did not feature in Witt's (1999) analysis.

Improvisation is an important dimension of the second aspect of an innovation, especially where new products, techniques, or methods are involved to adapt a distinct invention for exploiting or reacting to a specific new situation, such as a new market or market condition. Certainly, one important type of new situation is an investment and/or a change in market conditions. In Schumpeterian economics, the role of improvisation is recognized as pivotal (see Cunha & Cunha, 2006; Tzeng, 2009). More importantly, Schumpeterian innovation entails a process channeling resources from normal circular flows to situations outside the circular flow, *but* until innovative experiments can be *brought back* to the normal circular flow for economic gain, Schumpeterian innovation may not necessarily be useful; inventing just for the sake of being different diverts resources to activities that may not have widespread uses.

Schumpeter (1934) describes the dual process of innovation in detail. Thus it is not the purpose of this chapter to repeat his argument. What is interesting, perhaps, is another feature of Schumpeter's innovation that can pose a challenge to the process of how innovation can be channeled back into the normal circular flow; this also relates to *creative destruction*. Creative destruction, which displaces something for the benefit of something with higher value, is commonly understood as a process which comes about via market competition. However, in many businesses, particularly in a franchised protected monopoly, this process can come from *within* the company because useful innovations are investments. They increase productivity, add resources, and can be a matter of progressive business practices independent of market competition. Thus, the process can entail "intrapreneurs" rather than entrepreneurs.[1] This fundamentally Schumpeterian concept of flow will be captured in our model.

SCHUMPETERIAN INNOVATION AND AUSTRIAN ECONOMICS

Schumpeterian innovation offers many insights that complement mainstream economic thought, particularly when it comes to the issue of uncertainty. First and foremost, the Austrian school of thought believes that (Misesian) human action affects economic outcomes. In contrast, the mainstream economic approach of modeling the uncertainty of innovation via probability distributions has failed to capture this important characteristic of innovation, as its formulation is entirely mechanical. The mainstream approach fails to recognize that human actions are not driven entirely by expected benefits and costs. It is true that the mainstream approach can salvage this shortcoming by introducing the notion of subjective probabilities that are based on the subjective risk preferences of the innovators (or the innovating firms). But this does not help one understand the nature of an inventive process in terms of people's interactions with their environments, as well as with other people.

A mechanical formulation of innovation via probabilities limits the very idea of innovation. Consider the question of whether robots are able to replace all functions of human beings. If innovations can be sufficiently modeled by probability distributions with given assumed subjective risk preferences, these features can *certainly* be embedded in a central operating system (i.e., the brain) of a robot, and innovations may thus be effectively generated by robots, just like if they were humans with the assumed subjective risk preferences. This being unlikely, given our current technologies, innovations are something that cannot be entirely captured by a probability formulation.

The mainstream approach also examines innovation by way of examples and case studies. Again, these studies do not address the heart of the issue. Such an approach cannot describe the inner logic of the black box of innovation; it only describes what goes in and what comes out of a black box. What happens inside the black box remains unknown. Studies of success stories are ubiquitous, but they cannot suggest a code or a formula for imitating an Albert Einstein, a Thomas Edison, a Bill Gates, or a Li Ka-shing.

Schumpeterian innovation can be a fruitful concept that opens alternative channels of thinking beyond probability formulations by addressing issues of what is inside the black box. Entrepreneurship in Schumpeter (1934) requires a conscious action on the part of an individual to divert resources from their normal circular-flow activities. This concept is also different from what is emphasized in the mainstream development economics literature, in which education and various infrastructure investments are viewed as the essence of development. In the context of a textbook treatment of the subject, education and infrastructure investments are most likely exogenously provided by governments or groups such as the World Bank. Yet such investments may fail to bring about true development as Schumpeter envisioned it, because actions and decisions take place in highly uncertain environments. This is something that is perhaps uniquely the responsibility of humans. Failure to recognize a self-motivating necessity to try something different can result in the mismanagement of a development program while relying on exogenous subsidies that provide the form, but not the substance, of development.

Schumpeterian innovation is a major contribution to the Austrian approach since it emphasizes a process rather than the comparative statics used in many mainstream analyses. The proposition here is that refutable implications not only apply to the scientific testing of theories, but also guide entrepreneurial actions. Lorne (2010) describes how this (refutability-based) methodology can be derived from a paradigm of constrained maximization, and is in line with a school of thought that was initiated by Steven Cheung.

THE RELATIONSHIP BETWEEN SCHUMPETERIAN INNOVATIONS AND SUSTAINABLE DEVELOPMENT

During the 1930s, the term "sustainable development" had yet to be coined. Indeed, it was almost 40-odd years after the death of Schumpeter – in 1987 – that the first definition of sustainable development was introduced by the Brundtland Commission (World Commission on Environment and Development, 1987). (If Schumpeter had been alive, we believe that he would have complemented his *Economic Development* with an additional treatment of sustainable development.)

It is here that this chapter has to resort to another great economist, Ronald Coase (who also might have much to say about sustainable development). Sustainable development requires that one addresses environmental issues, which, in Coasean terms, are extra-contractual spillover effects that are caused by undefined or vague ownership. Coase (1960) suggests that with sufficiently low transaction costs, such spillover effects can be internalized via a process of contracting.

However, at this point we are still unable to link Schumpeter and Coase, because they seem to address two different things. The gap can be closed by invoking a newer definition of sustainable development that came after Brundtland – one that explicitly recognizes the intersection of economy, environment, and society as being at the heart of sustainable development (Lai, Chau, Ho, & Lorne, 2006; Lai & Lorne, 2003, 2006; Lorne, 2009) rather than being merely a present-versus-future generation issue, as Brundtland proclaimed.

Schumpeterian innovation is thus relevant to Coasean thinking, because in order to fully address sustainable development, society (or the human resources affected) must also be taken into consideration. In this context, *creative destruction poses a challenge in that the very essence of innovation is to creatively destroy some existing capital, human as well as non-human*. The basis for developing a win–win strategy is thus jeopardized.

This problem has resurfaced in recent years due to the development efforts of major cities around the world, where a key consideration in many local and regional development projects has to do with methods of *preserving* – not replacing or developing – relics and heritage buildings. This is, in principle, contrary to the spirit of Schumpeterian innovation, at least in terms of its creative destruction characteristics.

The suggestion that we have made in our past writings is to extend the Coasean argument on contracting regarding the environment to the societal sector, which would address the methods for formulating strategies and building infrastructure in a way that would result in a win–win outcome for all three sectors. The suggestion can therefore be extended in light of our discussion of Schumpeterian innovation in the previous section, so that we must also address the possibility that new capital will replace old capital in the spirit of creative destruction, which can be mitigated in the spirit of developing win–win outcomes. Win–win outcomes are contractual in nature, and thus also Coasean. Such outcomes are possible because competition and cooperation are not mutually exclusive concepts. The increasingly popular concept of "co-opetition" (Brandenburger & Nalebuff, 1996) that has been brought up by management scholars from various camps is very much in line with this type of thinking as well.

How can all these factors be synthesized into a uniform framework? Building on the earlier work of Yu, Shaw, Fu, and Lai (2000) on investments in mariculture as a means of privatizing open-access oceanic resources (Lai, 1993), Lai and Lorne (2006) characterize Schumpeterian innovations as problems involving *shifts* rather than *movements along* given cost or production functions. In this chapter, we address these Schumpeterian shift problems through the history of franchised public buses in colonial Hong Kong. Before we elaborate on how Yu's (2000) model can be modified to address the bus-franchise problem, we need to reiterate some relevant facts: the innovations in Hong Kong's bus industry involved *improvisations* and *adaptation* besides the direct introduction of purchased new products after their *experimentation* by bus engineers. The institutional framework for such innovations was provided contractually and was Coasean under a state franchise.

To provide the theoretical background for the case study, the next section shall explain the structure of Yu's model and explain how it is a *Schumpeterian re-interpretation of the Coase Theorem* as it applies to real life, followed by an account of the idea that monopolies "protected" under state franchises will still innovate to lower their costs rather than content themselves with the extraction of economic rent.

SPATIAL RELEVANCE

The question of space is often neglected in economics, and its treatment in Austrian economics is still in its formative stages, with Desrochers (1998, 2001, 2004) and Andersson (2005) as prominent pioneers. It is metaphysically easy to say that all economic agents and activities occupy space and have spatial implications. This line of thinking articulates with urban planning, which deals with the spatial division of labor in land use, which entails the type of transportation problem that is the subject matter of this chapter. The challenge is to show how such ontological facts and implications are communicated, using standard economic vocabulary and techniques. Our spatial example is the breaking up of a geographically insulated franchised area that at the same time induced both economic opportunities and risks. Furthermore, our case study was conducted in a political-economy context in relation to land (and hence "spatial" in that abstract sense[2]), in which state-regulated private monopolies in the public utilities market have been condemned by Poon (2006) – under the spell of Henry George – as merely making profits by exercising their market power. One of the sources of such "profits" is the land that is used as bus garages and is obtained from the state at a low price. While recent research (Lai, Davies, & Cheung, 2011) refutes the cheap-land thesis, it remains necessary to show how such land is actually used for innovative purposes.

THE MODEL

This section modifies Yu's model (Yu et al., 2000) as shown in Fig. 1, which is a phase diagram with four quadrants. The northeast quadrant has a production function that is not linear (as in the case of neoclassical economics) but a probabilistic area. It may be called Schumpeterian as far as innovations – successful and unsuccessful – are embodied. Coasean entitlements are assumed to enable such innovations to come into existence, implying that the model involves more than just pure exchange. Yu's model is modified here by factoring in the twin Schumpeterian ideas of *inside circular flow* versus *outside circular flow* as well as creative destruction.

Extending the Coasean Model to Schumpeterian Innovation and Sustainable Development

In itself, the Coase Theorem is based on the revised generalization by Stigler (1987), which was "officially" recognized by Coase (1988), as exemplified by

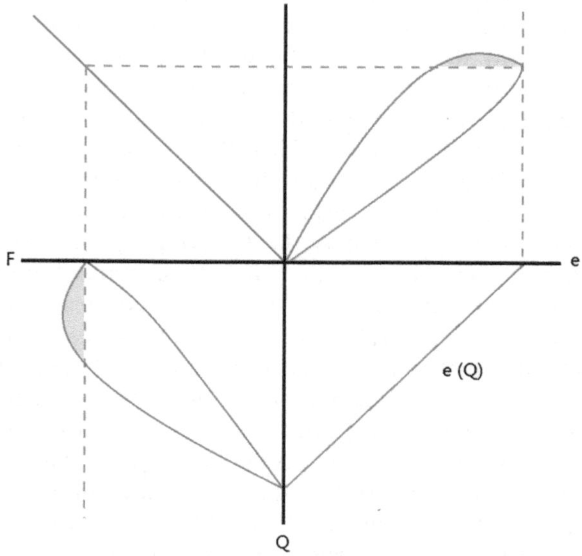

Fig. 1. Yu's (2000) Original Model of Sustainable Development.

Coase's (1960) cattle-ranching and wheat-farming parable. It is a theorem that addresses pure exchange in a world of zero transaction costs. Since there is no uncertainty, it has no room for any inventions or innovations that affect production.

The theorem is in this sense a tautology or purely definitional. However, institutional economics as a policy-relevant program pertains to a world of uncertainty and positive transaction costs. Due to this connection, it is the so-called "corollary of the Coase Theorem" (Lai, 2007) that has been appreciated by researchers as a means to operationalize the theorem (Lai & Hung, 2008). Among other things, it has been used to examine how urban renewal that is enabled by government seizures of land affects property values (Lai et al., 2007); how variations in the lifespan of planning permissions affect investment decisions (Lai, Wong, Ho, & Chau, 2008); and how different reasoning by engineers led to decisions to reject plans for zones with different objective topographical and hydraulic backgrounds (Lai, Wong, & Chau, 2011). In simple terms, innovations are compatible with Coasean thinking in a world of positive transaction costs, in which Schumpeterian innovations are essential for bringing about sustainability.

Let us examine the theoretical constructs for this discussion. Yu's (Yu et al., 2000) model of sustainable development (Fig. 1) is a phase diagram with the northeast quadrant representing production functions that transform an input, *e*, which is a dimension of the "environment" as represented by the horizontal axis, into a good, *F*, electricity, as represented by the vertical axis. The southwest quadrant displays a trade-off relationship between *e* and another good, *Q*, which is fish production.[3] The Schumpeterian nature of the production function in the northeast quadrant is indicated by its characterization as a probability area that is created by innovations on the basis of a given neoclassical production function that is derived from a given invention (say, a new bus model). In the northwest quadrant there is a 45-degree line that transposes the shape of the production function from the northeast to the southwest quadrant. This reveals an area of joint maximization or "win–win" combinations between goods *F* and *Q*. Insofar as *e* is a dimension of the environment, this area can be said to have satisfied the requirement of hard sustainability, as there is no trade-off between the two goods with respect to the environment.

How should one perceive the shift problem, as represented by the phase diagram of sustainable development in the context of Hong Kong's bus industry? We shall formulate this argument step by step, starting with a

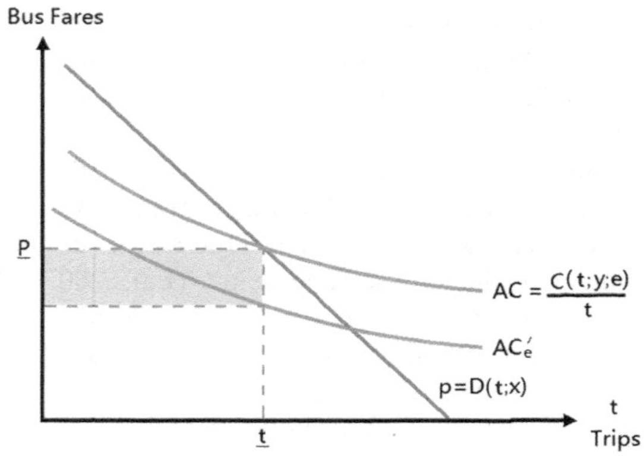

Fig. 2. Gains from Schumpeterian Innovation under Regulated Natural Monopoly.

neoclassical treatment of the conventional natural monopoly problem,[4] as depicted in Fig. 2. Let the demand for public transportation, trips, be denoted by t, with the inverse of the demand curve expressing bus fare, p, as a function of trips, t, and other factors affecting demand, x, that is, $p = D(t; x)$.

The cost of providing rides is captured by a cost function, C, which is a function of trips, t, other exogenous factors, y, and a key variable of Schumpeter innovative efforts, so that total cost $\mathrm{TC} = C(t; y; e)$, with the average cost per trip represented by $\mathrm{AC} = C(t; y; e)/t$, as shown in the diagram.

The traditional regulated-natural-monopoly model depicts a regulated fare price of $\underline{p}$, as the intersection of the demand curve for trips and the average cost curve of trips, while the corresponding number of trips under regulated-fare conditions is labeled $\underline{t}$. Schumpeterian innovation enters this model in terms of a shifting AC curve, which is a function of e. The higher the innovative effort is, the lower the shift of the AC will be. The maximum gain from innovative efforts is denoted by the shaded area. This is the *perceived profit* for the natural monopoly, since the bus fare is regulated and fixed at $\underline{p}$. It is perceived and not necessarily realized because with fixed demand and a fixed bus fare, the shaded area represents the maximum profit only if the innovative effort can be fully integrated back into the normal circular flow as trip use (more on this in a later section).

Investment Behavior of Monopolies Created by State Franchises

Many people do not like the concept of a monopoly, especially when it is created or protected by the state. The key reason for the public's mistrust of monopolies is that they are assumed to invariably use their market position to extract rent without any motivation to innovate; when they are protected by the state, they would have no incentive to improve their products, as there is no competition.

This view is problematic, for in reality, not only is there potential competition, an idea that underlies the so-called "Coase Conjecture" (Gul, Sonnenschein, & Wilson, 1986; Yu, 1981), but there is also no theoretical possibility of innovation in the neoclassical perfect competition model, in which products are homogeneous and production methods identical.

When a monopoly is protected by the state, its performance will really come to depend on whether the monopoly becomes an integral part of the state or whether it remains a private enterprise doing business under a charter or franchise agreement with a definite time span.

In the former case, it is likely that the monopoly will behave like any ordinary government department: breeding red tape and reluctance while lacking in innovation. In the latter case, however, private enterprise would innovate. The fear of losing the charter or a franchise due to poor performance, state-imposed performance standards, and price ceilings are all examples of constraints that would challenge the *intrapreneurs*, and the result of this is innovation.

Our case study focuses on the manner that China Motor Bus (CMB) transformed its fleet into an all double-deck one under uncertain supply conditions and growing market demand in the face of competition, which was due to the de facto opening up of its once physically and legally protected market that was constrained by a price ceiling.

However, before dealing with the details of CMB's innovations in terms of improvisation, one should not lose sight of the fact that both CMB and Kowloon Motor Bus (KMB) introduced new bus models throughout their franchise lives from 1993 to 1998. From 1946 to 1998, a total of 12 models of buses were imported by CMB, as compared to 19 models by the larger KMB (a larger firm innovates more). These facts should help dispel the myth that a state-enforced monopoly is incompatible with innovation. From 1967 to 1998, the key models of new 14-seat (later 16-seat) minibuses were made in Japan and included four automakers (Isuzu, Nissan, Mitsubishi, and Toyota), and were owned largely by individual drivers and were independently operated. The minibuses competed with the franchised bus lines.

Yu's Model Modified

With cost-shifting (rather than charging the right price), the significance of Schumpeterian innovation can be *represented* by a modified Yu model, which is depicted in Fig. 3. The positive *y*-axis represents the *regulated fare-induced trips*, which is labeled *tL*, the quantity of benchmark trips. Intrapreneurs treat the preconditions of their industry as some sort of benchmark for deciding how much innovative effort to expend. Thus, it is conjectured to be a function of *y*, which is the other factor besides innovative effort that would affect the cost curve.[5]

The quantity of benchmark trips scales in descending order of *y* in that high factor costs would result in a low level of regulated trips.[6] The *L* in the symbol denotes the trips as the lowest benchmark from which Schumpeterian innovation would aim to reduce costs. Thus, the maximum value that *tL* can have is the *x*-intercept of the demand curve for trips in Fig. 2, which, if *y* is a value that allows that to be the lowest benchmark, essentially means that there would be no need for any Schumpeterian innovation in that situation.

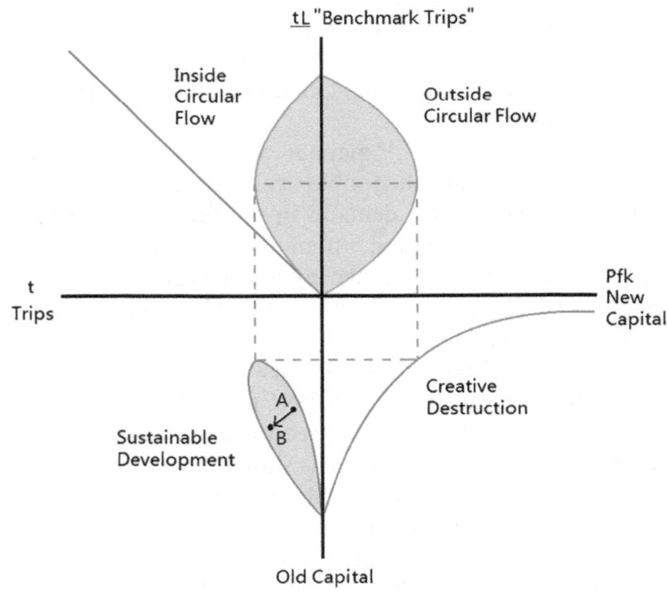

Fig. 3. Schumpeterian Innovation and Sustainable Development.

While only a theoretical possibility, the maximum value of the benchmark can help identify the "corner" properties for the phase diagram.

The positive *x*-axis represents an index for the Expected New Capital (*Pfk*) created by Schumpeterian innovation. It is approximated by the expected profit that is perceived to be generated by innovative effort, *e*. The symbol Pfk^*, shown in Appendix A, is the maximized profit function with respect to *e* rather than to trips, *t*. Thus, Pfk^* is uniquely the value created by Schumpeterian innovation, which is the emphasis required if the shifting of curves in Fig. 2 is the focus.

The negative *x*-axis represents the actual trips brought about by Schumpeterian Innovation. The reason for introducing this as an explicit dimension of analysis is to recognize the *dual* circular flow properties of Schumpeterian innovation, as in Schumpeter (1934).

The positive *y*-axis stands for the regulated-fare-induced trips and is used only for the purpose of benchmarking the expected innovation (i.e., expected new capital, Pfk^*). These are not actual trips until the innovation is integrated into the normal circular flow.

The negative *y*-axis represents old capital, or the status-quo methods used in providing trips. This is also an important consideration in Schumpeterian innovation, and can spearhead the relevance of Coase to the concept of sustainable development, based on whether or not a win–win contractual outcome is possible.

The meanings of the four axes are significantly different from those in Yu's model (Yu et al., 2000), which emphasize the interaction between production and the environment. However, Fig. 3 is similar to Yu's model in that it is an attempt to characterize the shift dimension, as opposed to the quantity dimension of adjustment in neoclassical economics. However, unlike Yu's model, in which Schumpeterian innovation is introduced as *an area of probabilities*, the formulation here explicitly brings in the analysis of the salient features of Schumpeterian innovation through the four quadrants of the phase diagram in the following manner:

- *The northeast quadrant: Schumpeterian "outside circular flow"*

This quadrant outlines the potential of new capital created by innovative efforts. The shape of the potential, as shown in the diagram, can be intuitively explained by noting the two corner points – zero trips and maximum quantity of trips – as bounded by a given hypothetical[7] demand for trips and will entail very little (zero) innovative effort. Zero trips correspond to a precondition in which the AC-curve of trips intersects the demand curve at the *y*-intercept of the demand, thus denoting a small (perhaps nonexisting) industry situation in which inventive efforts will not be incurred because of extremely low perceived uses. Likewise, the other corner with the maximum quantity of trips is caused by a precondition of a very low AC-curve of trips such that innovative activities cannot push the AC-curve any further down. Thus innovative efforts for these two corner points can be expected to be zero for a given demand curve. The trip level that would most probably result in innovative effort is intermediate, with the precondition that the size of the industry is not insignificant, and that there is plenty of room for cost reductions (see further elaboration in Appendix A).

- *The northwest quadrant: Schumpeterian "inside circular flow"*

An important consideration in Schumpeterian innovation is not only whether an experiment has been run, but also whether any of the new capital created can be brought back into the circular flow in terms of the uses of t. With respect to inventions in bus design and bus technology, chances are that the use of a brought-in particular bus model comes in two steps timewise – first with light use, and, if it is found to be versatile and useful, a more extensive adoption. Note, however, that because of regulated bus fares, the maximum use of the new capital would be bound by the benchmark trips of $\underline{tL}$.[8] The probability that affects the outside-circular-flow activities is different from the probabilities of how outside-circular-flow activities can be channeled back inside the circular flow. Thus, the area of possibilities in the northwest quadrant is not symmetrical to the area of possibilities in the northeast quadrant. The curvatures can be generally shown as a function of demand elasticities, industry preconditions, and cost structure considerations (see Appendix A).

- *The southeast quadrant: Schumpeter's creative destruction*

How new capital will replace old capital is the essence of creative destruction. When the amount of new capital added is very small (or zero), one expects old capital (or the status quo) to be fully preserved. Conversely, when there is much new capital, one can expect the possibility of replacement to be high. Thus, the line in the southeast quadrant represents the trade-off between new and old capital. The curvature drawn in the phase diagram accommodates the fact that while an analysis can start with a fixed quantity of old capital (status quo), the possibility of new capital is unlimited, particularly if the exogenous parameters of demand in the model are relaxed and allowed to grow.[9] Thus, the trade-off is not to have an intercept at the positive x-axis, but to only approach it asymptotically.

- *The southwest quadrant: Sustainable development*

This is the sector where Schumpeter can meet Coase to establish a win–win contractual relationship. How can trips with new capital coexist with old capital? It is useful to introduce a conjecture here by examining the corner conditions again.

For either zero or maximum benchmark trips, Schumpeterian innovation is expected to be small, with old capital expected to be largely if not fully preserved. Thus, the zero-new-trip corner point of reference in the southwest quadrant starts with the maximum amount of old capital preservation. Along with the forces of creative destruction, as more and more new buses are brought into use, the old buses will be replaced, some perhaps prematurely, and the general trend is expected to be negative. In other words, there is a trade-off between new buses and old buses, with the maximum expected amount of new capital (including newly bought buses, equipment, and human capital) completely replacing the old capital, reducing its stock to zero. Within the middle range, as the number of newly generated trips increases (through demand increases or cost decreases), more old capital is likely to be replaced. However, because of various shift factors for trip demand and trip supply as well as the uncertain nature of Schumpeterian innovations, all outcomes come with probabilities. Therefore, there is an area that is induced by the probabilities that provides a certain "width" to the trade-off, which achieves sustainable development (with both t and old capital moving in the same direction). In this framework, sustainable development that produces win–win solutions for t and old capital can only be addressed for *a particular win–win development path*, but not generally as *an area of win–win combinations* as envisaged in Yu's model (Yu et al., 2000),[10] for example, from point A to point B within a probability area, which shows the general features of a negative trade-off.

CHINA MOTORBUS CASE STUDY

This section presents our investigation into the innovations effected by the improvisation and purchase of new bus models by CMB in the face of market opportunities and threats. The case shows how a double-decking strategy to capture more passengers in the face of competition with KMB was achieved as well as the importance of bus depots as a factor in the innovation process. This is followed by an account of how the CMB case fits into Yu's modified model. A natural monopoly was chosen since a falling-average-cost firm articulates best with innovations; quasi-rent is recoverable from industry growth and as the demand side is controlled, it helps us focus on the supply side.

The Drive to Double-Decking under Changing Market Conditions

The double-decker has a long history in Hong Kong. The year 1933 saw the division of Hong Kong into two geographical franchises for public buses operated by private firms. KMB won the franchise license for Kowloon and the New Territories, while CMB obtained the exclusive right to operate buses on Hong Kong Island. Both KMB and CMB were owned by Chinese majority shareholders.

KMB introduced the double-deckers as early as 1948, when Daimler CVG5s were imported and used on urban routes. CMB did not purchase its first double-decker, a Dennis Loline III, until 1962, and this belated introduction of a higher-capacity bus was due to government regulations based on the consideration that Hong Kong Island was hillier. There was a specific clause in the early CMB franchise licenses[11] stating that special permission must be obtained from the Governor in Council to run double-deckers. Not until after 30 years, in 1962, and following road improvements which included the raising of traditional vertical shop signs and tree pruning, was permission granted for the introduction of double-decker buses on Route Two between Vehicular (later Macau) Ferry Pier and Shaukeiwan, a route that was almost entirely level (except at Quarry Bay) and on roads without tight bends. On that route at least, it was revealed that the previous consideration was more psychological than technical. Route Ten between North Point Ferry Pier and Central Street (Sai Ying Pun) also saw the use of double-deckers. The conversion of the whole bus fleet into double-deckers to cope with rising demand under escalating cost conditions and fare ceilings by CMB during the 1970s provides a good example of Schumpeterian entrepreneurial improvisation backed by imagination and the technical competence of engineers working for a transport monopoly.

The salient features of the institutional background to such an improvisation were:

a) The public bus companies were private firms listed on the stock exchange and controlled by two Chinese families.
b) Bus fares were regulated and remained constant for 30 years until the first major general upward revision in 1976, due to the government's social considerations.

c) Sites for bus depots/garages, essential for the assembly and maintenance of buses using "completely knocked down" (ckd) kits and modifications to buses, were obtained by the bus companies from the government and no land premium concession was made (Lai, Davies, & Cheung, 2011).
d) The government did not simply allocate curb rights as if it were a predatory monopoly seeking royalties, but provided a subsidy in kind in the form of free bus terminals planned in tandem with ferry piers and new housing developments (Lai, Davies, & Cheung, 2011).
e) The geographical franchises were physically protected by the natural barrier of Victoria Harbor, which separates Hong Kong Island from Kowloon and its hinterland, the New Territories. Kowloon and the New Territories have a much larger population than Hong Kong Island. The last factor was important, as this physical separation of the market by the Harbor was altered when the government went ahead with the idea of the first cross-harbor road tunnel in the 1960s. This was completed in August 1972 and permitted both bus companies to jointly operate "tunnel bus routes" that cross the harbor. This, in effect, allowed for reciprocal incursions by each bus company into the once protected market of its counterpart.

Another major incursion into the geographical franchise and, hence, the monopoly position of CMB, which basically segregated and shielded it from KMB before the tunnel was opened, was the emergence of the illegal nine-seat "minibus" during the Communist riots of 1967. "Controlled" by the triads and tolerated by the government at the time, these minibuses provided at least a minimal service while the regular buses were strikebound. Their eventual legalization, which violated the terms of the franchises for both CMB and KMB, destroyed the geographical franchise concept. However, they offered guaranteed passengers seats without having them stand, as in the case of the full-size buses, and offered flexible pickup and drop-off points at market prices.

Meanwhile, the population of Hong Kong continued to grow at a pace of one million per decade and urban densities increased. Per capita income also grew nonstop after the end of World War II, and real wage growth accelerated during the 1970s. As bus fares were capped, the way for the bus companies to protect their markets and make a profit was to expand capacity.

The common constraint facing them was not a lack of incentive or capital to import British buses, but the peculiar capacity limit of the British bus chassis and bus body suppliers of the time. Britain had also entered the climactic phase of its labor activism, which reduced productivity, and its government's policy of subsidizing purchases by local bus operators of new rear-engine buses meant that new buses produced in the United Kingdom were quickly absorbed by the domestic market, leaving less for the export market.

Before we continue, one should understand that a typical bus is a combination of four key components: a chassis, a body, an engine, and a gear box. There are specialist suppliers for each or all of these, and it is a commercial and technical decision to choose the right combination. Besides, the livery of a bus is important as it is a good way of differentiating one's product in the face of competition. Innovation involves experimentation with different combinations of these components and liveries.

Innovation by Improvisation

In an attempt to retain its market share, if not increase it due to the phenomenal expansion of the market offered by the new tunnel, CMB sought every opportunity to transform its much smaller fleet into a larger and wholly double-decker fleet by persuading the government to relax its controls on its use of double-deckers on Hong Kong Island. This was achieved in the mid-1970s. It should be emphasized that CMB made a strategic decision in the midst of the 1967 local communist riot, which drastically reduced bus travel by the public. This fact renders the criticism that CMB was reluctant to invest unwarranted.

By 1967, CMB had, besides some obsolete single-deckers (Tilling Stevens and Guy Arab UF buses), a modern fleet of four types of front-engine Guy Arab V buses: 106 short 7,645.4 mm single-deckers (which carried 48 passengers each), nicknamed "hydrofoils" due to their power; 40 long 10,845.8 mm single-deckers (which carried 79 passengers each), nicknamed "Long Dragons" due to their length; 1,15 9,144 mm double-deckers (which carried 93 passengers each) and 44 8,534.4 mm double-deckers (which carried 82 passengers each). All of these were equipped with Gardner 6LW or the more powerful Gardner 6LX diesel engines and Metal Sections steel and aluminum bodies.

Both the hydrofoils and the long dragons had "externality" problems. The former were under-capacity but overpowered. The long dragon had structural problems due to the excessively long span behind its rear axle, and the whole bus was hard to maneuver on most urban and rural routes.

In 1968, CMB engineers made two innovative moves. In the first case, they added an upper-deck to transform one – later to include 105 – of their 106 short wheelbase Guy Arab Mk Vs single-deck buses into a double-decker to become the S class. The second conversion involved the reduction of the wheelbase of each Long Dragon from 6,705 mm to 5,486 mm, as well as its conversion into a double-decker that was added to the LX class. This second conversion was devised by Chief Engineer Trevor Williams. It involved cutting through the chassis mainframe just behind the fluid flywheel mounting brackets and removing the unwanted 1041.4 mm and reuniting the front and rear sections by welding[12] (Davis, 1994, p. 74). The bus body for the upper deck of the S class was obtained by utilizing the original roof and body of the single-decker and that for the lower deck was built new by CMB contractors.

The bus body for the converted Long Dragons came from three sources:

1. "Wong Chau" bodies constructed from scratch by CMB contractor Wong Chau to three slightly differing designs;
2. bodies purchased second-hand from UK dealers; and
3. new ckd kits purchased from the British Aluminium Co. (BACO).

The influence of certain individuals was pivotal.[13] By 1969, Lyndon Rees had joined CMB as Traffic Manager from southern Wales where double-deck buses were operated on routes that ran in steep-sided valleys with sharp bends, similar in many respects to those encountered on Hong Kong Island's roads, particularly at Mid-levels and around the Peak (Davis, 1994, p. 60). In the early 1970s, Rees was joined by John Blay, who replaced Trevor Williams as Chief Engineer. Together Rees and Blay set about transforming CMB from being an operator of largely single-deck buses to all-double-deck fleet and it was with their knowledge of the British bus industry that they were able to purchase many of the second-hand buses necessary both to increase the number of double-deckers and to provide buses for the rapidly expanding Cross Harbor Tunnel routes.

The bus body for the upper deck of the S class was obtained by transposing the original roof and body of the first deck and that for the lower deck was built by CMB contractors. One variant, the LS class, had a lower body to allow it to pass under a bridge on the Peak.[14] The best and least costly option was to buy new ckd kits, but the British suppliers could not cope with CMB's demand. The existing double-deckers were also gradually upgraded with Gardner 6LX engines. All the complicated conversion work took place locally in CMB's depots, which the company purchased from the government through open auctions that proved successful. No government subsidy in land values was involved. From Davis (1994) and the memory of the first author of this chapter, the key depots used for conversion work were the two sites along King's Road, North Point (Lai, Davies, & Cheung, 2011). At the same time, CMB adopted "one man operation" (OMO) to reduce labor costs by making the conductors (two on each double-decker) redundant.

At the same time, CMB placed orders for second-hand front-engine buses when a front-engine bus chassis ceased to be the norm in the British bus industry. Seventeen 8,534.4 mm and eleven 9,144 mm Guy Arab IVs were imported from 1970 to 1972, along with ten 9,448.8 mm Guy Arab Vs (chassis only) and 76 Leyland Titan PD3/4s and 28 PD3/5 9,144 mm (with a permitted carrying capacity of 84 persons) from 1971 to 1975. These were far from adequate to meet growing demand in CMB's franchise area, much less the expanded market. Therefore Rees arranged for CMB to import its first batch of second-hand rear-engine buses from British sources, such as the 9,144 mm Leyland Atlantean second-hand. A total of 21 low bridge and 50 high bridge versions were imported between 1972 and 1975.

Although the Atlantean had fared badly in London, the similar Daimler Fleetline had performed better.CMB boldly ordered a new rear-engine 9,448.8 mm double-deck Daimler Fleetline for trials in 1972 before placing contracts for as many as 305 9,753.6 mm to 10,058.4 mm buses, which were delivered between 1974 to 1979. These "LF class" buses were fitted with Gardner 6LXB engines, Metal sections, and Walter Alexander bodies.[15] Called locally "Jumbo buses" due to their huge capacity, each had a carrying capacity of as many as 121 passengers. A total of 30 shorter 9,448.8 mm and lower models, the "SF class" with a capacity for 105 passengers each, were introduced from 1979 to 1980 to operate on the Peak route.

The development of the Cross-Harbor Mass Transit Railway (MTR) by the government during the late 1970s was a mixed blessing for CMB. It exerted the first serious blow on CMB in 1985 when its Island Line was completed, as it competed directly with most CMB routes. However, from 1980 to 1985, the connection of Central and Admiralty of the Initial Modified Line to Kowloon created a feeder-route market for passengers who preferred to cross the harbor by train. To cope with the demand, a total of 206 9,448.8 mm second-hand rear-engine ex-London Transport Daimler/Leyland Fleetline ("DMS"), built between 1970 and 1974, were purchased by CMB and introduced in Hong Kong from 1980 to 1984, where they each had a permitted capacity of 100 passengers. Unlike KMB, CMB specified that these buses were to be fitted with the CMB standard Gardner 6LBX engines and Park Royal bodies.[16]

OMO was introduced in 1972 prior to the tunnel's opening. In Hong Kong, the transition to OMO was smooth and there was no labor union opposition to it.

Interestingly, while the Daimler "DM/DMS" class (classified XF by CMB) Fleetline was not regarded as a success in London (where the long Hong Kong version has never been used), it was well received by bus companies and passengers in Hong Kong. London Transport experimented with OMO for the Fleetline, but decided in 1978 to replace them with Leyland Titans and MCW Metrobuses. "The London argument was that the types were withdrawn because they were not suited to the arduous conditions there" (Booth, 2009, p. 91).[17]

CMB avoided London's problems with the Fleetline by removing a number of technical modifications to the Fleetline that had been specified by London Transport. CMB utilized the OMO fare collection method of a coin box (which was augmented during the 1990s by the e-money Octopus) and a flat fare (the level of which was fixed until 1972). These two apparently trivial technical matters sped up boarding time, and hence, bus running time tremendously.[18] The success of the Fleetlines in Hong Kong is a good real-life example of how a less-than-welcome product in one place can become a successful product elsewhere.[19]

The story of the Guy Arab double-deckers should be concluded by pointing out that the second-hand Guy Arabs were retired in 1980, but a fleet of 167 new front-engine double-deckers, tailor-made for hilly Hong Kong use, the "Victory 2," was bought by CMB in increments from 1978 to 1982 and they were classified as "LV" buses (30 Dennis Jubilants with a design and body appearance similar to that of the LV buses were introduced as the "DS" class in 1980.) One hundred and fifty LX Guy buses were given new lighter, steel-and-aluminum Walter Alexander bodies and new seats from 1979 to 1985. The re-bodying exercise did not only modernize the appearance and render the interior more comfortable (Lidstone, 2002), but also presented the Guy as if it were the Fleetline.

Experimentation with Different New Bus Models

It should be emphasized that CMB did not simply improvise by improving new or second-hand buses, but it also *experimented* with new bus models and bulk-purchased only those that it found suitable for Hong Kong's topographical, climatic (humid in the spring and hot and rainy in the summer), and traffic conditions. Davis (1994, p. 186) notes that there was a company policy "of assessing as many types of new vehicle as possible in order to provide its passengers with the most suitable bus for each service (route)" (It was also company policy to assign specific models of buses to specific routes and drivers to these buses to achieve specialization). The Dennis Loline III, bought in 1962, was found to be unsuitable, and no further orders were placed. The same applied to the Indian-built Ashok Leyland Titan and Seddon Model 236 Midibus, both of which were introduced in 1974; the Albion Viking Midibus, introduced in 1975; the codenamed B15 Leyland Titan, which was introduced in 1980; and two Metro Cammell Weymann (MCW) Metroriders, which were introduced in 1988.[20]

The standard Hong Kong bus at the turn of the millennium was the OMO, three-axle, low floor, rear-engine, air-conditioned bus with "Octopus" e-money charger (besides the coin box) and environmentally friendly (European standard) engines. There has also been a revival of the single-decker bus, air-conditioned and low-floored, due to competition from the MTR, so capacity has ceased to be the sole concern. The investment polices of CMB evolved and matured before it lost all its franchised routes in 1998.

CMB, Coase, and Sustainability

The saga of CMB also fits well into the modified Yu model that was outlined in this chapter, bearing in mind that the original Yu model (Yu et al., 2000) was designed to examine sustainability within the environment, which is understood not only from an ecological point of view, but includes old and new capital components. Since one dimension of sustainability is *human-centered* (Lai & Lorne, 2003), technological unemployment can be a key issue in economic development. The above case study showed that during the period 1960–1985, CMB managed to increase its total trip-carrying capacity by t through a combination of old and new improvised capital.

This case study shows that innovation by improvisation is *not* a technological displacement of workers and old capital, which means it can indeed achieve a win–win outcome. In the employment of CMB mechanics, old capital stood for the carrying capacity of the imported British bus models that needed no improvisation, while new capital (Pfk) stood for those that were improvised. When old capital was at its maximum, innovative effort was not required.

The change in the exogenous conditions that actually brought about Schumpeterian innovation were due to (a) a shortage of old capital, a shock or a change in the situation (e.g., a shift in demand, as during the 1967 Communist riots), and (b) the addition of new roads and tunnels. These changes in conditions spurred improvised changes to an existing bus model that expanded the Schumpeterian innovation in the northwest quadrant of the phase diagram of the modified Yu model. However, when CMB mechanics simply added more seats to the upper decks of the Fleetlines (in a $2+3$ instead of the standard $2+2$ arrangement) or removed some seats from the lower deck of the MCW to create more standing room, there was no obvious innovation as this was simply a capacity expansion movement along a neoclassical production function. Regardless, the type of exogenous change that truly induced certain mechanical changes (notably shortening the Long Dragon and hydrofoil and adding a deck to them, and adoption of coin boxes to OMO buses) was far different from that which led to adding more seats to an existing bus fleet. The mechanical changes were successful Schumpeterian improvisations which shifted the production functions and expanded the "new capital area" in the northeast quadrant and, as shown in the case study, successfully entered into the normal circular flow in the northwest quadrant. Sustainable development was achieved by having more t without displacing old capital. Likewise, obsolescence and the replacement of old capital (e.g., the replacement of Metal Section by Alexander bodies for the double-deck LX buses and the introduction of the LV buses) also occurred.

DISCUSSION AND CONCLUSION

From the 1960s to the 1990s the public bus scene on Hong Kong Island was dominated by the Guy Arab V and Daimler Fleetline. Both bus models contributed significantly to CMB's operations and had an economic lifespan of 33 and 28 years, respectively. Both witnessed key improvisation work. The former was initially a mix of double-deckers and single-deckers that were longer and shorter. The single-deckers were all converted locally into double-deckers by the mid-1970s and re-bodied by the mid-1980s. The latter was introduced together with the coin box-OMO and avoided the problems encountered by London bus drivers and their passengers.

The key finding of this case study is that a franchised monopoly can innovate even when its franchise license does not specify such a requirement and can complement the discovery about the behavior of the state that grants the franchise. The state does not merely allocate curb rights (Klein, Moore, & Reja, 1997), but also actively engages in the provision of other factors by investing in road infrastructure and bus terminals (Lai, Davies, et al., 2011).

What were the key theoretical lessons learned?

First, a monopoly governed by a *prior contract* (Yu, 1981) with the state, like CMB's, did innovate. Its larger competitor KMB innovated more in terms of the number of new bus models it purchased. In comparison, the free minibus market introduced just a few models. This finding is consistent with the "Schumpeter Hypothesis" on the size of a firm and its propensity to innovate.

Second, regarding Kirzner's view that Schumpeterian entrepreneurs may be individuals without special traits, we found that key individuals played prominent parts in bringing about the improvisation and double-decker policy. Indeed, they are good examples of *intrapreneurs*. The most successful years of CMB were when expatriate bus engineers were recruited and retained. The key personalities were Chief Engineer Trevor William and his successor, John Blay, who came from Swedish Motors in Bangkok and was previously an engineer with London Transport; and Traffic Manager Lyndon Rees. Rees had substantial industrial experience in Wales, where double-deckers operated on routes that ran in steep-sided valleys with sharp bends, which were similar to those on Hong Kong Island's roads (Davis, 1994, p. 60). They were able to persuade the family-operated CMB to embark on bold plans of innovation. It is interesting to note that during this period, CMB maintained a cordial relationship with the government, with which exchanges of human capital were common. Rees had worked in the Transport Department and Blay later went to the Transport Department.

What came after 1985 appeared to be a different story. CMB fell so far behind the competition in the increasingly congested public transport market that some of its routes were eventually revoked by the government, which led to its demise as a transport operator. However, the company continued to earn profits by switching to real estate using its depots, which were once used for improvisations and the assembly of bus parts. CMB's reported profit has always been positive, which is a rarity for public utility companies around the world, which often require government subsidies. Apparently, the loss of its franchised bus business in 1998 did not affect CMB's profitability, as it had shifted its major revenue source to real estate development in strategic partnership with Swire Properties, starting in 1993. That year, on the grounds that CMB bus management had lagged behind the times, the government's Transport Department re-assigned 26 of its lucrative Southern District routes, which were insulated from the reach of the rival Island Line of the Mass Transit Railway (MTR), to CityBus.

Both MTR and CityBus were fully or mostly air-conditioned, but CMB's bus fleet was only partially so. In any event, as soon as the Island Line commenced operations in 1985, CMB's passenger count and revenue fell sharply.

Interestingly, CMB is still operating a small fleet of air-conditioned single-deck Dennis Dart buses as free lunchtime shuttles on working days to ship passengers from near the North Point Government Offices to Island Place to promote the business of an Island Place shopping complex. Island Place was built on the location of one of CMB's former urban franchised bus depots.

Epilogue: The Schumpeter Paradox

If Schumpeterian innovation is characterized as a conscious effort to shift down cost (and the associated supply) curves, the characteristic of "trying to become a natural monopoly" gives rise to an interesting theoretical problem. If final product prices are flexible, a lower cost structure will lower prices (the process of creatively destroying the status quo method), but a lower price will also make the effort incentive-incompatible, as the firm practicing it will not be perceived as trying to maximize profits.[21] Hong Kong's bus industry has saved itself from this paradox because bus fares were regulated. Had this constraint been relaxed, the relevance of the outcome to providing evidence in support of the insights raised by Schumpeter would be an interesting and open question, but this is beyond the scope of this study.

NOTES

1. The term "intrapreneur" first appeared in writings by Gifford and Elizabeth Pinchot. Gifford Pinchot III, an environmentalist and descendant of the first Chief of the United States Forest Service under Teddy Roosevelt, is known for his management philosophy of internalizing changes and is the founder of the Bainbridge Graduate Institute in Washington, United States. One of the authors of this article has long provided examples of "*intrapreneurship*" in illustrating Schumpeter's inside versus outside circular flow activities in his MBA courses in the 1990s, mostly at the City University of Hong Kong. The approach was also further extended in Lorne (2009).

2. The notion of "spatiality" depends on the levels of inquiry, which can be purely ontological (hence all-embracing); transportation-related (hence it can be reduced to time); industrial (space as land/sites and as an input factor, as in the case of bus depots discussed in this chapter); real estate; urban (regarding agglomeration as

canvassed by Andersson, 2005), social psychological; and political economy (the context for this chapter). A great challenge to Austrian economists regarding spatial inquiry has been posed by the difficulties in fitting its methodological subjectivist individualism to cities or regions which are essentially collective wholes related by, in a Coasean terminology, "a nexus of contracts" (Webster, 2003). The gap is typically plugged by the idea of "knowledge." Knowledge, however, though individualized necessarily has a public dimension. Therefore, it is the opinion of the first author that Austrian philosopher Ferdinand Ebner's notion of "language" would be helpful. The concept of "communicative planning" that was derived from Habermasian philosophy, which compromises empiricism, had Ebner's work as one of its foundations.

3. The idea here is that electricity production, F, is assumed to "consume" natural resources, thus "eating" into the environment, e. This degradation of natural resources has an impact on fish habitats, causing a quantitative reduction of the fish yield, Q. The limiting case is that the environment is so badly exploited that the quantity of the fish yield becomes zero due to ecological collapse.

4. The assumption of a natural or decreasing cost monopoly is for theoretical exposition and based on the findings that there were economies of scale for franchised bus and ferry companies in Hong Kong from 1933 to 1998.

5. The way to think of this is to recognize that $\underline{t}$ in Fig. 2 is a function of different levels of AC based on various preconditioned values of y. Thus, $\underline{tL}$ spans the whole scale of rides in Fig. 2 up to the maximum of the x-intercept of the demand curve that is the same as t. But in a reduced form, it is labeled as $\underline{tL}$ rather than t. This is an important conceptual feature of Yu's phase diagram – to move analysis from the neoclassical diagram in Fig. 2 to the phase diagram addressing shifts, with neoclassical analysis at "the back of the mind."

6. We abstracted from shifts in demand (i.e., changes in the values of x) in this phase diagram for a simplistic exposition that can be included in the mathematics in Appendix A. Considering changes in y here, holding x constant, is equivalent to the *ceteris paribus* condition.

7. Again, the term "hypothetical" needs to be inserted here to emphatically abstract from the reality of changing demand due to population growth and the addition of new routes.

8. We can further denote this innovation adoption rate as a percentage of the benchmark trips and integrate this into the mathematics in Appendix A. This remains a very simplistic view of how inventive efforts can flow back into the normal circular flow, and is indicated here as a first approximation only. In reality, the bus company can open new routes to attract new ridership even at fixed regulated fares so that the 45° line is not an artificial boundary. Indeed, how an invention is duplicated and repeated in the normal circular flow can be presented by the tilting of the 45° line to the left, so that rides perceived as benchmarks in the outside circular flow quadrant are transformed into much more numerous rides in the normal circular flow.

9. Note again that the phase diagram is drawn for a given demand. When other factors, such as x in the argument of the demand curve, change, the area of probabilities will change accordingly.

10. The analysis here may be generalized as an implication for real estate and urban development in that while locational heritage can be preserved to produce a win–win situation, the broader economic region as a whole is driven by many other economic factors, including the powerful force of Schumpeterian creative destruction.

11. That would be Clause 6 in the 1933 and 1948 licenses. Clause 14 of the 1959 license delegates the power to the Commissioner of Police.

12. Photo 1, Appendix B shows a photo of a to-scale model of a Long Dragon before conversion. Photo 2, Appendix B shows a photo of a double-deck LX bus converted from the Long Dragon with a "Wong Chau" body. Photo 3, Appendix B shows a photo of a double-deck LX bus from the Long Dragon which initially looked like that in Photo 2, Appendix B and was later modernized with an Alexander Body.

13. We thank Mike Davis for providing the information for this paragraph.

14. The four models in Photo 4, Appendix B show how the Hydrofoil evolved from a single-deck bus with conductor to "One Man Operation" (OMO) mode and then became a double-decker and OMO.

15. Photos 5 and 6 in Appendix B show to-scale models of the LF with two types of body and livery.

16. Note that by 1968, the key UK bus chassis producers – Guy, Daimler, Leyland, AEC, Albion, and Bristol – and body builders – ECW, Park Royal, and Roe – had been combined into the British Leyland Corporation (BLMC). By the 1970s British Leyland was a failing corporation and in an attempt to save it, it was nationalized in 1975 by the Labour government (see Booth, 2009, p. 113). Photo 7 in Appendix B shows a scale model of an ex-London Transport DMS in the CMB fleet as an XF.

17. In a careful analysis informed by Hong Kong's experience, London Transport found that its real problem was not bus design, but its means of fare collection. Mike Davis did not share this view on the grounds that all subsequent buses have front entrances and OMO. It was the maintenance of London's first bus not designed by LT – the "not-invented-here syndrome" – that was the problem. Certain elements had decided that they were not going to like it on principle. Passengers were not accustomed to boarding buses at the front, so boarding time and, hence, bus movement, were slowed by the need for the bus to stop longer to allow passengers to buy tickets at a ticket machine or from the driver-conductor, who also had to give change. The rigid maintenance practice of London Transport to completely separate the Fleetline's body from its chassis rendered it troublesome. It was thus withdrawn and sold before its service life was over. A bus expert classified the Fleetline as a "blunder" (Booth, 2009). They were exported to Hong Kong during the 1980s after only about ten years of service.

18. KMB also purchased some Fleetlines, but CMB's Fleetlines enjoyed a much longer service life than their KMB counterparts due to their tried Gardner 6LWB engines. This choice of engine proved correct, as parts for repairs could easily be scrounged from retired buses if overseas supplies hit a snag. CMB's XF (DMS) Fleetlines were retired in 1996, but the LF and SF Fleetlines survived for a few years after New World First Bus took over CMB's fleet at a cost in September 1998. In comparison, although KMB's new Fleetlines ran until 1997, its 100 second-hand

DMS Fleetlines (equipped with Leyland engines and MCW bodies) ceased operations by 1990 due to a shortage of parts. In 1979, the European-owned private bus company, Passengers Transport Services (Asia) Limited, trading as "City Buses" (renamed CityBus in 1981), obtained six second-hand 10,058.4 mm Daimler Fleetlines from the United Kingdom. Eventually it bought a total of 42 Daimler/Leyland Fleetlines, of which the bulk (33) were the ex-London Transport DMS class (Davis, 1995).

19. What has happened to the Fleetlines? They were all sold to New World First Bus when CMB lost its franchise in 1998. The LFs were retired by the new owners in 1999 due to its policy of adopting an entirely air-conditioned bus fleet. The SFs, due to their capability to serve the Peak routes, were not retired until 2000, when the long successful history of Daimler/Leyland Fleetlines in Hong Kong, which survived the absorption of Leyland into Volvo in 1988, ended. More significantly, before the Chinese government banned the importation of second-hand buses in the mid-1990s, some retired CMB Daimler/Leyland (LF and XF) Fleetlines found their way to the bus fleets of such cities as Guangzhou, Dalian, and Harbin (Chan, 1997) as an innovation that assisted China's program to produce double-decker buses domestically. Apparently CMB's Fleetlines lasted longer than those of KMB because the former's GB340 gear boxes proved superior to the SCG-4 gearboxes used by KMB under Hong Kong road conditions.

20. Some bus models were not bulk-purchased because there were changes in the production policies or in the ownership of the manufacturers. Good examples were the dual rear-engine, air-suspended MCW-Scania Metropolitan ("MS") buses, introduced in 1975, and the eight front-engine Ailsa-Volvo ("AV") buses, which were introduced from 1975 to 1978. Regarding accepted buses, we discussed the story of the Leyland Guy Victory 2 above and shall not repeat it here.

21. This statement is contingent upon flexible product prices. It is true that cost-cutting is compatible with profit-seeking if we assume costly and time-consuming entry due to scale economies and/or imitation difficulties – say production technology transfer from innovator A to imitator B. However, if there were entry costs or imitation costs, which an idealized public good such as innovation would not entail, product prices would not be flexible. We thank David Emanuel Andersson for this useful comment.

ACKNOWLEDGMENTS

We are grateful for the invitation by Professor David Emanuel Andersson to write this chapter and the useful comments of three anonymous referees. We presented the model and key features of this chapter at the Eight International Symposium on Management Engineering. That event was organized by the International Society of Management Engineers and was held in Taipei from August 22 to August 25, 2011. The presentation is forthcoming in the *International Journal of Information Systems for Logistics and Management* (Lorne & Lai, 2012). The revision of the draft was funded by a Public Policy Research Grant, No. HKU7007-PPR-11, which was awarded to the first author. We are grateful to Mr. Jason Kwong for alerting us of and obtaining for us the work by Lidstone (2002) on the Guy Arabs V. We thank Mr. Polycarp Cheung for assisting in the compilation of bus model data and Mr. Jason Kwong for art work and technical support. We are indebted to Mr. Mike Davis for his expert advice on the technical side of CMB and other buses and information on individuals who played the role as innovators in the local bus industry and his permission for using Photos 2 and 3.

REFERENCES

Andersson, D. E. (2005). The spatial nature of entrepreneurship. *Quarterly Journal of Austrian Economics*, *8*(2), 21–34.

Booth, G. (2009). *Bus blunders*. Hersham: Ian Allan.

Brandenburger, A. M., & Nalebuff, B. J. (1996). *Co-opetition: A Revolution mindset that combines competition and cooperation*. New York, NY: Double Day.

Chan, D. C. Y. (1997). *China double-deck bus handbook*. Hong Kong: Northcord Transport.

Cheung, S. N. S. (1968). Private property rights and sharecropping. *Journal of Political Economy*, *76*(6), 1107–1122.

Cheung, S. N. S. (1973). The fable of the bees. *Journal of Law and Economics*, *16*(1), 11–33.

Cheung, S. N. S. (1975). Roofs or stars: The stated intents and actual effects of a rents ordinance. *Economic Inquiry*, *13*(1), 1–21.

Coase, R. H. (1959). The federal communications commission. *Journal of Law and Economics*, *2*(1), 1–40.

Coase, R. H. (1960). The problem of social cost. *Journal of Law and Economics*, *3*(1), 1–44.

Coase, R. H. (1974). The lighthouse in economics. *Journal of Law and Economics*, *17*(2), 356–376.

Coase, R. H. (1988). *The firm, the market and the law*. Chicago, IL: Chicago University Press.

Coase, R. H. (2000). The acquisition of Fisher body by General Motors. *Journal of Law and Economics*, *43*(1), 15–32.

Cunha, M. P., & Cunha, J. V. (2006). Towards a complexity theory of strategy. *Management Decision*, *44*(7), 839–850.

Davis, M. (1994). *Hong Kong buses volume one: China Motor bus 1933 to 1993*. Croydon, UK: DTS Publishing.

Davis, M. (1995). *Hong Kong buses volume three: Citybus Limited*. Croydon, UK: DTS Publishing.

Desrochers, P. (1998). A geographical perspective on Austrian economics. *Quarterly Journal of Austrian Economics*, *1*(2), 63–83.

Desrochers, P. (2001). Geographical proximity and the transmission of tacit knowledge. *Review of Austrian Economics*, *14*(1), 25–46.

Desrochers, P. (2004). Cluster-based economic strategy, facilitation policy and the market process. *Review of Austrian Economics*, *14*(1), 25–46.

Giersch, H. (1984). The age of Schumpeter. *American Economic Review*, *47*(2), 103–109.

Gul, F., Sonnenschein, H., & Wilson, R. (1986). Foundations of dynamic monopoly and the Coase conjecture. *Journal of Economic Theory, 39*, 155–190.

Holcombe, R. G. (2003). Progress and entrepreneurship. *Quarterly Journal of Austrian Economics, 6*(3), 3–26.

Hornby, A. S., Gatenby, E. V., & Wakefield, H. (1973). *The advanced learner's dictionary*. London, UK: Oxford University Press.

Johannessen, J. A., Olsen, B., & Lumpkin, G. T. (2001). Innovation as newness: What is new, how new, and new to whom? *European Journal of Innovation Management, 4*(1), 20–31.

Kim, J., & Mahoney, J. T. (2006). How property rights economics furthers the resource-based view: Resources, transaction costs and entrepreneurial discovery. *International Journal of Strategic Change Management, 1*(1-2), 40–52.

Klein, D. B., Moore, A., & Reja, B. (1997). Curb rights: Eliciting competition and entrepreneurship in urban transit. *Independent Review, 2*(1), 29–54.

Lai, L. W. C. (1993). Marine fish culture and pollution: An initial Hong Kong empirical study. *Asian Economic Journal, VII*(3), 333–351.

Lai, L. W. C. (2007). "The problem of social cost": The Coase Theorem and externality explained: Using simple diagrams and examples to illustrate the role of land use planning in tackling externalities. *Town Planning Review, 78*(3), 335–368.

Lai, L. W. C., Chau, K. W., Ho, D. C. W., & Lorne, F. T. (2006). A "Hong Kong" model of sustainable development. *Property Management, 24*(4), 16–18.

Lai, L. W. C., Chau, K. W., Yiu, E. C. Y., Wong, S. K., Wong, W. S., & Chan, P. Y. L. (2007). Measuring and interpreting the effects of a public-sector-led urban renewal project on housing prices: An empirical study of a comprehensive development area zone developed upon taking in Hong Kong. *Environment and Planning B: Planning and Design, 34*(3), 524–538.

Lai, L. W. C., Davies, S. N. G., & Cheung, P. A. C. W. (2011). Government transport land use planning and development by implicit contract for franchised buses and ferries in Hong Kong: 1933 to 1972. *Planning Practice and Research, 26*(4), 435–464.

Lai, L. W. C., & Hung, C. W. Y. (2008). The inner logic of the Coase theorem and a Coasian planning research agenda. *Environment and Planning B: Planning and Design, 35*(2), 207–226.

Lai, L. W. C., & Lorne, F. T. (2003). Implementing sustainable development: Institutional features. In L. W. C. Lai & F. T. Lorne (Eds.), *Implementing and understanding sustainable development* (pp. 1–30). New York, NY: Nova Science.

Lai, L. W. C., & Lorne, F. T. (2006). The Coase theorem and planning for sustainable development. *Town Planning Review, 77*(1), 41–73.

Lai, L. W. C., Wong, S. K., & Chau, K. W. (2011). Are engineering reasons zoning neutral? An empirical inquiry into development proposals in green belts and agriculture zones. *Environment and Planning B: Planning and Design, 38*(2), 322–337.

Lai, L. W. C., Wong, S. K., Ho., E. C. K., & Chau, K. W. (2008). "Time is of the essence?" An empirical application of the corollary of the Coase theorem. *Review of Urban and Regional Development Studies, 20*(1), 34–51.

Lidstone, J. G. (2002). The last guys on earth. *Bus and Coach Preservation*, October, 41–45.

Lorne, F. T. (2009). Macro-entrepreneurship &sustainable development: The need for innovative solutions for promoting win-win interactions. *Environmental Economics and Policy Studies, 10*(2), 69–85.

Lorne, F.T. & Lai, L. W. C. (2012). Schumpeterian innovation for regulated natural monopoly as a corporate strategy. *International Journal of Information Systems for Logistics and Management*, 11 (Forthcoming).

Poon, A. (2006). *Land and the ruling class in Hong Kong*. Richmond: Alice Poon.

Ruttan, V. W. (1959). Usher and Schumpeter on invention, innovation, and technological change. *Quarterly Journal of Economics*, *73*, 596–606.

Schumpeter, J. A. (1934). *The theory of economic development*. Cambridge, MA: Harvard University Press.

Stigler, G. J. (1987). *The theory of price* (4th ed). New York, NY: Macmillan.

Swedberg, R. (1991). *Joseph A. Schumpeter: His life and work*. Oxford, UK: Polity Press.

Tzeng, C. H. (2009). A review of contemporary innovation literature: A Schumpeterian perspective. *Innovation: Management, Policy & Practice*, *11*(3), 373–394.

Webster, C. J. (2003). The nature of the neighbourhood. *Urban Studies*, *40*(13), 2591–2612.

Witt, U. (1999). Do entrepreneurs need firms? A contribution to a missing chapter in Austrian economics. *Review of Austrian Economics*, *11*, 99–109.

World Commission on Environment and Development. (1987). *Our common future*. Oxford, UK: Oxford University Press.

Yu, B. T. (1981). Potential competition and contracting in innovation. *Journal of Law and Economics*, *24*, 215–238.

Yu, B. T., Shaw, D., Fu, T., & Lai, L. W. C. (2000). A property rights and contractual approach to sustainable development. *Environmental Economics and Policy Studies*, *3*(3), 291–309.

Yu, T. F. L. (2001). Entrepreneurial alertness and discovery. *Review of Austrian Economics*, *14*(1), 47–63.

APPENDIX A: SCHUMPETERIAN INNOVATION FOR A REGULATED NATURAL MONOPOLY

Let the demand for trips D be written as an inverse function of price p:

$$p = D(t;\ x) \tag{A.1}$$

where t represents the quantity of trips, and x represents factors that will shift the demand curve.

The total cost (TC) of trips is written as:

$$\text{TC} = C(t;\ y;\ e) \tag{A.2}$$

where y represents factors that shift the cost function, and e is the innovative effort.

$$\text{AC} = \frac{C(t;\ y;\ e)}{t} \tag{A.3}$$

Regulated monopoly will set price by equating D with AC:

$$\text{that is, } D(t;\ x) = \frac{C(t;\ y;\ e)}{t} \tag{A.4}$$

Label the t that satisfies the above equation as $\underline{tL}$:

$$\underline{tL} = L(x; y; 0) \tag{A.5}$$

with e set equal to zero without loss of generality.

Substituting Eq. (A.5) into Eq. (A.1), the regulated price, $\bar{p}$, can be represented by Eq. (A.6):

$$\bar{p} = D(\underline{tL}; x) \tag{A.6}$$

$\underline{tL}$ corresponds to "benchmark trips" at the regulated price, $\bar{p}$, because the natural monopolist will use that to decide on the innovative efforts to be incurred, and thus the new capital expected to be generated. It is for this reason that setting e equal to zero refers to the precondition before innovative efforts are to be incurred. It also avoids the paradox that the return to innovation will not be wiped out by equating D with AC for every step of innovation effort adjustment.

The perceived profit from the Schumpeterian innovative effort can be specified as:

$$Pfk = \bar{p} \cdot \underline{tL} \cdot A(y; e) - C(\underline{tL}; y; e) \tag{A.7}$$

Eq. (A.7) integrates the inside versus outside circular flow characteristics of Schumpeterian innovation in that while e affects costs with $\underline{tL}$ as the benchmark in outside circular flow, plus the adoption of the innovation effort in the form of new capital is a percentage, A, of the benchmark trips. We further make the plausible assumptions of $Ay > 0$ and $Ae > 0$. The first assumption says that when exogenous conditions increase costs, they also make innovative efforts easier to adopt. The second assumption says that when e increases, the likelihood of these efforts being adopted also increases.

The first derivatives of the cost function in Eq. (A.7) can be further interpreted as C_t, the marginal cost of a trip; C_y, the cost change due to an exogenous factor increase; and C_e, which denotes how much the trip cost is reduced, inclusive of the opportunity cost of the innovation effort, e.

Economic reasoning suggests that C_t is small, $C_y > 0$, and C_e is assumed to be negative (i.e., investment efforts reduce production costs) but decreasing in absolute value until the opportunity cost of the effort is greater than the gain, turning C_e positive.

The natural monopolist chooses e so as to maximize Pfk when generating new capital by setting:

$$\bar{p} \cdot \underline{tL} \cdot A_e - C_e = 0 \tag{A.8}$$

The profit-maximizing e^* from Eq. (A.8) can be written as $e^*(x;y)$. Note that equation Eq. (A.8) also can be interpreted as a marginal-gain-equals-marginal-cost condition, with marginal gain being affected by revenues from benchmark trips.

New capital can be represented by Pfk^*

$$Pfk^* = \bar{p} \cdot \underline{tL} \cdot A(y; e^*) - C(\underline{tL}; y; e^*) \tag{A.9}$$

One can examine the curvature of the possibility frontiers of the northeast and the northwest quadrants in Fig. 3 with the following equation:

$$\begin{aligned}\frac{\partial Pfk^*}{\partial y} &= \underline{tL} \cdot A \cdot \frac{\partial \bar{p}}{\partial t} \cdot \frac{\partial L}{y} + \bar{p} \cdot A \cdot \frac{\partial L}{\partial y} + \bar{p} \cdot \underline{tL}\ A_y \\ &\quad - C_t \cdot \frac{\partial L}{\partial y} - C_y - C_e \cdot \frac{\partial e^*}{\partial y} \\ &= \left[A\left(\underline{tL} \cdot \frac{\partial \bar{p}}{\partial t} + \bar{p}\right) - C_t\right]\frac{\partial L}{\partial y} - C_y - C_e \cdot \frac{\partial e^*}{\partial y} + \bar{p} \cdot \underline{tL}\, A_y\end{aligned}$$

By introspection, the factors that drive the curvature of the new capital frontier in the phase diagram can be shown to consist of three categories:

Elasticity considerations, E:

$$E = \left[A\bar{p}\left(\frac{1}{\eta} + p\right) - C_t\right]\frac{\partial L}{\partial y}$$

where η is the elasticity of demand.

Industry considerations, I:

$$I = \bar{p} \cdot \underline{tL}\, A_y$$

and Schumpeterian cost considerations, S:

$$S = C_y + C_e \cdot \frac{\partial e^*}{\partial y}$$

APPENDIX B: SMB BUS MODELS

Photo 1. The Long Dragon before Conversion. *Note*: This model is in its original cream and dark red livery.

Photo 2. A Double-Decker LX Bus Converted from a Long Dragon. *Source*: Davis (1994, p. 90); reprinted with permission from Mike Davis. *Note*: This model was in the early 1970s livery of cream and orange.

Photo 3. A Double-Decker LX Bus Converted from a Long Dragon and Equipped with an Alexander Body. *Source*: Davis (1994, p. 75); reprinted with permission from Mike Davis. *Note*: This model bus was in its final CMB cream and blue livery.

Photo 4. The Evolution of the "Hydrofoil."

(a) Single-Decker with Conductor, Central Doorway, to
(b) Single-Decker, OMO, Doorway Relocated to the Front, to
(c) Double-Decker, Low Body LS Class or
(d) Double-Decker S Class

Note: (a) was in cream and dark red livery and the rest in cream and orange livery adopted during the early 1970s. The S and LS classes were all re-painted in the standard cream and blue during the late 1970s.

Photo 5. A "Jumbo" Fleetline with a Metal Section Body. *Note*: This model is in its early 1970s orange and cream livery, which was later replaced by the standard blue and cream livery.

Photo 6. A "Jumbo" Fleetline with an Alexander Body. *Note*: All Alexander-bodied buses were in the final standard blue and cream livery of CMB buses.

Photo 7. A DMS Bus in CMB Service. *Note*: In blue and cream livery.

PART III
INSTITUTIONS AND SPATIAL ORDER

SPONTANEOUS CITIES

Peter Gordon

Their intricate order – a manifestation of the freedom of countless numbers of people to make and carry out countless plans – is in many ways a wonder. – Jane Jacobs

The rules and institutions that shape our lives have come about via bottom-up as well as top-down forces.[1] The relative merits of each have been argued and elaborated for a very long time and the discussion continues. This chapter will consider both of these phenomena as they shape our cities. Many observers take it for granted that cities are the work of designers and planners via top-down authority. Others see top-down as futile and emphasize the ubiquity and power of bottom-up currents. The latter have been characterized as order from human action rather than from human (intentional) design.[2]

Some of the confusion stems from the simple fact that *planning* is a universal activity. We cannot imagine many human endeavors that move forward without a plan. Economists think of markets as the mechanism that coordinates large numbers of plans and construe the outcome as the result of decentralized bottom-up planning. But to many others "planning" simply denotes top-down central planning. And whereas central planning at the national level is not as fashionable as it was in years between the end of World War II and the fall of the Berlin Wall, this is not so for the planning of cities. Indeed, in several languages a city map is called a "city plan."[3] In the United States and elsewhere, city planning is a profession, complete with university curricula and an associated body of research. Most of the latter presumes that top-down planning is essential. To be sure, many of the

The Spatial Market Process
Advances in Austrian Economics, Volume 16, 181–209

ISSN: 1529-2134/doi:10.1108/S1529-2134(2012)0000016010

world's great cities (especially the capitals) have touches of the Grand Manner[4] planning tradition. But monumental citadels, public halls, public squares and spaces, the occasional City Beautiful monument, and similar elements along parade grounds or ceremonial axes are not where most of the world's city people live and work. In fact, most cities (even the great capitals) are populated by spontaneous fill-in, much of which cannot be easily linked to any grand plan or vision.

In the second section of this chapter, some of what we should know about cities for background to this chapter is discussed. The third section elaborates some of the relevant ideas associated with planning. The fourth section highlights some of key insights on the causes of economic growth. The fifth section returns to cities and examines the way they contribute to economic growth. The sixth section discusses the division of labor between orders from human design and spontaneous orders: Human design in the service of profit-seeking activities *is* subject to market-based error correction; "mega projects" are defined and seen as the prominent exceptions. There will always be some projects that fall into this category. This means that bottom-up and top-down necessarily coexist even though we can expect more from the bottom-up efforts. Concluding thoughts are noted in the seventh section.

CITIES

"Unplanned city" (and its relation "unchecked growth") is the way many people describe cities of which they disapprove. They usually mean too little top-down planning, assuming that this is the only planning possible. But Stephen Davies, describing urbanization in England, shows that this was not always so. He notes that,

> [t]he years between 1740 and 1850 therefore saw an unprecedented amount of urban growth. Cities and towns of all kinds and sizes grew more rapidly and on a greater scale than ever before in history. The rapidly increasing population was drawn into the towns in ever larger numbers with the rise of industry, creating an enormous demand for housing and the urban fabric in general. This was the kind of situation that, when its like happens today, is regularly described in terms of "crisis" or even "catastrophe". And yet the challenge was largely met. Housing and other facilities were built and provided. The towns of Britain grew to meet the new demands of a growing population and a transformed economy. There were no great shantytowns around growing cities such as Manchester and Birmingham. Instead a tidal wave of brick and stone swept over fields, turning them into new urban areas. Moreover, the period also saw the creation of great architectural achievements of lasting value in both the great cities and the new towns … .

> The elegance of Bath and Cheltenham, the West End of London and Bloomsbury, the New Town in Edinburgh, and the centers of Glasgow and Newcastle-upon-Tyne – all were built in this period. As this was the first instance of such wide-spread urbanization our understanding of its nature is crucial for our thinking about the process of urbanization in general, whether historically or today. In particular this instance raises the question of how urbanization can happen in the absence of an apparatus of planning and controls, by voluntary means, and what the results of this may be. (Davies, 2002, p. 19)

But the pendulum has swung. Not only is there now a widespread intellectual presumption that the bottom-up planning that Davies describes should be replaced with top-down approaches, but there is also the fact that when it comes to cities, top-down planning is the international standard. The day-to-day activities of large numbers of professional city planners involve regulation of how private property is to be used.[5] Rules to enforce the "separation of land uses" were typically justified by concerns over presumed widespread negative externalities – coupled with a general unwillingness to address these via pricing or property rights clarifications. There is also significant government involvement prompted by the desire to promote "affordable" housing projects. The details of both of these activities are beyond the scope of this chapter. But, to get our bearings, it is worth pointing to the dominance of suburban development in major cities of the developed world despite the widespread idea among planners and policy makers that it is their task to contain such "sprawl." The data in Table 1 suggest the international (developed-country) dominance of large-city suburbanization.[6]

This is how the middle classes have been able to move into the types of housing that were once thought to be elite. Except for the fact that the trend overrides conventional planning doctrine, which is to promote more

Table 1. Spatial Organization – Population Growth in Metropolitan Areas (Population > 1 Million).

Country or Region	Since	Areas	Core (%)	Suburbs (%)
Western Europe	1965	42	−13.0	+113.0
Israel	1965	1	−1.6	+101.6
Canada	1951	4	+5.3	+94.7
Australia and New Zealand	1965	6	+7.2	+92.8
Japan	1965	8	+7.6	+92.4
United States	1950	52	+8.4	+91.6
Hong Kong	1965	1	+55.0	+45.5

Source: http://www.demographia.com/db.highmetro.htm

intensive development of built-up areas, this outcome should not be surprising. Rybczynski (2010, p. 170, italics added) has noted that "[v]irtually every technological innovation of the last fifty years has *facilitated*, if not actually encouraged urban dispersal."

Explicit recognition of a top-down mandate to limit the spreading out of cities came with the United Kingdom's Town and Country Planning Act of 1947 and the various British "Greenbelt" plans that followed. This type of growth management and urban growth boundary approach to city planning has since been mimicked throughout most of the industrialized nations. Consider this sentiment by Filion and McSpurren (2007, p. 501): "A supportive distribution of residential density is perceived to be an essential component of strategies aimed at increasing the use of public transit. To alter substantially land use-transport dynamics in a fashion that favours public transit patronage, residential density policies must be deployed over long periods and unfold at local and metropolitan levels simultaneously." Many planners are eager to support "transit villages" as part of "coordinated efforts" to support the use of public transit (Bernick & Cervero, 1997).

Much of this is inspired by concerns over the air quality consequences of widespread auto use. But pollution pricing is avoided while reshaping cities is embraced. The Smart Growth movement seeks a stronger role for top-down urban and regional planners.[7] Environmental and "sustainability" concerns (and environmental impact hurdles) have been added to the mix, usually involving even more fear or skepticism over market outcomes. At the same time, public sector "redevelopment" activities have been growing in importance and recently given wide sanction via the United States Supreme Court's expansion of the eminent domain power of governments.[8] Nevertheless, it appears that significant policy efforts and contrasts around the world make little difference. There are big plans, to be sure, but they do not seem to matter. Market forces trump apparent policy differences – to the deep consternation of many observers, most of whom conclude that existing top-down plans have to be toughened.[9]

PLANNING

In most societies top-down planning and bottom-up planning co-exist. Even the formerly "East-bloc" regimes that had outlawed private property and formally assigned all planning to central authorities had unwittingly spawned numerous black markets.[10] It is quite plausible that the failed centrally planned economies persisted as long as they did because of black market activity. And while many observers grossly over-simplify by referring to the United States as a "laissez-faire" or "free market economy," it is much more likely to be an amalgam of top-down and bottom-up. It is hard to imagine anything else because it is the nature of politicians and bureaucrats to want to increase their influence and power, but it is the nature of almost everyone else to look for ways to avoid their power and influence.

The socialist calculation debates of the early-to-mid twentieth century challenged the neoclassical "nirvana economics" (Demsetz, 1969) approach as well as the aspirations of Marxist economic planners. It is now recognized that the final intellectual blow was struck by Friedrich Hayek when he emphasized the wide dispersion of critical knowledge, much of it tacit, and the impossibility that central planners could grasp or gather enough of it.[11] It is left to individuals to respond to market price signals. Most of the centrally planned economies did collapse, as expected, just over a half-century after Hayek delivered his decisive blow. Nevertheless, neoclassical economic analysis or faith in central planning persists in many quarters. It is not at all strange that the former is often used to support the latter. By positing a grossly unrealistic economic universe and finding that reality falls short, neoclassical economists have incited a large literature on "market failure."[12] The latter has been absorbed and even celebrated by statists and central planners. Austrian school economists, in contrast, reject the simplifications of the neoclassical model and avoid its central planning implications. This is summed up in Hayek's (1988, p. 76) famous observation that the "curious task of economics is to demonstrate to men how little they really know about what they imagine they can design."

The second challenge to top-down planning comes from the public choice school of economics, which acknowledges the self-serving motivations of political actors (including politically sanctioned "experts") and consequent wasteful rent-seeking (Krueger, 1974) – and even "rent extraction" (McChesney, 1997) – about which neoclassical economics is mostly silent. Most "capitalist" economies foster widespread "crony capitalism," whereby the essential profit-loss dynamic is lost. Even when and where markets "fail," there is little reason to expect that the simple public sector remedies prescribed by neoclassical economists will come about.[13]

The conceptual problems of modern city planners were addressed by Britton Harris in a series of articles that explored the analogy between city planning and mathematical programming. Harris (1971) argues that advances in mathematical programming reveal problem-solving challenges and opportunities that could help us better understand the work of city planners. But these thoughts were not a return to the calculation debates – they did not claim that planners could replace markets for the allocation of goods and they did not allude to planners computing prices – but they did reflect the technocratic optimism of the mid-twentieth century. Harris can be seen as devoting considerable energy to refining and updating Progressive Era impulses.

GROWTH, DEVELOPMENT, AND COMPLEXITY

It is almost a cliché of modern growth economics that "institutions matter." Growth is not simply about applying more labor and capital. Deron Acemoglu presents a schematic summary (Fig. 1) that shows institutions (he defines them, as does Douglass North, as rules of the game that are humanly devised and that shape human activities) as the "ultimate cause"; his simple graphic sums up much of what we know about economic growth.[14] People respond to incentives, but the incentives are clearest when the institutions are

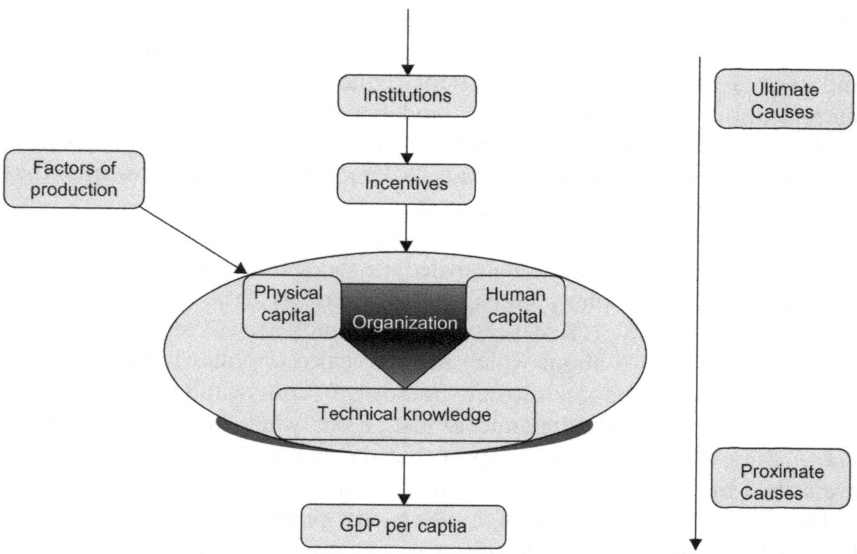

Fig. 1. Economic Growth. *Source*: Adapted from Acemoglu (2009).

favorable. There are inevitably various definitions of "institutions," but the most robust empirical results are those that define institutions via "economic freedom" indices.[15] Recent work by the World Bank (2006) attempts to value "good" institutions, calling them "intangible wealth." It turns out that most of the world's wealth is intangible wealth, with substantially more of it in the developed countries. Responding to incentives, people combine human and physical capital in auspicious ways – but only *after good ideas are formed.* Good ideas are promising *new combinations of old ideas.* And "[e]conomic growth occurs whenever people take resources and rearrange them in ways that are more valuable" (Romer, 2007). It is always about the *discovery of better combinations.* One could add that the number of possible combinations grows over time as there is ever more to choose from.

The graphic also shows the role of organizations. Coase (1937) famously shows that organizations emerge to reduce transactions costs. It is then that we get better technologies. Economists suggest that "organizational capital" is an important contributor to productivity. It involves a firm's capacity to discover economies in production and distribution. But this is linked to our interest in spatial order, because organization involves many shells, including the ones that describe *spatial* organization. And just as with Elinor Ostrom's (2010) emphasis of local institutions, local spatial arrangements emerge that respond to local conditions.

The big picture story is how we might obtain the favorable circumstances. Some analysts (see Bhalla, 1994) have even suggested a positive feedback, from growth to the demand for improved institutions. But only when the institutions are favorable can we expect the benefits of Smithian comparative advantage, Schumpeterian discovery as well as the formation of complex Hayekian supply chains prompted by prices and more discovery – supply chains that often span the globe.[16] All three of these phenomena describe highly complex processes that rely on market signals and decentralized decision making.

Jane Jacobs (1961) famously called attention to the nature and the extent of the complexity of spatial organization, cities, and successful neighborhoods. She argued for diversity of land uses and explained her fears that city planners of her day, who had taken on the task of large-scale city redevelopment projects, could not cope with all of the intricacies involved.[17] But whether it is Leonard Read explaining the complexity of constructing a simple pencil[18] or Jacobs trying to explain urban neighborhoods, each one addresses the wide gap between popular understandings and the extent of the underlying complexities. Emphasizing how complicated things really are underscores Hayek's skepticism of grand designs. Paul Romer illustrates complexity in this way:

> There have been 10**18 seconds since the Big Bang, and there are 10*88 particles in the known universe. Those are very large numbers ... but they are dwarfed by the number of ways that things or ideas can be combined. Even something as simple as a deck of cards can be arranged in unimaginably numerous ways. There are 10**68 possible card decks, which means that any order you happen to shuffle has probably never appeared before. (Romer, 1994, cited in Postrel, 1998)

And "[t]he naïve intuition that people have about limits to growth is profoundly wrong .... There is a scarcity of physical objects but that's not the constraint on what we can do" (*ibid.*). This suggests that the "real constraint is not the number of objects, but the ways of combining objects or ideas – a number of possibilities that makes the number of atoms in the universe look close to zero in comparison. We are limited in a very real sense, only by our imagination and the time in which we have to exercise it" (Postrel, 1998, p. 64).

All these thoughts are relevant to the economic growth discussion. The biggest question in economics is still the one that asks why some people and places are rich and some poor. Going back to at least Adam Smith, the discussion continues to the present and looks at how so many (notably in the West) became so rich so quickly over the last 200–300 years. Steven Landsburg notes:

> Modern humans first emerged about 100,000 years ago. For the next 99,800 years or so, nothing happened. Well, not quite nothing. There were wars, political intrigue, the invention of agriculture – but none of that stuff had much effect on the quality of people's lives. Almost everyone lived on the modern equivalent of $400 to $600 a year, just above the subsistence level. True there were always aristocracies who lived far better, but numerically, they were quite insignificant. (Landsburg, 2007)

Landsburg could have added the important fact that population growth was accompanied by *increasing* resource supplies. Bjørn Lomborg illustrates it this way:

> It is remarkable that the fall in the proportion of people starving in the world should have come at the same time as the population of developing countries doubled. What is more astounding is that the actual number of people starving in the Third World has fallen. While in 1971 almost 920 million people were starving, the total fell below 792 million in 1997 .... In 2010 it is expected to fall to 680 million. (Lomborg, 2001, p. 61)

Events have undermined countless "doomsday" forecasts. Yet, they remain in vogue; "[t]he most astonishing thing about the extraordinary growth and innovation that the United States and other economies have achieved over the past two centuries is that it does not astonish us"

(Baumol, Litan, & Schramm, 2007; p. 1). Scarcity is a fundamental fact of life, but we see receding (never disappearing) scarcity. Julian Simon has famously ascribed this to the power of the only *infinite* resource – human ingenuity. When allowed to flower in a context of economic freedom (i.e., protection of property and credible contract enforcement), the application of human ingenuity explains what would otherwise be a paradox: ever more consumers, but ever greater availabilities.

Anticipating Simon, Joseph Schumpeter famously assigned the key *discovery* activity to entrepreneurs. In a world of considerable uncertainty, those with a comparative advantage in pursuing it and also accepting its risks are indispensable. All of this is consistent with Romer's (2007, p. 128) point that "[e]conomic growth occurs whenever people take resources and rearrange them in ways that are more valuable."[19] It is about new combinations and about rearranging previously unrelated items. But this is again a problem of choosing from a near infinite number of combinations. We somehow get people to *rearrange ideas* from a near infinite set so that they can facilitate the beneficial *rearrangement of resources* from a very large set. Entrepreneurs are the ones who typically take the lead and show the way. They develop insights and take action. Whereas developing economies can execute high-growth catch-up strategies (the recent example of China) by implementing existing technologies "off the shelf," economies already on the frontiers grow via new ideas and new methods that are implemented by entrepreneurs.

Flashes of insight are actually a novel assembly of ideas that takes place within *and also among* inspired brains. Consider Duggan's description of creativity:

> Clausewitz gives us four steps for how strategic intuition works. First, you take in 'examples from history' throughout your life and put them on the shelves of your brain. Study can help, by putting more there. Second comes 'presence of mind' where you free your brain of all preconceptions about what problem you're solving and what solution might work. Third comes the flash of insight itself. Clausewitz called it *coup d'oeil*, which is French for 'glance'. In a flash, a new combination of examples from history fly off the shelves of your brain and combine. Fourth comes 'resolution', or determination, where you not only say to yourself, 'I see', but also, 'I'll do it'! (Duggan, 2010, p. 10)

But we do even better if we are able to select (mix and match) ideas, even the seemingly disparate ones, from the "shelves" of many brains. We do that best once we have created modes and networks by which we interact – or as in Matt Ridley's (2010, p. 6) colorful expression: "I believe that at some point in human history, ideas began to meet and mate, to have sex with each other."

Duggan and Ridley seemingly anticipate Johnson's discussion of the "adjacent possible." Here is his summary:

> The adjacent possible is as much about limits as it us about openings. At every moment in the timeline of an expanding biosphere, there are doors that cannot be unlocked yet. In human culture, we like to think of breakthrough ideas as sudden accelerations on the timeline, where a genius jumps ahead fifty years and invents something that normal minds, trapped in the present moment, couldn't possibly have come up with. But the truth is that technological (and scientific) advances rarely break out of the adjacent possible; the history of cultural progress is, almost without exception, a story of one door leading to another door, exploring the palace one room at a time. But of course, human minds are not bound by the finite laws of molecule formation, and so every now and then an idea does occur to someone that teleports us forward a few rooms, skipping some exploratory steps in the adjacent possible. But those ideas almost always end up being short-term failures, precisely because they have skipped ahead. We have a phrase for those ideas: we call them 'ahead of their time'. (Johnson, 2010, p. 16)

CITIES AND THE "ADJACENT POSSIBLE"

The ideas of the thinkers cited in the previous section help us to appreciate the insight of Jacobs quoted at the beginning of this chapter. Cities exist because most of us are more productive when clustered. But simple clustering is inadequate. People must be able to develop contacts and networks that work for them. This can involve private or public spaces. Peculiar spatial arrangements that facilitate all this must be possible. When this occurs, cities can be the engines of growth and innovation: "Cities enable the collaboration that makes humanity shine most brightly. Because humans learn so much from other humans, we learn more when there are more people around us" (Glaeser, 2011, p. 247; see also Storper & Venables, 2004). The great port cities have always had an additional advantage, being able to draw on even more ideas from abroad and adding them to the interaction that naturally happens in cities. Economists have been accused of neglecting how innovation happens. Looking at cities would be a good way to proceed.

Urban economists label all of the benefits of nearness "agglomeration economies."[20] Just as there may be scale economies within firms, there may also be scale economies among firms, in both similar and different industries. The comparative benefits of clusters of similar versus dissimilar firms in terms of which is best for the incubation of new ideas have fed a minor controversy among urban economists.[21] But nearness between *any* two parties reduces their transaction costs, and there are also gains when both are near valued third parties. This includes proximity to common vendors, customers, or labor pools. Everyone involved also benefits from lower search costs.

Lee (2006) found that the longest average commutes in the United States (in minutes) are those experienced by residents of the New York metropolitan area, particularly those who commute to its downtowns. But why do these people put up with long commutes and high prices? Partly because they are rewarded with high wages. But why are high wages available? Because these workers are productive. And they are extraordinarily productive because they work in areas of New York where agglomeration opportunities abound.

New ideas spawn new businesses, new processes, new products, and new wealth. The ever-increasing value of information explains the fact that ever more agglomeration economies spring from information exchange. Note that while the first two types of agglomeration economies involve transactions, the third is more complex. Edwin Mills has remarked that electronic information exchange is good for transmitting unambiguous information (data is an example), but face-to-face interaction is still necessary for the transmission of ambiguous information. He cites seminars as an example. The feedback is quick and ongoing and complex, including the tone, facial expressions, and body language. Could all of these ever take place electronically? Can relationships be formed via teleconferencing? What would be the "new normal?" No one really knows. But the discussion evokes Johnson's "adjacent possible" and its importance to the spread and sharing of ideas. For any setting, *the adjacent possible that works best* involves complexities that are beyond the capabilities of top-down planners.

It is not simply clustering, but propitious clustering that matters. Many analysts worry about what the "best" clusters might be. But the content and the arrangement of clusters are very complex, and the best ones for each setting are most likely to emerge spontaneously. The shortcoming of much existing research on cities is that – instead of examining cities and what it is about their *emergent spatial juxtapositions* that facilitate the development of new technical knowledge – most analysts have settled on an oversimplified and extreme shortcut: the idea of city (or metro area) size or simply overall "density" to explain success. Higher (usually population) densities presumably facilitate interactions – so let's have higher densities. Urban economists have noted "human capital externalities" (Rauch, 1993) and have done considerable work to test the links between metropolitan area education levels and productivity or growth (Gordon & Richardson, 2012, survey some of this literature).

But this is much too simple. Overall density variations within any city or metropolitan area are huge; simply relying on the means and ignoring large variances oversimplifies and ignores essential information. For the United States, the Los Angeles urbanized area has been more densely populated than the New York urbanized area since at least 1980.[22]

Density has been taken up by Smart Growth planners who routinely prescribe "compact development" and higher densities than the market demands. The latter is often dismissed as "urban sprawl." But this approach involves various misunderstandings. Bruegmann reminds us that "sprawl" is not new:

> Most American anti-sprawl reformers today believe that sprawl is a recent and peculiarly American phenomenon caused by specific technological innovations like the automobile and by government policies like single-use zoning or the mortgage interest deduction on the federal income tax. It is important for them to believe this because if sprawl turned out to be a long-standing feature of urban development worldwide, it would suggest that stopping it involves something much more fundamental than correcting some poor American land-use policies .... I will argue that the characteristics we associate today with sprawl have actually been visible in most prosperous cities throughout history. Sprawl has been as evident in Europe as in America and can now be said to be the preferred settlement pattern everywhere in the world where there is a certain measure of affluence and where citizens have some choice in how they live. (Bruegmann, 2005, p. 17)

Growth means outward expansion. But the word "sprawl" is problematic because it is vague and pejorative. We are in the automobile age. Around the world, as people reach middle-class status, they want private mobility (Dargay, Gately, & Sommer, 2007). As more people acquire the range and mobility afforded by cars, origins and destinations disperse. And as origins and destinations disperse, the demand for private autos increases, and so forth. The objection to "sprawl" is really an objection to auto-oriented development as well as to autos. Along these lines, it is usually presumed that developing more compact forms (such as "transit villages" or "transit-oriented development") will cause auto use to decline, to be replaced by transit use, walking, bicycling, and so on. "Coordinated" development of public transit and transit stations is now a favorite theme.

But there are problems with this view. First, causation may run the other way; historically dense areas may have lower auto use, but making developed areas denser is not likely to reduce auto use. Second, high-density development accounts for greater street congestion and slower, less efficient, auto use. Third, even if higher densities make distances shorter, this could increase the quantity of travel demanded, including auto travel. In the United States, Manhattan is by far the densest urban place. It is also by far the nation's largest transit market and also has the slowest auto traffic. As mentioned, Lee (2006) shows that the longest auto commutes in America are among those of the New York commuters who *drive* to work into Manhattan's downtowns.

The limited ability of planners and policy makers to impact these phenomena is fairly clear in Table 1. As 2010 census data become available, it appears that suburbanization continues in spite of significant efforts by planners to stop it. Most of them conclude that they have just not been able to try hard enough. The popular antidote to the spread of cities is "smart growth" or "new urbanism," each of which prescribes more compact urban forms. All of this is presented as in the interests of "sustainable development" and "livable communities." Advocates are not reluctant to suggest "regional urban design" (see, e.g., Porter, 2008).

This goes with the belief that top-down planners can arrange "jobs" and "housing" to be "balanced", that is, in closer proximity so that commuting distances can be reduced (Cervero, 1996). This view assumes that planners can do the matching and that they can do so in light of all of the trade-offs that would be involved. But individuals' choices of job and home location are much too complex for any of this to be achieved top-down. The same goes for employers' location choices. But the bigger problem is that these discussions leave little room for the "serendipitous connections" that foster so many of the agglomeration economies (McArdle, 2010).

Theoretical discussions of cities are still hobbled by the convenient and dated assumption of monocentric cities, in which all households send a worker to a job in the downtown. This tradition still prompts analysts to look for central city versus suburb distinctions. But these gross divisions bear very little resemblance to actual modern cities. For the United States since 1980, most commuting has been suburb-to-suburb. But when we examine the personal travel data, no matter how it is reported, we find some remarkable results. First, overall commuting times have been remarkably stable; 25.1 minutes in 2000 and 25.3 minutes in 2007 (Pisarski, 2006). Second, differences between central city versus suburban average work-trip durations are moderate. The 2001 and 2009 National Household Travel Surveys defined *four* classes of metropolitan location: "urban," "suburban," "second city," and "town and country" along an "urban continuum" – "town and country" being exurban-rural. Reported average travel (one-way, all modes) times for commuters living in these places were 28, 24, 21, and 24, respectively in 2001; the corresponding numbers from the next time the survey was taken in 2009 were 28, 24, 23 and 25 (Table 2). The "urban" and "suburban" travel times did not deteriorate in spite of more people and

Table 2. Mean Commute Times (Minutes, One-Way, All Modes), 2001 and 2009.

	Urban	Suburban	Second City	Town and Country	All Metro	USA
2001						
Commute time	28	24	21	24	24	
Population[a]	39,757,000	61,105,000	43,140,000	60,757,000	204,050,000	253,131,000
Population share	15.7%	24.1%	17.0%	24.0%	80.6%	100.0%
2009						
Commute time	28	24	22	25	25	
Population[a]	49,563,000	69,223,000	45,322,000	65,532,000	229,639,000	283,017,000
Population share	17.5%	24.5%	16.0%	23.2%	81.1%	100.0%

Source: Author calculations from 2001 and 2009 NHTS.
Note: NPTS defines an "urban continuum" from "urban" to "suburban" to "second city" to "town and country."
[a]Excludes ages 0–4.

more drivers, and "suburban" commutes were of shorter duration than "urban" in both years. There is no sign of "traffic doomsday" and there is no sign that "suburban sprawl" prompts more time consuming work trips. Both results can be explained by the co-location of employers and employees in ways that prevent overly costly travel. In a world where policy makers avoid pricing the roads, these benign results can be seen as markets coming to the rescue of policy failures.

Lee (2006) provides a more complex analysis, first identifying places of work in greater detail and then noting the commuting time differences. For the fourteen largest (3 million and more in 2000) American metropolitan areas, 18 percent of workers were employed in the main center, 15 percent were employed in various subcenters and 68 percent were "dispersed," that is, not working in a major center.[23] The "dispersed city" is a much more widespread phenomenon than many suppose. The respective average commuting times for the three groups were 35 minutes, 30 minutes, and 26 minutes (also one-way and drive-alone only). Again, the variations are not great; many in the first group were commuters to Manhattan's two centers, where many use public transit and still experience a more time-consuming trip. But how is it that on average the dispersed workers had the shortest commute? Contrary to the fear that "sprawl" causes long commutes, many employers apparently found it to their advantage to locate in places that were convenient to large numbers of workers. Lee found similar patterns for all of the 79 metropolitan areas that he studied. It is doubtful that top-down land use planning could have achieved this benign result.

A similar market process apparently applies to the location of shopping opportunities. Consider that the idea that centers and subcenters have evolved. Rybczynski writes:

> To understand the implications of an urbanism based on popular demand, it helps to look at an environment where the consumer is paramount: the places we shop. Shopping habits have changed radically over time. A century ago, shoppers dressed up and took a streetcar to a downtown department store; fifty years ago they drove the station wagon to a suburban shopping center; twenty-five years ago they might have spent the afternoon at the mall. Today, many young people have never seen a true department store … and I suspect in another twenty-five years many shopper will never have set foot in a mall. (Rybczynski, 2010, p. 93)

But he also reports that "even as dispersal appears to be the order of the day, concentration is making a comeback. Sometimes concentration takes new forms: power centers, office parks, theme parks, and village-like planned communities in the middle of nowhere" (*ibid.*, p. 171).These are multi-purpose places. Shopping and entertainment are hard to separate. So even if people do not rely on a traditional downtown, they still enjoy being among others and can do so in a variety of suburban places. The critics have not noticed that people seek and find "community" in all sorts of places.

The International Council of Shopping Centers reports that there are about 100,000 "shopping centers"(including many "Lifestyle Centers"), which account for about 50 percent of America's retail gross leasable area. Whereas some of the centers are Edge Cities that include many of the functions once associated with downtowns, many others are developed at low densities that are seemingly under the radar (as in Edgeless Cities; see Lang, 2003). So, rather than downtown and the burbs, it is an extremely complex arrangement. The many small "centers" are spatially distributed so that the average shopping trip by central city versus suburban residents in the United States were of similar duration, 14 minutes for central city residents and 16 minutes for residents of suburbs (2009 NHTS data; see Zhu, 2012). In fact, the 2001 and 2009 travel surveys by the U.S. Department of Transportation show that the average shopping trip distance in 2001 and 2009 was the same, at 6.7 miles each way. In the intervening years, the American population had grown by 7.8 percent but shopping access had not gotten out of reach in spite of significant growth and development.

It should not be surprising that emergent orders have an important spatial dimension. Emergent "spatial orders" have been described by Chris Webster and Lawrence Wai-Chung Lai:

> The creative order that emerges as individuals interact to discover, test and exchange new knowledge has been termed catallaxis and involves innovation. It happens when resource owners, however meager their assets, find others who want something that they possess and discover how to process their assets to supply that need in return for remuneration. Catallaxis as an economic model contrasts to the traditional neoclassical maximization model by being open ended and relatively unconstrained. In the comparative static neoclassical world, profit and utility maximization is limited by endowment constraints including production technology. In the catallactic world, knowledge evolution, innovation and adaptation guarantees a constant supply of new wealth-enhancing opportunities for those willing and able to use their resources productively in exchange or in combination. (Webster & Lai, 2003, p. 35)

This spatial order allows for the internalization of many positive externalities and the avoidance of many negative externalities. In fact, land markets are the only mechanism that we have for pricing these (see Pennington, 2002). As we will see in the discussion of private land use planning (below), the spatial order also involves the supply of many "public" goods and spaces.

Urban economics began with *equilibrium* models that describe economizing behavior with respect to job access. There are several problems with this approach. First, it skirts the important question of how cities change to facilitate growth and development – the topic that is taken up in the previous pages. But the simple model is incomplete on its own terms. Economizing behavior in space involves access to all sorts of places and activities. Bids for space at any location are formed as the bidders evaluate various sites for their interaction potential with large numbers of other locators. These interactions *may or may not* involve explicit transactions. *Potential* externalities are carefully considered. The emergent spatial arrangements determine which of the potential externalities become *realized* externalities. All of this requires open-endedness, which is what it takes for better arrangements to emerge as the world changes. So it is not simply clustering or size or density; what matters is the specific nature of each cluster. Is it a place that is congenial to inventiveness and productivity?

How do we get such places? There is no choice. The fortunes of cities rise or fall, depending on how well they provide opportunities for greater productivity. The productivity of most enterprises is often linked to location with respect to suppliers, workers, customers, and information opportunities. This involves complex trade-offs that each locator has to evaluate.

But spatial organization is the key ingredient missing from most discussions of the sources of economic growth (Fig. 1). "Bad" institutions have been cited as retarding growth while flexibility has been cited as essential (Acemoglu's argument); the same applies to the malleability of location patterns. This brings us back to the importance of trial-and-error experimentation, feedback, and discovery opportunities – and the fact that market participants are most sensitive to feedback. These do the important work in a profit-loss system. To be sure, Jacobs (cited in Rybczynski, 2010, p. 60) wrote that "[c]ities are an immense laboratory for trial and error, failure and success, in city building and city design."

As already noted, events in the United States and elsewhere (as Fig. 1 shows) have overwhelmed the ideas as well as the efforts of top-down planners. Rybczynski writes:

> [Herbert] Gans, who had taught in a city-planning department, took issue with Jacob's critique of city planning. Not because he was particularly sympathetic to planners – although he pointed out that most city planners probably agreed with her proposals – but because he felt that she exaggerated the power of planning in American society. "The truth is that the new forms of residential building – in suburb as well as city – are not products of orthodox planning theory," he wrote, "but expressions of middle-class culture which guides the housing market, and which planners also serve." In an entrepreneurial society where people are free to choose how, and where, to live, they will ultimately get what they want, not what planners think they need. (Rybczynski, 2010, p. 91)

Gordon and Ikeda (2011) challenged analysts' focus on whole cities or metropolitan areas and the various studies that linked city-wide or metropolitan-area-wide descriptors, especially population densities and the skill set of resident workers, with metropolitan success (examples of metropolitan-wide analyses include Dalton & Zabel, 2009; Glaeser & Ressenger, 2010; Ihlanfeldt, 2007; Kok, Monkkonen, & Quigley, 2010; Malpezzi, Chun, & Green, 1998; Schuetz, 2009). Unlike these analysts, Gordon and Ikeda studied the top *submetropolitan* destinations of United States migrants with advanced academic training (those with Masters degrees and higher) by considering arrivals at the over 2000 Public Use Microsample Areas (PUMAs) that are classified as "metropolitan" by the U.S. Census Bureau. These areas are useful because they are much smaller than most cities; density variations are significant enough to undermine the usefulness of large-area averages. The authors found that

> [s]ubstantial human capital (as measured by people with advanced degrees) can be seen to migrate to parts of Manhattan as well as to areas such as Silicon Valley. These people are seemingly attracted to opportunities found in 'low density' as well as in 'high density' places. Four of the top 25 (out of 2069 areas included after discarding ones with only

> partial data) were in Manhattan and four of the top 25 were in Silicon Valley; other top-25 destinations included West Los Angeles or suburban Washington DC, suburban Seattle, Boston, suburban Chicago, Austin or San Diego. The densest receiving area (in Manhattan) was thirty-eight times as dense as the most spread out (in Silicon Valley, California), yet each one succeeded in attracting highly educated, (and presumably creative) people ... the sizes of areas ... vary from below ten square kilometres (in Manhattan) to one just over 300 square kilometres (in the Washington DC suburbs) and one just over 250 square kilometres (in Silicon Valley). (Gordon & Ikeda, 2011)

Clearly, the simple idea of "density" is not adequate. And favorable spatial arrangements can occur in a wide variety of settings. Silicon Valley is still an agglomeration, albeit one that spans San Francisco Bay.

There are many kinds of proximity. Easy auto access rather than pedestrian access may be sufficient and is widely available in many areas. Electronic networking is clearly a plus; it is a complement and not a substitute for conventional networking. Gordon and Ikeda (*ibid.*) introduced the idea of

> 'Jacobs density' ... The drawback to this measure is that data on Jacobs density may be hard to get, because it would have to combine measures of distance travelled per hour (say) of the average user of public space and the average number of public stopping points in which informal contacts could take place. ... However, we can say that the informal contacts that form social networks valuable for entrepreneurial discovery would be hard to imagine taking place absent an environment of economic freedom ..."[24] (Gordon & Ikeda, 2011)

DIVISION OF LABOR

The variety as well as the ubiquity of emergent orders is clear. But it is also true that almost everything within reach of our senses is designed by humans. How much of the order in our lives is from human action and how much is from human design? What should be the proper division of labor? Holcombe has taken a stab at providing an answer for the American context. He writes:

> A strong argument can be made for leaving the government out of the land use planning process altogether, and allowing private landowners complete freedom to use their land as they want, so long as their land use does not create a nuisance for others. ... the law of nuisance is superior to zoning for preventing conflicting uses of land. Still, under current institutions, the government must play a crucial role in land use planning, because it owns nearly all the roads. But for optimal land use policy, the government must play a role considerably different from the role recommended by the New Urbanists. It should plan more for its own infrastructure development – especially roads – and do less planning about how private landowners can use their land. If government does a good job planning for the location of transportation corridors, private landowners will be led by market forces to make efficient land use choices. (Holcombe, 2004, p. 295)

In this view, top-down planners set the "rules of the game" via published infrastructure plans. Private land owners are then free to plan and develop land uses subject to these specifications. To be sure, the New Urbanists often insist that they are critics of poorly conceived top-down planning. But they part company with Holcombe's approach because they are optimistic that it is possible to replace "bad" top-down planning with "good" top-down planning.

That aside, there are two ways to parse Holcombe's argument. First, consider his mention of "government." In a world of increasingly dispersed knowledge involving people with strong demands for property rights, we should expect that at least some authority is also decentralizing. While the demand for property rights has been used to explain the early twentieth-century adoption of zoning codes in the United States, their recent privatization in many places fits the view that many large-city governments have lost credibility and trust in this area. Discussions of modern American cities must acknowledge the phenomenal growth of private communities (revealingly labeled "master-planned") as well as privately organized business improvement districts.[25] There are presumably now 900 of the latter in the United States.[26] In addition, almost 20 percent of the American population reside in privately governed communities (most of them *not* "gated"); between 1980 and 2000 one-half of new housing was placed in such communities (Briffault, 1999; Nelson, 2005; Pennington, 2002). People do vote with their feet. Both of the cited privatization phenomena are essentially spontaneous orders. When relatively small units can be formed, novel institutional arrangements can emerge spontaneously to create property rights, as Elinor Ostrom has found on more than one occasion.

Most private business or residential communities include all manner of "public" spaces, "public" facilities and "public" services that are supplied in response to market signals. Foldvary (1994) points to the fact that local public goods have benefits that are available over a limited space. He calls them "territorial goods." In that case, the benefits are capitalized in land values and provide market signals to guide developers. Once again, events have overtaken academic discussions of the public versus private divide, as well as standard definitions of "market failure."

Private communities involve governance that generates and makes available rights versus protections trade-offs. Members are keen to protect the value of their homes and rightly see neighborhood change and neighborhood quality as a commons. This explains homeowners' natural demand for rules of property. The various "Not in My Backyard" (NIMBY) battles reported in the popular press are simply disagreements over neighborhood property rights when the rights are not adequately clear. While elaborate community-level rules have been criticized by many as intrusive, they represent the emergent trade-offs vetted by markets. Private zoning can internalize externalities in the same way that a private shopping center operator tries to match stores with locations so as to maximize overall profitability. NIMBY conflicts are less likely to occur in this situation. Homeowners will have sorted for broadly similar development tastes.

So whereas private planning diminishes a serious problem, conventional "public" zoning and related regulations have added to the problem of development limits that have contributed to the housing affordability difficulties of recent years (Glaeser & Gyourko, 2003; see also Gruen, 2010, for a summary of recent research). This may seem ironic because one of the popular rationales for interventions in land markets is that markets supposedly fail to adequately meet what are usually referred to as "broader social goals."

But the main point is that in light of the growing popularity of private districts and communities, we can modify Holcombe's approach: not all roads are government-owned; considerable land use and infrastructure planning are jointly executed and private. Private developers are motivated to internalize various externalities and determine economic scales of infrastructures and other features.[27]

Nevertheless, at some point elements of private infrastructure link up with their public counterparts. At some point there will be conventional governmental units that supply the remaining public goods. But the further up the supply chain this occurs, the better. Nonprivate actors, as already suggested, face an information deficit as well as politicization problems.

The second reaction to Holcombe's proposal is more general. Most of the artifacts that we are in touch with involve *human design subject to market forces*, benefiting from price signals. Most human designers, therefore, interact with market forces via trial-and-error feedback and learning. The visions of entrepreneurs and the designers in their employ benefit from continuous feedback and error-correction opportunities. People will make mistakes and thus error-correction opportunities must be available. This is why emphasizing discovery and having discovery opportunities are so important. This view of design greatly expands the domain of emergent orders. All of the elements that make up private communities have designers and they are all subject to market forces.

Rapid change in consumer electronics provides a useful and obvious example of market dynamism. Profit-seeking, competition, and market feedback account for amazing product improvements, for example continuously superior designs. These are very basic concepts – even though some writers have noted that trial-and-error learning is not the focus of neoclassical economics – and essential elements of the market economy.[28]

But how scalable is this model of human design subject to market forces? Which are the cases or situations where the error-correction process is *not* to be counted on? Such cases have two attributes. First, market demand is harder to identify when it comes to large and unique projects. Second, project scale or uncertainty can limit the possibility of attracting enough private capital. These two attributes define the urban "mega-projects" that are removed from trial-and-error as well as market discipline by their very nature. They are not amenable to small steps or easy reversibility. That's the trouble with grandiosity.[29] Not surprisingly, the urban mega-projects have a mixed record of success. Americans rightly celebrate the Erie Canal, New York's Central Park, the Interstate Highway System and a few others. But we also know about all of the ill-fated "public-private" projects whereby public moneys (including tax breaks) subsidize private sports arenas, convention halls, or even aquaria (see, e.g., Siegfried and Zimbalist, 2000). Peter Hall (1982) even devoted a book to *Great Planning Disasters*,[30] in which he documented various mega-project failures and noted that they were each conceived with the hope that they would alter the shape of their city, but failed to do so. The mega-projects have a notoriously poor record in terms of the gaps between their costs and benefits – and the misallocations of public funds allocated to make up the difference (see, e.g., Altshuler & Luberoff, 2003; Flyvbjerg, Holm, & Buhl, 2002). And as public choice analysis suggests, crony capitalism becomes a concern.

Mega-projects, then, are the only logical exceptions to market-guided human design. To be sure, there was a time in our past when most transportation and infrastructure services were private (Beito, 2002). Even now, a moderate reversion to private ownership is underway, especially in places where public providers are trying to raise revenues by selling facilities. Indeed, Winston (2010) titles the first chapter of his recent book "Back to the Future to Improve U.S. Transportation."[31] Anything that can be metered can possibly be privatized, so the widespread presumption of public planning and ownership can be reconsidered. There are, of course, also many nonmetered private facilities available to the public, because these are bundled with private facilities. The private shopping center, again, includes many obvious examples. The more privatization, the more innovation, and improved productivity will be forthcoming.

This discussion parses Holcombe's proposed division of labor. Top-down planners remain responsible for the urban mega-projects as well as infrastructure requirements beyond private projects, be they residential, commercial, or any other. All of the rest is better left to bottom-up planners. This approach is appealing because city forms around the world are fairly durable and much too diverse to be subject to common top-down planning principles.

But the world we live in is not divided between bottom-up and top-down responsibilities in this simple manner because of ideological attachments. Enduring optimism over the prospects of top-down urban planning reaches back to the Grand Manner idea and is still popular among abstraction-prone High Modernist architects who are ready and eager to design whole cities. Fishman describes the tradition in this way:

> [Ebenezer] Howard, [Frank Lloyd] Wright, and Le Corbusier had a different outlook. They were not afraid to ask basic questions about the structure of cities and of societies; or to consider large-scale problems; or to envision and work for the social changes that might be necessary to carry them out. They still believed that human efforts could solve human problems. They had the confidence to think that an advanced industrial society could create an urban environment worthy of its highest values. Inevitably, they were disappointed, but I hope that their ideals are not irrelevant to our present tasks. (Fishman, 1994, p. xii)

In fact, writing about Le Corbusier, Rybczynski notes:

> Major American cities such as Los Angeles and New York had adopted zoning legislation before the First World War, but Le Corbusier gave zoning an aesthetic rationale. Henceforth, not only would residential and commercial uses be placed apart, but a variety of other functions would be isolated in self-sufficient 'centers' – shopping centers, convention centers, cultural centers, government centers, sports centers, and so on. The modern city would no longer be a hodgepodge of activities; it would be ordered, logical, and *planned*. … The Soviet Union, which had rejected his architecture in the 1920s, adopted his idea of mass-produced housing and high-rise urbanism and exported them to its ally Communist China. In America, the designers of the public housing projects that were built in almost every major city also adopted Le Corbusier's vision. (Rybczynski, 2010, p. 49)

In many quarters, city planning is *presumed* to be the natural preserve of top-down planning and bottom-up is preempted as a matter of policy. The Smart Growth movement builds on this presumption. To be sure, top-down cannot entirely ignore market forces, because capital and labor are mobile, but these forces are slow-moving and often beyond the time-frame of political decision makers.

There are real mega-projects, but there is also the view that eagerly places all sorts of other projects in the same category. This approach discards market-based error correction opportunities. And it invites rent-seeking and politics. This means Bootleggers-and-Baptists phenomena (Yandle, 1983). In that case, we have well-meaning professionals who are simply on the wrong side of the calculation debate allied with those in the private sector who seize on opportunities for self-dealing.[32]

CONCLUSIONS

Many would like to assume that the socialist calculation debates were won by market economists many years ago. But whereas top-down central planning no longer enjoys the intellectual approval that it once had, the same cannot be said for the top-down planning of cities. Today's city planning literature features considerable concern over "urban sprawl" and presumably associated market failures – including inadequate open space, traffic congestion, air pollution, high cost of services, and improperly patterned land uses. The fact that many of these problems can be mitigated by privatization is seldom acknowledged. And while sprawl remains poorly defined, suburbanization is widespread and notable in the large cities of the developed countries, thereby undermining the presumption that variations in policy approaches make a difference. In fact, to the extent that people's preferences trump international policy differences, it appears that it is the spontaneous orders seen in cities that matter most.

NOTES

1. "Top-down" versus "bottom-up" characterizations of institutional change have been adopted by institutional economists (see Easterly, 2008).
2. Horwitz (2001, p. 82) summarizes the Austrian tradition: "the study of human action leads to a focus on three issues: the limits of human reason arising from the inarticulate nature of much human knowledge; the institutional arrangements that evolve to enable humans to make use of dispersed and tacit human knowledge; and the processes that hamper or foster the evaluation of such institutions."
3. The Germans say *Stadtplan*; the French say *Plan de la Ville*. I am told that Koreans also refer to the city map as a plan, whereas Chinese do not.
4. "It thrived because it could stage easily perceived strong urban images that were at once modern and resonant with authority. This is what appealed to the City Beautiful movement of the United States, as Daniel Burnham, Charles Mulford Robinson, Edward Bennett and their associates sought to civilize the anarchic growth of the American city seized by the demon of commercialism and the unabridged tolerance for the laissez faire" (Kostof, 1991, p. 218).
5. Rybczynski (2007) is a case study summary of all of the regulatory twists and turns that one modern residential development goes through.

6. As recently as 1995, the *Economist* (pp. 5–6) in its "Survey of Cities" reported; "Clearly there is a difference between the European city with its dense historic heart based on walking and public transport, and America's unfocused sprawl based on the car. Even so, European cities are subject to the same processes as American ones. They too are generating new suburbs and allowing old areas to decay."

7. For the United States, Carruthers and Ulfarsson (2008, p. 1797) report: "As of 2005, legislation had been adopted by 20 states and many other initiatives have been implemented independently at the local level."

8. *Kelo v. City of New London* (see Epstein, 2008).

9. One observer who is not surprised is Rybczynski (2010, p. xiii) who writes that the "urban vitality that she [Jane Jacobs] espoused – and correctly saw as a barometer of healthy city life has found new expressions in planned commercial and residential developments, whose scale rivals that of the urban renewal of which she was so critical. These developments are the work of real estate entrepreneurs, who were absent from the Jacobite city described in *Death and Life*, but loom large today, having long ago replaced planners as our chief urban strategists." And "[i]f the first half of the twentieth century in American urbanism – the era of the City Beautiful movement, the garden suburbs and urban renewal – can be characterized as the Age of Planning, the period after 1970 was the Age of the Market" (*ibid.*, p. 93).

10. Where there are cracks, there are usually growing vines: "Despite North Korea's obstinate commitment to central planning, the market is growing like a vine in the cracks of the socialist edifice" (*The Economist*, Jan. 1, 2011, p. 70).

11. Ikeda (2004) argues that various interventions not only ignore local knowledge, but may also distort it.

12. Google Scholar comes up with 82,000 mentions of "market failure" and 24,100 mentions of "government failure." To be sure, there are probably some references that cite both and not all references accept either as established fact.

13. Not only do socialists reject or ignore these two points, but many of them sincerely believe that socialists and socialism are morally superior.

14. A timely summary of growth economics is in Wight (2011).

15. De Han and Sturm (2000) note that there is more than one index, but that they yield similar results in tests of the links between greater economic freedom and economic growth.

16. The formation of complex supply chains without price signals cannot be imagined, but it was not until Hayek (1945) forcefully made this point that the basic idea was widely appreciated.

17. Jacobs was particularly concerned with urban redevelopment planning: "What will the projects look like? They will be spacious, park-like and uncrowded. They will feature long green vistas. They will be stable, symmetrical and orderly. They will be clean, impressive and monumental. They will have all the attributes of a well-kept, dignified cemetery" (Jacobs, 1961, cited by Rybczynski, 2010, p. 55).

18. "I, Pencil, simple though I appear to be, merit your wonder and awe, a claim I shall attempt to prove. In fact, if you can understand me ... I have a profound lesson to teach. And I can teach this lesson better than can an automobile or an airplane or a mechanical dishwasher because – well, because I am seemingly so simple. Simple? Yet, *not a single person on the face of this earth knows how to make me*. This sounds fantastic, doesn't it? Especially when it is realized that there are about one and

one-half billion of my kind produced in the U.S.A. each year". Leonard Read: http://en.wikipedia.org/wiki/I,_Pencil (accessed March 23, 2012).

19. Kohn (2004) discusses the limits of neoclassical economics, including its neglect of entrepreneurial activities.

20. Paul Krugman (1991) and others have modeled economies with "agglomeration economies" that only consider pecuniary externalities. These ("new economic geography") models also omit land markets. The analysis in the rest of this chapter does require land markets as well as externalities beyond the pecuniary type.

21. See Desrochers (2001) for a summary of the two sides' findings.

22. As reported by the U.S. decennial census. The "urbanized areas" do not follow the boundaries of political jurisdictions, as distinct from the bureau's "metropolitan areas," which are made up of one or more counties. The urbanized areas are thought to more closely define the areas that are actually settled at densities to merit the label.

23. Lee used two statistical methods to define centers and subcenters. For the second method, the respective proportions were 7, 15, and 78.

24. More than one study has determined that a doubling of *metropolitan-area* density increases productivity by about 6 percent (see Ciccone & Hall, 1996; Harris & Ionnides, 2000). A previous literature went so far as to speculate on an optimum urban size.

25. There have also been discussions of how older established neighborhoods, including those in the inner city, could be privatized (see Nelson, 2005).

26. http://en.wikipedia.org/wiki/Business_improvement_district (accessed March 23, 2012).

27. Many more roads and highways could (some say should) be privatized (see, e.g., Winston, 2000).

28. Coyne (2010) elaborates the contrasts between neoclassical and Austrian economics: the former emphasizes allocation while the latter focuses on exchange. Tullock's (1965) analysis of bureaucracies describes the objectives of bureaucrats and demonstrates that bureaucrats' interests are not likely to involve feedback from market tests.

29. Tim Harford's *Adapt* (2011) discusses this general class of problems beyond the urban examples.

30. In response, John Landis has recently written about "Ten Planning Successes" (2009). He includes various new downtown ballparks that he reports attracted ancillary investments.

31. In a previous paper (Winston, 2000), he argued for privatization based on his conclusion that hoping for better public policy or management was futile.

32. Gruen (2010) includes summaries of the state of current land use regulation.

REFERENCES

Acemoglu, D. (2009). *Introduction to modern economic growth.* Princeton, NJ: Princeton University Press.

Altshuler, A., & Luberoff, D. (2003). *Mega-projects: The changing politics of urban public investment.* Washington, DC: The Brookings Institution.

Baumol, W. J., Litan, R. E., & Schramm, C. J. (2007). *Good capitalism, bad capitalism and the economics of growth and prosperity*. New Haven, NJ: Yale University Press.

Beito, D. T. (2002). The private places of St. Louis: Urban infrastructure through private planning. In D. T. Beito, P. Gordon & A. Tabarrok (Eds.), *The voluntary city* (pp. 47–75). Ann Arbor, MI: The University of Michigan Press.

Bernick, M., & Cervero, R. (1997). *Transit villages in the 21st century*. New York, NY: McGraw-Hill.

Bhalla, S. S. (1994). Freedom and economic growth: A virtuous cycle? In A. Hadenius (Ed.), *Democracy's victory and crisis: Nobel symposium 1994* (pp. 195–241). Cambridge, UK: Cambridge University Press.

Briffault, R. (1999). A government for our time? Business improvement districts and urban governance. *Columbia Law Review*, *99*(2), 365–477.

Bruegmann, R. (2005). *Sprawl: A compact history*. Chicago, IL: University of Chicago Press.

Carruthers, J. I., & Ulfarsson, G. F. (2008). Does "smart growth" matter to public finance? *Urban Studies*, *45*(9), 1791–1832.

Cervero, R. (1996). Jobs-housing balance revisited: Trends and impacts in the San Francisco Bay Area. *Journal of the American Planning Association*, *62*(4), 492–511.

Ciccone, A., & Hall, R. E. (1996). *Productivity and the density of economic activity*. National Bureau of Economic Research Working Paper No. 4313. NBER, Cambridge, MA.

Coase, R. (1937). The nature of the firm. *Economica*, *4*(16), 386–405.

Coyne, C. J. (2010). Economics as the study of coordination and exchange. In P. J. Boettke (Ed.), *Handbook of contemporary Austrian economics* (pp. 14–29). Cheltenham, UK: Edward Elgar.

Dalton, M. & Zabel, J. (2009). *The impact of minimum lot size regulations on house prices in eastern Massachusetts*. MIT Center for Real Estate Working Paper, Cambridge, MA.

Dargay, J., Gately, D., & Sommer, M. (2007). Vehicle ownership and income growth, worldwide: 1960–2030. *Energy Journal*, *28*(4), 163–190.

Davies, S. (2002). Laissez-faire urban planning. In D. T. Beito, P. Gordon & A. Tabarrok (Eds.), *The voluntary city* (pp. 18–46). Ann Arbor, MI: University of Michigan Press.

De Han, J., & Sturm, J.-E. (2000). On the relationship between economic freedom and economic growth. *European Journal of Political Economy*, *16*, 215–241.

Demsetz, H. (1969). Information and efficiency: Another viewpoint. *Journal of Law and Economics*, *12*, 1–22.

Desrochers, P. (2001). Local diversity, human creativity, and technological innovation. *Growth and Change*, *32*(3), 369–394.

Duggan, W. R. (2010). Strategic intuition: East meets west in the executive mind. *Clarendon Global Insights*, (first quarter), 10–14.

Easterly, W. (2008). Institutions: Top down or bottom up? *American Economic Review*, *98*(2), 95–99.

Epstein, R. A. (2008). *Supreme neglect: How to revive constitutional protection for private property*. New York, NY: Oxford University Press.

Filion, P., & McSpurren, K. (2007). Smart growth and development reality: The difficult co-ordination of land use and transport objectives. *Urban Studies*, *44*(3), 501–523.

Fishman, R. (1994). *Urban utopias in the twentieth century: Ebenezer Howard, Frank Lloyd Wright, Le Corbusier*. Cambridge, MA: MIT Press.

Flyvbjerg, B., Holm, M. S., & Buhl, S. (2002). Underestimating costs in public works projects: Error or lie? *Journal of the American Planning Association*, *68*(3), 279–295.

Foldvary, F. E. (1994). *Public goods and private communities.* Northampton, MA: Edward Elgar.
Glaeser, E. L. (2011). *Triumph of the city: How our greatest innovation makes us richer, smarter, greener, healthier and happier.* New York, NY: The Penguin Press.
Glaeser, E. L., & Gyourko, J. (2003). The impact of building restrictions on housing affordability. *Federal Reserve Bank of New York Economic Policy Review*, *9*(2), 21–39.
Glaeser, E. L., & Ressenger, M. G. (2010). The complementarity between cities and skills. *Journal of Regional Science*, *50*(1), 221–244.
Gordon, P., & Ikeda, S. (2011). Does density matter? In D. E. Andersson, Å. E. Andersson & C. Mellander (Eds.), *Handbook of creative cities* (pp. 435–455). Cheltenham, UK: Edward Elgar.
Gordon, P., & Richardson, H. W. (2012). Urban structure and growth. In N. Brooks, K. Donaghy & G.-J. Knaap (Eds.), *The Oxford handbook of urban economics and planning* (pp. 98–122). New York, NY: Oxford University Press.
Gruen, C. (2010). *New urban development: Looking back to see forward.* New Brunswick, NJ: Rutgers University Press.
Hall, P. (1982). *Great planning disasters.* Berkeley, CA: University of California Press.
Harford, T. (2011). *Adapt: Why success always starts with failure.* New York, NY: Farrar, Straus, and Giroux.
Harris, B. (1971). Planning as a branch and bound process. *Proceedings of the Tenth European Congress of the Regional Science Association*, *26*, 53–63.
Harris, T. F., & Ionnides, Y. M. (2000). Productivity and metropolitan density. Working Paper. Available at http://ase.tufts.edu/econ/papers/200016.pdf
Hayek, F. A. (1945). The use of knowledge in society. *American Economic Review*, *35*(4), 519–530.
Hayek, F. A. (1988). *The fatal conceit: The errors of socialism.* Chicago, IL: University of Chicago Press.
Holcombe, R. G. (2004). The new urbanism and the market process. *Review of Austrian Economics*, *17*(2/3), 285–300.
Horwitz, S. (2001). From Smith to Menger to Hayek: Liberalism in the spontaneous-order tradition. *Independent Review*, *6*(1), 81–97.
Ihlanfeldt, K. R. (2007). The effect of land use regulation on housing and land prices. *Journal of Urban Economics*, *61*, 420–435.
Ikeda, S. (2004). Urban interventionism and local knowledge. *Review of Austrian Economics*, *17*(2/3), 247–264.
Jacobs, J. (1961). *The death and life of great American cities.* New York, NY: Random House.
Johnson, S. (2010). *Where good ideas come from: The natural history of innovation.* New York, NY: Riverhead Books.
Kohn, M. (2004). Value and exchange. *Cato Journal*, *24*(3), 303–339.
Kok, N., Monkkonen, P., & Quigley, J. M. (2010). *Economic geography, jobs, and regulations: The value of land and housing.* Program on Housing and Urban Policy Working Paper No. W10-005, University of California, Berkeley.
Kostof, S. (1991). *The city shaped: Urban patterns and meanings through history.* New York, NY: Bulfinch Press.
Krueger, A. O. (1974). The political economy of the rent-seeking society. *American Economic Review*, *64*(3), 291–303.

Krugman, P. R. (1991). Increasing returns and economic geography. *Journal of Political Economy*, *99*, 483–499.

Landis, J. (2009). *Ten planning successes*. Samuel Zell and Robert Lurie Real Estate Center at Wharton Research Paper No. 656.

Landsburg, S. (2007). A brief history of economic time. *The Wall Street Journal*, June 9, p. A8.

Lang, R. F. (2003). *Edgeless cities: Exploring the elusive metropolis*. Washington, DC: Brookings Institution Press.

Lee, B. (2006). *Urban spatial structure and commuting in U.S. metropolitan areas*. Paper presented at the 45th annual meeting of the Western Regional Science Association, Santa Fe, New Mexico.

Lomborg, B. (2001). *The skeptical environmentalist: Measuring the real state of the world*. Cambridge, UK: Cambridge University Press.

Malpezzi, S., Chun, G. H., & Green, R. K. (1998). New place-to-place housing price indexes for U.S. metropolitan areas, and their determinants. *Real Estate Economics*, *26*(2), 235–274.

McArdle, M. (2010). Serendipitous connections. *The Wall Street Journal*, Oct. 5, p. A21.

McChesney, F. S. (1997). *Money for nothing: Politicians, rent extraction and political extortion*. Cambridge, MA: Harvard University Press.

Nelson, R. H. (2005). *Private neighborhoods and the transformation of local government*. Washington, DC: Urban Institute Press.

Ostrom, E. (2010). Beyond markets and states: Polycentric governance of complex economic systems. *American Economic Review*, *100*(3), 641–672.

Pennington, M. (2002). *Liberating the land: The case for private land-use planning*. London, UK: Institute of Economic Affairs.

Pisarski, A. E. (2006). *Commuting in America III*. Washington, DC: Transportation Research Board.

Porter, D. R. (2008). Regional urban design: A form too far? *Urban Land*, *Nov./Dec.*, 42–48.

Postrel, V. (1998). *The future and its enemies*. New York, NY: The Free Press.

Rauch, J. E. (1993). Productivity gains from geographic concentration of human capital: Evidence from the cities. *Journal of Urban Economics*, *34*, 380–400.

Ridley, M. (2010). *The rational optimist: How prosperity evolves*. New York, NY: Harper.

Romer, P. M. (1994). Economic growth and investment in children. *Daedalus*, *123*(4), 141–154.

Romer, P. M. (2007). Economic growth. In D. M. Henderson (Ed.), *The concise encyclopedia of economics* (pp. 128–131). Indianapolis, IN: Library of American Liberty.

Rybczynski, W. (2007). *Last harvest*. New York, NY: Scribner.

Rybczynski, W. (2010). *Makeshift metropolis: Ideas about cities*. New York, NY: Scribner.

Schuetz, J. (2009). No renters in my suburban backyard: Land use regulation and rental housing. *Journal of Policy Analysis and Management*, *28*(2), 296–320.

Siegfried, J., & Zimbalist, A. (2000). The economics of sports facilities and their communities. *Journal of Economic Perspectives*, *14*(Summer), 95–114.

Storper, M., & Venables, A. J. (2004). Buzz: Face-to-face contact and the urban economy. *Journal of Urban Geography*, *4*(4), 351–370.

Tullock, G. (1965). *The politics of bureaucracy*. Washington, DC: Public Affairs Press.

Webster, C., & Lai, L. W.-C. (2003). *Property rights, planning and markets: Managing spontaneous cities*. Cheltenham, UK: Edward Elgar.

Wight, J. B. (2011). Public policy, human instincts, and economic growth. *Independent Review*, *15*(3), 351–365.

Winston, C. (2000). Government failure in urban transportation. *Fiscal Studies*, *21*(4), 403–425.

Winston, C. (2010). *Last exit: Privatization and deregulation of the U.S. transportation system.* Washington, DC: Brookings Institution Press.

World Bank. (2006). *Where is the wealth of nations? Measuring capital for the 21st century.* Washington, DC: World Bank.

Yandle, B. (1983). Bootleggers and Baptists: The education of a regulatory economist. *Regulation*, *7*(3), 12.

Zhu, P. (2012). Are telecommuting and personal travel complements or substitutes? *The Annals of Regional Science*, *48*(2), 619–639.

THE RISE AND FALL OF AGGLOMERATION ECONOMIES

Randall G. Holcombe

Agglomeration economies exist because there are economies of scale in economic activities that occur in close proximity to each other. Some economies of scale are static, in the sense that large-scale economic activity can have lower unit costs than smaller-scale activity. Some are dynamic, in the sense that they generate entrepreneurial innovation and increase economic progress. These dynamic economies of scale are produced by positive spillovers in the production and use of knowledge. The knowledge that drives economic progress is often tacit, and can only be conveyed when people sharing it are in close proximity to each other. One result of agglomeration economies is that some geographic locales exhibit more economic progress, and more prosperity, than others. Institutional differences across locales account for a substantial part of the differences in the creation of agglomeration economies, and as a result, prosperity, in different locations. Good institutions foster agglomeration economies and generate prosperity.

Because of the geographic nature of agglomeration economies, once they are established they are difficult to move, and governments can exploit the wealth created by agglomeration economies by taxing and regulating them. Over time the prosperity produced by the agglomeration economy will fade if institutions do not remain favorable, because economic progress will leave the old agglomeration economies behind, in favor of new ones. The rise and fall of agglomeration economies occur as good institutions foster the growth of agglomeration economies, after which government-imposed

The Spatial Market Process
Advances in Austrian Economics, Volume 16, 211–232

ISSN: 1529-2134/doi:10.1108/S1529-2134(2012)0000016011

changes in institutions to exploit the resulting prosperity lead to the fall of agglomeration economies as they are overtaken by agglomeration economies in other locations.

For hundreds of years before the Industrial Revolution began in Britain, China was more technologically advanced than Europe, but as Heilbroner (1962) notes, China's tradition-based economic institutions were not conducive to economic progress. While China enjoyed the benefits of static agglomeration economies, its institutions prevented those dynamic agglomeration economies that are generated by entrepreneurship and supported by the production of knowledge. The Industrial Revolution began in Britain, rather than in China or in other parts of Europe, because Britain had economic institutions conducive to the creation of dynamic agglomeration economies. As Mokyr (1990) and Landes (1998) note, institutions such as Britain's common law legal system and decentralized government that fostered Tiebout (1956) competition led to the innovation that started the Industrial Revolution.

Economic progress in Britain was concentrated in areas such as London and Manchester, where agglomeration economies allowed manufacturing to advance because of localized knowledge. In the twentieth century, institutional advantages shifted to the United States, which had lower tax and regulatory barriers to entrepreneurship than Europe. In the first part of the century, Detroit became the center of automobile manufacturing. It is no coincidence that the "big three" US auto manufacturers of Ford, General Motors, and Chrysler – and lesser manufacturers like Studebaker and Packard – were located in close proximity to each other. Because agglomeration economies are geographically based, once established they are subject to exploitation, and institutional changes eroded the advantages that Detroit had. Partly, this was due to tax and regulatory costs imposed on the industry by Michigan's government, and partly institutional changes were imposed by the United Auto Workers union, which had the support of the federal government.[1]

Detroit was never alone as the only area in which agglomeration economies existed in auto production. Advances were made in Britain, Germany, and other locations. As innovation in the automobile industry slowed in Detroit and that created an opening for Tokyo to emerge as a competing location that generated agglomeration economies in automobile manufacture. Meanwhile, new industries emerged as innovation leaders. The Silicon Valley region of California has been at the forefront of the computer revolution for half a century, with competing agglomeration economies in that industry in Austin and Boston. It appears that California's high tax and regulatory costs imposed on businesses there may lead Silicon Valley to a fate similar to Detroit.

The pattern is: favorable institutions lead to innovation and agglomeration economies. Governments impose tax and regulatory costs on innovators to appropriate some of the wealth generated by agglomeration economies. Old agglomeration economies lose their advantages and fall behind as new agglomeration economies take their place. Because of the nature of economic progress, successful agglomeration economies cannot remain successful by just continuing their old ways. Progress means that what is successful today will become increasingly obsolete in the future, so continued success can occur only with continued innovation to stay ahead of other innovators. Institutions need to foster innovation and entrepreneurship for agglomeration economies to endure, and too often, those with political power are able to impose costs on agglomeration economies for their short-term benefit. The long-term cost is that those agglomeration economies become increasingly less competitive, and are replaced by agglomeration economies elsewhere.

The success of agglomeration economies often means not just keeping the lead in a particular industry, but rather creating an environment such that as new industries emerge, they are able to thrive. Silicon Valley overtook Detroit not by producing better automobiles, but by laying the foundation for a new industry. In a world characterized by economic progress, maintaining the benefits of an agglomeration economy always means maintaining an environment within which knowledge is continually generated, and entrepreneurship is continually supported to apply that knowledge for productive purposes. This introductory discussion provides some background and context for discussing the rise and fall of agglomeration economies.

STATIC AND DYNAMIC AGGLOMERATION ECONOMIES

One aspect of agglomeration economies is economies of scale. When automobile production centered in Detroit in the early part of the twentieth century, this allowed more efficient production methods, which lowered the per-unit cost of output. Arrow (2000) emphasizes the tension between increasing returns to scale and equilibrium models, and as Young (1928) noted, increasing returns to scale is at the foundation of economic progress.

Kaldor (1972), building on Young's insights, noted that static neoclassical economic models did not do a good job of depicting the economic progress that results from increasing returns to scale in production. This insight goes at least as far back as Adam Smith (1776), however, who noted the increased productivity that comes with an increased division of labor. Smith's example of the pin factory, where individuals specializing in one small part of a larger manufacturing operation increase productivity by, perhaps, hundreds of times, shows the benefits of agglomeration economies. The division of labor is limited by the extent of the market, Smith argued, so enlarging the extent of the market allows for a greater division of labor, which increases productivity and generates prosperity. By concentrating automobile production in Detroit rather than having automobiles locally built, the extent of the market is increased from one locality to an entire nation, and in some cases an entire world. The resulting agglomeration economies increase productivity and produce prosperity.

These static factors that generate increasing returns are economically significant. As Marshall (1890) notes, a concentration of economic activity lowers transportation costs for intermediate goods and lowers labor market search costs. Ellison, Glaeser, and Kerr (2010) estimate that static factors like reduced transportation costs and labor market pooling account for the bulk of the benefits from concentrations of economic activity. But Ellison et al. (2010) also note the importance of intellectual spillovers, which are dynamic in nature.

Agglomeration economies generate increased economic progress, which is more than just a static increase in productivity. This dynamic increase in economic welfare perpetuates itself through time. This is the creative destruction described by Schumpeter (1934, 1954). Entrepreneurs try to gain a competitive advantage by introducing new and improved products, and by developing better and lower-cost methods of production. Because some entrepreneurs are innovating, all firms must continually update their production methods and product offerings, or they will fall behind those that do. Thus, in contrast to static equilibrium models, competitive markets are ever-changing, and as Holcombe (2009) notes, are characterized by product differentiation and innovation that are the primary drivers of economic progress. Firms have to continue to introduce innovations into their production methods and into the products they sell, or they will lose market share to innovators, until eventually the market for their output vanishes.

The neoclassical model of the competitive firm assumes that firms produce a homogeneous output through a given production technology, using given inputs. In the real world of economic competition, entrepreneurs realize that none of these are given. Firms can change their production technology, their product characteristics, and the types of inputs they use. A look at any intermediate microeconomics textbook reveals a non-sequitur in the explanation of profit maximization for competitive firms. A chapter on competitive firms concludes that in the long run the best a firm can do is to earn a normal rate of profit, which firms should be satisfied to get. This normal profit is the maximum profit a competitive firm can expect in the long run. Then, a few chapters later appears a chapter on monopoly that tells readers a monopoly can earn above-normal profit as long as the monopoly power is retained. Reading the two chapters together, the profit-maximizing strategy of a competitive firm is not to choose the optimal mix of inputs to minimize cost and receive a normal profit; it is to look for ways to gain some monopoly power to earn a higher profit.

In fact, this is how competitive firms in the real world – as opposed to the textbook world – actually behave. They look for ways to differentiate their products, for improved production methods, and for different mixes of inputs to lower costs and enhance productivity. This may mean looking for higher-quality inputs, such as hiring labor with more human capital. It may also mean looking for lower-quality inputs that can be bought at lower cost. For example, half a century ago cashiers keyed prices into cash registers, which would give the total amount due, and the cashier had to calculate the change. Today, cashiers scan prices into computerized cash registers, eliminating keying errors, and the cash register calculates the change due the customer, so the cashier does not have to. This reduces errors, but in addition means that cashiers require less human capital today than they did previously.

To remain competitive, firms must continually innovate, improving their production processes and improving their products, to keep up with a dynamic market in which their entrepreneurial competitors are continually improving. However, firms are already doing the best they can with the knowledge they have on hand. If entrepreneurs knew how to make a better product, they would already be doing it. If they knew how to produce more efficiently, at lower cost, they would already be doing it. How do they come up with the innovations that can help them keep up with an ever-improving marketplace? Partly, they can do this in-house, through their own formal or informal research and development efforts. Additional information can come from others in the same market who are innovating. They can watch the activities of their rivals, and they can get ideas from suppliers and customers. If a supplier of inputs has a better idea for the production of an input that may lead to an improvement in the firm's production process. Some of this information will be plainly visible in the marketplace, but some will be tacit knowledge, which is best gained by being in close proximity to those with the knowledge. The sharing of this tacit knowledge is one factor that leads to agglomeration economies.

TACIT KNOWLEDGE AND AGGLOMERATION ECONOMIES

In a market economy, firms must continually innovate to keep up with the economic progress that has characterized capitalism since its origin in the Industrial Revolution. If firms are already making best use of the knowledge they have to produce the best products at the lowest cost that they can, any improvement means coming up with new ideas. Kirzner (1973) characterizes entrepreneurship as the noticing of a previously unnoticed profit opportunity, but how does one spot something that has not been noticed by anyone previously? Some people are more observant and more insightful than others, but in almost all real-world cases the person who spots a profit opportunity will be someone who has specialized knowledge related to that profit opportunity. An auto mechanic is unlikely to spot an opportunity to introduce a profitable new drug into the market, and a pharmacist is unlikely to spot an opportunity to introduce a profitable refinement to an internal combustion engine.

Even what may appear in hindsight as obvious profit opportunities may not be easy to spot beforehand. Ray Kroc was a seller of restaurant equipment who was surprised by a large order for milkshake mixers from a small restaurant in San Bernadino, California, named McDonalds. Because of his experience in the restaurant industry, Kroc saw a profit opportunity that even the owners of the restaurant did not, bought the restaurant in 1954, and turned McDonalds into a world-wide chain. The restaurant was in plain sight of its customers, its other suppliers, and of course, its founders, but it was Kroc who was the entrepreneur who saw the extent of the profit opportunity it represented. Desrochers (2001) describes several other examples of such entrepreneurial insight, where a key element in the entrepreneurial action was some tacit knowledge produced by personal observation. One example Desrochers relates was a meeting Steve Wozniak, cofounder of Apple Computer, attended in which a color computer monitor was being demonstrated. Wozniak stated that if he had not seen the demonstration, the Apple II, Apple's first commercial product, would likely have had a monochrome monitor.

The Kroc and Wozniak cases have in common that both entrepreneurs had a specialized body of knowledge that enabled them to recognize an entrepreneurial opportunity that could be observed – but not recognized – by others. In both cases, it was first-hand observation that led the entrepreneurs to see the profit potential in the opportunity. Had Kroc been selling restaurant equipment on the east coast, he would not have observed the McDonalds restaurant, and would not have acted on the profit opportunity. Had Wozniak not observed first-hand the advantages of a color monitor, the Apple II likely would have been less successful with a monochrome monitor – and possibly would not have been profitable – partly because of the appeal color gave to computer games.

Much of the knowledge people have is tacit knowledge that, as Hayek explained, is specific knowledge of time and place that some people have, but that is difficult to articulate and pass along to others. Hayek (1945, pp. 521–522) notes that everyone has "knowledge of the particular circumstances of time and place... which use can be made only if the decisions depending on it are left to him or are made with his active cooperation." This tacit knowledge is knowledge that cannot be articulated, verbally or in writing, because otherwise, to use Hayek's description, it would not depend on the active cooperation of the person with the knowledge. If the knowledge were not tacit, the person with the knowledge could pass it on to others who could then act in place of the person with the knowledge.

Hayek's description of this knowledge also indicates how it can be acquired. Because it is knowledge of the particular circumstances of time and place, someone else who shares that time and place can absorb the knowledge by observing it in use. This explains the mechanism behind agglomeration economies. People in close proximity can absorb the knowledge of others by being in the same place at the same time, which is especially important when that knowledge is tacit – that is, not easily communicated by other means. What, exactly, constitutes the same time and place will vary depending on the knowledge. As Audretsch (1998, p. 21) notes, "knowledge is vague, difficult to codify, and often only serendipitously recognized. While the marginal cost of transmitting information has been rendered invariant by the telecommunications revolution, the marginal cost of transmitting knowledge, and especially tacit knowledge, rises with distance." In some cases that knowledge might be contained within a firm's boundaries, and not easily acquired by those outside the firm. In other cases, such as Silicon Valley for computers, New York for the financial industry, and Detroit for automobile production, the place is a larger geographic area. Firms in close proximity to each other can absorb some tacit knowledge held by others in their line of work, resulting in agglomeration economies.

People learn through experience, but like riding a bicycle or hitting a baseball, one cannot pass that knowledge to someone else without their also having the experience. Based on past experiences, businesspeople have ideas about how to best respond to the unique present situation, but those ideas come from a stock of past experiences that cannot be distilled into an instruction manual. Similarly, scientists and engineers build a stock of experience, enabling them to spot innovations that others cannot see, even though the reasoning behind the entrepreneurial insight cannot be clearly articulated. Being nearby, and able to see that knowledge being used, facilitates its transmission.

Small differences can make the difference between profits and losses, and nobody can know ahead of time whether an innovation will be profitable. The brief history of handheld computing devices is a case in point. Apple was an early innovator, having brought their handheld Newton, with handwriting recognition, to market in 1993, but it failed to be profitable. In 1996 US Robotics introduced the Palm-Pilot handheld computer, also with handwriting recognition, which was hugely successful and very profitable. In 2000 Palm was spun off into a separate company, which was bought by Hewlett Packard in 2010, because Palm's products were eclipsed by other innovators, including Apple with its iPod, iPad, and iPhone. Products by Google and Microsoft, among others, entered this competitive market in 2011. The products are similar, but the differences among them will determine which will be profitable.

Nobody can know ahead of time which products, and which features, will ultimately succeed on the market, because it depends on consumer demand for them, and this demand cannot be observed before the products are available for purchase. Steve Jobs, when asked whether Apple relied on consumer opinion to determine what products they would bring to market, said: "A lot of times, people don't know what they want until you show them."[2] Entrepreneurs must use their stock of specialized knowledge to make judgments about future conditions that have never been observed. Tacit knowledge plays a key role in keeping up with an ever-changing market. Were this not the case, experience would be worth no premium on the market, and boards of directors could hire recent college graduates with management degrees to run their firms, rather than pay substantial premiums to hire experienced people. This is true not only of the entrepreneurs who run the firms, but of every employee all the way down the line. One can marvel at the entrepreneurial insight of Ray Kroc, but anyone visiting a McDonalds can also see that experienced workers are more productive, faster, and more reliable than new hires. One can show a new hire what to do, but through experience they become more proficient because they acquire tacit knowledge that can only be gained by experience.

Adam Smith (1776, p. 9) made this same observation about entrepreneurs, noting, "[a] great part of the machines made use of in those manufactures in which labour is most subdivided, were originally the inventions of common workmen, who, being each of them employed in some very simple operation, naturally turned their thoughts towards finding out easier and readier methods of performing it." Echoing Smith's observation, Richard Florida (2005b, p. 194) writes that "Japanese manufacturing firms leaped ahead of ours with their 'creative factory' methods, which tap the intelligence of every worker on the factory floor to make continuous small improvements in the production process. U.S. firms – stuck in the Fordist system, whereby the engineers and top managers do all the thinking while the masses are paid to execute – nearly had their doors blown off. Many of our firms have now caught on to the new way." Tacit knowledge exists in every employee, and the challenge for the entrepreneur is to continue acquiring sufficient new knowledge to stay ahead of the continual economic progress of the firm's competition.

This is the dynamic aspect of agglomeration economies. Tacit knowledge exists within the firm, but it also exists in other firms within the market. Sometimes these other firms are direct competitors, sometimes they are suppliers, and sometimes they are customers. By locating in an area where other similar economic activities are taking place, entrepreneurs are more likely to be in a position to observe and take advantage of the tacit knowledge of others. One reason is that there will be a pool of knowledgeable employees in the local job market, an idea that goes back at least as far as Marshall (1890). The job market in the Silicon Valley has many people who have experience, and tacit knowledge, in the computer industry, and the job market in Detroit (still) has people who are experienced auto workers. Entrepreneurs can observe first-hand what their competitors, suppliers, and customers are doing in the local market; they can talk informally with others in the same industry; they are in a good position to hire people who have experience and tacit knowledge in the industry, and for all these reasons firms can be more successful when they locate in close proximity to others who are engaging in the same type of activity. That attraction creates agglomeration economies.

CREATING AN ENVIRONMENT FOR AGGLOMERATION ECONOMIES

Because of the obvious advantages of agglomeration economies, policy makers try to foster them. They have offered tax incentives, development grants, low-cost sites, industrial parks, and many other incentives to try to lure economic activity to their areas. What policies actually work in laying a foundation for agglomeration economies?

A recent literature initiated by Florida (2002) emphasizes the role of creative individuals in laying the foundation for economic prosperity – both their own prosperity and the prosperity of the areas in which they live. Florida defines the creative class in economic terms, as Holcombe (2011) discusses, identifying them as people who earn their incomes through creative work. Florida (2005a, pp. 3–4, emphasis in original) observes that "the single most overlooked – and single most important – element of my theory is that *every human being is creative. …* Tapping and stoking the creative furnace inside every human being is the great challenge of our time."

Florida's idea complements Hayek's insight about individuals having specific knowledge of time and place. All individuals have that knowledge, following Hayek, and Florida's "challenge" is getting them to make best use of it. Hayek championed the market allocation of resources as a way of coordinating that knowledge of time and place, whereas Florida emphasizes an environment that attracts creativity, laying the foundation for agglomeration economies.

Florida emphasizes amenities that attract creative individuals, such as restaurants, museums, an active nightlife, and other cultural attractions. But amenities like this will be produced in places where there is a demand for them, by creative entrepreneurs who see them as profit opportunities. Despite the appeal of such amenities, policies will meet with more success when they are oriented toward attracting the creative population who will demand those amenities, rather than pursuing the idea that subsidizing such amenities will attract the creative class and lay the foundation for agglomeration economies. Florida's emphasis on creativity hits the mark, however, because entrepreneurship is the fundamental creative economic activity, and because the knowledge that lays the foundation for entrepreneurial activity is a product of creative work.

If Florida is correct that everyone is creative, then fostering agglomeration economies is a matter of enticing individuals to use their creativity in economically productive ways. While everyone has creative impulses, entrepreneurial innovation is necessarily characterized by uncertainty.

Because entrepreneurial activity means doing something differently from the way it has been done before, there is no way to know whether an attempt at entrepreneurship will succeed. Past experience can be a guide, if the entrepreneur has observed similar innovations in the past, but it cannot provide direct evidence on something that has never occurred before.

When Henry Ford decided to manufacture automobiles on an assembly line, he could observe other goods being manufactured on assembly lines, but could only conjecture on how well assembly line production would work for automobiles. Similarly, Ford's idea that he could produce automobiles at lower prices and attract a larger number of buyers was also a conjecture. He could not observe the actual elasticity of demand for automobiles at the price he planned to sell them, because they never had been sold that cheaply, so any conjecture was an extrapolation beyond actual experience and real-world observation.

As this is being written in 2011, Boeing's 787 Dreamliner composite body aircraft – an innovative design change from the aluminum body airliners that preceded it – is more than two years behind schedule. Smaller composite body aircraft had been produced before, and Boeing has extensive experience in aircraft design and manufacture, but it is apparent that they could not foresee the manufacturing problems they would face in this project. Such uncertainty is necessarily a feature of entrepreneurship, because entrepreneurial activity means doing something that has not previously been done.

The primary issue in creating an environment for agglomeration economies is creating an environment in which people are willing to take the risks involved in being entrepreneurial. People will be more entrepreneurial when they are able to reap the benefits of their creative activity. Cultivating the creative class means creating an environment where creative people keep the profits from their entrepreneurial actions, and also one in which they bear the losses from entrepreneurial attempts that are unsuccessful.

Subsidizing a firm to build a facility in a particular area, through tax breaks or providing a site at an attractive price, provides an incentive to build the facility, but will not necessarily produce a facility that is worth more than it costs, nor will it necessarily bring with it the entrepreneurship and innovation that lays the foundation for agglomeration economies. Governmental economic development organizations rarely make the distinction between facilities that provide jobs to an area and facilities that engage in entrepreneurial activity. Government-provided economic incentives may be sufficient to bring a manufacturing facility to an area, for example, that provides manufacturing jobs, while the innovative and entrepreneurial functions of the company remain elsewhere. The facility will provide employment to some, but will not bring in the kind of creative work that produces knowledge spillovers that foster agglomeration economies.[3]

If the entrepreneur takes all the risks in the entrepreneurial activity, then the individual who has the information behind the innovation has the incentive to see that the benefits are worth the costs. Needless to say, because of uncertainty entrepreneurs are often wrong, but that does not detract from the necessity of providing the appropriate incentives. Entrepreneurial individuals will tend to move to locations where they can reap the rewards of the entrepreneurial risks they take, and all individuals in an area have an incentive to be more entrepreneurial when the institutions in that area place few barriers in the way of acting entrepreneurially, and enable them to keep the profits from successful ventures they undertake.

Consider the examples from the introductory section of this chapter, from the beginning of the Industrial Revolution in Britain to the rise and fall of the automobile industry in Detroit, to the rise of the electronics industry in California's Silicon Valley. Those agglomeration economies were not created by government policies underwriting them, but rather by government remaining out of the way and not impeding the entrepreneurs who were generating economic progress. One can point to some apparent successes of government-directed entrepreneurial efforts, such as the industrial policies pursued by Japan and South Korea in the second half of the twentieth century. To analyze them in detail would digress from this chapter's subject, but note that the Japanese industrial policy that appeared so successful from the 1950s to the 1980s led to what has been referred to as Japan's lost decade of the 1990s. One might question whether South Korea, which began its industrialization in the 1970s, is following Japan's path toward stagnation and slower growth.[4] Examples like this notwithstanding, the often-celebrated agglomeration economies of Silicon Valley, Austin, and Boston occurred independently of government intervention, and without their governments anticipating those outcomes.[5]

WHAT INSTITUTIONS FOSTER AGGLOMERATION ECONOMIES?

The short answer to the question that heads this section is: Capitalist institutions. Mokyr (1990) and Landes (1998) have given detailed historical analyses of the successes of capitalism, and have argued that places that have adopted capitalist institutions have become wealthy, while those that have not have remained poor. What, exactly, are these capitalist institutions? One answer has been given by Gwartney and Lawson (2005), who have summarized those institutions as low taxes, government expenditures, and transfers; rule of law and protection of property rights; stable money; freedom to trade internationally; and low regulatory barriers to engaging in voluntary exchange. Gwartney and Lawson have been putting together an economic freedom index based on these factors for more than a decade now, allowing researchers to empirically measure the benefits of capitalist institutions, as they define them. There is little reason to go into detail to explain that index here, because there is a substantial literature that uses the index, and that has shown that economic freedom, as Gwartney and Lawson define it, produces higher incomes, higher economic growth, and a substantial list of other good outcomes, including better health, longer life expectancy, and greater income equality. Berggren (2003) wrote a survey of studies using the index, which is now a few years old, but that shows the advantages of institutions of economic freedom.

The specific institutional structure that lays the foundation for agglomeration economies is an important issue, but because it has been addressed elsewhere this section simply notes that agglomeration economies that generate economic progress occur where there are minimal tax and regulatory barriers to economic exchange, and where property rights are protected.

From a policy perspective, agglomeration economies are important because they imply that even when public policies are homogeneous across jurisdictions, economic activity, innovation, and entrepreneurship will not be uniformly distributed in space. Agglomeration economies imply that creative people benefit from clustering together, so two cities might be identical from the public policy standpoint and yet one is able to attract entrepreneurs and innovative activity while the other sees an out migration of creative individuals. Why? Because creative people want benefit from agglomeration economies, so cities with clusters of entrepreneurial activity start with an advantage in attracting more entrepreneurs. One cannot hope to replicate Boston, or Silicon Valley, by imitating the public policies of those areas. Agglomeration economies must begin with a nucleus of creative activity in place for those agglomeration economies to be cultivated. But, everybody has the potential to be entrepreneurial, so the cultivation of entrepreneurship starts by reinforcing the entrepreneurial impulses of an area's existing population. Agglomeration economies then build by making it easy and attractive for other entrepreneurial individuals to migrate in.

AGGLOMERATION ECONOMIES ARE A SPONTANEOUS ORDER

When considering policies that foster agglomeration economies, it is important to recognize that agglomeration economies are the product of a spontaneous order. The benefits of agglomeration economies exist precisely because they cannot be foreseen. People cluster together because of the advantages of sharing tacit knowledge, and that sharing leads to the innovation that produces economic progress.[6] Because that knowledge is decentralized, as Hayek (1945) emphasized, no one individual can foresee the direction that the aggregated knowledge will lead. Entrepreneurs must always be alert to new ideas, to remain on the forefront of an ever-evolving economy. As Joseph Schumpeter (1954, p. 82) said; "[t]he essential point to grasp is that in dealing with capitalism we are dealing with an evolutionary process. ... Capitalism, then, is by nature a form or method of economic change and not only never is but never can be stationary." In a market economy, success can never mean finding a successful formula and sticking with it. Entrepreneurs always need to be picking up new ideas and moving forward, and locating in the midst of other innovators gives them the best chance of remaining profitable in a continually evolving economy.

Because agglomeration economies produce a spontaneous order, fostering agglomeration economies means creating conditions that make it inexpensive and easy for people to act on their creative impulses. Creativity, by its very definition, provides unexpected results. Economic planning, in the sense of planning for a particular outcome, is an impediment to cultivating creativity. Yet despite this recognition, government planning with the hope of fostering economic prosperity is common at all levels of government. At the local level, many cities offer tax breaks, industrial development grants, and other enticements to attract specific businesses to their area. At the national level economic planning goes by the name of industrial policy. In these examples of planning, government picked and supported particular firms, giving them economic assistance with the goal of making them competitive in world markets.

The spontaneous order of the market often produces unexpected outcomes. Who would have foreseen, in the 1960s and 1970s when IBM dominated the computer market, that Microsoft, founded in 1975, would be the dominant firm in that market 20 years after its founding? If US industrial policy had supported IBM in the 1960s and 1970s the way Japan supported Sony and Korea supported Samsung, the advantages given to the dominant firm might have snuffed out emerging competitors like Microsoft and Apple. Similarly, because of Japanese and Korean industrial policy, the world economy may never see entrepreneurial firms like Microsoft and Apple emerge in Japan or Korea. The dominant firms have too many government-supported advantages over entrepreneurial start-ups. This example is, along the lines of Bastiat (1995), unseen. People can see the successes of IBM, Sony, and Samsung. They will never miss – because they cannot see – the entrepreneurial start-ups that would have been created in Japan and Korea had they not been inhibited by those countries' industrial policies. Because agglomeration economies produce unforeseen results, due to their combining of the tacit knowledge of a large number of individuals, planning stifles rather than cultivates creativity. The spontaneous order of the market cultivates creativity.

The challenge any economy faces, whether we are talking about a city or a nation or the global economy, is coordinating the economic activities of all its participants. As Hayek (1945) notes, everybody has some specific knowledge that others not only do not know, but cannot know without sharing their specific time and place. People have tacit knowledge that allows them to know how to accomplish particular tasks, even though they may not be able to articulate that knowledge to pass it on to others. A market economy makes best use of that knowledge and coordinates the activities of everyone, for the benefit of everyone.

Cities are concentrations of knowledge. Because much knowledge is tacit, being in close proximity with those who have complementary tacit knowledge can enable people to observe and learn from them. For some knowledge, being in the same city means being in the same place, as Hayek (1945) uses the term. The concentration of tacit knowledge that gives rise to agglomeration economies facilitates the best use of that knowledge. Individuals are more likely to find their best employment match when that match is in the same city because, first, it is easier to change jobs, and second, it is more likely that information about the job match will be available because of the proximity. This creates agglomeration economies, making those locations more attractive for others with complementary tacit knowledge. Agglomeration economies give cities an advantage in maintaining their creative edge. This makes it difficult for other cities to join their ranks, but also creates localized rents that can be exploited by governments. These locational rents give rise to predatory government, which over time erodes the advantages that support agglomeration economies.

People tend to take a short-sighted view of the factors that produce prosperity. Agglomeration economies give creative cities such as New York and San Francisco an edge, but not necessarily a permanent one. Fifty years ago Detroit was prosperous as a result of the agglomeration economies produced by the automobile industry, and it would have taken quite a visionary to foresee not only the rise of agglomeration economies in other cities as Detroit fell, but also to foresee the computer industry overtaking the auto industry as the anchor of many new agglomeration economies. The best way to be a part of the next wave of agglomeration economies is to provide an environment conducive to entrepreneurial activity, and reap the rewards that will be the result of an unplanned order. Cities can create an environment that will cultivate entrepreneurship, but they cannot plan an outcome that is of necessity the result of bottom-up individual activity.

AGGLOMERATION ECONOMIES ARE DIFFICULT TO RELOCATE

Agglomeration economies create concentrations of wealth that are geographically bound. One company could choose to leave Silicon Valley, but it could not take the advantages of the agglomeration economies with it, and the entire Silicon Valley could not migrate to another more entrepreneur-friendly location. Partly, this is due to the physical infrastructure that is tied to the agglomeration economies. Indeed, some physical attributes are a part of the geography rather than the built environment. One cannot move a harbor or a navigable river, for example. Once constructed, moving a factory is also difficult. The owners cannot simply let the factory wear out, because physical capital must be continually upgraded to remain competitive. If the firm is expanding, it could choose to locate a new facility in a different location, but doing so might give up some advantages of the agglomeration economies in the old location. There are, however, advantages to having facilities in different locations – reducing shipping costs to geographically dispersed customers, for example – which could lay the foundation for a move from an overly taxed and regulated jurisdiction to a less-restrictive environment.

Some businesses will be more mobile than others. A firm involved in heavy manufacturing will have firm-specific and difficult-to-move capital, whereas a service-oriented firm may be able to rent office space and move at low cost when its lease is up. A move to a different geographic area will be complicated by the fact that all the firm's employees may not want to move, for family reasons or other reasons of geographic preference. Furthermore, moving away from the agglomeration economy severs those benefits, so any institutional costs – the taxes, regulation, and other institutional impediments – in that location must be weighed against the benefits of remaining to take advantage of the agglomeration economies. Residents of New York are heavily taxed, for example, but those in the financial industry stay, even though they could easily move when their leases are up, because of the advantages of being in close proximity to the rest of the industry.

Reductions in transportation and communication costs, and the growth in the production of services relative to manufacturing, will make it easier for agglomeration economies to relocate. Of course, an entire local economy is not going to pick up and move. In addition to the reasons given above, relocation is a bottom-up individual decision, not a top-down decision. But as new agglomeration economies develop, firms will find it feasible to relocate some of their operations from old ones. Financial firms operating on a global scale can locate in New York or London, but can shift more of their operations from one city to another in response to institutional changes, for example. Thus, Charlotte is becoming a financial center. As China develops, Shanghai has the potential to compete with Hong Kong as a financial center, so agglomeration economies can migrate, although slowly.

THE FALL OF AGGLOMERATION ECONOMIES

Agglomeration economies have sufficient geographic roots that they cannot just pick up and move. This geographic immobility gives governments the power to extract some of the economic benefits of the agglomeration economies in the form of taxes and regulatory burdens. People can obtain income in two ways: they can engage in productive activity to generate income for themselves, or they can plunder income and wealth from those who have produced it. Government receives its revenue through taxation: that is, by using its coercive power to require that those who have resources tender some of those resources to the government. This creates the institutional structure for entrepreneurial individuals to use the force of government to obtain transfers for their benefit. As Baumol (1990; 1993) notes, if the institutional structure prevents some individuals from using force to plunder others, entrepreneurs have an incentive to engage in productive activity, and to keep the profits from their productivity. If the institutional structure provides mechanisms whereby some people can engage in plunder and transfer wealth from productive individuals to themselves, then entrepreneurial people will engage in destructive entrepreneurship. They will find it more privately profitable to work to obtain political power and favoritism in the legal system, to claim a share of what other people produce, rather than be producers and see their production taken from them.

Capitalist institutions limit the ability of people to engage in destructive entrepreneurship, but over time, if production is tied to a given geographic location, that provides the incentive for those with political power in those locations to turn that power to their advantage by using it to command the resources of productive individuals. Those with political power can use it to enrich themselves directly, by taking a share, and indirectly, by using the proceeds to buy the political support of others. Olson (1982) describes a process whereby, as political systems mature, interest groups gain increasing power, and are able to increasingly use that power to direct the force of government to provide themselves with benefits. Thus, the wealth of income-generating agglomeration economies increasingly is transferred away from productive individuals toward those with political power. Agglomeration economies generate locational rents, and those rents can be taxed away.

In autocratic governments the plundering class is limited to the rulers and those who keep them in power, such as the military, the police, and the judges. As Bueno de Mesquita, Smith, Siverson, and Morrow (2003) and Niskanen (2003) note, in democracies the group that needs to be supported to maintain power is larger, because democratic leaders need to maintain a majority to retain their power. The productivity of the agglomeration economy provides the resources those with political power can target to provide benefits to themselves and those whose support allows them to maintain their power. Thus, the above-normal returns that are produced by the entrepreneurs in the agglomeration economy are taxed and regulated so that all of the advantages of their entrepreneurship can be taxed away.

Because of its ties to a specific geographic location, the creative class in the agglomeration economy cannot just move away. However, because of the creative destruction that accompanies economic progress, the economic benefits that accrue to a particular set of activities will decline over time. Unless that entrepreneurial energy continues to produce innovations, the productivity of the agglomeration economy will decline until it is overtaken by agglomeration economies in other jurisdictions. Agglomeration economies do not just get up and move. Rather, their decline tends to come from two different sources. First, as noted in the previous section, multiple agglomeration economies often exist in the same industry. If one location loses some of its advantages relative to another, firms in that industry can expand in the more advantageous location, and eventually the center of innovation will move from its previous location to a new one. Second, as industries mature, advances become rarer, and it becomes easier for firms away from the center of activity to match the productivity of those in an overly taxed agglomeration economy.

In the early twentieth century, when there was rapid innovation in the automobile industry, geographical proximity to other producers made a bigger difference. Meanwhile, as that industry matured, new industries became more innovative. In part, automobile manufacturing moved and became more dispersed, but in part the electronics industry rose as the leader in innovation. Silicon Valley replaced Detroit as the center of innovation not because it stole Detroit's industry, but because it created a new, more innovative, industry that could hardly have been imagined when Detroit was an industrial leader. This process continues to be repeated, as formerly high-tech industries lose that status through the spread of technology. The Industrial Revolution began in Britain largely as a result of the development of the textile industry, which migrated into, and then out of, the United States, and now primarily is in the Asia-Pacific.

As another example, Los Angeles was once a manufacturing center, and home to many automobile manufacturing plants. California saw its last large-scale automobile manufacturing facility close in 2009, and as of 2011 California has no major automobile manufacturing facilities. High taxes, burdensome regulations, and a unionized workforce imposed sufficient institutional costs to cause a substantial industry, with its associated agglomeration economies, to relocate.

Because they are geographically bound, agglomeration economies provide a target for political entrepreneurs, who can use the power of government to transfer income and wealth from productive individuals to themselves and their political supporters. Institutions change and the conditions of economic freedom that provided the environment within which the agglomeration economy was born and began to thrive give way to higher tax and regulatory burdens, which push entrepreneurs to other less burdensome locations. The agglomeration economy cannot pick up and move, but as economic progress marches on the agglomeration economy becomes increasingly less productive and entrepreneurial. Meanwhile, other agglomeration economies rise where institutional conditions are more favorable.

CONCLUSION

Agglomeration economies are spontaneous orders that are produced by the sharing of the tacit knowledge of creative and entrepreneurial individuals who are in close proximity to one another, sharing the same "time and space," to use Hayek's terminology. Other factors contribute to agglomeration economies, to be sure. Geographic factors, such as natural harbors, and being in close proximity to major markets and to suppliers, can be significant, but these were not the factors that made Manchester a major textile manufacturing center around 1800, or that made Detroit a major automobile manufacturing center in the mid-twentieth century, or that made California's Silicon Valley the nucleus of the computer industry's development in the second half of the twentieth century. In all those cases, agglomeration economies occurred because those locations had institutions that were supportive of markets and capitalism, that imposed low tax and regulatory burdens on economic activity, and that allowed entrepreneurs to reap the benefits of their productive activities. The tacit knowledge produced by innovative individuals was more easily transferred to those in close geographic proximity, giving everyone in that area an advantage over people in other areas. Imitators could not hope to keep up – except in other areas that also had concentrations of those activities that produced their own agglomeration economies.

Agglomeration economies produce advantages to those in a specific geographic area, and those advantages are tied to the area. In the short run, agglomeration economies are not mobile, and that creates an opportunity for those who wield political power in that area to use that power to transfer income and wealth from productive individuals to themselves, as well as to those whose support those with political power rely on to maintain their power. Over time, the advantages that were going to entrepreneurs as a result of their innovative activity become increasingly captured by the political class, reducing the advantages of innovation and entrepreneurship. As economic progress renders the past innovations of the agglomeration economy increasingly obsolete, the productivity of the agglomeration economy fades as other locations with institutions more favorable to innovation overtake the fading agglomeration economies of the past. Thus, goes the rise and fall of agglomeration economies.

NOTES

1. See Holcombe and Gwartney (2010) for a discussion of the United Auto Workers in this context, and also the impact of government-mandated union costs on the decline of other unionized industries in the United States and around the world.

2. Jobs said this in a *Business Week* interview in 1998. This sounds a lot like Galbraith's (1958) dependence effect in *The Affluent Society*.

3. The division here may not be as clear-cut as this paragraph makes things sound. For example, if factory workers are encouraged to use their on-the-job knowledge to suggest improvements in the processes at the facility, they could play a role in fostering innovation. Furthermore, having skilled workers of any type in an area means other firms looking for the same skill set can move into the area and have a pool of potential employees. And, the management in any facility will have to be engaged in some independent and creative decision making, no matter how centralized the firm's overall management structure.

4. Holcombe (forthcoming) analyzes the South Korean case in more detail and concludes that South Korean industrial policy (like the similar Japanese policy) is not a model for sustainable economic growth.

5. One can point to the concentration of universities in Boston as a causal factor, and the government in North Carolina has tried to replicate that with some success in their Research Triangle. Silicon Valley has a similar concentration of universities, and the University of Texas in Austin has undoubtedly contributed to Austin's success. These observations strongly suggest the advantages of concentrations of human capital, which makes sense when one considers agglomeration economies as taking advantage of knowledge spillovers. However, many centers of higher education have not produced similar results.

6. This also implies that agglomeration economies may exist anywhere where there is a concentration of population for any reason, so as Harris and Todaro (1970) show, agglomeration economies can persist in areas with poor institutions.

REFERENCES

Arrow, K. J. (2000). Increasing returns: Historiographic issues and path dependence. *European Journal of the History of Economic Thought*, *7*(2), 171–180.

Audretsch, D. B. (1998). Agglomeration economies and the location of innovative activity. *Oxford Review of Economic Policy*, *14*(2), 18–29.

Bastiat, F. (1995). What is seen and what is not seen. In G. B. de Huszar (Ed.), *Selected essays on political economy* (Chapter 1). Irving-on-Hudson, NY: Foundation for Economic Education.

Baumol, W. J. (1990). Entrepreneurship: Productive, unproductive, and destructive. *Journal of Political Economy*, *98*(5:1), 893–921.

Baumol, W. J. (1993). *Entrepreneurship, management, and the structure of payoffs*. Cambridge, MA: MIT Press.

Berggren, N. (2003). The benefits of economic freedom: A survey. *Independent Review*, *8*(2), 193–211.

Bueno de Mesquita, B., Smith, A., Siverson, R. M., & Morrow, J. D. (2003). *The logic of political survival*. Cambridge, MA: MIT Press.

Desrochers, P. (2001). Geographical proximity and the transmission of tacit knowledge. *Review of Austrian Economics*, *14*(1), 25–46.

Ellison, G., Glaeser, E. L., & Kerr, W. R. (2010). What causes industry agglomeration? Evidence from coagglomeration patterns. *American Economic Review*, *100*(3), 1195–1213.

Florida, R. (2002). *The rise of the creative class: And how it's transforming work, leisure, community, & everyday life*. New York, NY: Basic Books.

Florida, R. (2005a). *Cities and the creative class*. New York, NY: Routledge.

Florida, R. (2005b). *The flight of the creative class*. New York, NY: HarperCollins.

Galbraith, J. K. (1958). *The affluent society*. New York, NY: Houghton Mifflin.

Gwartney, J., & Lawson, R. (2005). *The economic freedom of the world: 2005 Annual Report*. Vancouver, BC: Fraser Institute.

Harris, J. R., & Todaro, M. P. (1970). Migration, unemployment, and development: A two-sector analysis. *American Economic Review*, *60*(1), 126–142.

Hayek, F. A. (1945). The use of knowledge in society. *American Economic Review*, *35*(4), 519–530.

Heilbroner, R. L. (1962). *The making of economic society*. Englewood Cliffs, NJ: Prentice-Hall.

Holcombe, R. G. (2009). Product differentiation and economic progress. *Quarterly Journal of Austrian Economics*, *12*(1), 17–35.

Holcombe, R. G. (2011). Cultivating creativity: Market creation of agglomeration economies. In D. E. Andersson, Å. E. Andersson & C. Mellander (Eds.), *Handbook of creative cities*. Cheltenham, UK: Edward Elgar.

Holcombe, R. G. (forthcoming). South Korea's economic future: Industrial policy, or economic democracy? *Journal of Economic Behavior & Organization*.

Holcombe, R. G., & Gwartney, J. D. (2010). Unions, economic freedom, and growth. *Cato Journal*, *30*(1), 1–22.

Kaldor, N. (1972). The irrelevance of equilibrium economics. *Economic Journal*, *82*, 1237–1255.

Kirzner, I. M. (1973). *Competition and entrepreneurship*. Chicago, IL: University of Chicago Press.

Landes, D. S. (1998). *The wealth and poverty of nations: Why some are so rich, and some so poor*. New York, NY: W.W. Norton.

Marshall, A. (1890). *Principles of economics*. London, UK: Macmillan.

Mokyr, J. (1990). *The lever of riches*. Oxford, UK: Oxford University Press.

Niskanen, W. A. (2003). *Autocratic, democratic, and optimal government*. Cheltenham, UK: Edward Elgar.

Olson, M. (1982). *The rise and decline of nations*. New Haven, CT: Yale University Press.

Schumpeter, J. A. (1934). *The theory of economic development*. Cambridge, MA: Harvard University Press.

Schumpeter, J. A. (1954). *Capitalism, socialism, and democracy* (4th ed). London, UK: George Allen & Unwin.

Smith, A. (1776/1937). *The wealth of nations*. New York, NY: Modern Library.

Tiebout, C. M. (1956). A pure theory of local expenditures. *Journal of Political Economy*, *64*(October), 416–424.

Young, A. (1928). Increasing returns and economic progress. *Economic Journal*, *38*(December), 527–542.

INSTITUTIONS, AGGLOMERATION ECONOMIES, AND INTERSTATE MIGRATION☆

David Emanuel Andersson and James A. Taylor

One of the seminal contributions of Friedrich Hayek was his explication of the role and nature of spontaneous orders (Hayek, 1973). The term *spontaneous order* refers to social structures that have emerged through human interaction but that have not been designed by anyone in particular. Such orders do not have any overarching objective. Instead, they coordinate the actions of individuals acting alone or on behalf of organizations, some of whom may have contradictory goals.

Central to the operation of a spontaneous order is the existence of a *systemic resource*, which informs order participants about their success in using the order for their own purposes. Success is order-specific, and corresponds to systemic resource accumulation. Such accumulation also functions as a signaling device, in that it enables other order participants to imitate successful strategies while pursuing their individual goals.

The market order or *catallaxy* is the spontaneous order to which Hayek devoted most of his writings. The rules of market participation are the rights and obligations associated with the protection and exchange of property

☆The views expressed by James A. Taylor in this chapter do not necessarily represent those of Jones Lang LaSalle.

The Spatial Market Process
Advances in Austrian Economics, Volume 16, 233–263

ISSN: 1529-2134/doi:10.1108/S1529-2134(2012)0000016012

rights. The systemic resource of markets is money, which not only enables market participants to imitate successful accumulators of wealth but also disseminates exchange ratios (market prices) that reflect relative resource scarcities within interconnected but anonymous networks of widely dispersed traders (Hayek, 1945).

DIFFERENT SPONTANEOUS ORDERS

The market is not the only spontaneous order. Hayek himself drew attention to language and English common law as other examples, noting that they had first been identified as such by Scottish Enlightenment philosophers such as Adam Smith and Adam Ferguson. Hence, such orders "are made with equal blindness to the future; and nations stumble upon establishments, which are indeed the results of human action, but not the execution of any human design" (Ferguson, 1782, sec. II). In the 20th century, Michael Polanyi used the term spontaneous order for the polycentric feedback system that explains the growth of scientific knowledge (Polanyi, 1962).

Gus diZerega (1989) contends that liberal democracy is yet another spontaneous order. According to this view, democracy is not about achieving predetermined joint goals. It should instead be construed as a rule-governed method for reconciling conflicts regarding the funding and organization of various jointly consumed goods. Liberal democracies have orderly and predictable features, despite disagreements about the legitimate role of government in society. They resemble markets in that it is equally difficult to predict the long-run quantitative outcomes that result from the interaction of order participants under the guidance of order-specific rules. Moreover, the "producers" of public policies gauge their performance by assessing election results in a way that brings to mind the way profit-seeking firms assess their performance with the help of revenue and cost flows.

But a democracy is not a market. There are certain systemic problems that exist in democracies that have no real counterpart in the operation of markets. These problems can be divided into two classes. The first class consists of problems that are the direct result of the *incentives* that reflect the rules of the democratic game. The second class are incentive-independent and arise from the *knowledge* deficiencies that are inevitable in an order where preferences are signaled as one discrete choice per voter and where the aggregate outcome is a single bundle of public policies.

Incentive problems are central to public-choice theories of the political process. Such theories conclude that the incentives that rational voters face make them rationally ignorant. This is because the expected pay-off from being well-informed about political options is approximately equal to zero, since it is extremely unlikely that a single vote will sway the outcome of an election. The key actors are instead small and well-organized rent-seeking coalitions that offer politicians financial and other support in exchange for policies that cater to their interests.

The combination of ignorant individuals and selectively informed interest groups yields a set of policies with concentrated benefits and dispersed costs as the most likely outcome (Olson, 1965). In the aggregate, the bundle of policies that benefit various small and well-organized groups may become quite costly. The totality of policies may even constitute a net loss to those groups that disproportionately benefit from one or more specific public policies. Mancur Olson (1982) claims that stable and durable democracies can be expected to produce an ever-increasing number of successful "distributional coalitions," with general economic decline as its long-run consequence.

Knowledge problems are not incentive problems. They remain in force even if politicians endeavor to act in the common interest and voters consider it a civic duty to be well-informed about the political programs of various candidates and political parties. The first knowledge problem – as compared with markets – derives from the indivisibility of the systemic resource and its resulting inadequacy as a signaling device of consumer preferences. Mild and strong preferences for a political program result in the same vote intensity, namely, one vote.

The second knowledge problem occurs when preferences are aggregated. Consider the case where a democratically elected government funds schools and designs their curriculum. Even in the unlikely case where education expenditures and curriculum priorities correspond to the preferences of the average voter, there will be a homogenization of consumption that will deviate from disaggregated individual preferences in the likely case where different people want different types and amounts of schooling. Giving markets a greater role in state-funded education – as in the case of school vouchers or local control of school curricula – increases the qualitative responsiveness to individual preferences but does not address the quantitative aggregation problem concerning the amount of money to be spent.

The only redeeming feature of democracies – in the sense that democratic choices may convey more dispersed knowledge than market choices – occurs when local knowledge and material resources are distributed among individuals in very different ways (Andersson, 2008). In that case, much of the local individual knowledge that may be useful to others cannot be conveyed through market price signals because the individuals in question do not have access to sufficient capital. But this regrettable feature of markets is only likely to be a serious problem when ownership of land and capital is concentrated in the hands of a small minority and reflect predation and luck rather than skill, diligence, and foresight (see De Soto, 2000, for a related discussion).

The incentive and knowledge problems of liberal democracy would seem to cause a rather dismal forecast about the performance of any real-world democracy. But the overall performance of the mature democracies is not quite as cataclysmic as these systemic problems suggest. The discrepancy between the omnipresent rent-seeking and ignorance that is suggested by the intrinsic features of democracy and the performance of real-world democracies arises both from the simultaneous presence of several democracies and the permeability of their borders. Interest groups seek to influence politicians and individuals vote, but those are not the only signals that influence political decisions. There is also the *exit option*, which implies that there are two democratic spontaneous orders.

The second spontaneous order is *polycentric democracy*,[1] in which individuals signal their dissatisfaction by relocating themselves or their movable assets to jurisdictions that offer more attractive local conditions. Jurisdiction-specific accumulation of people and capital thus becomes a systemic resource that performs the same function in this order that accumulation of votes does in a single "monocentric" democracy. There is therefore a limit to politicians' willingness to accommodate the demands of interest groups, even if the offered inducements would seem very attractive on a case-by-case basis.

Table 1 compares the systemic features of markets, monocentric democracy, and polycentric democracy. The table shows that polycentric democracy falls between the market order and a single democracy as regards individuals' ability to disseminate knowledge for the benefit of unknown others. While the choice of residence is (almost) as discrete as the choice of whom to vote for, capital can be allocated between jurisdictions in a continuous manner that resembles a portfolio approach to equity investments. And there is no longer one unique policy bundle that everyone must consume. Rather, there will be several distinct policy bundles where the scope for individual choice is an increasing function of the number of jurisdictions and the heterogeneity of bundles on offer, as well as a decreasing function of the transaction costs associated with interjurisdictional migration.

While Table 1 demonstrates the general systemic superiority of markets over political allocation of resources, this should not be interpreted in a

Table 1. Systemic Attributes of Three Spontaneous Orders.

Attribute	Market	Monocentric Democracy	Polycentric Democracy	Knowledge Dissemination Effectiveness
Systemic resource	Money	Votes	Mobile human and material capital	1 Market 2 Polycentric democracy 3 Monocentric democracy
Systemic resource distribution	Roughly equal to highly skewed	Equal (for insiders)	Equal to highly skewed	1 Monocentric democracy 2 Polycentric democracy 3 Market
Signaling of preferences	Continuous (willingness to pay)	Discrete (one person, one vote)	Discrete (residence) or continuous (capital)	1 Market 2 Polycentric democracy 3 Monocentric democracy
Aggregation of preferences	No (individual choice)	Yes (one size fits all)	Intermediate (different jurisdictional bundles)	1 Market 2 Polycentric democracy 3 Monocentric democracy
Typical *taxis*	Business firm	Political party	Local government	
Effect of abolishing *cosmos*	Central planning	Autocracy	Centralized and autarkic democracy	

Source: Adapted from Andersson (2010).

universal sense. As has been shown most persuasively by James Buchanan and Gordon Tullock (1962), voluntary exchange in markets cannot be expected to provide certain public goods other than to a very limited extent. These undersupplied goods are those that have transaction costs that are high relative to their expected value.

In a constitutional sense, this implies that well-informed people become more likely to assent to the tax-funded supply of a good when the number of affected individuals increases (*ibid.*). And the number of affected people is an increasing function of the spatial extent of the impact of the good on land values, other things being equal. In practice, this means that the strongest justification for government as opposed to market provision is for goods such as law enforcement, large-scale transportation and utility infrastructures, and scientific research (Andersson, 2011).

INSTITUTIONAL COMPETITION

The insight that jurisdictions compete for mobile human and capital resources is not new.[2] Already in 1923, Max Weber wrote that "the competitive struggle [among states] created the largest opportunities for modern western capitalism. The separate states had to compete for mobile capital, which dictated to them the conditions under which it would assist them to power" (Weber, 1923/1961, p. 249). While Weber's observation does not require the presence of multiple democracies, it does require multiple jurisdictions and mobile capital.

While Hayek never investigated the spontaneous-order attributes of either monocentric or polycentric democracy, he did come to conclusions regarding political decentralization that mirror the systemic properties that are presented in Table 1. In *The Constitution of Liberty*, Hayek writes that

> [t]here are strong reasons why action by local authorities generally offers the next-best solution where private initiative cannot be relied upon to provide certain services and where some sort of collective action is therefore needed; for it has many of the advantages of private enterprise and fewer of the dangers of the coercive action of government. Competition between local authorities or between larger units within an area where there is freedom of movement provides in a large measure that opportunity for experimentation with alternative methods which will secure most of the advantages of free growth. Though the majority of individuals may never contemplate a change of residence, there will usually be enough people, especially among the young and enterprising, to make it necessary for the local authorities to provide as good services at as reasonable costs as their competitors. It is usually the authoritarian planner who, in the interest of uniformity, governmental efficiency, and administrative convenience, supports the centralist tendencies and in this receives the strong support of the poorer majorities, who wish to be able to tap the resources of the wealthier regions. (Hayek, 1960, p. 263)

Hayek's argument complements Weber's in that it explicitly mentions mobile people rather than mobile capital. It goes without saying that the flow of people and the flow of capital goods both generate relevant feedback by making it possible for governmental decision makers to discern the relative attractiveness of their jurisdiction.

Interjurisdictional competition has also been mentioned as being among the reasons that certain regions of the world have developed at a more rapid pace than others. In *The European Miracle*, Eric Jones argues that the political fragmentation of Europe as compared with China and India is the main cause of Europe's superior economic performance over the past millennium:

> [H]ow did Europeans escape crippling exploitation by their rulers? … The rulers of the relatively small European states learned that by supplying the services of order and adjudication they could attract and retain the most and best-paying constituents … European kings were never as absolute as they wished. The power dispersed among the great proprietors was a check on them, as was the rising power of the market. (Jones, 1981, p. 233; quoted in Vaubel, 2008, p. 50)

The rulers of medieval Europe may have had a greater wish to exploit their subjects than modern democratic governments. It is nevertheless still the case that a decision to move elsewhere is the most effective strategy for escaping the exploitation of governments that are unreceptive to consumer preferences or beholden to interest groups.

It is instructive to note that successful distributional coalitions were especially influential in post-war Australia, Britain, and New Zealand, which are also three of the world's most stable and durable democracies. As a result of the accumulation of rent-extracting legislation, the three economies nearly ground to a halt in the 1970s (Olson, 1982). Faced with brain drains and capital flight, the governments of these three nation states deregulated their economies in the 1980s. This was as true of the Labor governments of Australia and New Zealand as of Margaret Thatcher's Conservative government in Britain. Faced with an even more mobile world from the 1990s onward, their successors in power (center-right in Australia and New Zealand and center-left in Britain) by and large continued policies that were designed to attract rather than repel capital and skilled labor.

What is important to note, however, is that the *transaction costs* associated with relocation matter. The success of protectionist and subsidy-seeking groups in post-war Australia, Britain, and New Zealand was facilitated by the high cost of exercising the exit option. Both Britain and New Zealand are unitary and centralized democracies. Although Australia is a federation, there are only six states, each of which has less fiscal and regulatory autonomy than American states or Canadian provinces.

Polycentric democracy works most effectively when exit-related transaction costs are low and when the number of viable jurisdictional options is large. The closest approximations of a genuine polycentric democracy are the 50 American states and the 26 Swiss cantons. In both cases, there is a substantial degree of policy autonomy at the regional and local levels of government. It is also possible for mobile individuals and firms to combine similar informal institutions (e.g., a shared language or shared business customs) with dissimilar formal laws and regulations.

Jurisdictional Competitiveness and the Size and Scope of Government

Given that democratic decision making is subject to both incentive and knowledge problems, we should expect a smaller government – above the threshold where the marginal benefit of government intervention equals its marginal cost – to be more attractive in attracting inflows of people and capital, other things being equal. The threshold corresponds to the spending that is necessary for engaging in governmental activities that are truly productive.

It is however unlikely that any existing government is too small to provide the generally desirable functions of government, typically the protection and delineation of private property rights, investments in productivity-enhancing physical infrastructures such as airports, highways, and power grids as well as some subsidization of scientific research without immediate commercial applications. Even Hong Kong's government, consistently rated as offering the most economic freedom in the world, regulates housing markets and subsidizes education.

The individual American states are especially suitable jurisdictions for the analysis of jurisdictional competitiveness in a polycentric democracy for three reasons. First, the American population is unusually mobile[3] (Borjas, Bronars, & Trejo, 1990), thereby contradicting Hayek's (1960, p. 263) statement that "the majority of individuals may never contemplate a change of residence." Second, American states have greater political autonomy than in most other federations. Third, the combined government interventions at the local, state, and federal levels are of sufficient size and scope – even in the least interventionist locality in the least interventionist state – to ensure that these governments have means that are in excess of what is required for fulfilling those functions that may increase their institutional competitiveness. Of course, that they have the means at their disposal does not imply that all governments give priority to their most essential roles. What it implies is that they could reduce overall spending and regulations *and* simultaneously increase spending on public goods. Thus in the American context, smaller is better.

Two organizations have undertaken the effort to measure the relative size and scope of state and local governments. The first such organization is the

Fraser Institute in Vancouver, British Columbia, which is widely known for its annual index of economic freedom in countries around the world (Gwartney, Hall, & Lawson, 2010). It also produces an annual index of economic freedom in the states and provinces of the United States and Canada (Ashby, Karabegović, McMahon, & Bueno, 2010). This index comprises a limited number of components that are grouped into three categories: size of government, takings and discriminatory taxation, and labor market freedom.

The other organization is the Mercatus Center at George Mason University in Fairfax, Virginia, which produces three indices that measure the relative interventionism of state (and aggregate local) governments: an economic freedom index, a personal freedom index, and an overall freedom index that combines states' scores on economic and personal freedom (Ruger & Sorens, 2009).

The Mercatus Center economic freedom index is more comprehensive than the index from the Fraser Institute. Apart from fiscal components and labor market regulations, it includes health insurance regulations, occupational licensing, eminent domain, liability rules, land and environmental regulations as well as utility regulation. The personal freedom index encompasses a wide range of paternalistically motivated regulations, such as gun control laws, marijuana laws, tobacco regulations, alcohol regulations, gambling laws, same-sex partnership laws, and school regulations. The overall index is the average score of the economic and personal freedom indices.

While both the Fraser Institute and the Mercatus Center are serviceable measures of the size of government, the Mercatus Center indices offer more information about the scope of the various state governments. But the designation of one half of the Mercatus Center overall freedom index as "personal" rather than "economic" is unfortunate in that it contradicts the conclusions of property rights theory.

While the motivation behind public policies such as gambling bans or alcohol taxes may be paternalistic, their effects are every bit as economic as those regulations that are conventionally classified as being of an economic nature. Armen Alchian and William Allen (1977), for example, contend that a consistent application of the economic theory of property rights shows that so-called "human rights" are a subset of property rights. Consider freedom of speech. To the extent that an individual values such freedom she should, ceteris paribus, exhibit a higher willingness to pay for land in locations that protect that freedom compared with other locations. The market valuation of free speech will therefore gradually be capitalized in land values. Such freedoms are thus also economic freedoms since they are all potential real estate attributes with implicit market prices.

Perfect enforcement of a banned activity implies that the ban corresponds to the imposed penalty, which means that it will be equivalent to an unusually high tax. Imperfect enforcement will reduce the magnitude of the implicit tax, although an implicit uncertainty cost will have to be added for risk-averse consumers.

The economic effects of paternalist taxes and regulations are perhaps even more burdensome in the case of entrepreneurs. Not only will taxes and expected fines make penalized production less profitable, but the enactment of a ban on, say, gambling is likely to curtail the ability of the entrepreneur to raise capital through transparent and legal channels for the purpose of investing in casinos or racetracks. The likely effect is that some prospective entrepreneurs are diverted to the illegal economy, while others are diverted to pursue profits in other fields than those where they anticipate the greatest returns. Such adverse effects on entrepreneurship cannot be assumed to be trivial, given the scope of such taxes and regulations in some states. Many kinds of entrepreneurial activity are in some cases banned, heavily taxed, or constrained in ways that preclude many types of innovation, especially within the education, gaming, hospitality, and retailing industries.

There is also a substantial literature – much of it Austrian-inspired – that explains the general inhibitory effects of taxes and regulations on entrepreneurship. For example, taxes on capital gains make some ventures that entrepreneurs might otherwise have perceived as profitable insufficiently promising (Harper, 2003), while zoning regulations inhibit the discovery of new land uses that are more valuable, where what is more valuable depends on the various accessibility attributes that are associated with each location (Andersson, 2011).

The conclusions are that taxes and regulations frequently benefit special interest groups at the expense of the general population and potential entrepreneurs; that government consumption for the most part is not receptive to individual consumer preferences; and that governmental paternalism imposes additional burdens on some consumers and additional constraints on opportunities for entrepreneurial innovation. We should therefore expect the whole array of taxes and regulations that are measured by the overall freedom index to influence the competitiveness of a state. Other things being equal, this would make New Hampshire the most competitive state and New York the least competitive one.

But other things are not equal. The most important noninstitutional difference between jurisdictions is the extent to which they benefit from various agglomeration economies, which is the subject of the next section. Such agglomeration economies tend to reflect investments in the distant past, and change at a much slower pace than state governments or legislators.

AGGLOMERATION ECONOMIES AND THE INSTITUTIONAL SYSTEM CONSTRAINT

It is not only low taxes and well-protected property rights that can be expected to attract people to a jurisdiction. Perhaps most important is a set of factors that together constitute *agglomeration economies*, or the various benefits that spring from the colocation of individuals and firms in the same region. While the affected areas almost never coincide with the spatial extent of jurisdictions, they nevertheless influence the competitiveness of one or more of them. By way of example, the agglomeration economies associated with the Chicago metropolitan area affect parts of three states (Illinois, Indiana, and Wisconsin), but the institutional attributes of each state only affect that part of the Chicago area that is located within the same state.

Economists with an interest in regional development invariably mention agglomeration economies as an important source of competitiveness. In the early twentieth century, Alfred Marshall enumerated the benefits that firms in the same or related industries gain by locating in close spatial proximity to one another (Marshall, 1920). Such benefits include specialized suppliers of intermediate goods, joint labor markets, and interfirm knowledge externalities. In the 1960s, Jane Jacobs extended economists' understanding of agglomeration economies by examining the beneficial effects of local economic diversity on creativity and innovation (Jacobs, 1961, 1969).

Traditional economic models of migration typically assume that the location of jobs is the most important factor influencing the migration decisions of individuals. In contrast, Richard Florida (2002) argues that there is more to an individual's choice of location than expected employment opportunities. In Florida's view, individuals in what he calls the "creative class" (individuals with creative occupations) are attracted by cities that exhibit above-average creativity. Traditional pull factors such as tax breaks and an abundance of sport franchises and shopping malls are – according to Florida – not as attractive to people with creative occupations as "abundant high-quality amenities and experiences, an openness to diversity of all kinds, and above all else the opportunity to validate their identity as creative people" (Florida, 2002, p. 218).

Florida (*ibid.*) contends that individuals choose a location based on both economic and lifestyle factors. His "creative capital theory" therefore assumes that the location choices of households rather than firms drive economic development. The theory distinguishes between general human capital and a more creative or entrepreneurial type of human capital that is called "creative capital." In addition, creative capital theory enumerates a number of factors that people with high levels of creative capital take into account when they choose a location. Thick labor markets, social interaction opportunities, and population diversity are three such factors.

In order to measure the relative attractiveness of states or cities to creative people, Florida (*ibid.*) uses his specially designed Creativity Index. This index encompasses the so-called "3 Ts" of economic development, where the 3 Ts refer to measures of talent, technology, and tolerance. Talent is a composite measure consisting of the share of the workforce with creative occupations and the share of the population having attained (at least) a bachelor's degree. The technology measure consists of the Milken Institute Techpole Index and patents per capita. The tolerance component includes the share of households that consists of same-sex couples, the share of the workforce in artistic occupations, and the share of the population that was born outside the United States.

Florida's theory implies the hypothesis that states that score high on the Creativity Index should be most successful at attracting individuals with creative occupations, other things being equal. The Creativity Index for states tends to reflect relative urbanization, since patents per capita and returns to human or creative capital are positively associated with the population size of metropolitan regions.

In the previous section, we hypothesized that jurisdictions with low taxes and few regulations should be expected to be more attractive to prospective migrants. In this section, the hypothesis is that individuals with creative occupations are attracted by agglomeration economies as measured by the Creativity Index. The least interventionist states are however not necessarily the states with the most agglomeration economies. While good institutions facilitate the gradual accumulation of agglomeration economies, the process is both slow and path-dependent (Holcombe, 2012). Consequently, the massive agglomeration economies that are associated with locations such as Manhattan or Silicon Valley reflect favorable institutions at an earlier stage of economic development.

Above-average agglomeration economies have two important effects: they are not easily depleted and they enable governments to pursue more value-destructive policies than are feasible in inaccessible and sparsely

Table 2. State Rankings on the State Creativity Index (SCI) and the Mercatus Center Overall Freedom Index (MOFI) 2006.

MOFI Rank	SCI Rank				
	1–10	11–20	21–30	31–40	41–50
1–10	Colorado Virginia	Idaho New Hampshire Texas	Arizona	Missouri Tennessee	North Dakota South Dakota
11–20		Georgia Michigan	Kansas Pennsylvania Utah	Indiana Iowa Oklahoma	Montana Wyoming
21–30	Oregon	Florida	Delaware Nevada North Carolina	Alabama Nebraska	Arkansas Mississippi South Carolina
31–40	Minnesota	Vermont	Maine New Mexico Ohio	Alaska Wisconsin	Kentucky Louisiana West Virginia
41–50	California Connecticut Maryland Massachusetts New York Washington	Illinois New Jersey Rhode Island		Hawaii	

Sources: Stolarick (undated); Ruger and Sorens (2009).

populated regions. It is therefore not at all surprising that there is a significant negative correlation ($r = -.314$) between the Creativity Index and the Mercatus Overall Freedom Index (MOFI) at the state level. But the negative correlation is not perfect. Table 2 shows the bivariate distribution of states divided into quintiles according to the State Creativity Index (SCI) and the MOFI.

The table is a clear illustration of the negative but imperfect correlation between government interventionism and agglomeration economies. Particularly striking is the cell in the extreme south-west corner of the table, which includes seven states that are simultaneously among the ten most creative states and among the ten states where residents are most constrained by government taxes and regulations. The only state with a below average SCI score among the ten most institutionally restrictive states is Hawaii, but note that that state is generally considered to be endowed with one of the world's most comfortable climates.

Richard Langlois (1986) introduces a concept that is particularly helpful for understanding the feasible choice domain in a wide variety of contexts, including the domain of policy choices. This concept is called the *system* constraint, and refers to the constraints that natural or social environmental conditions impose on individual choice. For example, neoclassical models of perfect competition impose the strictest possible system constraint, since individual producers have to adopt an exogenously given price and production technology. In boundedly rational and imperfectly competitive models of the behavior of firms, the system constraint is looser, since the choice set is expanded to encompass all those choices that are good enough for survival, which generally encompasses a range of production plans. These plans include the profit-maximizing plan as a special case, but all plans that at least break even are feasible choices.

Roger Koppl and Douglas Glen Whitman (2004) explain how the relative "tightness" of the system constraint simultaneously determines the appropriate behavioral assumptions and the expected predictive accuracy of individual choice models. In their view, a tightening of the system constraint makes it possible for the social scientist to use more restrictive behavioral assumptions and arrive at more precise predictions of the effects of individual behavior. Using ideas from the phenomenology of Alfred Schutz (1932/1967), this implies that a tighter system constraint is associated with increasing anonymity of the relevant *ideal type* and greater applicability of rational-choice models of individual behavior.

To illustrate their reasoning, Koppl and Whiteman (2004) use the hypothetical example of unconstrained basketball players as their starting point:

> Suppose we wish to describe the on-court behavior of professional basketball players. We construct a model under the assumption that basketball players are motivated solely by the desire to win basketball games. With this assumption we have defined an ideal type, which we will call *homo basketballicus*. This ideal type, combined with knowledge of the rules of basketball, leads us to certain conclusions about his play. For instance, he will pass the ball to another player when the other player clearly has a better chance of making a basket. How useful is such a model? Let us first consider the example without considering the system constraint. In that case, the value of the model would depend on how many basketball players actually approximate the profile of *homo basketballicus*. This ideal type is reasonably broad, but not nearly as broad as it could be. It implicitly assumes that a number of other factors that could motivate a basketball player, such as his desire to make a good living and his desire to impress fans, are either non-existent or unimportant relative to the goal of winning games. (Koppl & Whitman, 2004)

But professional basketball players are in fact subject to a relatively – albeit not perfectly – tight system constraint, which means that it is reasonable to assume that players are exclusively motivated by the desire to win games:

> Now let us consider the same issue, but without ignoring the role of the system constraint. Professional basketball players may be motivated by many goals besides winning. But to get and retain a place on the team, they must contribute to winning. The owner will lose ticket revenue if he does not have a winning team. Any player who consistently mortified the goal of team victory for other ends would be cut from the team. Thus, the professional players we see have a strong (though imperfect) tendency to pass the ball when a teammate has a better chance to score. (Koppl & Whitman, 2004)

The system constraint that lawmakers face in a pure monocentric democracy would have to be classified as being very loose. The viability of a government would then only depend on its being able to offer a bundle of policies that appeal more to the median voter than that of the opposition. The winner's policy mix may even be generally unattractive to that voter, although it will not be the mix that she perceives as the single worst one. One consequence is that it becomes difficult to predict the likely evolution of future government policies. The personal identities of the main players matter. Any prediction of future policy choices will have to take account of such personal characteristics as an individual policy-maker's responsiveness to lobbying, her normative goals, and her personal theories regarding the effects of various policies. The relevant ideal type therefore has a very low level of anonymity, and in extreme cases interpretations of unique personal motivations and objectives are most efficacious for generating pattern predictions. In spite of being effective in a relative sense, such predictions will tend to be unreliable, especially if the relevant individuals are not very transparent about their motivations, objectives, or theories. Thus, monocentric democracies will tend to be subject to *big player* instability (cf. Koppl, 2002).

The system constraint is tighter in a polycentric democracy, although usually nowhere near as tight as in a perfectly competitive market or a professional basketball game. In addition to the periodic challenge of defeating the political opposition, lawmakers face competition from other jurisdictions, some of which may compete for the same human capital, consumption spending, and entrepreneurial investments.

Increases in the mobility of capital, consumption goods, or people have the effect of tightening the system constraint, since substandard institutions then become more likely to cause a reduced tax base. Interstate or international agreements that allow people and capital to flow without institutional restrictions hence have the predictable effect of making it more difficult to maintain value-destructive laws and regulations. Such laws and regulations include those that opportunistic lawmakers initiate in response to rent-seeking but also well-intentioned policies with perverse indirect effects (see Moroni, 2012).

Different jurisdictions in a polycentric democracy face system constraints of unequal "tightness." Substantial agglomeration economies – mainly local knowledge externalities and good interregional accessibility – offer politicians opportunities to pursue value-destructive policies that are beyond the reach of politicians in less well-endowed locations. Attractive natural endowments – an mild climate; natural beauty; valuable natural resources – cause a similar loosening of the relevant system constraint. The most constrained politicians are therefore to be found in jurisdictions that are inaccessible, sparsely populated, cold, and lacking in natural resources.

The differentiated system constraint means that actual policy choices become more difficult to predict the more inherited advantages a jurisdiction possesses. Not only can well-endowed jurisdictions accommodate more rent extraction from productive economic activities; they also facilitate (but by no means guarantee) the pursuit of ideologically motivated policies with value-destructive indirect consequences. In the best-endowed jurisdictions, there is therefore more freedom of political choice; politicians still have the option of limiting themselves to market-enhancing policies, but they can also afford more redistribution than elsewhere. In this context, it is immaterial whether the redistribution reflects rent-seeking, welfare-state entitlement programs, or paternalist conceptions of right and wrong.

Government policies are sometimes classified according to four possible functions: the protective, productive, redistributive, and paternalist functions. In fact there are only two. While it might make some sense to label the protection of property rights as the protective function of government, it is also productive. Better delineation and enforcement of property rights reduce the transaction costs that producers and consumers face, which will be reflected in higher land prices, other things being equal. The protective function of government is therefore a subset of its productive function[4] (arguably, the most important subset).

Paternalism is usually separated from redistribution, but this obscures an important commonality. The separation makes sense on motivational but not on consequentialist grounds. If an activity is taxed or banned because certain influential actors consider it a "demerit good," then a redistribution of the *economic property rights* that govern the activity must have occurred. A legislature cannot avoid redistributing property rights when it introduces legislation such as compulsory seatbelts or a ban on home schooling. In all such cases, lawmakers redistribute property rights from individuals to the government, with attendant utility gains being redistributed to all those individuals who both disapprove of the activity (e.g., driving without seatbelts) *and* have interpersonal (i.e., meddlesome) preferences. In contrast, individuals who have a positive valuation of the banned activity lose their individual property rights over one or more resource attributes and suffer utility losses (cf. Barzel, 1989).

Jurisdictions can sustain redistributive policies to the extent that it benefits from inherited agglomeration economies and various nature-given endowments. But this does not imply that they are insured against economic decline. Holcombe (2012) notes that the City of Detroit has been suffering from depopulation and other symptoms of decline as the predictable consequence of rent-seeking among firms and employees in its automotive cluster. In the long run, institutional vicious cycles such as the one in Detroit should be self-correcting in a polycentric democracy. Persistent losses of people and capital will in the long run leave a jurisdiction if it has depleted its resources for profitable rent-seeking. The jurisdiction will then either be forced to reform or else become an irrelevant spatial option. In the case of Detroit, this self-correcting process has been slowed down by federal subsidies, which alludes to the way that federal intervention in state or local affairs endangers the self-correcting properties of a genuine polycentric democracy.

INSTITUTIONS, AGGLOMERATIONS, AND MIGRATION

We have identified institutional quality and agglomeration economies as two factors that may repel or attract people. There are others. Everett Lee (1966) distinguishes between four classes of factors that may influence an individual's decision to migrate. These are:

1. Factors associated with the area of origin;
2. Factors associated with the area of destination;
3. Intervening obstacles;
4. Personal factors.

Lee draws attention to the first two factors by identifying a bad climate as a push factor (Factor No. 1) and a good climate as a pull factor (Factor No. 2). Examples of intervening obstacles are legal restrictions on migration as well as space-bridging costs associated with geographical distance.

Personal factors reflect social networks that connect individuals with their families, friends, and coworkers.

In traditional models of migration, the local availability of jobs often features as the most important variable. But from a spatial or an Austrian perspective, the size and scope of a regional labor market is a proximate rather than an underlying causal factor. Spatial economists would assert that regional labor market conditions reflect regional agglomeration economies. And both Austrian and institutional economists would point out that favorable formal and informal institutions provide the impetus for the gradual accumulation of agglomeration economies (Holcombe, 2012), although the precise location of major cities also reflect the path dependencies that discrete large-scale infrastructural investments occasionally initiate (Batten, 2000).

For the purpose of investigating the effects of current institutional quality and accumulated agglomeration economies, we estimated a regression model where net domestic interstate migration from 2005 to 2007 is a function of one of three freedom indices (as alternative measures of institutional quality) and Richard Florida's SCI (as a measure of state-level agglomeration economies). Numerous studies have shown that regional climate (e.g., Partridge, Rickman, Olfert, & Kamar, 2010) and criminality (e.g., Gabriel & Mattey, 1996) also affect the relative attractiveness of regions. The number of heating degree days (HDD) and the homicide rate in the largest city are therefore included as control variables. In addition, there is a dummy variable for Alaska and Hawaii in order to account for the possible effect of inferior interregional accessibility.

Migrating individuals and households can also be analyzed with the help of system constraints and Schutzian ideal types. If the system constraint facing politicians is loose, it is even looser for potential migrants. While self-imposed occupational and consumption preferences might rule out several possible relocation choices, the system constraint is minimal; a film director may feel that he is constrained to the Los Angeles region, but in fact he could also choose to work in unskilled occupations such as being a street sweeper in South Dakota or a janitor in Mississippi. The only genuinely *systemic* constraints that limit migration choices are those labor market interventions that create labor costs that exceed the marginal product of labor for some workers with lower-than-average productivity. The system constraint therefore only applies to a subset of all migrants and is mainly limited to the effects of state minimum wages and health insurance coverage mandates. It applies to the extent that these regulations price migrants out of employment opportunities.

One of the main contentions in this chapter is that relatively laissez faire institutional environments attract more individuals than they repel. The rationale for this contention covers two aspects. First, beneficiaries of rent-seeking legislation tend to be long-established residents with good local connections. Thus this group should have a lower relocation propensity. Rent-extracting legislation also tends to discriminate against recent arrivals. The expectation is therefore that an increase in such legislation reduces the attractiveness of a jurisdiction to potential in-migrants.

Second, the effects of regulations are not symmetric. For example, a same-sex marriage ban imposes a disadvantage on same-sex couples, but its legalization does not mandate its application. In other words, regulations imply a loss of variety. The implication is that a prohibition is likely to repel some people for whom the prohibited activity is a valued consumption good, but it is unlikely to affect the migration decisions of those who are indifferent or have a negative valuation. No matter in which state you live, it is easy to avoid what some consider to be unsavory environments, be they casinos, brothels, smoke-filled bars or schools with unusual curricula. For the same reason, we assume that even those individuals who support high taxes or minimum wages will not avoid states with low taxes or deregulated labor markets.

These considerations leave us with four hypotheses that correspond to ideal types of unknown prevalence:

1. Ideal Type No. 1 consists of those entrepreneurs (and the workers they employ) who are attracted by agglomeration economies. Agglomeration economies create location-specific returns such as transfers of tacit knowledge. This type can be expected to be most over-represented in those occupations and industries where agglomeration economies are most pronounced, such as knowledge-intensive services.
2. Ideal Type No. 2 consists of those entrepreneurs and workers who are attracted by free-market institutions, on the grounds that an increase in the size and scope of government reduces the profitability and scope of market entrepreneurship. The expectation is that this type is common within private profit-seeking firms.
3. Ideal Type No. 3 consists of migrants who are mainly consumers, for example, retirees. Lower taxes and less intrusive regulations increase attainable consumption choices, and thus free-market institutions should attract this group. While agglomeration economies benefit producers they also raise land values, which makes housing and local services more expensive. Agglomeration economies should therefore repel this type.

4. Ideal Type No. 4 consists of those who do not take agglomeration economies or institutions into account when making their migration decisions. This could be caused by ignorance or by a focus on other factors, such as the location of family members or the attractiveness of the local climate.

It is possible to add ideal types that correspond to combinations of types 1, 2, and 3. Whether one does so or not, one should not expect any spatiotemporal stability in the quantitative effects of the ideal types. Subjective and heterogeneous individual preferences and knowledge – together with a loose system constraint – make it all but certain that we have to limit our conclusions to broad pattern regularities rather than point estimates (Koppl & Whitman, 2004; see also Hayek, 1967).

Table 3. List of Variables.

Variable	Code	Source
Dependent variables		
Net domestic in-migration, 2005–2007, as percentage of 2005 state population	ALL	The Pew Research Center
Net domestic in-migration ages 22–39, 2005–2007, per 1,000 of 2005 state population	YOUNG	National Center for Higher Education Management Systems
Net domestic in-migrants ages 22–39, with advanced degrees, 2005–2007, per 1,000 of 2005 state population	MA+	National Center for Higher Education Management Systems
Institutional quality		
Fraser Economic Freedom Index	FEFI	Fraser Institute
Mercatus Economic Freedom Index	MEFI	Mercatus Center at George Mason University
Mercatus Overall Freedom Index	MOFI	Mercatus Center at George Mason University
Agglomeration economies		
State Creativity Index, 2006	SCI	Stolarick (not published)
Control variables		
Mean number of annual heating degree days in the largest in-state city (30-year average)	HDD	www.worldclimate.com
Homicide rate per 100,000 population in the largest in-state city, 2005	KILL	Federal Bureau of Investigation
Alaska or Hawaii (dummy variable)	AKHI	–

Table 4. Descriptive Statistics.

Variable (Code)	Mean	Standard Deviation	Minimum	Maximum
ALL	.216	2.510	−9.100	5.100
YOUNG	2.428	3.362	−7.093	10.191
MA+	.331	.444	−.972	1.370
FEFI	6.910	.624	5.700	8.200
MEFI	.000	.224	−.596	.385
MOFI	.000	.265	−.784	.432
SCI	.529	.204	.135	.917
HDD	2793.000	1222.538	.000	5872.000
KILL	15.866	12.897	1.900	47.300

Table 3 presents all dependent and independent variables that are included in the empirical analysis. Net domestic in-migration is analyzed as three distinct flows: all domestic interstate migrants regardless of age; a subset that is limited to migrants between 22 and 39 years of age; and a second-order subset that consists of 22-to-39-year-olds with an advanced degree. The description of the ideal types makes clear that we expect institutional quality to affect all groups, but that the relative importance of agglomeration economies should be stronger among the younger group (a larger share of producers), and stronger still in the highly educated subset (a larger share of knowledge workers).

Table 4 conveys descriptive statistics of all dependent and independent variables, with the exception of the Alaska/Hawaii dummy. The highest and lowest net in-migration rates (ALL) in the studied period were recorded in Idaho and Alaska; Idaho's gain corresponded to 5.1 percent of its 2005 population, while Alaska lost 9.1 percent of its initial population to other states. In the 22–39 age group (YOUNG), net domestic in-migration ranged from a low of −.71 percent in Alaska to a high of +1.02 percent in Arizona. The corresponding figures for highly educated young adults (MA+) were −.01 percent in North Dakota and +.14 percent in Washington .

Independent variables of special interest are the three freedom indices and the SCI. New Hampshire scores highest on the MOFI, whereas South Dakota scores highest on the Mercatus Economic Freedom Index (MEFI). New York is the most interventionist state according to both indices. The less comprehensive Fraser Economic Freedom Index (FEFI) ranks Wyoming as most free and Rhode Island as least free (South Dakota ranks 2nd and New York 49th according to FEFI). The SCI, finally, implies that

California benefits from the most agglomeration economies, followed by Massachusetts and New York. The three lowest SCI scores were recorded in Arkansas (48th), Mississippi (49th), and West Virginia (50th).

Table 5 shows that the existence of our hypothesized ideal types for the most part are borne out by the empirical results. Overall freedom as measured by the Mercatus Institute is the most important variable for explaining net domestic migration among the 48 contiguous states. Using one of the other two freedom indices yields similar but slightly weaker effects (the freedom measures are highly correlated[5]). A one-unit increase in the MOFI score was associated with a net population gain of 4.02 percent over the analyzed time period (this corresponds to the MOFI difference between New York and Kansas). The associated pattern prediction is that a reduction in the size and scope of government can be expected to render a state more attractive to residents of other states, other things being equal.

Agglomerations of human capital, creative resources or technology do not seem to make much of a difference to overall migration patterns. It is likely that the insignificant result derives from a canceling-out of Ideal Type No. 1 and Ideal Type No. 3 tendencies. While knowledge workers such as scientists, engineers, and financial professionals are likely to be disproportionately attracted to the agglomeration economies of places such as New York City, Los Angeles, and Chicago, many others have to accept a substantial reduction in their purchasing power if they choose to live in a major metropolitan area. This is especially true for those who give priority to housing consumption. The wage premiums associated with large metropolitan areas tend to be highest for workers with advanced cognitive or managerial skills, but negligible for workers that rely on motor skills (Johansson & Klaesson, 2011). We should expect retirees and other "pure consumption migrants" to be even warier of large metropolitan regions.

As expected, there is a positive Sunbelt and a negative crime effect. For example, 1,000 extra HDD are associated with a net loss of 1 percent of a state's population. This climatic difference corresponds to a move from North Dakota to Maine or from North Carolina to Louisiana. Clearly, the system constraint of polycentric democracy is tighter in northern than in southern states, other things being equal (which they are not) (Table 5).

The results associated with migrants in the 22–39 age group tell a partly different story. Institutions are still important, but agglomeration economies have a comparable impact on a state's overall attractiveness. For this group, the narrower MEFI yields the most significant results, and implies that an MEFI improvement of one point (approximately equivalent to the difference between the highest-ranking and lowest-ranking states) is

Table 5. Net Domestic In-Migration as a Function of Institutional Quality, Agglomeration Economies, Climate, and Criminality, 2005–2007.

Variable (Code)	ALL		YOUNG		MA+	
	Estimate	*t*-value	Estimate	*t*-value	Estimate	*t*-value
Constant	3.481		4.550		−.973	
Institutional quality						
FEFI					.133	1.537*
MEFI			6.207	3.700***		
MOFI	4.020	3.955***				
Agglomeration economies						
SCI	.518	.397	6.505	3.693***	1.254	5.011***
Control variables						
HDD	−.001	−3.859***	−.001	−4.977***	−.0001	−1.739**
KILL	−.060	−2.881***	−.084	−2.932***	−.055	−1.180
AKHI	−5.907	−4.490***	−2.407	−1.296	.480	1.800†
Regression statistics						
R^2	.561	.543	.428			
N	50	50	50			

*$p < .10$; **$p < .05$; ***$p < .01$ (one-tailed); †opposite sign.

associated with a .62 percent gain in the state's total population. The corresponding population gain gap between the highest-ranking and lowest-ranking state according to the SCI is .51 percent. Warm weather and crime effects are very similar to those of the overall population of migrants.

The group of young professionals with at least a master's degree is the most deviant subgroup. In that particular group, Ideal Type No. 1 seems dominant. This is not unexpected. Highly skilled professionals benefit disproportionately from the transmission of advanced tacit knowledge that is concentrated in large urban centers such as New York City and Los Angeles. They do this in two ways. First, knowledge externalities raise the productivity of knowledge workers, with greater returns to human capital as the predictable result (Johansson & Klaesson, 2011). Second, these same knowledge externalities give rise to a greater number of discoverable but localized entrepreneurial profit opportunities. Such opportunities arise both within and in the interstices between various specialized production and consumption clusters (Andersson, 2005). More speculative is Florida's (2002) contention that knowledge workers (the "creative class") are more appreciative of the consumption opportunities afforded by urban agglomerations (theaters, galleries, etc.), which would in that case reinforce the attractiveness of states that score high on the SCI.

For this group it seems as if all factors other than agglomeration economies are negligible. The three economic freedom indices exhibit the expected sign in alternate models, but none of them is significant (at $p < .05$). Nor is a high homicide rate a deterrent. Even a warm climate is only weakly significant, with an estimated effect that is only one tenth as great as the effect on all migrants or all migrants in the same age group. A somewhat cynical conclusion is that it is the most sophisticated and creative group of interstate migrants that contributes most to the viability of sustained political mismanagement in interventionist states. New York lost 3.4 percent of its total population to other states between 2005 and 2007, but in-migrants aged 22 to 39 with an advanced degree accounted for a net population gain of .033 percent. The latter figure is small, but its probable economic impact is not as small as other groups with the same number of people. It is exactly this demographic group that tends to have the greatest ability to influence the creativity and innovativeness of a regional economy.

Extending the Time Period: Qualitative Stability but Quantitative Flux

Samuli Leppälä and Pierre Desrochers (2012) argue that mainstream regional economists tend to engage in too much aggregation, overemphasizing regional division of labor and specialization at the expense of the corresponding individual phenomena. Their preferred remedy is the consistent application of methodological individualism. In empirical analyses, this implies a shift toward case studies of individual behavior as well as quantitative microeconometric analyses.

We think Leppälä and Desrochers raise a valid point as regards mainstream practice, but nevertheless overstate their case. The empirical analysis in the preceding section is an example of a simple macroanalysis that we believe can be reconciled with Austrian conceptions of individual subjective preferences, knowledge, and expectations. The problem, as we see it, is not that mainstream regional scientists use spurious empirical methods. It is rather that they misinterpret the results when applying them to real-world observations.

Mainstream models often implicitly assume that the economy is in approximate general equilibrium and, as a result, that individuals face a tight system constraint. Consequently, mainstream economists often hope that their estimated coefficients are general in the sense that they can be used for quantitative predictions of future states of the world. They hope in vain. The most important methodological message of our discussion so far is that the system constraint, when it exists, is more often weak than strong. A weak system constraint enables individuals to choose between alternative courses of action, which rules out a deterministic interpretation of empirical results.

The particular ideal types that were described in the previous section are less anonymous than the ideal type that is the foundation for Austrian economic theory as put forward by Ludwig von Mises (1949). In Misesian terms, our ideal types are "historical." But we would rather label them fallible behavioral hypotheses that build upon reasonable but potentially erroneous generalizations about subsets of populations. For example, the hypothesis associated with Ideal Type No. 2 is that jurisdiction-specific production and consumption opportunities affect the likelihood of choosing a jurisdiction. More specifically, fewer feasible production and consumption choices reduce the attractiveness of the jurisdiction in the eyes of those individuals who conform to the assumptions of Ideal Type No. 2. But the exact extent of the institutional restrictions that must be imposed to keep those people away who would otherwise choose a specific jurisdiction is inherently uncertain. It also varies among the individuals who belong to this subset of the population.

Generalizations in situations where a weak system constraint governs an ideal type of less than perfect anonymity are thus always conjectural and describe pattern regularities rather than inevitabilities. Such generalizations describe the direction of an effect rather than its magnitude. To illustrate this, let us consider what happens when we extend the time period of our analysis from three years (2005–2007) to ten years (2000–2009). Obviously, some of the independent variables – the MOFI and the SCI – will be less synchronized with the longer than with the shorter time period. The maximum chronological difference between these independent variables and the dependent variable increases from one to six years when the time period is extended to ten years (the two indices refer to the year 2006). This temporal mismatch is nevertheless likely to be at most a minor problem, since institutional and agglomeration variables are more stable over time than individual relocation decisions.

Table 6 compares the states that gained and lost the most domestic in-migrants in the two periods. There are some commonalities, but the lists are not identical, nor does each three-year figure correspond to three tenths of the ten-year figure. Six of the top ten states that gained population in the ten-year period are also among the top ten states in the three-year period.

Table 6. Rank-Ordered Net Domestic In-Migration as a Percentage of the State Population; 2000–2009 and 2005–2007; Rank 1–10 and 41–50.

Rank	2000–2009		2005–2007	
	State	In-Migration (%)	State	In-Migration (%)
1	Idaho	+8.6	Idaho	+5.1
2	North Carolina	+8.4	Arizona	+4.6
3	South Carolina	+7.7	Nevada	+3.6
4	Florida	+7.4	Georgia	+3.4
5	Georgia	+6.9	South Carolina	+3.3
6	Delaware	+5.9	North Carolina	+3.2
7	Oregon	+5.2	Oregon	+2.6
8	Colorado	+4.9	Delaware	+2.5
9	Tennessee	+4.6	Arkansas	+2.3
10	Wyoming	+4.5	Montana	+1.9
41	North Dakota	−3.1	Mississippi	−1.7
42	Ohio	−3.2	Illinois	−1.8
43	Rhode Island	−4.2	California	−1.9
44	Massachusetts	−4.3	New Jersey	−1.9
45	California	−4.4	Massachusetts	−2.0
46	Illinois	−5.1	Michigan	−2.1
47	Michigan	−5.4	Hawaii	−2.2
48	New Jersey	−5.5	New York	−3.4
49	Louisiana	−7.1	Louisiana	−6.4
50	New York	−8.9	Alaska	−9.1

Among the ten states that lost the greatest shares of their original populations to other states, there are also six states that show up in both time periods.

Apart from different rank orderings, there are fluctuations in the year-on-year rate of change for each state. Idaho gained more new residents than any other state in relative terms, but about 60 percent of its ten-year net gain occurred in the three years from 2005 to 2007. Conversely, Alaska lost 9.1 percent of its 2005 population to other states between 2005 and 2007, but the net ten-year loss was only 1.4 percent, so that there was a net gain of in-migrants during the remaining seven years. All these migration instabilities are illustrations of the fact that there is no deterministic functional relationship. There are no objective conditions that make people choose as if they were allocated to their optimal spatial slots by an omniscient casting director. Different individuals have different preferences, knowledge, and expectations, and these subjective factors may themselves change as people learn from or forget the past.

Table 7. Net Domestic In-migration as a Function of Institutions, Agglomeration Economies, Climate, and Criminality, 2000–2009 and 2005–2007.

Variable (Code)	2000–2009		2005–2007	
	Estimate	*t*-value	Estimate	*t*-value
Constant	6.436		3.834	
MOFI	8.115	4.163***	4.512	3.813***
SCI	−1.721	−.648	−.001	−.001
HDD	−.001	−2.495***	−.001	−3.386***
KILL	−.276	−2.154**	−.165	−2.124**
R^2	.386		.380	

$N = 50$; *$p<.10$; **$p<.05$; ***$p<.01$ (one-tailed).

Table 7 compares the estimated in-migration effects of the same independent variables in the two time periods. The Alaska/Hawaii dummy variable of Table 5 has been removed, since both Alaska and Hawaii experienced atypical population losses between 2005 and 2007 for unknown reasons. The SCI has however been retained, in spite of its low *t*-values in the two functions (the rationale for its inclusion is the continuity of its insignificance). Interestingly, the MOFI has the strongest association with net domestic in-migration as compared with the other two freedom indices regardless of time period chosen.

A comparison of the two functions reveals that there is considerable qualitative functional consistency between the two time periods (with the exception of the Alaska-and-Hawaii effect), but that the quantitative point estimates of three of the effects fluctuate in unpredictable ways. One of the four point estimates happens to be the same for both time periods, but this does not invalidate our conclusion; the possibility of change does not rule out its intermittent absence.

CONCLUSION

With the help of hypotheses formulated as ideal types with system constraints, we arrive at our interpretation of the empirical results. This interpretation is as follows and consists of three tentative pattern predictions. First, more fiscal and regulatory freedom increases the net domestic in-migration rate, but does not seem to affect most migrants with an advanced degree between 22 and 39 years of age. Second, greater agglomeration economies neither attract nor repel in-migrants *in general*, but do disproportionately attract in-migrants in the 22–39 age groups, particularly if they have an advanced degree. Third, the results lend empirical support to earlier studies that indicate that migrants tend to prefer warm and peaceful locations. In sound bite terms: Most Americans seek freedom, warmth, and peace, but some seek knowledge.

The results also allow us to make some pattern predictions about what type of locations are in the best position to benefit from the individual migration choices of Americans. In the empirical analyses, agglomeration economies as measured by the SCI reflect state rather than metropolitan-area averages. This can be misleading, since the spatial extent of agglomeration economies tends to coincide with labor market areas. Actual commuting flows, center-periphery time distance limits, and rent-distance gradients – not state boundaries – reflect the extent of local labor markets. In America, the closest approximation of a local labor market is the Metropolitan Statistical Area (MSA), which is based on observed commuting flows between an urban core and outlying counties. It is these MSAs that benefit from agglomeration economies, rather than the entirety of the state or states in which an MSA is located.

We have seen that small-government states gain population in general, whereas high-creativity states gain young and educated residents. In practice, this means that a high-creativity MSA in a small-government state should be especially competitive by being attractive to in-migrants across all demographics. And if this same MSA happens to be warm and have a low homicide rate, it seems a safe bet that it will be a magnet to migrants, as long as state politicians do not stray from their small-government course. In other words, the prediction of future population gains only holds as long as state lawmakers shun the slippery slope that would make them end up like New York (as we have seen, economic success facilitates such slippage, as does warmth).

There is one MSA that combines all four desirable features. The name of its core city is Austin. Boulder may be colder but scored even higher on the 2006 Creativity Index. And Boulder is located in Colorado, which ranked second on overall freedom in 2006. Cities such as Austin and Boulder are thus in an especially advantageous position, since they operate in a much less regulated institutional environment than otherwise similar conurbations of knowledge workers in California or the Northeast. Like their bicoastal counterparts, Austin and Boulder are known for their left-wing liberalism and environmentalism. But unlike Boston or San Francisco, they are hemmed in by their conservative hinterlands. Hence a more general pattern prediction might be that the future will favor blue cities in red states.

NOTES

1. The idea that polycentric democracy is a separate spontaneous order is introduced for the first time in this chapter.
2. Interjurisdictional competition is most often associated with Charles Tiebout (1956), who formulated an equilibrium model where residents "vote with their feet" and end up in the jurisdiction that offers the best bundle of public services. Since the Tiebout model deals with an optimal end state rather than with a spontaneous process of gradual and boundedly rational adjustments, it is not very relevant to Austrian theorizing.
3. The lifetime domestic interstate migration rate has been stable at slightly above .3 over the past 100 years. In other words, there is a 31 or 32 percent probability that a US native will move to another state during her lifetime.
4. The productive function usually refers to the tax-funded production of public goods, such as defense, roads, and vaccination programs. The protective function includes defense, but does not include roads or vaccination programs.
5. The specifications in Table 5 use the freedom index with the highest *t*-value. The three freedom indices are all highly correlated and yield the same qualitative conclusions when included in isolation. Correlations between each freedom index and the other variables as well as between each pair of nonfreedom variables are much lower. The estimation method is ordinary least squares.

REFERENCES

Alchian, A., & Allen, W. R. (1977). *Exchange and production: Competition, coordination, and control.* Belmont, CA: Wadsworth Publishing Company.

Andersson, D. E. (2005). The spatial nature of entrepreneurship. *Quarterly Journal of Austrian Economics, 8*, 21–34.

Andersson, D. E. (2008). *Property rights, consumption and the market process.* Cheltenham, UK: Edward Elgar.

Andersson, D. E. (2010). Cosmos and taxis in religious life: Pattern regularities and new challenges. *Studies in Emergent Order, 3*, 172–194.

Andersson, D. E. (2011). Creative cities need less government. In D. E. Andersson, Å. E. Andersson & C. Mellander (Eds.), *Handbook of creative cities.* Cheltenham: Edward Elgar.

Ashby, N. J., Karabegović, A., McMahon, F., & Bueno, A. (2010). *Economic freedom of North America 2010.* Vancouver, BC: Fraser Institute.

Barzel, Y. (1989). *Economic analysis of property rights.* Cambridge, UK: Cambridge University Press.

Batten, D. F. (2000). *Discovering artificial economics: How agents learn and economies evolve.* Boulder, CO: Westview Press.

Borjas, G. J., Bronars, S. G., & Trejo, S. J. (1990). *Self-selection and internal migration in the United States*. Washington, DC: Bureau of Labor Statistics.

Buchanan, J. M., & Tullock, G. (1962). *The calculus of consent: Logical foundations of constitutional democracy*. Ann Arbor, MI: University of Michigan Press.

De Soto, H. (2000). *The mystery of capital: Why capitalism triumphs in the West and fails everywhere else*. New York, NY: Basic Books.

diZerega, G. (1989). Democracy as a spontaneous order. *Critical Review*, *3*(2), 206–240.

Ferguson, A. (1782). *An essay on the history of civil society*. London, UK: T. Cadell.

Florida, R. (2002). *The rise of the creative class*. New York, NY: Basic Books.

Gabriel, S. A., & Mattey, J. P. (1996). *Leaving Los Angeles: Migration, economic opportunity, and the quality-of-life*. San Francisco, CA: Federal Reserve Bank of San Francisco.

Gwartney, J. D., Hall, J. C., & Lawson, R. (2010). *Economic freedom of the world: 2010 Annual Report*. Vancouver, BC: Fraser Institute.

Harper, D. A. (2003). *Foundations of entrepreneurship and economic development*. London, UK: Routledge.

Hayek, F. A. (1945). The use of knowledge in society. *American Economic Review*, *35*(4), 519–530.

Hayek, F. A. (1960). *The constitution of liberty*. Chicago, IL: The University of Chicago Press.

Hayek, F. A. (1967). Degrees of explanation. In F. A. Hayek (Ed.), *Studies in philosophy, politics and economics*. Chicago, IL: The University of Chicago Press.

Hayek, F. A. (1973). *Rules and Order* (Volume I of *Law, Legislation, and Liberty*). Chicago, IL: The University of Chicago Press.

Holcombe, R. G. (2012). The rise and fall of agglomeration economies. In D. E. Andersson (Ed.), *The spatial market process*. Bingley, UK: Emerald.

Jacobs, J. (1961). *The death and life of great American cities*. New York, NY: Random House.

Jacobs, J. (1969). *The economy of cities*. New York, NY: Random House.

Johansson, B., & Klaesson, J. (2011). Creative milieus in Stockholm. In D. E. Andersson, Å. E. Andersson & C. Mellander (Eds.), *Handbook of creative cities*. Cheltenham, UK: Edward Elgar.

Jones, E. (1981). *The European miracle*. Cambridge, UK: Cambridge University Press.

Koppl, R. G. (2002). *Big payers and the economic theory of expectations*. London, UK: Palgrave Macmillan.

Koppl, R. G., & Whitman, D. G. (2004). Rational-choice hermeneutics. *Journal of Economic Behavior and Organization*, *55*(3), 295–317.

Langlois, R. N. (1986). The new institutionalist economics: An introductory essay. In R. N. Langlois (Ed.), *Economics as a process: Essays in the new institutionalist economics*. Cambridge, UK: Cambridge University Press.

Lee, E. S. (1966). A theory of migration. *Demography*, *3*(1), 47–57.

Leppälä, S., & Desrochers, P. (2012). Regional economic analysis: The case for methodological individualism. In D. E. Andersson (Ed.), *The spatial market process*. Bingley, UK: Emerald.

Marshall, A. (1920). *Principles of economics*. London, UK: Macmillan.

Mises, L. von (1949). *Human action: A treatise on economics*. New Haven, CT: Yale University Press.

Moroni, S. (2012). Land-use planning and the question of unintended consequences. In D. E. Andersson (Ed.), *The spatial market process*. Bingley, UK: Emerald.

Olson, M. J., Jr. (1965). *The logic of collective action: Public goods and the theory of groups.* Cambridge, MA: Harvard University Press.

Olson, M. J., Jr. (1982). *The rise and decline of nations: Economic growth, stagflations, and social rigidities.* New Haven, CT: Yale University Press.

Partridge, M. D., Rickman, D. S., Olfert, M. R., & Kamar, A. (2010). Dwindling U.S. internal migration: Evidence of spatial equilibrium? Discussion paper. Retrieved from http://mpra.uk.uni-muenchen.de/28157. Accessed in May 2011.

Polanyi, M. (1962). The republic of science: Its political and economic theory. *Minerva, 1*, 54–73.

Ruger, W. P., & Sorens, J. (2009). *Freedom in the 50 states: An index of personal and economic freedom.* Fairfax, VA: Mercatus Center at George Mason University.

Schutz, A. (1932/1967). *The phenomenology of the social world.* Evanston, IL: Northwestern University Press.

Stolarick, K. (undated). *State creativity index 2006*, unpublished data. Personal correspondence with C. Mellander, Martin Prosperity Institute, University of Toronto.

Tiebout, C. (1956). A pure theory of local expenditures. *Journal of Political Economy, 64*(5), 416–424.

Vaubel, R. (2008). A history of thought on institutional competition. In A. Bergh & R. Höijer (Eds.), *Institutional competition* (pp. 29–66). Cheltenham, UK: Edward Elgar.

Weber, M. (1923/1961). *General economic history.* New York, NY: Collier.

LAND-USE PLANNING AND THE QUESTION OF UNINTENDED CONSEQUENCES

Stefano Moroni

The unintended consequences of intentional human actions are given insufficient consideration in any form of planning, particularly in land-use planning. The traditional interpretations of the city, and the rules usually employed in governing it, seem to underestimate the fact that the unintended side-effects of human action play a pivotal role in the overall outcome. In this chapter, my aim is to show how a more insightful approach to land-use issues must take into account the role of unintended consequences – not simply as a caveat, but as the very core of an appropriate vision of the urban market system and of land-use regulation. I use the term "urban market system" here in order to identify the totality of voluntary market relationships that occur in a city – in this sense, the urban market system clearly includes the land and real estate market.[1]

I will separate what can be termed the *generic* theory of unintended consequences (first section) from two more *specific* theories of unintended consequences (second section). The idea is that the generic theory is fairly obvious and needs little further discussion. In contrast, the two specific theories present a serious challenge to accepted mainstream planning theory and practice, and particularly to those concerned with spatial planning

The Spatial Market Process
Advances in Austrian Economics, Volume 16, 265–288

ISSN: 1529-2134/doi:10.1108/S1529-2134(2012)0000016013

and its system of regulation. Land-use planning is still largely exercised in an orthodox way, that is, as a mode of rational, deliberate intervention in the form of a plan. This is, in its turn, a directional set of authoritative rules that are established with the aim of achieving a desired overall state of affairs by means of deliberate coordination of the contents of private independent urban activities (Moroni, 2010a).

By a "directional set of rules" I mean a batch of guidelines that aim at defining a certain arrangement within a socio-spatial system, and that also aim at orienting various private activities. The rules that are deemed necessary to achieve this aim are particular and concrete ones, that is, rules that apply not to a class of actions by any individual, but rather to specific actions concerning specific land. Note that such rules are indispensable if we want to reach a predefined state of affairs: each component within a system must play its own specific and complementary role toward that end. (The opposite of "directional" rules are rules that are "relational," which refer to rules that are abstract and general. Relational rules contain no reference to particular objects or lots and apply to cases that are as yet unknown; thus, they do not try to attain a specific end state.)

By "coordination of contents" I mean a form of coordination whose aim is to coordinate not only the typical features of private actions but also their unique features. The actions of individuals are then coordinated not only with regard to their general, repeatable (time-independent) aspects but also as regards their specific, unrepeatable (time-dependent) ones. (The opposite of "coordination of contents" is "pattern coordination", where only the typical, repeatable aspects are coordinated; O'Driscoll & Rizzo, 1985.)

Before entering into the heart of the issue, three crucial points should be underscored. First, unintended consequences are not typical of complex systems per se, but they are typical of social complex systems. Second, to focus attention on unintended consequences – accepting that these by-products have a fundamental role in social dynamics – has an important implication: it entails acknowledging that the social sciences cannot be completely reduced to psychology.[2] The third point is that methodological individualism[3] is perfectly compatible with the idea of the importance of unintended effects, but it is not a necessary precondition. Note that while the irreducibility of the social sciences to psychology stems from the hypothesis of unintended effects, in the case of methodological individualism the relation is the reverse. In other words, methodological individualism is integrated and enhanced by accepting the hypothesis of the importance of unintended effects.

THE GENERIC THEORY OF UNINTENDED CONSEQUENCES

What I will call the *generic theory* basically affirms that there often exists a disparity between the intentions of the actors and the outcome of their actions that gives rise to side-effects that are neither expected nor predictable.[4] Unintended consequences are "incongruent" consequences, because what is in place in this case is a disparity between an action's original purpose and its results (Ermolaeva & Ross, 2011). This occurs because whenever we carry out our intentions in a complex world, there will be countless side-effects that could only partly be foreseen; most of the outcome depends on a series of combined reactions of a largely random nature. In other words, the interplay of forces and circumstances are so numerous and complex that it is impossible to consider all possible outcomes in advance. We can therefore say that any action has immediate effects – to some extent intentional and predictable – along with remote side-effects that are not necessarily intended or predictable. By acting we (intentionally) bring about certain things, while (unintentionally) provoking other things.

The generic theory has been reiterated by many authors in the course of the last century.[5] As formulated in such general terms, the theory seems neither particularly original nor revolutionary.

It is not as original as many would claim, simply because it has always been acknowledged.[6] Even in the distant past, various authors openly recognized the distinction between intentional action and its unintended consequences. Boethius, for one, noted in his *De consolatione philosophiae* (Book V, Ch. 1) that what humans in their activities call "chance" is often the upshot of the "unforeseen and unexpected coincidence" of various intentional actions, that is, the final outcome comes from a combination of converging and overlapping causes and "not from the intention of the actor [*non ex gerentis intentione*]." Boethius sums up his argument: "We may therefore define chance as an unexpected result from the coincidence of certain causes in matters where there was another purpose [*Licet igitur definire casum esse inopinatum ex confluentibus causis in his quae ob aliquid geruntur euentum*]." He concludes by observing that the reason why such things happen is known only to Providence, which oversees all human actions. A similar perspective on unintended consequences was held by Dante[7] and Vico.[8] Frédéric Bastiat (1850/2006) and Vilfredo Pareto (1916/1935) recognized and described the same phenomenon in secular sociological terms.

It should be added that the generic theory of unintended actions is hardly revolutionary, given that it does not involve any deep or surprising repercussions. For example, we cannot get very far by generically saying – as some writers uncritically do – that the scope of social theory is by and large to inquire into the unintended effects of intentional human action.

Note moreover that the generic theory merely furnishes a banal – but nonetheless relevant – criticism of planning, namely that the implementation of any given plan (such as a comprehensive land-use plan) is inevitably compromised along the way, since the plan itself triggers a great many unexpected side-effects. Jeffrey Pressman and Aaron Wildawsky (1984) offer a classic inquiry into this problem by looking at a number of specific American programs that generated outcomes that were dramatically different from the envisaged aims. As Pressman and Wildawsky (1984) note, there is no mode of organizing social and economic life which is not subject to unintended and unanticipated consequences. What happens is that "policies with unforeseen consequences are being implemented daily" (*ibid.*, p. 223). They further observe that the "lack of concern for the side effects of a policy may be attributed to a common human characteristic, the limited 'capacity for attention' beyond initial purposes. The effects of many policies are not foreseen" (*ibid.*, p. 220).

TWO MORE SPECIFIC THEORIES OF UNINTENDED CONSEQUENCES

The generic theory considered in the previous section has been developed into two more specific theories of a more surprising nature. One is what I call the *theory of perverse (unintended) consequences* and the other is what I call the *theory of virtuous (unintended) consequences*. Each of these two sub-theories will be subjected to the following five questions: (i) What does the theory actually entail? (ii) Who advanced the theory? (iii) What task does it envision for social theory? (iv) What implications does it have for planning? (v) What sort of criticisms has it elicited?

The Theory of Perverse Unintended Consequences

First Question: What Does the Theory Actually Entail?

The theory of perverse unintended consequences claims that actions often generate undesired by-products that are counterintuitive and do not merely go in a different direction, but in the *opposite* direction to the one originally intended. The action causing these side-effects is therefore counterproductive and self-defeating. Consequences backfire. According to this theory, any intentional action to improve some feature of social or economic reality "only serves to exacerbate the condition one wishes to remedy" (Hirschman, 1991, p. 7). Albert Hirschman writes that "[i]t is not just asserted that a movement or a policy will fall short of its goal ... rather, so goes the argument, the attempt to push society in a certain direction will result in its moving all right, but in the opposite direction" (*ibid.*, p. 11). The perverse outcome is therefore a special and extreme case of unintended consequences. In such cases, the idea of unintended consequences ends up acquiring a predominantly negative connotation: "'unintended' easily slides over to 'undesired' and from there to 'undesirable'" (*ibid.*, p. 38). Hirschman (*ibid.*) also notes how astonishingly simple this theory is.

Second Question: Who Advanced This Theory?

The theory of perverse side-effects was propounded most effectively by Edmund Burke (1790/1999), Joseph de Maistre (1797/1994), and Gustave Le Bon (1895/2001).[9]

Reflecting on the events of the French Revolution, De Maistre was prompted to attribute the phenomenon of the perverse side-effects of human action to a subtle notion of Providence bringing about its own ends by using human beings as its unwitting servants. As de Maistre himself wrote (1797/1994, p. 80): "One may ... notice that it is an affectation of Providence [*une affectation de la Providence*] ... that the efforts of a people to obtain a goal are precisely the means that Providence employs to keep them from it." He continues:

> If one wants to know the probable result of the French Revolution, it suffices to examine that which united all parties. They have all wanted the debasement, even the destruction, of the universal Church and the monarchy, *from which it follows* that all their efforts will culminate in the glorification of Christianity and the monarchy. All men who have written on or reflected about history have admired this secret force that makes sport of human plans [*cette force secrète qui se joue des conseils humains*]. (1797/1994, p. 80)

Elsewhere he makes the observation that "[n]o free agent can thwart the plans of the Creator without incurring in the sphere of his activity evils proportionate to the extent of the crime" (*ibid.*, p. 84).

Niccolò Machiavelli recognized and described the same phenomenon in secular terms. After having recalled examples of unintended consequences of human intentional actions, Machiavelli writes in his *Discourses* that "thus it is seen in all human affairs, upon careful examination, that you cannot avoid one inconvenience without incurring another [*Ed in tutte le cose umane si vede questo, chi le esaminerà bene, che non si può mai cancellare uno inconveniente, che non ne surga un altro*]" (Book I, Ch. 6).

In more recent times, the theory of perverse side-effects was reformulated – stripped of any metaphysical implications – by Raymond Boudon (1977). In a well-known book, Boudon emphasizes how the intentional actions of the individual always tend to generate numerous unintended consequences. But Boudon's focus is on the outcome which to his mind is theoretically and practically relevant, which is that such side-effects are basically undesired and run counter to the wishes of the actors. Thus the most important unintended side-effects at the social level are those that produce undesired outcomes, that is, perverse ones. The expression "*effets pervers*" is the technical term that Boudon uses for this phenomenon; his term has come to enjoy wide currency and it is the one that I have chosen to use here.

The theory of perverse side-effects has been further developed by Jay Forrester (1971), Michel Crozier and Erhard Friedberg (1977),[10] Charles Murray (1984), Nathan Glazer (1988), Edward Tenner (1997),[11] and William Sherden (2011).

Third Question: What Task Does It Envision for Social Theory?
Boudon (1977) argues that social theorists have given scant attention to perverse effects. He observes that in spite of the frequency of perverse effects in daily social life, attempts at modern sociological analysis are scarce. For this reason Boudon urges social theory to give priority to the analysis of perverse effects. However, if social theory ought to occupy itself mainly with perverse effects, the risk arises that by dealing only (or mainly) with perverse effects – outcomes that are not merely different but contrary to those intended – this would entail overlooking a sizeable number of other fundamental social phenomena.

Fourth Question: What Implications Does It Have for Planning?
This theory implies that it is difficult to coercively plan a complex system such as the urban market system. Steering a system toward the ends envisaged by a given plan (a comprehensive land-use plan, for example) is difficult, because the implementation of the plan generates unpredictable perverse effects that lead in the opposite direction from the initially intended one. This happens for two reasons: the particular behavior of complex social systems as well as the coercive nature of public intervention.

First, complex social systems frequently mislead us (Forrester, 1971). This is due to the great number of components that are connected in a nonlinear way with numerous feedback loops. In a simple system, the cause of a problem is usually close to its symptoms. In a complex system, the causes are often far removed – in both time and space – from the symptoms we experience. Therefore, the attention of decision-makers and planners often focuses on spatiotemporal "influence points" within a complex system at which attempts to interfere inevitably fail. Complex systems often mislead us, since we are accustomed to thinking about simple systems. They do this by presenting us with apparent causes that meet our immediate and surface expectations. Typically, complex social systems contain a very small number of influence points at which their behavior can be significantly changed. These influence points are usually not where we expect them to be. The "urban market system" is a good example: it involves a highly complex system of exchanges and interactions that is often treated as a simple system. Its true complexity is often deceptive; public intervention is consequently applied to the wrong elements, with counterproductive results (Holcombe & Powell, 2009; Holcombe & Staley, 2001).

As regards the coercive nature of public intervention, the point is that the likely occurrence of perverse effects depends not only on the intrinsic complexity of the system. It also depends on the fact that the state intervenes as a monopoly supplier of lawful coercion (DeMuth, 2009). This fact causes a certain resistance as well as contrarian actions by private actors, who are obliged to modify their behavior to bring it in line with the public directives. In particular, "the greater the divergence between public and private purposes, the greater will be the tendency for private responses to nullify government rules" (DeMuth, 2009, p. 18). For example, state power over land-use planning has been and continues to be a particularly strong form of power that can have substantial effects on individual freedom and private property rights, as in the case of property rights over land. Land-use planning often tries to intervene *directly* in land-use markets, in an attempt to obtain specific outputs through directional rules (that are concrete and specific, rather than abstract and general); this causes reactions on the part of the urban actors and developers: they "work against" the plan, creating the condition for chains of perverse unintended consequences. In the case of the directional rules that are employed to guide land-use markets, the aforementioned divergence between public and private purposes tends to be unusually pronounced.

Let us look at some more concrete examples of these perverse effects in land-use planning. A relevant example concerns the effects from land-use planning as it is applied to old urban neighborhoods. William Sherden writes:

> City planners' efforts to improve old – but otherwise healthy – urban neighborhoods have unintentionally caused their decline ... Older cities that have grown organically are social ecosystems consisting of numerous individuals in pursuit of business, pleasure, and domestic matters. They have thrived unplanned and are self-sustaining, vibrant, safe, adaptive places. Urban planners with the best intentions to improve these cities have caused a number of them to collapse, leaving behind decaying structures that once housed a diversity of human activities. (2011, pp. 146–147)

As is well known, this kind of criticism of orthodox land-use planning was developed in depth by Jane Jacobs (1961).

Another example can be seen in policies aimed at fostering greater cohesion within towns, which have resulted in further disintegration. Stephen Macedo writes that

> [a]mong the great complaints of our time is the decline of neighborhoods and neighborliness, of informal social ties, voluntary cooperation, and mutual aid. There is no doubt in my mind that well-intended but misguided government interventions have had a significant deleterious impact on the quality of civil society in metropolitan areas: without intending it, governments have positively encouraged urban decline.[12] (1999, p. 292)

Another example is so-called "inclusionary zoning" – a policy promoted by many local governments in the United States and Europe. The point of inclusionary zoning is the forced imposition of a desired social mixture at the neighborhood level. This is achieved by coercing developers to include within their new residential settlements a quota of buildings that are intended for people from low-income groups. The quota is usually composed of price-controlled units. It is called "inclusionary zoning" to contrast it with "exclusionary zoning" (for instance, zoning that imposes large-lot requirements in order to *exclude* low-cost housing).

The aim of inclusionary zoning is twofold: to promote social mixture and to guarantee affordable housing. As regards the issue of social mixture, inclusionary zoning often fails: an imposed mix does not necessarily promote a real mix, which would be one characterized by reciprocal tolerance and effective integration. In many cases, policies that impose a specific social mixture merely add to the tensions, increasing the perceived distance between groups. In urban areas where this type of mix is "forced," the dwellings that are reserved for low-income households become even more easily recognizable in the proximity of dwellings that are intended for other social classes. Residents' perceived isolation becomes even stronger than previously (Ruming, Mee, & McGuirk, 2004).

The intent of providing affordable housing is often a failure too: the irony of inclusionary zoning is that, in the places where it has been adopted, "its net effects are apt to be the opposite of the ones advertised" (Ellickson, 1981, p. 1216). The overall effect is that "these programs are essentially taxes on the production of new housing. The programs will usually increase general housing prices, a result which further limits the housing opportunities of moderate-income families" (*ibid.*, p. 1170). The inclusionary burden does not simply reduce the developer's profit (as the proponents of inclusionary zoning believe) but, instead, increases housing prices in general. The conclusion is that inclusionary zoning "is a misguided undertaking that is likely to aggravate the housing crisis it has ostensibly been designed to help solve" (*ibid.*, p. 1215); "despite the assertions of inclusionary zoning proponents, most inclusionary ordinances are just another form of exclusionary practice" (*ibid.*, p. 1216).[13]

Another interesting example can be found in programs for public control over rental agreements, which are introduced to favor households with little financial support. Such programs have made house rentals less profitable, thereby reducing the stock of rented accommodation. The result is thus that they have exacerbated the situation for those seeking a place to live (Brown, 2009; Ikeda, 2005; Kasper & Streit, 1998).

Perverse effects have also been generated by smaller projects. One example is the promotion of skywalks. City planners introducing skywalks – for instance in Des Moines, Iowa, where three miles of skywalks were built in 1983 – thought about them as instruments for saving the inner city by providing safer public places. But what happened was that skywalks made cities more dangerous, since they reduce pedestrian street-level traffic, thereby causing street-level shops to close and street-level property values to decline. A side-effect is the creation of unsafe street-level areas (Sherden, 2011).[14]

In general terms, Milton Friedman (1988) calls government policies and plans that produce effects contrary to those intended the "invisible foot of government."

Fifth Question: What Sort of Criticisms Has It Elicited?

Taken in its less extreme form (an action *can* generate perverse effects), the theory of perverse effects is a compelling one: every public intervention – such as land-use planning, especially if top-down detailed zoning – can induce unexpected effects that run counter to the original goals. Taken in its extreme form (an action *always* generates perverse effects), the theory is less persuasive: if *all* actions produced perverse effects, namely an outcome that goes against the actor's intentions and is completely undesired, the world would be impossible to live in; ours would indeed be a dire world.

More importantly, in some cases the unintended effects of actions can actually be positive – prevalently positive, or at any event significantly positive (Gillon, 2000; Hirschman, 1991).[15] Hirschman (1991) observes that ours is certainly not "the best of all possible worlds," but neither is it "the most perverse of all possible worlds" – a point which leads us to the next topic.

The Theory of Virtuous Unintended Consequences

First Question: What Does the Theory Actually Entail?

The theory of unintended virtuous consequences claims that there can be orderly social structures – advantageous ones from the individuals' point of view – as an unintended effect of particular ways that intentional human actions tend to combine. These social structures are emergent "spontaneous orders." As Chandran Kukathas observes, the notions of unintended consequences and spontaneous order are therefore not equivalent:

> Not all unintended consequences of human action result in the formation of spontaneous orders. The notion of unintended or unanticipated consequences is a far broader notion which refers not only to the stable patterns or formations which issue from human action, but to all unforeseen results which follow. The notion of a spontaneous order, however, refers more narrowly to those results which form complex orderings or patterns ... While we may find that, within society, many human actions will have unintended consequences, only some of them will lead to the formation of regularized patterns of behaviour or orders.[16] (1990, p. 89)

Spontaneous orders make up a very particular subset of unintended consequences. They exhibit the following characteristics. First, a single individual's action is not sufficient to bring about spontaneous orders; to have them we need a multiplicity of individuals interacting, and, additionally, they must be able to bridge spatial discontinuities by exchanging information. Second, the individuals that make up a spontaneous order do not pursue the same end, and the overall consequences are not intended by the individuals. Third, the consequences are located at the social level, which is to say that they constitute a social phenomenon – specifically, an emergent macro-social structure. Fourth, consequences are generally beneficial for the individuals involved (cf. Aydinonat, 2008, pp. 11–126).

The theory of unintended virtuous effects is exemplified by the spontaneous market order.[17] Social systems such as the market order generate emergent patterns of behavior; the orderliness of the ensemble of actions that spontaneously emerges is in no sense part of the aim of any single individual. It is interesting to note that the greater is the diversity of the individuals in a system, the richer are the emergent global patterns. As a specific instance of spontaneous order, the market order is clearly the most efficient, productive, and creative economic mechanism yet discovered. The reason that the market system is so efficient and productive is because it is able to spontaneously activate and make use of dispersed knowledge. Thanks to a decentralized self-adapting mechanism we are able to make use of more knowledge. And this is true also for urban market systems.

Over a century ago the question was broached by Frédéric Bastiat (1846/2001, pp. 79–80), who wrote:

> On entering a very large city … I said to myself: Here are a million human beings who would all die in a short time if provisions of every kind ceased to flow towards this great metropolis … How does each succeeding day bring what is wanted …? What, then, is the ingenious and secret power which governs the astonishing regularity of movements so complicated, a regularity in which everybody has implicit faith …? That power … is the principle of freedom in transactions. (1846/2001, pp.79–80)

Discussions about cities and urban market systems are often hampered by the widespread acceptance of a distinction first introduced in ancient Greece: In modern terms, the distinction separates what we call *natural phenomena* from *artificial phenomena*. Friedrich Hayek (1982, vol. I, p. 20) observes that the original Greek terms were "*physei*, which means 'by nature' and, in contrast to it, either *nomō*, best rendered as 'by convention,' or *thesei*, which means roughly 'by deliberate decision.'" The use of these last two quite different terms (*nomō*/*thesei*) to capture the second element of the dichotomy (*the artificial phenomena*) has generated confusion that still affects many theorists.

For example, Joseph Rykwert (2000) writes that cities are not a natural phenomenon (as some – in Rykwert's opinion – seem to think, speaking of cities as spontaneous phenomena), since they depend on human actions and decisions. Rykwert (2000, p. 10) states that "[a]lthough no town or city I live can possibly be exactly as I wish it … yet the way it looks and the way it works has been determined by people like myself, not by impersonal forces … What sometimes looks like an impersonal force is often a vector … resulting from all our decisions."

In contrast to Rykwert, I believe that we should distinguish clearly and decisively among three – not two – kinds of phenomena. First, there are natural phenomena which have nothing to do with human decisions and actions, such as an earthquake. Second, there are artificial phenomena which are the direct result of deliberate human decisions and actions, such as the construction of a bridge. Third, there are artificial phenomena which are the unintentional result of the interplay among intentional decisions and actions, such as the urban market system.

What we should also consider is the fact that the theory of virtuous unintended effects is by no means simple like its perverse counterpart, but is highly complex. It employs a particularly sophisticated version of the so-called "invisible hand explanation."[18]

Second Question: Who Advanced This Theory?

Hayek was most important for developing this theory[19] even though the groundwork had been laid much earlier by others. Early contributors not only included Bernard Mandeville (1723/1997), Adam Ferguson (1767/1995), David Hume (1740/2000), Adam Smith (1776/1993), and Carl Menger (1883/1986), but also the less-famous theorists Pierre de Boisguilbert (1707/2004) and Anders Chydenius (1765/2009).[20] Chydenius (1765/2009) contends that "[e]very individual spontaneously tries to find the place and the trade in which he can best increase National gain, if laws do not prevent him from doing so" (*ibid.*, § 5). In that situation "[e]very man seeks his own gain … . The work that has the greatest value is always best paid, and what is best paid is most sought after" (*ibid.*, § 5). Thus, "[w]hen I consulted experience, I soon realized that the more liberty had been allowed to reign in a trade, the greater was always its increase, and vice versa, and the more evenly this liberty was distributed, the more naturally were the trades balanced against each other" (*ibid.*, § 33).

Third Question: What Task Does It Envision for Social Theory?

In this case, the idea that social theory must deal with unintended effects becomes more interesting and precise, inasmuch as it is concerned with the fundamental task of dealing with unintended effects that combine in spontaneous orders, such as in urban market systems. Hayek's view – in particular – is that "to provide an 'invisible-hand explanation' of social order, to show how social order can emerge as an unintended outcome of separate individual choices, is the most challenging task for social theory" (Vanberg, 1994, pp. 225–226). Actually, we might say that it is *only* in this specific case that the assertion that social theory must tackle unintended effects becomes truly innovative and full of surprises.

Fourth Question: What Implications Does It Have for Planning?

The theory of unintended virtuous effects – especially the theory of the market as a form of spontaneous order – gives rise to a more sophisticated and incisive critique of planning, particularly land-use planning. I should stress here that the current conventional approaches to land-use planning remain for the most part top-down and are based on a form of "constructivistic rationalism," to use Hayek's (1982) terminology. In fact, in many countries planning practice is still based on the idea that it is possible to steer and manage urban development in a top-down and detailed manner, by way of some sort of general, more or less flexible plan.[21]

The general critique of attempts at guiding markets contends that it is not possible to use intentional organization of activities in a way that makes efficient use of dispersed knowledge in the same way as it is possible to (spontaneously) obtain it through the unplanned market order. In other words, it is impossible to intentionally concentrate the dispersed knowledge that enables complex economic systems to function. It is impossible because the relevant knowledge is both situated (know-how specific in space and time) and tacit (know-how acquired through "learning by doing" and therefore internalized in the mind of the individual, who makes use of it without deliberate, explicit reflection). The consequence is that this social knowledge can never be made "public." Any attempt to do so – that is, to intentionally centralize knowledge and guide the economy – would result in reduced productivity and efficiency. Centralization implies that we would be forcing the system to use less than the knowledge that is actually available in society, thereby reducing opportunities for experimentation.

This critique holds for land-use planning too: all-embracing land-use planning tends to impede the activation and use of the intrinsically dispersed and dynamic knowledge of how to use urban land. In particular, orthodox land-use planning centered on zoning tends to reduce both the efficiency of urban market systems (by introducing arbitrary connections between the demand and supply of land and buildings[22]) and their creativity. Creativity is impeded because both society as a whole and the economy are intrinsically rooted in change: a fixed land-use pattern will not only become quickly obsolete, but will in itself impede social and economic experimentation (Moroni, 2007, 2010a, 2011a).[23]

Hayek (1960) contends that

> [w]e must not overlook the fact that the market has, on the whole, guided the evolution of cities more successfully ... than is commonly realized and that most of the proposals to improve upon this, not by making it work better, but by superimposing a system of central direction, show little awareness of what such a system would have to accomplish, even to equal the market in effectiveness. (p. 342)

Moreover,

> [o]nly a method which operates mainly through the inducements and data offered to the private owner and which leaves him free in the use of a particular piece of land is likely to produce satisfactory results, since no other method will make as full use of the dispersed knowledge of the prospects and possibilities of development as the market does. (*ibid.*, p. 352)

Interestingly, whereas the theories discussed earlier – the generic theory of unintended effects, and the specific theory of perverse unintended effects – have attracted a degree of interest in the field of land-use planning,[24] the theory discussed here – the specific theory of unintended virtuous effects – has been largely ignored by planning theorists and practitioners. A large part of orthodox and current land-use theory can be re-interpreted as a position that denies the very existence and possibility of spontaneous orders.[25]

Fifth Question: What Sort of Criticisms Has It Elicited?

We saw earlier how the theory of unintended perverse effects tends to overstate the (unintended) *negative* repercussions. What we might ask now is whether, by the same token, the theory of unintended virtuous effects has the same, opposite, tendency of overstating the (unintended) *positive* outcomes. Some writers have pointed out that Hayek fails to give due attention to the possibility that social situations unintentionally created can wreak havoc on the same individuals who helped them come about (Buchanan, 1977; Hodgson, 1993). Similar criticisms have been raised against attempts to transpose the Hayekian idea of spontaneous orders to the city and the urban market (Camagni, 2008; Cusinato, 2009).

Two observations can be made in response to these criticisms. First and foremost, Hayek does not claim that all spontaneously generated situations or configurations are positive (Vanberg, 1994). Second, for Hayek a spontaneous order – for instance, a spontaneous market order – is not just any orderly situation, but a particular stable structure that requires certain conditions. The conditions include the existence of determinate rules of conduct that *exclude* from the outset certain possible outcomes, even though it is *not* possible to *determine* the overall desirable consequences (Moroni, 2007, 2010a, 2011a).

It is true that even the theory of virtuous unintended consequences can be inappropriately radicalized, which would imply the fallacy of seeing always and only the positive outcomes of pluralistic social action. But it is also true that Hayek's views comprise decisive elements for a more balanced and insightful interpretation of spontaneous-order theory.

CONCLUSIONS: TWO THESES

There are two central theses in this chapter. First, it is important to distinguish between two different (specific) theories of unintended consequences. Both are relevant, and they are compatible if appropriately and nonradically interpreted. Second, if we use *directional rules* to intervene in urban market systems we are likely to generate perverse effects. Conversely, if we limit ourselves to *relational rules*, we are more likely to reap the rewards of beneficial unintended effects.

The Relevance of the Proposed Distinctions

To summarize, I believe it is essential to distinguish the generic theory of unintended consequences from the two specific theories. It is even more essential to distinguish between the latter two. In support of this position, I refer to Amartya Sen's statement regarding the Hayekian position:

> The Hayekian claim regarding the profundity of the insight provided by the perspective of "the results of human action but not of human design" seems to me to be difficult to sustain ... It is, I fear, an *un*profound thought to recognize that any action has many results that were not part of the design of the agent. This cannot but be the case. (1984, p. 92)

Sen illustrates his point by imagining someone crossing a road, who finds himself on the other side according to his intentions; but the act of crossing the road has spawned various unintended effects, such as slowing down a passing car, causing the motorist to be slightly late in getting home, and therefore affecting the series of actions the latter completed in and around his house. "If this discourse is generating boredom," notes Sen, "then I have succeeded in making my point. The recognition that many results of our actions are not reflections of our design can, in itself, scarcely be one of great profundity" (*ibid.*, p. 93).

If the *only* thing Hayek aimed to highlight was that our actions often have unintended consequences, Sen would be right. This fact has been acknowledged all along. But the point is that Hayek above all focused on the fact that, under certain conditions, our intentional actions unintentionally give rise to overall ordered phenomena that take advantage of dispersed knowledge, thereby guaranteeing dispersed benefits. I am referring here to the theory of unintended virtuous effects. This theory is neither banal nor obvious.[26]

I note that from his earliest systematic attempts to tackle the issue of unintended consequences, Hayek (1967, p. 97) is not interested in the generic theory, and focuses exclusively on "unintended patterns and regularities."

Trying to Minimize Perverse Unintended Effects While Facilitating Beneficial Unintended Effects

By way of conclusion, the topic of unintended consequences is crucial both for interpreting the way in which cities and, in particular, urban market systems function, and for understanding how local government should – or should not – intervene in them. As we have seen, if the theory of perverse unintended consequences is interpreted in a non-extreme way, and the theory of virtuous unintended consequences is also interpreted appropriately, the two theories are compatible rather than contradictory. They are thus both useful at the same time.

From this perspective – bearing in mind the definitions used – we can say that perverse unintended consequences tend to increase if we intervene in the urban market system mainly through *directional rules* in order to attain *coordination of contents* (i.e., through rules that are intended to achieve substantive predefined urban patterns and that are mainly based on the abstract knowledge of experts). Perverse unintended consequences can be expected to decrease, together with an increase in benign unintended consequences, if we limit ourselves to *relational rules* that aim at *pattern coordination* (in this case, only the reciprocal sphere of the free action of urban actors is specified, and ample leeway is allowed for the activation of local, dispersed knowledge) (Moroni, 2010a).

The point then is not rules versus laissez-faire, but rules of one kind (directional rules to directly obtain an order of urban actions) versus rules of another kind (relational rules to indirectly favor self-coordination of urban actions). As I have suggested, the issue involves jettisoning an *instrumental idea of the law* in favor of a *framework idea of the law*. It entails abandoning a "teleocratic" approach to regulating land use in favor of a "nomocratic" approach (Moroni, 2010a). In addition, this implies that orthodox plans should be replaced by "urban codes" of a more abstract and general nature, which are limited to excluding (a small subset of) outcomes with evident and direct harm to others, while leaving ample room for experiments such as new economic activities and new urban lifestyles (Moroni, 2011a).

The relational rules collected in the urban code refer to typical situations and are based on knowledge of typical facts. They are mainly negative rules that impede certain kinds of externalities in the construction and use of buildings – that is, external effects that stem from development, and which directly and tangibly affect someone. Such an urban code is thus solely concerned with the impersonal and impartial framework of social activities, not their concrete trajectory. It accommodates the unforeseen. The aim of the relational rules that make up an urban code is pattern coordination, not content coordination (Moroni, 2007). In this case the set of rules and the order of actions *do not* coincide.

Because we are dealing with *unintended* consequences, it is impossible to pin down the exact way of inducing the greatest number of positive unintended consequences. That said, I believe that the lesson of the two specific theories is that it shows us what instruments to *avoid* in order to minimize perverse effects – that is, orthodox urban plans – and what situations to *encourage* in order to favor benign urban outcomes: We should encourage self-organization through the application of abstract and general relational rules.

NOTES

1. Obviously, each urban market system is part of more comprehensive market system.

2. In other words, the problem of social interaction cannot be entirely confined or reduced – without the "rest" – to problems related to what the individuals themselves think. If a large part of all social effects are indeed unintentional, we cannot get very far if we focus exclusively on individual intentions and on the laws that regulate how they are formed (Popper, 1945).

3. The familiar notion of methodological individualism asserts that all social phenomena must be explained only in terms of individuals' goals and actions (Mises, 1933/1960; Popper, 1957).

4. Here individuals are taken to be "purposive actors," that is, acting on the basis of motives and making choices between alternatives.

5. These authors took their cue from a renowned essay by Merton (1936), which placed the theme firmly at the center of the debate.

6. Vernon (1979, p. 57) writes: "That actions regularly bring about consequences unintended by the actor is scarcely a controversial point."

7. Let us look at what Dante says in the *Convivio* (Book IV, Ch. 5): "It is no wonder if divine providence, which wholly transcends angelic and human powers of perception, often proceeds in ways that are hidden to us, inasmuch as human actions frequently conceal their meanings from men themselves [*Non è maraviglia se la divina provedenza, che del tutto l'angelico e lo umano accorgimento soperchia, occultamente a noi molte volte procede, con ciò sia cosa che spesse volte l'umane operazioni a li uomini medesimi ascondono la loro intenzione*]."

8. Here are the words of Vico in his *Principi di scienza nuova* (Conclusion): "It is true that men have themselves made this world of nations ... but this world without doubt has issued from a mind often diverse, at times quite contrary, and always superior to the particular ends that men had proposed to themselves; which narrow ends, made means to serve wider ends, it has always employed to preserve the human race upon this earth [*Perché pur gli uomini hanno essi fatto questo mondo di nazioni ... ma egli è questo mondo, senza dubbio, uscito da una mente spesso diversa ed alle volte tutta contraria e sempre superiore ad essi fini particolari ch'essi uomini si avevan proposti; quali fini ristretti, fatti mezzi per servire a fini più ampi, gli ha sempre adoperati per conservare l'umana generazione in questa terra*]."

9. Actually, the theory of unintended perverse effects is extensively covered in literature (novels). In *Bleak House* by Charles Dickens, one of the characters, Richard Carstone, describes himself thus: "You must know that I have done no good this long time. I have not intended to do much harm, but I seem to have been capable of nothing else." Likewise, in Goethe's *Faust*, Mephistopheles describes himself as a "part of the force that always tries to do evil and always does good [*Ein Teil von jener Kraft, die stets das Böse will und stets das Gute schafft*]."

10. Crozier and Friedberg (1977) speak of a fundamental mechanism at work in human activities: a mechanism by which in aiming to do good, we do the opposite – like some kind of "black magic" accompanying all human action, and leading to the opposite effect of the one we aimed for.

11. Edward Tenner (1997) focuses on this perverse logic in the area of technology: "The real revenge is not what we do intentionally against one another. It is the tendency of the world around us to get even, to twist our cleverness against us. Or it is our own unconscious twisting against ourselves. Either way, wherever we turn we face the ironic unintended consequences of mechanical, chemical, biological, and medical ingenuity – revenge effects, they may be called." Tenner explains that a revenge effect is not the same thing as a side-effect; a revenge effect is something diametrically opposed to original intentions. He observes moreover that technology does not produce a revenge effect in itself: only when we "anchor" technology in laws, regulations, and habits does a revenge effect reach its full potential (*ibid.*, p. 9).

12. As is well known, several recent studies (e.g., Putnam, 2000) have observed that social capital has been declining steadily from the second half of the twentieth century to the present. As David Beito, Peter Gordon, and Alexander Tabarrok (2002, p. 7) point out, "[i]t would be a mistake, however, to correlate this decline with 'capitalism,' as it coincides more closely with the rise of the welfare state. The rise of the welfare state and the diminution of property rights crowded out the private provision of many collective goods and social services that had shown considerable merit."

13. See also Powell and Stringham (2009, p. 110): inclusionary zoning is essentially "a price control on a percentage of units and a tax on the remaining

market-rate units and it leads to decreased production and increased prices for the vast majority of buyers."

14. In more general terms, the same perverse effects can be found in the failure of certain welfare policies: specific measures taken to reduce poverty have completely backfired, causing instead a rise in poverty (Glazer, 1988; Murray, 1984). As Murray (1984, p. 9) writes: "We tried to provide more for the poor and produced more poor instead. We tried to remove the barriers to escape from poverty, and inadvertently built a trap." Glazer (1988, p. 3) writes that "[o]ur efforts to deal with distress are themselves increasing distress." Similar perverse effects have emerged with the failed policies for helping so-called Third World states: policies intended to help the population (for instance, money transfers) did not help them but instead their national gatekeepers while creating a situation of unending dependence (Bauer, 2004; Moyo, 2009). For other examples of perverse effects of public policies and planning, see James (1980), Scott (1998), O'Toole (2007), Holcombe and Powell (2009), Dahrendorf, Elkana, Neier, Newton-Smith, and Rév (2000), Ermolaeva and Ross (2011).

15. On the fact that the unintended consequences can have both *negative* and *positive* outcomes, see also Margetts, 6, and Hood (2010).

16. See also Petsoulas (2001, p. 12): "The fact that spontaneous orders are unintended consequences of human action does not mean ... that every unintended consequence can be considered a spontaneous order. A spontaneous formation can be characterised as an order when it has a structure, and also when it is beneficial for the individual involved." (cf. Smith, 2006, pp. 1–14.)

17. Other cases of spontaneous order can be used to illustrate the same point, but for the time being I will consider the exemplary case of the market, because it is crucial to my basic argument about the city and the forms of land-use regulation.

18. The aim in the case of invisible-hand explanations (Koppl, 1994; Langlois, 1986; Nozick, 1974, 1997; Ullmann-Margalit, 1977, 1978) is to oppose the idea that a good explanation of situations and of existing social patterns must always try to pinpoint the "responsible" element behind such situations or patterns; in other words, the purpose is to "downsize" the role and importance of visible-hand or conspiratorial explanations. It is no wonder therefore that the invisible-hand explanations often supplant the visible-hand ones, inferring complex and indirect cause-and-effect relations in the place of more simple and direct ones. According to Nozick (1974), invisible-hand explanations are good because they make no use of notions "constituting" what is to be explained – or, at least, minimize the use of notions constituting the phenomenon to be explained. (The opposite happens with visible- and hidden-hand explanations).

19. Polanyi (1951) also helped develop the theory of spontaneous order. The two theorists – Hayek and Polanyi – knew each other and were familiar with their respective work. Contrary to what some writers claim (Gray, 1980), I believe that Hayek's reflections in this regard are for the most part original, and that he should be credited with having constructed an innovative theory of spontaneous order (see also Bladel, 2005).

20. The theory of spontaneous (market) order was further developed, in the wake of Hayek's contribution, by contemporary Austrian economists such as O'Driscoll and Rizzo (1985), and Kirzner (1973, 1992). There are few discussions around this little-known (and not widely appreciated) notion of the market in the land-use planning literature: among the few, see Pennington (1999, 2002, 2003); Holcombe

and Staley (2001); Webster and Lai (2003); Holcombe and Powell (2009); Moroni (2010a, 2011a).

21. The public authorities tend to have great powers to dictate development: as land use planning is currently worked out, it usually involves detailed plans regarding how private landowners can use their properties. In such cases, central and local governments feel confident that they possess the information and skill necessary for managing the evolution of urban growth. The idea is that a top-down, conscious ordering process is the only one possible. It is important to emphasize here that both imperative land-use planning (the kind of planning that, e.g., is usual in Italy) and flexible land-use planning (the kind that is usual in Great Britain) assume the validity of this view (Moroni, 2007).

22. With the consequence, for example, of raising housing prices.

23. Another critique, focused on a more general level of discourse, concerns intervention in the "basic social institutions" (rather than specifically urban interventionism). This critique holds that it is not possible to consider the basic institutions as modifiable at will while pursuing specific ends. Many social institutions, such as the institution of private land ownership or rules regarding the sale and purchase of land parcels, have evolved spontaneously over time through trial and error, and encapsulate the accumulated wisdom of several generations (Hayek, 1988). We must, therefore, treat these institutions with a different type of awareness and respect, and act with greater caution. This critique likewise holds for many forms of meta-planning (institutional design), which often aim to completely restructure the basic institutions of the urban market (Moroni, 2010b, 2011b).

24. See, for instance, the famous work by Hall (1980) and, more recently, Sager (1994).

25. See, for instance, the classical work by Abercrombie (1943). Criticizing Adam Smith's idea of the invisible hand, he observes that the city should not be "under the domination of the muddler who will talk about the Law of Supply and Demand and the Liberty of the Individual," but under the control of planning: "Town and country planning seeks to proffer a *guiding hand* to the trend of natural evolution, as a result of careful study of the place itself and its external relationships" (*ibid.*, p. 27, emphasis added).

26. In some passages that follow those cited here, Sen (1984) appears to acknowledge (referring to Adam Smith, without revising his judgement of Hayek) that the invisible-hand effect in the market context is perhaps something different; but there too he attempts to minimize it, noting that in the case of economic exchanges in the market "[t]here is nothing startling or deeply illuminating in the recognition that not all the results were part of the design of every agent" (*ibid.*, p. 93).

REFERENCES

Abercrombie, P. (1943). *Town and country planning*. London, UK: Oxford University Press.

Aydinonat, N. H. (2008). *The invisible hand in economics: How economists explain unintended social consequences*. London, UK: Routledge.

Bastiat, F. (1846/2001). *Sophismes economique* [*Economic fallacies*]. Paris. Safety Harbor, FL: Simon.

Bastiat, F. (1850/2006). *Ce qu'on voit et ce qu'on ne voit pas* [*That which is seen and that which is not seen*]. West Valley City, UT: Waking Lion Press.

Bauer, P. T. (2004). *From subsistence to exchange and other essays.* Princeton, NJ: Princeton University Press.

Beito, D. T., Gordon, P., & Tabarrok, A. (2002). Toward a rebirth of civil society. In D. T. Beito, P. Gordon & A. Tabarrok (Eds.), *The voluntary city* (pp. 1–12). Ann Arbor, MI: The University of Michigan Press.

Bladel, J. P. (2005). Against Polanyi-centrism: Hayek and the re-emergence of spontaneous order. *Quarterly Journal of Austrian Economics*, *8*(4), 15–30.

Boethius, S. (undated/1902). *De consolatione philosophiae* [*The consolation of philosophy*]. London, UK: Dent.

Boisguilbert, P. de (1707/2004). *Dissertation de la nature des richesses, de l'argent, et des tributs.* Italian translation in O. Nicastro (Ed.), *Economisti francesi del primo settecento.* Pisa: ETS.

Boudon, R. (1977). *Effets pervers et ordre social.* Paris: PUF.

Brown, M. E. (2009). A brief survey of rent control in America: Past mistakes and future directions. In R. G. Holcombe & B. Powell (Eds.), *Housing America* (pp. 133–155). New Brunswick, NJ: Transaction Publishers.

Buchanan, J. M. (1977). *Freedom in constitutional contract.* College Station, TX: Texas A&M University Press.

Burke, E. (1999). *Reflections on the revolution in France.* Oxford, UK: Oxford University Press.

Camagni, R. (2008). Le ragioni del piano. Perché il divorzio fra liberalismo e pianificazione è insostenibile. *Scienze Regionali*, *7*(1), 101–122.

Chydenius, A. (1765/2009). *Den Nationnale Winsten.* [Italian Translation: *La ricchezza della nazione.*] Macerata: Liberilibri.

Crozier, M., & Friedberg, E. (1977). *L'acteur et le système.* Paris: Èditions du Seuil.

Cusinato, A. (2009). Le ragioni del piano, tra ideologia e storia. *Scienze Regionali*, *8*(2), 121–130.

Dahrendorf, R., Elkana, Y., Neier, A., Newton-Smith, W., & Rév, I. (Eds.). (2000). *The paradoxes of unintended consequences.* Budapest: Central European University Press.

Dante. (undated/1990). *Il convivio* [*The Convivio*] New York, NY: Garland.

DeMuth, C. (2009). *Unintended consequences and intended non-consequences.* Working Paper. American Enterprise Institute for Public Policy Research, Washington.

Dickens, C. (1977). *Bleak house.* New York, NY: Norton.

Ellickson, R. C. (1981). The irony of inclusionary zoning. *Southern California Law Review*, *54*, 1167–1216.

Ermolaeva, E., & Ross, J. (2011). *Unintended consequences of human actions.* Lanham, MD: University Press of America.

Ferguson, A. (1995). *An essay on the history of civil society.* Cambridge, UK: Cambridge University Press.

Forrester, J. W. (1971). Counterintuitive behaviour of social systems. *Technology Review*, *73*(3), 52–68.

Friedman, M. (1988). Social security: The general and the personal. *Wall Street Journal*, March 15.

Gillon, S. M. (2000). *That's not what we meant to do. Reform and its unintended consequences in twentieth-century America.* New York, NY: Norton.

Glazer, N. (1988). *The limits of social policy.* Cambridge, MA: Harvard University Press.

Goethe, J. W. von (1808/2000). *Faust* (English translation). New York, NY: Norton.
Gray, J. N. (1980). F.A. Hayek on liberty and tradition. *Journal of Libertarian Studies*, *4*(2), 119–137.
Hall, P. (1980). *Great planning disasters*. London, UK: Weidenfeld and Nicolson.
Hayek, F. A. (1960). *The constitution of liberty*. London, UK: Routledge.
Hayek, F. A. (1967). *Studies in philosophy, politics and economics*. London, UK: Routledge.
Hayek, F. A. (1982). *Law, legislation and liberty*. London, UK: Routledge.
Hayek, F. A. (1988). *The fatal conceit*. London, UK: Routledge.
Hirschman, A. O. (1991). *The rhetoric of reaction: Perversity, futility, jeopardy*. Cambridge, MA: Harvard University Press.
Hodgson, G. M. (1993). *Economics and evolution*. Ann Arbor, MI: University of Michigan Press.
Holcombe, R. G., & Powell, B. (Eds.). (2009). *Housing America*. New Brunswick, NJ: Transaction Publishers.
Holcombe, R. G., & Staley, S. R. (Eds.). (2001). *Smarter growth*. Westport, CT: Greenwood Press.
Hume, D. (2000). *A treatise of human nature*. Oxford, UK: Oxford University Press.
Ikeda, S. (2005). The dynamics of interventionism. In P. Kurrild-Klitgaard (Ed.), *The dynamics of intervention* (pp. 21–57). Oxford, UK: Elsevier.
Jacobs, J. (1961). *The death and life of great American cities*. New York, NY: Random House.
James, R. (1980). *Return to reason*. London, UK: Open Books.
Kasper, W., & Streit, M. E. (1998). *Institutional economics*. Cheltenham, UK: Edward Elgar.
Kirzner, I. M. (1973). *Competition and entrepreneurship*. Chicago, IL: University of Chicago Press.
Kirzner, I. M. (1992). *The meaning of market process*. London, UK: Routledge.
Koppl, R. G. (1994). "Invisible-hand" explanations. In P. J. Boettke (Ed.), *The Elgar companion to Austrian economics* (pp. 192–196). Aldershot, UK: Edward Elgar.
Kukathas, C. (1990). *Hayek and modern liberalism*. Oxford, UK: Clarendon Press.
Langlois, R. N. (1986). Rationality, institutions and explanations. In R. N. Langlois (Ed.), *Economics as a process* (pp. 225–255). Cambridge, UK: Cambridge University Press.
Le Bon, G. (1895/2001). *Psychologie des foules* [*The crowd*]. Kitchener, ON: Batoche Books.
Macedo, S. (1999). Hayek's liberal legacy. *Cato Journal*, *19*(2), 289–300.
Machiavelli, N. (1531/1882). *Discorsi sopra la prima deca di Tito Livio* [*Discourses*. The Historical, Political, and Diplomatic Writings of Niccolò Machiavelli]. Boston, MA: J.R. Osgood and Company.
Maistre, J. de (1797/1994). *Considérations sur la France* [*Considerations on France*]. Cambridge, UK: Cambridge University Press.
Mandeville, B. (1997). *The fable of the bees*. Indianapolis, IN: Hackett.
Margetts, H., 6, P., & Hood, C. (Eds.). (2010). *Paradoxes of modernization: Unintended consequences of public policy reform*. Oxford, UK: Oxford University Press.
Menger, C. (1883/1986). *Untersuchungen über die Methode der Socialwissenschaften und der politischen Ökonomie insbesondere*. [English translation: *Investigations into the Method of the Social Sciences with Special Reference to Economics*.] New York, NY: New York University Press.
Merton, R. K. (1936). The unanticipated consequences of purposive social action. *American Sociological Review*, *1*(6), 894–904.
Mises, L. von (1933/1960). *Grundprobleme der Nationalökonomie* [*Epistemological problems of economics*]. Princeton, NJ: Van Nostrand.

Moroni, S. (2007). Planning, liberty and the rule of law. *Planning Theory*, *6*(2), 146–163.

Moroni, S. (2010a). Rethinking the theory and practice of land-use regulation: Towards nomocracy. *Planning Theory*, *9*(2), 137–155.

Moroni, S. (2010b). An evolutionary theory of institutions and a dynamic approach to reform. *Planning Theory*, *9*(4), 275–297.

Moroni, S. (2011a). Land-use regulation for the creative city: The fact of complexity and the values of the liberal-democratic ideal. In D. E. Andersson, Å. E. Andersson & C. Mellander (Eds.), *Handbook of creative cities*. Cheltenham, UK: Edward Elgar.

Moroni, S. (2011b). The role of deliberate intervention on organizations and institutions. *Planning Theory*, *10*(2), 190–197.

Moyo, D. (2009). *Dead aid*. New York, NY: Farrar, Straus and Giroux.

Murray, C. (1984). *Losing ground: American social policy, 1950–1980*. New York, NY: Basic Books.

Nozick, R. (1974). *Anarchy, state and Utopia*. New York, NY: Basic Books.

Nozick, R. (1997). *Socratic puzzles*. Cambridge, MA: Harvard University Press.

O'Driscoll, G. P., & Rizzo, M. J. (1985). *The economics of time and ignorance*. London, UK: Routledge.

O'Toole, R. (2007). *The best-laid plans*. Washington, DC: Cato Institute.

Pareto, V. (1916/1935). *Trattato di sociologia generale* [*Treatise of general sociology*]. New York, NY: Harcourt Brace.

Pennington, M. (1999). Free market environmentalism and the limits of land use planning. *Journal of Environmental Policy and Planning*, *1*, 43–59.

Pennington, M. (2002). *Liberating the land: The case for private land-use planning*. London, UK: Institute of Economic Affairs.

Pennington, M. (2003). Land use planning: Public or private choice. *Economic Affairs*, *23*(2), 10–15.

Petsoulas, C. (2001). *Hayek's liberalism and its origins*. London, UK: Routledge.

Polanyi, M. (1951). *The logic of liberty*. London, UK: Routledge.

Popper, K. R. (1945). *The open society and its enemies*. London, UK: Routledge.

Popper, K. R. (1957). *The poverty of historicism*. London, UK: Routledge.

Powell, B., & Stringham, E. P. (2009). Inclusionary zoning. In R. G. Holcombe & B. Powell (Eds.), *Housing America* (pp. 109–130). New Brunswick, NJ: Transaction Publishers.

Pressman, J. L., & Wildawsky, A. (1984). *Implementation*. Berkeley, CA: University of California Press.

Putnam, R. D. (2000). *Bowling alone: The collapse and revival of American communities*. New York, NY: Simon & Schuster.

Ruming, K. J., Mee, K. J., & McGuirk, P. M. (2004). Questioning the rhetoric of social mix: Courteous community or hidden hostility? *Australian Geographical Studies*, *42*(2), 234–248.

Rykwert, J. (2000). *The seduction of place*. New York, NY: Vintage Books.

Sager, T. (1994). *Communicative planning theory*. Aldershot, UK: Avebury.

Scott, J. C. (1998). *Seeing like a state: How certain schemes to improve the human condition have failed*. New Haven, CT: Yale University Press.

Sen, A. K. (1984). *Resources, values and development*. Oxford, UK: Basil Blackwell.

Sherden, W. A. (2011). *Best laid plans: The tyranny of unintended consequences and how to avoid them*. Santa Barbara, CA: Praeger.

Smith, A. (1993). *An enquiry into the nature and causes of the wealth of nations*. Indianapolis, IN: Hackett.

Smith, C. (2006). *Adam Smith's political philosophy: The invisible hand and spontaneous order*. London, UK: Routledge.
Tenner, E. (1997). *Why things bite back: Technology and the revenge of unintended consequences*. New York, NY: Vintage.
Ullmann-Margalit, E. (1977). *The emergence of norms*. Oxford, UK: Clarendon Press.
Ullmann-Margalit, E. (1978). Invisible-hand explanations. *Synthese*, *39*, 263–291.
Vanberg, V. (1994). J. M. Buchanan and F. A. Hayek: The thought of two Nobel laureates. In P. J. Boettke & D. L. Prychitko (Eds.), *The market process* (pp. 225–228). Aldershot, UK: Edward Elgar.
Vernon, R. (1979). Unintended consequences. *Political Theory*, *7*(1), 35–73.
Vico. (1744/1948). *Principi di Scienza nuova* [*The new science*]. Ithaca, NY: Cornell University Press.
Webster, C., & Lai, L. W.-C. (2003). *Property rights, planning and markets*. Cheltenham, UK: Edward Elgar.

PART IV
MARKETS, INVESTMENTS, AND SPACE

NOVELTY-BUNDLING MARKETS

Jason Potts

Economic analysis of the problem of consumer choice over new goods – that is, of novelty consumption – is a troublesome domain of economic theory. It is widely acknowledged that it happens, and is modeled a form of utility substitution (Hicks, 1956; Morishima, 1973). But it also involves a lot of new choice domains, and these can be information-intensive and difficult for consumers, who can sometimes fail badly in this process (e.g., Bianchi, 1998, 2002; Earl, 1986; Witt, 2001). Consumers can succeed or fail in choice over novelty, and this is not the same as problems of risk or uncertainty. These have unknowns in the face of rational heuristics, but novelty presents a further problem, namely the choice of the heuristics themselves. Novelty requires a value judgment in choice over novelty. This can be seen as the creation of a preference, but it must also be seen as an act of discovery to conjecture or assess (i.e., evaluate) value. The consumer, in this context, must behave like an entrepreneur (Earl, 1986).

On the other hand, the *production* of novelty as new goods (Bresnahan & Gordon, 1997; Galenson, 2005; Magee, 2005; Witt, 2009) is extensively analyzed and grounded in Schumpeterian and evolutionary economic analysis. Much is known about the incentives to produce novelty, but within the same analytic confines, less is known about the consumer side of this same problem. Witt (2001) calls this the problem of "learning to consume" new or novel goods, where the consumer has no comparable experience and must proceed through incomplete preferences and missing information and uncertainties over expected value and yet still make a choice. The analytic question is how they do make these choices, both in reality and in theory.

The Spatial Market Process
Advances in Austrian Economics, Volume 16, 291–312

ISSN: 1529-2134/doi:10.1108/S1529-2134(2012)0000016014

Economic theory can show that a new good must increase utility where it accompanies an increased willingness to pay that, in aggregate, is greater than the costs of production, giving rise to a new market. For individual consumers, however, the decision necessarily takes place in time. It is an experience good. Consumers may not know what they want, they may not know the domain and range of new consumption possibilities, and they may not know how to evaluate the new goods and the potential opportunities they provide. Even when they know their *price*, they may have no idea of what these new goods are *worth*. Novelty is a hard consumer problem because the consumer needs to construct knowledge, not simply acquire information.

New or novel goods thus present a basic challenge to the standard microeconomics of rational choice and underscore the need for a process theory of the market. The problem specifically concerns: (a) how novel goods fit into the consumer's preference sets and utility functions; and (b) what organizational and institutional processes are required for integration. The standard analytic stratagem, employed in general equilibrium theory, is to assume that preference sets or utility functions already contain these as potentials. More sophisticated treatments variously decompose the novelty into characteristic components that are assessed using existing preferences (Lancaster, 1966), or suppose that consumers discover preferences over novel goods by experimental learning or by observation of others' consumption experiences and feedback (Bentley, Earls, & O'Brien, 2011; Earl and Potts, 2004).

There are of course degrees of novelty. But when faced with novel goods and services that require new thinking of the sort that consumes resources or affects other choices, novelty invariably presses on most consumers in any open economic order. Facing these novelties, agents either: (1) *already know* what to do (by the assumption of complete and sovereign preferences); or (2) they *individually learn* what to do (by intelligent decomposition and experimentation); or (3) they *socially learn* what to do (by observing other people's choices and outcomes). Latent rationality, experimentation, and social learning seemingly exhaust the microeconomic analysis of consumer interaction with new goods.

Note the hidden assumptions. First, these models assume that novel goods arrive individually and sequentially by an iterative and finite algebra. Novelty is marginally scarce here, not widely abundant. Novelty is assumed to present itself singularly. Consumers facing multiple novelties are analytically decomposed as singular novelty consumers times x. By this monotonic logic, multiple novelties cost more than singular novelties. In this reasoning there is no suggestion that multiple novelties are a "convex" solution in itself.

Second, the standard model assumes that the discovery or learning process is costly and is not in itself a good. It is assumed that individual utility is not enhanced by the social experience of discovering new ideas and their appropriate consumption. The problem with consumer novelty is that it is costly because it deals with the unknown, thus requiring trial and experimentation (a point trivially true on the producer side, but not necessarily true on the consumer side). This supposes that there is no learning aspect to novelty consumption; that there is no social dimension to that learning; and that no individual positive externalities accrue to this process of engagement. It assumes the absence of social learning.

Third, this framework assumes that producers play no role in this process, or that it is a consumer – not a producer – problem. Business models treat novelty as a cost of "informing" consumers, with no value created in the process of consumers acquiring this information and learning. The additional production cost of advertising and marketing is variously treated as another input expense (or from a political economy perspective, as some manner of exploitation). Novelty production and novelty consumption are distinct events with separable costs and pay-offs. This generalizes the classic industrial innovation model of R&D labs on one side and grateful expectant consumers on the other. Consumers play no important or value-creating role in this process, and do not contribute through their experimental consumption endeavors to the production and meaning of novelty or newness.

Fourth, and most strikingly, it assumes that a basic principle of economics does not apply; namely new specialization under changing incentives. Firms produce novelty at a cost of developing it, and consumers consume novelty at a cost of learning about it. When other agents are involved, they are agents for producers (e.g., advertisers) or for consumers (e.g., consumer advice). But missing are a further class of agents that specialize on *both* sides of the market to bundle multiple novelties from producers into a single *experience good* (an intermediate production over novelty) for consumers who value social learning as a good in itself and who value the experience of multiple simultaneous novelty. Individual producers of novelty can value the institutions such bundling agents produce to interact with consumers; at the same time consumers can value the expert bundling of high-quality novelty assembled by these intermediating agents. Specialization can emerge on these two fronts.

This intermediating role between the production and consumption of novelty is often diffused as special cases in existing markets (e.g., advertising, trade events, and so on), with each treated as a market imperfection in respect of its own production market. But taken together, and viewed through the lens of emergent specialization about abundant novelty, a new and distinct class of economic organization and institutions is suggested that I call *novelty-bundling markets* (NBMs).

Like the concept of a "market for preferences" (Earl & Potts, 2004) and "social network markets" (Potts, Cunningham, Hartley, & Ormerod, 2008), NBMs arise under the particular context of consumer choice over uncertainty and novelty in situations where it is difficult to make a good choice because these are experience goods, or because, being novel, consumers lack effective rules for choice. In such circumstances consumers often look to others to furnish missing information, recommendations, or even decision rules. Potts et al. (2008) argued that much of the creative industries can be classified as "social network markets," an idea suggesting a switch from an industrial production-based definition to a market or consumer-based definition of the creative economy (D. E. Andersson & Andersson, 2006; Caves, 2000; Pine & Gilmore, 1999; Vogel, 2007).

The concept of "novelty-bundling markets" extends this method to define a further class of market forms that meet the following criteria:

(1) Abundant flows of novelty on the *producer side*: novelty is in effect a "free good."
(2) An expert and often reputation-branded market form that intermediates and organizes (bundles) the flow of novelty production to a reduced form for consumption of novelty. Producers and consumers of novelty interact via an NBM in which *expertise is recognized* and rises.
(3) The novelties are subject to *multiple evaluative criteria*. Often they are "boundary objects" (Star & Griesemer, 1989) that are of conflicting, ambiguous, or uncertain value. Social interaction to resolve these uncertainties of value and *worth* (Stark, 2009) is instrumental in the value creation of NBMs.
(4) In NBMs, consumers are typically engaged in search where they *don't necessarily know what they are looking for*, yet will know it when they find it (Stark, 2009, pp. 1–3).

A paradigmatic example of an NBM is an arts-music festival such as *Burning Man* (United States), *Glastonbury* (United Kingdom), or *Woodford* (Australia). These are expertly bundled suites of novelty that are socially consumed, and from which consumers expect to be surprised and challenged by a bundle that presents reflexive opportunities for experience and discovery (Hutter, 2010; Sundbo & Darmer, 2008). Other examples include fashion magazines such as *Vogue* or technology magazines such as *Wired*. Many think tanks can be construed as NBMs, as can many blogs. There is an abundance of creative acts and styles that could be in these festivals, magazines, or think tanks, but only some are chosen for the bundle. These bundles are chosen by experts in the field, typically those with substantial reputation. The elements of these bundles are rarely simple to evaluate, containing multiple criteria of worth. Consumers search in festivals, magazines, and blogs, looking for exciting new things or opportunities without necessarily having a specific search target in mind; yet they nevertheless may expect to find something that is both surprising and valuable, even if it requires some effort at eliciting value or estimates of worth through reflexive engagement. While such instances (such as festivals and magazines, among other examples of NBMs) are clearly not major sectors of the economy, my argument is that NBMs play a significant role in facilitating the demand side of the innovation process in many sectors and particularly so in the creative industries.

The second purpose, beyond introducing and outlining the analytic concept of an NBM, is to contrast three analytic explanations of NBMs: (1) a neoclassical economic explanation, centered on market failure and bounded rationality; (2) an evolutionary/Austrian economic explanation, centered on the emergence of professional consumers and resultant endogenous transformation of preferences and market structure by the processing of distributed information; and (3) an economic sociology account, centered on the *dissonance of multiple evaluative criteria*.

Consider also the origin of the demand for novelty. Novelty is not costless for a consumer, containing risks associated with unknown expected value and the real possibility of costly error. Yet the demand for novelty can be attributed, in part, to *social competition*. Novelty consumption provides a mechanism for consumers to *signal* their ability to make good, interesting choices over novel goods as a play in the ongoing game of social competition. Note that this also predicts that those most engaged in NBMs will be those who are new entrants to the game of social competition, such as the young, or those who have been less successful in previous rounds. It is noteworthy that the underlying assumption of abundant novelty seems most evident in domains where social competition is strongest and most readily observable, such as in respect of choice in music, fashion, media consumption, leisure, political ideas, and such like.

WHAT ARE NBMs?

An NBM is a market form in that it is made of institutions and business models. It arises in a particular context where *abundant novelty* issuing from the producer side meets substantial *search costs* and *evaluation difficulties* on the consumer side. In a NBM consumers don't necessarily know what they are searching for. These difficulties on the demand side are specifically caused by the fact that novel goods, which are experience goods, often require new "rules for choice" as new suites of evaluative criteria.

While NBMs tend to concentrate around the creative industries, they potentially extend throughout the economy wherever these specific conditions in novelty supply and demand arise. Consider four examples of NBMs: (1) a branded music festival such as Glastonbury; (2) a branded garment retailer such as Zara or H&M; (3) a fashion magazine such as *Vogue*; and (4) a think tank such as the Cato Institute. In each case, these are ostensible bundles of novel goods: (1) new musical acts; (2) new ready-to-wear fashion; (3) new fashion concepts; (4) new policy ideas.

These "bundled markets" are assembled by experts, typically with substantial reputational assets, who have selected from the cornucopia of novelty flows in their respective domains to present a narrowed set of consumption prospects. This is often a complex mix of the more familiar and the more exotic but also, and crucially, organizes the space and form of the presentation of this novelty to embed implicit references, contrasts, tensions, and navigation cues, as for example in the organization of the lineup, the display, the spread, and the layout. In each case, these bundles are finite in not presenting an assemblage of all possible new things, but a bounded suite of novelties to be experienced. These bundles are typically complex: the consumer can expect a gradient of the familiar, partially familiar, and unfamiliar; all arranged in a predictable form but that yet equally contains predictable surprises. NBMs are not just lists or samples but assemblies in which the content will change each time, and in which the principles of organization will become known by consumers as a form of consumer "literacy"; they are a technology of choice over novelty. Table 1 offers a list of NBMs.

An NBM has the following features. First, it *intermediates* production and consumption of novelty. Consumers interact with novel goods via the NBM, and producers of novelty interact with consumers via the NBM. Producers and consumers no longer meet in an unmediated manner. An NBM is an emergent market form.

Second, a NBM is a specialist domain organized by *experts* – which includes enthusiasts, buffs, critics, and producers all – who are experienced

Table 1. Novelty-Bundling Markets.

Examples of Novelty-Bundling Markets	
Branded garment retailers	Policy think tanks
Fashion magazines; new technology magazines	Dating and introduction agencies
Arts festivals; music festivals; film festivals	Holiday tour packaging (some)
Degustation experiences	Boutique stores
Blogs (some)	Media channels, particular types of "shows"
Trade fairs	Showrooms (especially in consumer electronics)

and skilled in the particular domain of novelty that is abundantly produced. They are experts in the sense of deep knowledge and access to the range of novelty produced, and also of the rules for choosing or the evaluative principles applied in discriminating between different categories of value and worth in mapping novelty to consumer lifestyles and dimensions of social competition. This specialization and experience need not originate from their previous role in production but may issue from experience and specialization in consumption. NBMs induce experts to compete by accumulating reputational capital as the outcome of their ability to assemble and organize high-quality bundles that meet consumer demands.

Third, NBMs present organized complex structures of display. These presentations often embed the implicit rules for choice in the physical, spatial, or temporal organization of the novelty bundle. An NBM is thus more than an indexed searchable list of new novelties (as in the early days of the Yahoo portal or as exemplified in the Google search-bar, which presumes that you know what you're looking for) and is substantially embodied in an organized market *design*.

The key difference is that the NBM design is not intended to promote efficient search or shopping – it is not intended to create maximal efficiencies and minimize transaction costs; rather the NBM design is intended to be challenging by contextualizing the frictions, tensions, and uncertainties inherent in the novelty and presenting these so as to make the multiple evaluative criteria over value, or "orders of worth" (Boltanski & Thévenot, 2006), able to be navigated and actively engaged with by the consumer.

NBMs thus tend to be more complex, filigreed or even confronting and challenging than an "efficient search and shopping" model would suggest as ideal. This is the difference between a boutique store and a supermarket (where the former is not necessarily designed for ease of use); or between a fashion magazine such as *Vogue* and a mail-order catalogue (where the former is not necessarily intended for ease of search). This additional complexity in an NBM serves a purpose, as when they promote deliberate contexts of dissonance to provide effective contexts for creative discovery and evaluation of worth.

Fourth, consumers participate in NBMs not only for the: (a) filtered choice set, and (b) organization of novelty browsing(search); but also (c) for both the social opportunities and the generative possibilities afforded. NBMs are social spaces as well as market spaces. This matters because of the ambiguity, uncertainty, and multiplicity of evaluative judgments that are required over novel goods.

An organized and inviting social context facilitates local feedback mechanisms that are instrumental to such consumption opportunities. Clearly, not all markets involving novel goods require strong social feedback. In markets for new construction materials, for example, technical functionality requirements and price considerations dominate. But where novel goods are present in multiple registers of worth (economic, cultural, political, industrial, civic, spiritual, and so on; see Boltanski & Thévenot, 2006), and thus where value criteria are themselves part of what must be chosen, the social space of an NBM becomes a critical part of the value that is created.

DEMAND FOR BUNDLING MARKETS

What is the nature of demand for the organizational and institutional form of "bundling markets?" The following factors are suggested to differentiate individual novelty experiences from multiple or bundled novelty experiences.

First, a multiple or bundled novelty context differs from single novelty by reframing the experience from a *search context* dominated by the risk of failure (or loss aversion, see Kahneman, Knetsch, & Thaler, 1991), due to the binary nature of the search being either successful or not, to a context in which *failure is actually expected*, in the sense that some and perhaps many of the novelties bundled will not be desired. Yet this is expected before the experience and is thus not a salient focus. Instead, a portfolio approach to search is enabled, with the bundle as a sample portfolio. NBMs reframe search to enable the consumer to search without knowing what they're searching for (Stark, 2009). This reframing effect is well known in behavioral and experimental psychology and provides a plausible mechanism to explain the demand for multiple bundled novelties, where this same set experienced in a disaggregated sequential context would be less valued.

Novelty bundling shifts the risk function from down-side loss aversion (a powerful behavioral inhibitor) to one that already expects that loss and has discounted it, so that it no longer functions as a behavioral inhibitor, allowing attention to be refocused on the possibility of discovery. This reframing of the experience of novelty suggests a *cognitive mechanism* to explain the superiority of multiple bundled novelties over sequential single novelties.

Second, the search and information acquisition and processing costs associated with novelty will have *fixed* and *variable cost* aspects. Novelty bundling allows the fixed cost (associated with finding time to experience the novelty, involving travel and opportunity costs, for example) to be spread over a larger number of novelties. This lowers the marginal cost of each novelty experience, inducing a higher quantity of consumption, in turn increasing the likelihood of *discovery* of good novelties for adoption. Bundling distributes fixed costs, lowering the marginal cost of each novelty experience and thus increasing demand for novel experiences.

Third, NBMs enable consumers to access the specialized selection services of the *experts* who assemble the bundle (such as the editors of a fashion magazine, the producer of a music festival, and so on) in a way that they would often not be able to afford with respect to an individual choice over a specific novelty. That this service is also accessed by others does not necessarily diminish the value of that access to expertise. A multiple novelty presented at scale thus enables higher fixed costs to be sustained at constant unit costs, enabling greater specialized services to be offered. This induces the possibility of market-based outsourcing of bundle selection over an abundance of novelties to experts or specialists in a way that few individual consumers would normally find cause to make. Multiple novelties thus facilitate a greater *division of labor* in the novelty selection process, offering a direct consumer benefit. Consumers of novelty in a bundling market will be presented with a greater range of viable options, including some they had not considered previously due to their limited knowledge of the full range of possibilities. The value of the expert-selected bundle generally lies less with the high-profile novelties, which may already be well known to the consumers. Rather, the value lies with those on the periphery as ones that many consumers may not have considered, or may have had little awareness of, but which may now enter due to the imprimatur of expert suggestion. Thus, while nominally offering a reduced form of selection, NBMs may simultaneously *widen* the space of novelty selection, legitimating solutions not previously entertained. This may improve the *efficiency* of novelty consumption.

Fourth, NBMs are commonly socially consumed experience goods (Hutter, 2011). This brings the consumer of novelty into contact with other consumers of novelty, facilitating the exchange of local information, rules for choice, frameworks for understanding, and access to social networks that would be more costly to assess in the context of individual novelty search. This acquired *social network capital* acts to cross-subsidize the fixed costs of the novelty search. The value of this is revealed in consumers' willingness to pay for entering such markets.

A fifth point concerns the nature of the bundle assembled in an NBM. These do not necessarily map to producer definitions of markets, or to consumer definitions of search problems. Rather, each NBM is an entrepreneurial conjecture as to what novelties go together. These may not all be from the same market per se. This can be clearly seen in the case of fashion magazines and new technology magazines, which bundle together a variety of sources of novelty into a single bundle. Similarly, music festivals often mix very different genres of performance, along with things having at first sight little to do with new music, such as new political ideas or new social technologies. So the bundles are very much more than just "what's new" catalogues of a particular industry's latest output, but rather are conjectures of what novelties fit together in valuable ways. This is what renders them an entrepreneurial product (Holcombe, 2003). NBMs are both *infinitely contestable*, in the sense of the myriad of permutations of possible bundles that may be assembled, but also *monopolistically competitive*, in the sense of the futility of an exact imitation of another NBM. By these factors alone there is substantial microeconomic reason to expect that multiple novelties (i.e., bundles) offer a superior consumer experience to singular novelties, and that the added-value opportunity will induce entrepreneurial supply of such NBMs.

MICROECONOMICS OF NBMs

A standard microeconomic account of the existence of an NBM would turn on presumed *market failure* or imperfect competition. This would assume that an NBM can exist only where it is able to exclude or postpone competition, implying a temporary monopoly advantage by intermediating producers and consumers of novelty that makes the capture of rents possible. How might this happen? Perhaps the agents of the NBM may have preferential access to a key resource, for example a festival site, or to artistic talent, or to a distribution channel. By exclusive control over this key resource, an NBM could exclude direct access to producers as well as competition in bundling markets, allowing it to operate as a monopolist.

A further account of imperfect competition may be due to reputation or brand capital that new entrants may find it difficult to compete with. Long-standing festivals or widely known fashion brands are examples. By capturing key resources or creating exclusive assets on the supply side, an NBM may provide consumers with a monopolized or imperfectly competitive access to a particular novelty. The NBM agent can create consumer rents. The standard policy response would be to seek to regulate the NBM by limiting the prices it can charge (as in festivals), by legislating shared access to channels of distribution or sites of access, or by seeking antitrust action.

Apart from the "demand for variety" literature (e.g., Gronau & Hamermesh, 2008), which treats this as an efficiency problem arising from differential opportunity costs due to different investments in human capital, the standard microeconomic approach has little to say about the consumer side; indeed, the imperfect competition hypothesis presumes that NBMs are producer actions to capture consumer rents, with no consumer value to their existence. This is because of the assumption that more choice is always preferred to less, hence bundling, or any other choice reduction mechanism, is implicitly harmful to consumer interests. By treating any new good as "just another good," there is no *prima facie* reason to suppose that the particular situation of abundant novelty presents a consumer problem. The standard microeconomic framework assumes that new goods arrive "fully labeled." In essence, there is no consumer choice problem, only the risk of producer rent-seeking. Each individual consumer has no role for other consumers in figuring out what the new good is, what it means, what its value is, and whether or not it is worth experiencing.

This analysis views NBMs as a form of imperfect competition that subtracts from consumer surplus. Consumers have no need for them, and enter only when better alternatives are foreclosed. This occurs when NBMs are subject to regulatory capture (some festivals, for example) or when sustained first-mover advantages lock in critical inputs or complementary resources (e.g., exclusivity contracts, preferential access to sites or ownership of critical distribution channels or licenses). This opens a path to a welfare-theoretic or public choice analysis that runs NBMs through standard analytic set-pieces in applied microeconomics.

Departures from the model of imperfect competition begin when we introduce *bounded rationality*. This means that search is no longer a free good and that agents are not assumed to already possess effective rules for choice over domains of novelty. This affects the consumer side because, now, each additional novelty imposes a further cost on learning about the expected and experiential value of the novel good (Hutter, 2011). Novelty abundance no longer simply means a larger commodity space but is now manifestly a problem and a direct cost for the consumer who must survey and evaluate that larger space. Obviously, one way to avoid this cost is simply not to engage with *any* novelty. With unknown expected values, consumer disengagement and retreat is a legitimate and indeed common option. NBMs can thus offer consumers pathways into this space, potentially bringing them back into the market and thus facilitating innovation.

Bounded rationality can thus explain the existence of NBMs without reference to imperfect competition. The rationale of NBMs is due to the value-added to *consumers* (not to producers) by filtering abundant novelty down to a reduced set of high-average-quality novelty that is less risky and costly for consumers than any attempt they might otherwise make to sample from the unfiltered and mass flow. From the consumer perspective, an NBM is thus an extension of the production process that operates at the market level rather than that of the individual firm or novelty producer (Bhidé, 2008). Bounded rationality does not negate the prospect of imperfect competition where there is monopolized access to key input resources, but it does suggest a different explanation of branding or reputational capital. Rather than viewing these as further mechanisms of rent extraction, branding and reputational capital now function as "information shorthand" for consumers, signaling the particular attributes of particular bundles. Brands (including branded bundles) are not further instances of imperfect competition; rather they add value for consumers by simplifying their search and choice process (Earl, 2002). That NBMs are widely observed to be heavily branded is neither an incidental nor accidental aspect of their function; it is integral to the way they create value for consumers.

EVOLUTIONARY ECONOMICS OF NBMs

An evolutionary approach to NBMs builds on the behavioral approach, but shifts the focus from a simple "lowering of the costs of search" explanation to an unpacking of how it does this in terms of decision rules and their evolution in a market space. Entrepreneurial agents drive this market process. The emergence of an NBM is explained as a result of the entrepreneurial behavior of increasingly specialized consumers, or increasingly diverse producers, moving further into bundling and distribution niches. An evolutionary economic analysis of NBMs seeks to trace the pathways of their emergence and development from an initial state of abundant production of novelty to the varieties of consumer experience in facing this abundant novelty.

The hypothesis I propose is that NBMs are often an evolutionary consequence of *consumer* specialization with feedback, as expert consumers turn from amateur to professional with the entrepreneurial adoption of business models to create and occupy a new intermediating market space (Harper, 1996). The rationale is in part attributable to the previous explanation of the prospect of producer rents and the creation of consumer value-added (as profit). NBMs are the result of entrepreneurial conjectures about the value of particular combinations of novelty and particular organizational forms of presenting this (Holcombe, 2003). They can succeed and replicate – drawing imitation – or fail and exit by open-market selection processes. Viable NBMs add value for consumers, and the particular form in which they exist tells us what value they add.

An evolutionary account of an NBM can be stylized as such. In the beginning there are many consumers facing an abundant flow of novelty. Because of heterogeneity in taste and experience, some consumers soon become better than others at making good choices over this domain. These are the emerging experts who are distinguished from peers by demonstrated success and emergent recognition in a socially competitive context. The motive driving this emergent specialization need not be due to financial incentives. The social competition hypothesis may underpin this, as may intrinsic motivations with respect to aesthetic enjoyment, hobbies, social or reputational status, or the expression of native talent in the construction of such consumption as an art form. But whatever the motivating factor, other consumers in turn will come to notice this expertise and the choices it involves and, for bounded rationality reasons, they will begin to orient their own choices toward the choices made by these emerging specialists (Bentley et al., 2011). This gives rise to a *social network market* (Potts et al., 2008). The next step is the entrepreneurial decision by the amateur but specialized consumer to turn professional by developing a business model about their specialized niche and extant reputation.

Thus, an NBM emerges from a social network market; it is then fitted with a business model that is attached to a particular reputation and is expressed as a market offering. Consumers of novelty are free to choose whether to delimit their choices to those suggested by the NBM, while producers of novelty are free to solicit the brokerage of the NBM as an indirect channel to consumers. What particular configurations of NBMs will be successful cannot be known in advance, but will be revealed by market experimentation and consumer selection. NBMs thus emerge out of consumer specialization, perhaps beginning with an enthusiastic, loyal or even cult following. They emerge as intermediaries into an open market ecology with reputational capital and connection to consumers already established, making these agents attractive channels for novelty producers. The producers would otherwise seek to make these connections themselves, but without operating from a position of credibility. Both producers and consumers of novelty can potentially gain from their existence.

Also note that the "professional consumers" who enter this space are not entering a predefined latent space of NBMs. This was a tacit assumption in the neoclassical and behavioral models above, where there was a predefined opportunity for rent extraction as well as a predefined opportunity for reducing consumer search costs. Rather, from the evolutionary perspective the emergent NBMs are creating and occupying a new market space that previously *did not exist*, but instead represents a value conjecture about particular configurations of novelty and ways of organizing and presenting it. NBMs are suggested by the attention that specialist amateur consumers may receive and in turn recognize, but the emergence of an NBM is then an entrepreneurial conjecture about how to create profit by creating a new and specific organizational form that bundles particular novelties in particular ways. This may of course then attract imitators who seek to occupy different points in this dynamic market ecology. This will lead to the emergence of monopolistic competition in NBM space. Thus NBMs evolve.

Formally considered, the first professional consumer establishes a monopoly position that will eventually tend toward a competitive state, as imitators of the strategy enter the niche. Yet this is a somewhat misleading description of the emergence and evolution of a NBM, because exact imitation is largely impossible (remember, we are dealing with novelty bundling, not commodity bundling). What is instead occurring is the development and unfolding of new market niches, enabling and facilitating further specialization on both the consumer and producer sides (for an early account of this as a spatial process, see Hägerstrand, 1967). So where does this end? In an important sense, there is no end to this process and no final equilibrium. Some NBMs will continue to evolve into more general arbiters of taste, increasingly functioning as gatekeepers of new ideas. This will occur as reputation is developed and leveraged. Others will specialize in particular niches, while others still will exit.

While this happens, new amateur consumers may develop skills and turn professional to contest the market space. It may happen that a domain of novelty production expands, supplying an ever-richer market ecology of NBMs. Or the domain may normalize, devaluing the contribution of NBMs.

Or possibly the domain may cease to produce a sufficiently abundant flow of novelty, rendering little value to be added by NBMs. NBMs may unfold as a rich and flourishing ecology, or they may collapse. These are after all derivative markets; if there is reduced flow of novelty, or reduced consumer problems in processing it, they will cease to provide functional value. For example, this may account for the current difficulties faced by packaged holiday tour bundlers. Such bundlers had more monopolistic power prior to the affordances of internet search. The internet has enabled consumers to search, evaluate, and bundle holidays that were previously difficult to assemble, and where it was difficult even to know what options were available due to the abundance of new possibilities. This is an instance of a previously successful NBM that is now a less rich ecology. Yet within this, for example in relation to high-end adventure tours focusing on unique experiences, a new NBM has emerged and is flourishing.

NBMs are not an industry per se. Rather they are an evolutionary outcome that emerges under certain conditions that are associated with sufficient producer flows of novelty and consumer problems in dealing with this. They are a feature of an evolving economy. An evolutionary economic analysis emphasizes how NBMs create further opportunities for producers and consumers by furnishing not just a selected bundle of novelty but, as importantly, in furnishing rules for choice for consumers facing such novelty (Earl & Potts, 2004), enabling consumers to develop more sophisticated choices over this domain. NBMs facilitate an increase in the complexity of consumer choices, driving *preference evolution*. The effect of NBMs is not neutral on the development of other markets, as the very existence of an NBM shapes consumer preferences, enabling a higher degree of complexity than would otherwise be possible.

In the neoclassical account, NBMs are rent extraction mechanisms. In the bounded rationality account, NBMs are efficiency improvements on choice. However, in an evolutionary account NBMs drive change in the underlying structure of preferences in an economic order. If so, this will provide feedback to producers who may now also increase their complexity of creative offerings (Earl & Potts, 2011), further fueling the process of economic evolution.

ECONOMIC SOCIOLOGY OF NBMs

A further observation we can make on NBMs is that they are not always effortless and simple. Often they can be challenging and complex. Why is this?

NBMs often have characteristic forms; tending to be smallish, boutique, niche-orientated and often confrontational or challenging to mainstream consumer sensibilities. Not everyone will be comfortable at Glastonbury. Not everyone will be *au fait* with the ideas pitched by certain think tanks. Not everyone can enter a boutique fashion store with confidence. The examples of NBMs suggested above imply somewhat elite or at least challenging consumption environments, inviting a certain measure of consumer courage to enter and an expectation of a certain frisson in experience. Not everyone will necessarily be entirely comfortable entering such markets, unlike aggregation search markets such as supermarkets or department stores. This is not an incidental observation, but seemingly key to their functioning. To understand this property of NBMs, we turn to economic sociology.

The approach I pursue here to unpack the existence and nature of NBMs, which elaborate on the microeconomic and evolutionary economic explanations offered above, draws on a recent contribution to economic sociology by the economic sociologist David Stark, in particular *The Sense of Dissonance: Accounts of Worth in Economic Life*. Stark (2009) builds on Luc Boltanski's and Laurent Thévenot's (2006) *On Justification: The Economies of Worth* (they elaborate a sociological theory of value framework consisting of six "orders of worth" – civic, market, inspired, fame, industrial, and domestic – that applies to all calculative economic situations). Starting with Boltanski's and Thévenot's value theory, Stark proposes a new definition of entrepreneurship in *heterarchical* organizations based on the *dissonance* or frictions of multiple evaluative criteria of worth: "Entrepreneurship is the ability to keep multiple evaluative principles in play and to exploit the resulting friction of their interplay" (Stark, 2009, p. 15). Stark conducts ethnographic analysis of organizational contexts in three situations of organizational heterarchy (a socialist factory, a new media start-up, and an arbitrage trading room), in each case finding that the key driver of entrepreneurial discovery is the tensions and frictions or the dissonance created by the interplay of different evaluative criteria of worth. He offers a deep sociological account of how such spatially and structurally organized dissonance (often deliberately engineered) can contribute to the discovery and realization of entrepreneurial opportunities. He models this with the concept of "structural folds" (Balazs & Stark, 2010), contrasting it with Ronald Burt's (1995) entrepreneurial brokerage concept of "structural holes."

Stark's analysis of knowledge creation in three different (but all heterarchical) contexts is offered as a new framework for the study of entrepreneurship and innovation in organizations. But the underlying theoretical idea and insight of Stark's structural folds, as spaces of overlapping, diverse, and ultimately dissonance-creating evaluative criteria of worth, can also be extended to account for the value created by NBMs. However, where Stark focuses on producer organization for knowledge creation (by exploiting "the ability to keep multiple evaluative criteria in play"), we may recognize that a similar generative entrepreneurial process may also be at work on the consumer side, and particularly in the context of consumer adoption of novelty as a space of entrepreneurial knowledge creation.

NBMs would seem to be paradigmatic instances of "structural folds." They are institutional spaces characterized by deep uncertainty, in which multiple evaluative criteria of worth intersect and are socially processed as an endeavor to figure out what counts – and to assess what values and criteria of value are relevantly applied. As testimony to this, it is uncommon in an NBM that a particular offering is singled out and valorized as to its obvious choice context. NBMs don't tend to do this (even if producers of novelty may prefer them to). Rather NBMs work best and are seemingly most viable and valuable when they perform the more equivocal task of presenting and organizing multiple novelties across a well-constructed "structural fold"; in effect deliberately creating tensions and frictions and contrasting criteria (sometimes subtly, sometimes forcefully) of evaluative worth. Entrepreneurial consumers can then meet with ambiguous possibilities and arrive at consumption choices that work as strategic plays in further rounds of social competition. But like the private vice and public virtue arguments of Thomas Mandeville and Adam Smith, the result of this private social competition are worth assessments of novelties, which become public virtues in the worth assessment carried by NBMs to other consumers.

The result is a social space in which such measures of value can be explored and revealed, and in which entrepreneurial action can flourish. Searching consumers, who already know what they want, will by definition have no need for NBMs; they will be frustrated by their complexity and forced engagement as well as by the wastefulness of their deliberate inefficiencies. But for consumers who are searching for things they don't yet understand, the heterarchic forms and structural folds of NBMs are like the difference between pulp fiction and avant-garde literature, or Hollywood and art-house cinema; the challenge is the point when the challenges are deliberately designed to lead you to a place that you would not otherwise easily go by your own evaluative criteria. NBMs are thus sites of *consumer entrepreneurship* by way of creating complex spaces (structural folds) that enable consumers to engage with novelty and to process it in a complex social space, where other consumers are similarly attempting to do so (Moeran & Pedersen, 2011). Obviously, this requires constraints and boundaries, which is what NBM agents furnish, selecting this particular set of novelties and arranging them in this particular organizational and spatial form. This is art, not science; design, not engineering.

Stark's organizational dissonance framework of how creative friction yields organizational reflexivity thus suggests a model of entrepreneurship that may be further extended to consumer choice and action, as well as offering a compelling explanation for the emergence and properties of NBMs that intermediate the production and consumption of novelty. In an immediately obvious way, the dissonance model of overlapping and conflicting accounts of worth explains first of all why it is a "bundling" market in the first place; why consumer choice and adoption is facilitated by the creation of a structured environment of multiple novelties (more than the single novelty assumed in standard economic approaches; fewer than the abundant novelties the consumers potentially face in unmediated markets).

Furthermore, Stark's model explains the entrepreneurial content of NBMs. This has two aspects: first in the entrepreneurial role of the expert "bundler" of novelty who both filters from the abundant flows of novelty a select set and organizes the experience of this in particular ways; and second in the consumer who enters as an entrepreneurial agent, not simply passively consuming from a commodified set of goods, but engaged in a complex process of navigating the tensions and dissonance in the different orders of worth that have been set up in the NBM. Consumers are not just consuming another good, but are lead to be engaged by the specific organization of the NBM to engage in "reconstructions of the self" (identity dynamics) through their novel choices. NBMs are thus spaces that create "ecologies of knowledge," consisting of evaluative principles in which multiple and potentially conflicting criteria of worth are in play and are entrepreneurially resolved (Stark, 2009, p. 142).

The efficacy of NBMs does not therefore ultimately turn on their efficiency in expertly filtering novelty, as the economic explanation would point to, but more in terms of their ability to create organized spaces in which novelty with multiple registers of worth can enter and be effectively evaluated by the social interaction of agents with differing criteria and perspectives on that worth. In this way, abundant flows of novelty are transformed by the social interactions interior to NBMs into assessments of newness and value. One can thus appreciate why NBMs will tend to scale with city size, such that larger cities will provide more scope for these sorts of interactions and engagements. While NBMs do not *cause* economic evolution, in that they are not creative generators per se, they facilitate and ultimately shape the uptake of novelty by resolving multiple criteria of worth into singular assessments of value. Interestingly, this seems to require multiple novelties to be processed simultaneously by multiple people in a common social space. This is the spatial consumer side of the production function for novelty.

CONCLUSION

This paper has introduced the analytic concept of an NBM. This extends the concept of a social network market to incorporate three further special conditions. Specifically: (1) multiple novelties experienced at once; (2) a context of search where consumers don't necessarily know what they're looking for but will know it when they find it; and (3) an emergent market form that intermediates between producers and consumers of novelty. This intermediating form is typically the product of amateur (but expert) consumers turned professional. This may seem a rather minor subset of the broader economy, perhaps barely worth the designation of a special class of market. I am certainly not arguing here that arts and music festivals, eisteddfods, fashion and technology magazines, blogs, think tanks, dating and introduction agencies, and branded garment retailers, among other instances of NBMs constitute in any sense a "significant" part of total economic activity, jobs, exports, and so on. But I have sought to draw out the implications of several stylized observations on novelty and innovation in the creative industries. These are salient points because they are the near opposite of standard assumptions in innovation theory.

The first was the supposition of abundant novelty. This is the opposite assumption to most innovation studies where new ideas are scarce and valuable and are the outputs of significant investment. But in the context of art, music, fashion, and intellectual ideas, for example, the consumer experience is closer to a regular downpour of novelty. The "novelty problem" is *not* that of incentivizing production; it is the problem of dealing with this abundance. NBMs thus address the consumer problem of novelty abundance.

A second aspect is the consumer problem of search amidst such abundant novelty. Here it is reasonable to recognize that consumers will not necessarily know what they are looking for, although may recognize it when they find it. NBMs are not simply sites of shopping but are closer to browsing environments (Earl & Potts, 2001). Compounding this problem is the phenomenon that such novelties often present themselves in multiple registers of value, making novelty difficult to evaluate individually and in isolation. NBMs facilitate resolving this problem by bundling novelties and organizing a context of comparative choice that is often built into the organizational or spatial composition of the bundle (e.g., in the program, the layout, or in the cluster or spatial domain). NBMs are often highly social spaces that facilitate the sorts of interactions that bring the multiple evaluative criteria of value or worth to a level of consumer engagement. Unlike "standard" consumer markets that aim to minimize transaction costs in shopping (while maximizing spending), it is common in NBMs to find frictions, tensions, and sources of dissonance. These have often been deliberately induced into the market experience so as to provide the generative edge that enables consumers to engage with novel goods in an entrepreneurial manner. In doing so, they sometimes discover their own sense of value and worth within.

NBMs are not a "significant" part of the economy. But the particular context and needs they meet – abundant novelty; the sort of search beyond the capabilities of search engines; novelty in multiple registers of value and with multiple criteria of worth – are all contexts that we can expect to become more common in an evolving economy in which experience services continue to grow as a share of economic activity (D. E. Andersson & Andersson, 2006). NBMs are somewhat exotic economic specimens. They only manifest in a rapidly evolving economic order under the particular conditions of abundant novelty intersecting with intense social competition. This is commonly observed in the creative industries. These rarefied economic market forms are worthy of study because they illuminate the interaction of the production and consumption of novelty, as well as its organizational and institutional forms. Consumer entrepreneurship is a key aspect of this interaction – an aspect that influences and is influenced by the market process and its spatial organization.

ACKNOWLEDGEMENTS

Sincere thanks to two anonymous referees for helpful suggestions, and also to Peter Earl, Michael Hutter, David Stark, and John Hartley for discussion of the concept of an NBM.

REFERENCES

Andersson, D. E., & Andersson, Å. E. (2006). *The economics of experiences, the arts and entertainment*. Cheltenham, UK: Edward Elgar.

Balazs, V., & Stark, D. (2010). Structural folds: Generative disruption in overlapping groups. *American Journal of Sociology, 115*(4), 1150–1190.

Bentley, R. A., Earls, M., & O'Brien, M. (2011). *I'll have what she's having: Mapping social behavior*. Cambridge, MA: MIT Press.

Bhidé, A. (2008). *The venturesome economy: How innovation sustains prosperity in a more connected world*. Princeton, NJ: Princeton University Press.

Bianchi, M. (1998). *The active consumer*. London, UK: Routledge.

Bianchi, M. (2002). Novelty, preferences and fashion: When goods are unsettling. *Journal of Economic Behavior and Organization, 47*, 1–18.

Boltanski, L., & Thévenot, L. (2006). *On justification: The economies of worth*. Princeton, NJ: Princeton University Press.

Bresnahan, T., & Gordon, R. (Eds.). (1997). *The economics of new goods*. Chicago, IL: University of Chicago Press.

Burt, R. (1995). *Structural holes: The social structure of competition*. Cambridge, MA: Harvard University Press.

Caves, R. (2000). *Creative industries: Contracts between art and commerce*. Cambridge, MA: Harvard University Press.

Earl, P. E. (1986). *Lifestyle economics*. Brighton, UK: Harvester Wheatsheaf.

Earl, P. E. (2002). *Information, opportunism and economic coordination*. Cheltenham, UK: Edward Elgar.

Earl, P. E., & Potts, J. (2001). Latent demand and the browsing shopper. *Managerial and Decision Economics, 21*, 111–122.

Earl, P. E., & Potts, J. (2004). The market for preferences. *Cambridge Journal of Economics, 28*, 619–633.

Earl, P. E., & Potts, J. (2011). The creative instability hypothesis. In J. Potts (Ed.), *Evolutionary economics and creative industries*. Cheltenham, UK: Edward Elgar.

Galenson, D. (2005). *Old masters and young geniuses*. Princeton, NJ: Princeton University Press.

Gronau, R., & Hamermesh, D. (2008). The demand for variety: A household production perspective. *Review of Economics and Statistics, 90*(3), 562–572.

Hägerstrand, T. (1967). *Innovation diffusion as a spatial process* (A. Pred, Trans). Chicago, IL: University of Chicago Press.

Harper, D. (1996). *Entrepreneurship and the market process*. London, UK: Routledge.

Hicks, J. (1956). *A revision of demand theory*. Oxford, UK: Clarendon Press.

Holcombe, R. G. (2003). The origin of entrepreneurial opportunities. *Review of Austrian Economics, 16*(1), 25–43.

Hutter, M. (2010). Familiar surprises: Creating value in the creative industries. In P. Aspers & J. Beckert (Eds.), *The worth of goods*. Cambridge, UK: Cambridge University Press.

Hutter, M. (2011). Experience goods. In R. Towse (Ed.), *Handbook of cultural economics* (2nd ed). Cheltenham, UK: Edward Elgar.

Kahneman, D., Knetsch, J., & Thaler, R. (1991). The endowment effect, loss aversion, and status quo bias: Anomalies. *Journal of Economic Perspectives, 5*(1), 193–206.

Lancaster, K. (1966). A new approach to consumer theory. *Journal of Political Economy, 74*, 132–157.

Magee, G. (2005). Rethinking invention: Cognition and the economics of technological creativity. *Journal of Economic Behavior and Organization, 57*, 29–48.

Moeran, B., & Pedersen, J. S. (Eds.). (2011). *The negotiation of values in the creative industries: Fairs, festivals and competitive events.* Cambridge, UK: Cambridge University Press.

Morishima, M. (Ed.). (1973). *Theories of demand: Real and monetary.* Oxford, UK: Clarendon Press.

Pine, B. J., & Gilmore, J. (1999). *The experience economy.* Boston, MA: Harvard Business School Press.

Potts, J., Cunningham, S., Hartley, J., & Ormerod, P. (2008). Social network markets: A new definition of creative industries. *Journal of Cultural Economics, 32*(3), 166–185.

Star, S., & Griesemer, J. (1989). Institutional ecology, translations and boundary objects. *Studies of Social Science, 19*, 387–420.

Stark, D. (2009). *Sense of dissonance: Accounts of worth in economic life.* Princeton, NJ: Princeton University Press.

Sundbo, P., & Darmer, P. (Eds.). (2008). *Creating experiences in the experience economy.* Cheltenham, UK: Edward Elgar.

Vogel, H. (2007). *Entertainment industry economics.* New York, NY: Cambridge University Press.

Witt, U. (2001). Learning to consume: A theory of wants and the growth of demand. *Journal of Evolutionary Economics, 11*, 23–36.

Witt, U. (2009). Novelty and the bounds of unknowledge in economics. *Journal of Economic Methodology, 16*(4), 361–375.

SPATIAL CONCENTRATION IN THE FINANCIAL INDUSTRY

Johanna Palmberg

During the last two decades, the world has experienced increasing financial globalization, generating higher levels of industry consolidation and integration (Amel, Barnes, Panetta, & Salleo, 2004). The financial sector is characterized both by globalization and by spatial relationships and local embeddedness (Agnes, 2000). In 2009, the 10 largest stock exchanges in the world accounted for 86 percent of the total value of shares traded (World Federation of Exchanges). This spatial concentration of the financial sector can also be seen in the Global Finance Centres Index (GFCI). The index indicates that London and New York are the two most important financial centers,[1] followed by Hong Kong, Singapore, and Zurich. A similar spatial concentration of the financial sector is evident on the national level.

Another important development is the role of information and communication technology (ICT). The financial industry is completely dependent on ICT platforms and digital networks for its communication. In many instances, ICT development has had centrifugal effects on the location of firms and households. However, the industry's increasing spatial concentration shows that the effect has been different in the financial industry. Sophisticated ICT platforms make it possible to disseminate information worldwide in (almost) real time. In addition, increasing regulatory demands have forced firms to disclose detailed, regular, and dependable information; the amount of available information relevant to the financial industry has for this reason sky-rocketed in the last decade. The financial industry faces

The Spatial Market Process
Advances in Austrian Economics, Volume 16, 313–333

ISSN: 1529-2134/doi:10.1108/S1529-2134(2012)0000016015

more opaque institutional structures and heavier governmental regulation than at any time in the past (Levine, 2004). The opaque institutional framework and government regulation are two more explanatory factors in the analysis of regional concentration in the financial industry.

Based on these observations, I investigate factors that determine the level of spatial concentration in the financial industry. Why does the financial industry have such a high level of spatial concentration? The theoretical framework is based on theories from regional economics, with a focus on agglomeration effects, externalities, and the regional clustering of industry. The positive agglomeration effects arise from access to (i) specialized labor, (ii) specialized suppliers, and (iii) knowledge dispersion (Marshall, 1920). Jane Jacobs (1961, 1969) contributes to a discussion of the role of cities (urban economies) in terms of innovations and entrepreneurship. Jacobs (1969) argues that diversified urban economies are the best environments for innovative and entrepreneurial behavior. A similar argument can be found in Audretsch (1998), Malmberg and Maskell (2002), and Storper and Venables (2004). These studies show that the role of knowledge can explain why innovative activities benefit from co-location, which enhances the positive agglomeration effects for firms located in the same region.

The high degree of spatial concentration in the financial sector illustrates the importance of local embeddedness, networks, face-to-face communication, knowledge spillovers, and spatial proximity for the organization of the industry. These factors highlight the importance of local knowledge and the dispersion of knowledge – factors that have been thoroughly discussed and analyzed in the field of Austrian economics. Therefore, an Austrian view is included to examine the role of knowledge in the spatial concentration of financial centers. Economists such as Friedrich Hayek (1937, 1945) and Ludwig Lachmann (1956) contribute to our understanding of the economic role of knowledge.

Following Storper and Venables (2004), the concept of knowledge can be divided into two groups: (i) specialized/private knowledge and (ii) ubiquitous/transparent knowledge. In turn, specialized/private knowledge can be divided into two subcategories: (ia) tacit and (ib) codified. This analysis focuses on the role of private knowledge including the subcategories tacit and codified knowledge, respectively. The categorization is in line with Hayek's (1937, 1945) and Michael Polanyi's (1966) approaches.

The rest of this chapter is structured as follows. The second section provides an overview of the characteristics and spatial locations of financial industries and centers. I discuss the causes of the spatial concentration of the financial sector, followed in the third section by a discussion of why the financial sector is more spatially concentrated than most other sectors. This section also provides a theoretical framework, focusing on agglomeration economies and the importance of knowledge flows. The framework is based on spatial economics, new economic geography (NEG), and Austrian economics. The fourth section discusses the Hayekian knowledge problem and the role of tacit knowledge. The final section applies these concepts to the financial industry.

FINANCIAL CENTERS

The level of financial development is a key factor influencing long-term economic growth. A high level of financial development allows for the effective diversification of risk and allocation of capital, which, in the long run, improves the growth prospects of an economy. Schumpeter (1911) was one of the first to highlight the importance of financial development as a determinant of economic growth. Recent empirical work supports this relationship (see Beck & Levine, 2002; Levine, 2004; Mishkin, 2007). For example, Levine (2004) summarizes the empirical evidence on financial development and economic growth and states that "the level of financial development is a good predictor of future rates of economic growth, capital accumulation and technological change" (Levine, 1997, p. 689).[2] Thus, stock and forward markets spread knowledge about market expectations of factors and changes that are important for economic development (Lachmann, 1978).

Generally, a financial center is a city where financial activities are concentrated. Financial service firms only serve customers within the city and in adjacent areas. Despite the development of information technology during the last decades, contemporary definitions of financial centers have a clear spatial component. For example, Gehrig (2000, p. 416) defines financial centers "as geographical locations with agglomerations of branches and subsidiaries of banks and other financial intermediaries in narrowly defined regions." It is difficult to define financial centers more precisely, due to the vast diversity of the existing definitions. Kindleberger (1974) is one of the pioneers in research on financial centers. Prior to his research, discussions of banking innovation and financial intermediation or deepening lacked a spatial dimension. Kindleberger defines a financial center in the following way:

> Financial centers are needed not only to balance through time the savings and investments of individual entrepreneurs and to transfer financial capital from savers to investors, but also to effect payments and to transfer financial savings between places. Banking and financial centers perform a medium of exchange function and an

> inter-spatial store-of-value function (… [T]he specialized functions of international payments and foreign lending or borrowing are typically best performed at one central place that is also (in most instances) the specialized center for domestic interregional payments. (Kindleberger, 1974, p. 6)

The hierarchical structure of the financial sector is another important characteristic of financial centers. Reed (1981) identifies five distinctive categories. The first three are centers that serve (i) the immediate surroundings, such as the city, the county, and the province; (ii) an area larger than the immediate surroundings but smaller than the nation; and (iii) the nation. Categories four and five include international dimensions. The fourth category encompasses financial centers that provide national as well as international services to contiguous countries and are often referred to as regional international centers. Finally, in the last group (category five), we find global financial centers (GFCs), which serve customers around the globe. Goldberg, Helsley, and Levi (1988, p. 83) summarize the characteristics of international financial centers as "major urban concentrations of financial services with a large portion of those services directed toward international financial transactions. They are also leading domestic centers for financial services in their own countries."

Using this typology, category five includes London, New York, and Hong Kong – the global centers that coordinate global markets. Category four (regional international centers) includes cities such as Amsterdam, Frankfurt, Luxembourg, Milan, Paris, Sydney, Taipei, Tokyo, Toronto, and Zurich. It is important to note that there is increasing competition between financial centers, mainly because policy makers aspire to upgrade their national financial center to an international center (see, e.g., Latter, 2001 for Hong Kong and Lee, 2001 for Singapore).

Poon (2003) uses cluster analysis to show that the hierarchical structure of the financial centers strengthened between 1980 and 1998. During this period, there was also increasing dominance by London and New York as GFCs.[3] These two financial centers are still ranked first and second among the 75 largest centers in the world. Hong Kong is ranked as number three and Singapore as number four.

Table 1 presents the five key areas of competitiveness (people, business environment, market access, infrastructure, and general competitiveness). The top four centers are strongly competitive in each of the five areas. Sydney and Toronto are among the lowest ranked (within the top ten centers) in all areas.

Over the last four years, there has been a convergence in ranking among the top three GFCs, and today, there is no significant difference among

Table 1. The Ten Largest Global Financial Centers.

Rank and City		Rating	SubIndices				
			People	Business Environment	Market Access	Infrastructure	General Competitiveness
1	London	775	London	London	London	London	London
2	New York	769	New York	New York	New York	New York	New York
3	Hong Kong	759	Hong Kong	Hong Kong	Hong Kong	Hong Kong	Hong Kong
4	Singapore	722	Singapore	Singapore	Singapore	Singapore	Singapore
5	Shanghai	694	Shanghai	Chicago	Shanghai	Tokyo	Tokyo
5	Tokyo	694	Tokyo	Tokyo	Tokyo	Chicago	Shanghai
7	Chicago	673	Chicago	Shanghai	Zurich	Zurich	Chicago
8	Zurich	665	Zurich	Zurich	Chicago	Shanghai	Sydney
9	Geneva	659	Geneva	Toronto	Toronto	Geneva	Zurich
10	Sydney	658	Toronto	Sydney	Sydney	Sydney	Toronto
10	Toronto	658	Sydney	Geneva	Geneva	Toronto	Geneva

Source: Yeandle (2011).

them in terms of general ranking. It is interesting to note, however, the dominance of London in many subsectors: it has 37 percent of the foreign exchange markets and 46 percent of the over-the-counter (OTC) market. In addition, the London Stock Exchange is the largest in the world in the number of listed firms; it also leads several other rankings, such as equity options and electronic trading in global energy markets (Cooper, 2011). Yeandle (2011) reports that London is the highest-ranked GFC in the following industry sectors: asset management, government and regulatory, professional services and wealth management, and private banking. New York is the highest-ranked center in banking and ranks second in asset management, government and regulatory, and professional services and wealth management.

Although the top centers are likely to retain their dominant positions, there is increasing competition, especially from Asia. In the GFCI9 (2010), eight Asian financial cities are listed among the twenty largest centers, compared with only three Asian centers in the GFCI1 (2007). Furthermore, several Asian centers (Shanghai, Seoul, Hong Kong, and Beijing) are ranked highest in a survey of the financial cities that will become more significant in the coming years. These Asian cities are also the most attractive locations for new branches or offices. A breakdown of the GFCI shows that Asian financial centers are in the top three in the industry sectors of asset management (Hong Kong, rank 3), banking (Hong Kong, rank 2), government and regulatory (Singapore, rank 2), insurance (Shanghai, rank 2), and professional services and wealth management (Hong Kong, rank 3) (Yeandle, 2011).

FINANCIAL CENTERS AND REGIONAL CONCENTRATION

The contemporary rate of urbanization is the highest in world history, with more than half of the world's population living in cities in 2008 (United Nations Population Fund). Following this rapid urbanization, an extensive body of research on cities has developed (e.g., Andersson, 1985; Florida, 2002; Glaeser, Kolko, & Saiz, 2001; Jacobs, 1961, 1969).

Questions of firm location and regional concentration have been investigated since the late nineteenth century, focusing variously on transportation costs, labor costs, and agglomeration effects. Within this literature, cities are often analyzed as the equilibrium outcome of an ongoing process of centripetal agglomeration forces and centrifugal dispersion forces (Huriot & Thisse, 2000). It was however not until the early 1990s that spatial considerations were included in mainstream economic theories (Fujita, Krugman, & Venables, 1999). Much of the previous negligence was caused by technical difficulties in both the theoretical and econometric analysis (Krugman, 1998a, 1998b). Theories of city formation and their role in economic development can also be found in the research of, among many others, Jacobs (1969, 1984) and Florida (2002). Both authors argue that cities are centers where innovations are stimulated and that this tendency leads to economic growth on the national level in the long run. Jacobs (1984) even argues that the causation runs from economic productivity in cities to national economic growth, not the other way around.

Cities – A Jacobsian Approach

Jacobs defines a city as "a settlement that consistently generates its economic growth from its own local economy" (Jacobs, 1969, p. 262). In line with the Austrian approach, Jacobs defines the development of cities as a spontaneous order where the process is "self-ordering, self-sustaining, and self-regulating" (Ikeda, 2004, p. 253). In particular, Jacobs (1969, p. 122) contends that "[c]ities are settlements where much new work is added to older work and that this new work multiplies and diversifies a city's division of labor."

Jacobs's (1961, 1969) analysis is based on the idea that interacting people are the promoters of cities and, in the long run, of economic prosperity. The interactions take place on the streets, in public places, and in other arenas where people meet on a daily basis; these interactions form the building blocks of social order and development. Cities are vital to economic life because they are the primary arenas for its development and expansion – a process fueled by two forms of energy: innovation and import replacement. Innovations are essentially human insights, whereas import replacements represent a society's capability to adapt imitations. Jacobs (1984, p. 193) describes the benefits of cities by noting that "the usefulness of cities is that they supply contexts in which those inputs – insights and adaptations – can be successfully injected into everyday economic life." Jacobs's use of a methodologically individualist approach has many similarities with Austrian economics in that both believe that economic prosperity and development are generated by the interactions between individuals (Ikeda, 2004).

Knowledge spillovers (human capital externalities) generate entrepreneurship, innovation, and creativity – important factors that drive economic growth. Open and diverse cities attract individuals with diverse backgrounds, fostering entrepreneurship and innovations in the process. According to Kirznerian theory entrepreneurship is, in essence, about "alertness": "a tendency for an individual to discover what would be profitable to him/her if he/she were to discover it" (Sautet, 2000, p. 60). However, there is no spatial dimension in Kirzner's theory (1973) of entrepreneurship, and Andersson (2005) argues that the theory is incomplete without this dimension. The choice of location is, in itself, an act of entrepreneurship, because different profit opportunities are attributed to different locations. Andersson (2005) further notes that location may affect an individual's level of alertness; individuals located in "buzz-cities" (see below) have a higher probability of success compared with others. In line with this argument, we should expect the level of entrepreneurship (or the probability of entrepreneurship) to be much higher in London and New York than in other financial centers, since both London and New York provide environments that facilitate and improve alertness.

The inflow of a diverse and specialized workforce also attracts firms to a region, which, in turn, generates a diversified supply of services and commercial facilities to households. Cities facilitate both expected and unexpected meetings at formal, informal, and chance meeting places.[4] Labor mobility is yet another important source of knowledge spillovers in the financial industry. Agglomerations in the financial industry are associated with diversified labor markets consisting of highly skilled workers; these

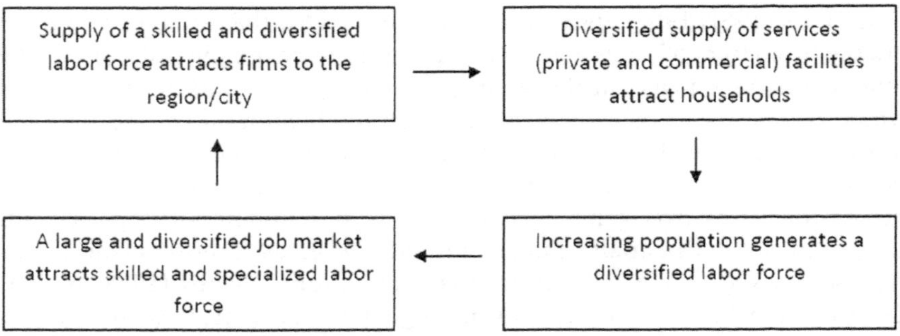

Fig. 1. The Cumulative Process of Agglomeration.

markets benefit both financial firms and finance professionals. Although individuals working in the industry have access to a large and diversified labor market that is suited to their requirements, firms in the cluster also benefit because they have access to a diversified labor force with industry-specific skills. The higher level of skilled labor increases the nominal wages, which is a real cost for the firms. Fig. 1 shows how the cumulative process of agglomeration may work.

According to the NEG, the positive agglomeration effects that benefit firms are a result of lower trading costs and nominal wages due to being in the proximity of a large market. Individuals benefit from the co-location of firms by having access to a larger and more diverse labor market, to greater product variety and to higher real wages. Costs associated with agglomeration effects are often referred to as congestion costs, which are caused by higher levels of competition (Fujita, 1993; Krugman, 1991; Venables, 1996).

The agglomerative milieu affects both the supply and the demand sides of the agglomeration process. The supply side consists of factors such as the willingness and ability to innovate and become an entrepreneur. The demand side consists of factors such as purchasing power and market size. Given the size of the city (the regional market), one can expect both the demand and supply factors to impact the innovation process positively.

Externalities and Agglomeration Effects

Jacobs (1969, 1984) presents a dynamic view of cities and argues that cities provide a beneficial environment for interaction between individuals, which, in turn, generates knowledge spillovers, innovations, and economic growth. In the literature on economic growth, externalities – especially knowledge externalities – are viewed as the primary driver of economic development (Lucas, 1988; Romer, 1986). For example, Lucas (1988) highlights the importance of human capital externalities and knowledge spillover effects in promoting positive agglomerative effects and economic growth. Because spatial proximity is important for the transmission of knowledge, one should expect stronger positive effects of knowledge spillovers in cities (Glaeser, Kallal, & Scheinkman, 1992).

Glaeser et al. (1992) discuss three different theories that address technological externalities:[5] (i) Marshall–Arrow–Romer (MAR), (ii) Porter (1990), and (iii) Jacobs (1969). These theories are relevant because they can be used to understand how cities form and why they grow; they are also relevant for understanding clustering in the financial industry. According to the MAR approach, cities grow because industrial concentration enables knowledge spillovers between firms in the same industry. Marshall (1920) uses increasing returns to scale as a prominent determinant of co-location. His analysis distinguishes between external and internal scale economies. Internal scale economies refer to scale effects that arise due to the level of production within a firm, whereas the size of the external market determines the magnitude of external scale economies. That is, firms gain both from internal and external economies of scale when they co-locate in a region. The causes of Marshallian externalities can be summarized in the following way:

> (1) mass production (the so-called internal economies that are similar to scale economies ... (2) the formation of a highly specialized labor force and the production of new ideas, both based on the accumulation of human capital and face-to face communications, (3) the availability of specialized input services, and (4) the existence of modern infrastructures. (Fujita & Thisse, 2000, p. 10)

In line with Schumpeter (1942), the MAR approach advocates *local monopoly* instead of *local competition* because local monopoly allows the innovator to internalize externalities. Porter (1990) agrees that growth is stimulated by the geographical concentration of an industry. However, Porter argues that local competition, not local monopolies, fosters economic growth. The third theory (Jacobs, 1969), which focuses on technological externalities, differs from the previous two by arguing that economic growth stems from diversity: the cross-fertilization of different geographically proximate industries that generates innovations and economic growth (Glaeser et al., 1992).

Industrial Agglomeration and the Role of Knowledge

Over the last decades, there has been tremendous development in the ICT sector. Together with globalization, the sophisticated digital communication systems that are available today have increased the importance of innovative and knowledge-based activities. These types of activities are also sensitive to distance; hence, new knowledge activities benefit from co-location (Audretsch, 1998).

Malmberg and Maskell (2002) use knowledge as an explanatory variable to elucidate the superior innovative and economic performance of co-located firms. This knowledge-based theory rests on the assumption that agglomeration leads to lower costs by providing (i) the ability to share costs with other firms in the same cluster; (ii) access to specialized labor, thus reducing the search costs for specialized skills; and (iii) geographical proximity, which lowers the costs of interaction and interfirm transactions. These mechanisms – related to knowledge and learning flows – occur within the cluster because of geographical proximity. Malmberg and Maskell (*ibid.*) argue that this exchange takes place through horizontal integration. Horizontally located firms generate knowledge and learning processes that lead to superior economic growth, as compared with single or network firms located at disparate geographical locations. The reason is that geographical proximity leads to superior *observability* and *comparability*.

First, by observing competitors' behavior, firms in adjacent industries can gain new knowledge. This happens more easily for co-located firms because the effort level is much lower compared with firms in disparate locations. Second, geographically co-located firms share the same conditions, opportunities, and threats, which make comparisons among firms more reliable. Various firms' strengths and weakness are more clearly detected when they operate in a similar environment. In other words, the co-location of firms increases the knowledge of how to improve production as well as the incentives to do so. Vertical agglomeration factors relate to the supply of knowledge and learning in the form of skilled and specialized labor and suppliers. These factors generate a greater degree of diversity because firms must diversify their products in order to prevail in the competition with other firms who have products in the same category (Cook, Pandit, Beaverstock, Taylor, & Pain, 2007; Malmberg & Maskell, 2002).

Tacit knowledge is the underlying cause of both horizontal and vertical agglomeration effects. The co-location of firms enhances the ability to generate and disperse tacit knowledge, a process that explains the superior economic performance among co-located firms (Gertler, 2003). The concept of tacit knowledge is closely connected to Hayek's analysis of the role of knowledge in society, to which we turn next.

Hayek's Knowledge Problem and Tacit Knowledge

Polanyi (1966) distinguishes between codified and tacit knowledge. Although codified (or explicit) knowledge can be expressed and communicated through symbols (written language), tacit knowledge is "a personal form of knowledge, which individuals only can obtain from direct experience in a given domain" (Augier & Thanning Vendelø, 1999, p. 254). Tacit knowledge can only be transferred through social interaction, for example, through conversation, imitation, and observation. This type of knowledge is difficult to communicate; thus its generation and dissemination benefit significantly from geographical proximity, especially "when such proximity is coupled with contextual homogeneity or 'common culture' that exists in agglomerations" (Cook et al., 2007, p. 1327). In economic geography, tacit knowledge is often discussed in terms of face-to-face contact. For example, Storper and Venables (2004, Table 1) highlight four effects of face-to-face communication (alternatively, tacit knowledge): (i) efficient communication, (ii) enhanced trust and incentives in relationships, (iii) improved screening and socialization, and iv) extra effort and motivation.

The importance of knowledge and its tacit characteristics are discussed thoroughly in Hayek's work. According to Hayek (1945), decentralized knowledge is the fundamental problem for social coordination; knowledge in a society is dispersed among a multitude of individuals. Contrary to the assumptions of modern neoclassical economics, information does not float freely among the members of any society. Information is discontinuous and is never costless. Therefore, the great problem of society is not the allocation of given resources but "the utilization of knowledge not given to anyone in its totality" (Hayek, 1945, p. 520).

To describe the organization of society Hayek uses the word "planning," by which he means the way that society allocates resources. This allocation involves a complex decision process by multiple interrelated individuals as well as planning decisions that are based on the type of knowledge that – generally speaking – is not transmitted to the planner from its source. Hayek describes this process and its importance for society in the following way:

> The various ways in which the knowledge on which people base their plans is communicated to them is the crucial problem for any theory explaining the economic process. And the problem of what is the best way of utilizing knowledge initially

> dispersed among all the people is at least one of the main problems of economic policy – or of designing an efficient economic system. (Hayek, 1945, p. 520)

In a market economy, "economic planning" is performed by thousands or millions of firms and individuals, whereas in a centrally planned economy, a small group of individuals does most of the planning. The main challenge for a society is to allocate the dispersed knowledge in the best possible way so that the members of the society can proceed with their plans. Hayek (1937, 1945, 1948) argues that a market economy is the system that generates the highest level of wealth. Market prices distill and disseminate local knowledge in a way that benefits individual market participants, each of whom combines their own unique knowledge with the generally available knowledge that the price system conveys (see also Mises, 1922).

Hayek (1945) notes that there are different types of knowledge; some types of knowledge (e.g., scientific knowledge) are more likely to be found among authorities or special groups of individuals (experts), whereas other types of knowledge are more likely to be dispersed among individuals (tacit knowledge). Hayek especially emphasizes "the knowledge of the particular circumstances of time and place" (Hayek, 1945, p. 521). This refers to knowledge about people, local conditions, and special circumstances. For example, a specific firm may have knowledge about a more effective production system, or a specific arbitrageur may have knowledge about a particular type of profitable transaction. It is important to note that both the firm and the arbitrageur use their special knowledge of the particularities of unique time-place combinations in their pursuit of profits.

Hayek (1945) further notes that all economic problems arise from change. Therefore, the economic problem of society is the problem of adapting to economic change. The most suitable individual to address this problem is one who is knowledgeable about particular conditions with respect to both time and place. To meet this requirement, Hayek advocates the decentralization of planning, as opposed to a system with top-down planning. A fundamental aspect of agglomeration economies and the creation of cities is the role of *dispersed* knowledge. In the next section, I therefore discuss the role of knowledge flows in the financial sector.

The Price System as a Mechanism for Knowledge Dissemination

Hayek (1945, p. 526) views the price system as "a mechanism for communicating information." In systems where knowledge is dispersed across individuals, prices can act as a coordinating entity. To make adequate decisions, each individual needs knowledge about the state of the art and about changes in the economy so that the individual decisions fit into the larger economic pattern. The fundamental question concerns how knowledge can be spread in a complex system, so that each actor accesses only relevant information that is important for *his or her* planning. This is a fundamental issue because individuals are solely interested in changes in the relative importance of factors that affect *their* planning. The numerical values that are assigned by the price system to commodities and factors of production are exactly the type of knowledge that is valuable to firms and households. That is, the price system only provides essential information to market participants. In this sense, the price system facilitates "a division of labor but also a coördinated utilization of resources based on an equally divided knowledge" (Hayek, 1945, p. 528).

The price system works to coordinate the expectations and plans of different individuals. This process does not always work smoothly. It can be affected by countervailing forces, such as price inflexibility (or economic inertia), time lags, and interpretation issues. However, if the economy is allowed to develop without political interventions, markets will develop institutions that protect the coordinating forces of the price system. The stock market and forward markets are two such examples (Lachmann, 1956).

The Price System and Expectations

Implicit in the above discussion about the price system as a "network of communication" is that the knowledge generated by the price system is based on past – rather than future – events. This deficiency is mitigated by forward and stock markets, in which knowledge about individuals' expectations concerning the future are spread. Although the forward market is quite restricted with respect to both traded goods and time intervals, the stock market deals with "continuous futures." By investing in the stock of a firm, the individual simultaneously expresses her expectations about the dividends of the specific firm as well as of all alternative investments that are forgone by the investor in order to buy shares in the specific firm. In this way, the stock market is seen as an instrument for bringing long-term expectations into consistency, like the price system in any other market. However, in the future and stock markets, a temporal aspect is included (Lachmann, 1956). Thus, forward and stock prices spread market opinions (rather than facts) about an uncertain future.

The stock market is seen by many economists as the most important market and also as an important economic indicator since it "in its relative valuation of the various yield streams reflects, in a suitable 'objectified' form, articulate expectations of all those who wish to express them" (Lachmann, 1956, p. 68). The stock market not only aligns individual expectations; it also works to bring forth economic growth through the constant revaluation of capital. The constant revaluation of capital signals – to both the capital owners and the managers – the opinion of the market regarding the firm-specific use of capital in production. Capital owners and managers who do not act in accordance with market opinion will be replaced by more productive entrepreneurs in the long run. That is, the stock market is a prime distributor of knowledge in society.

KNOWLEDGE FLOWS IN THE FINANCIAL INDUSTRY

We have discussed different types of knowledge. A commonality in both types of theories – spatial and Austrian – is the importance of tacit or local knowledge for social order and economic development. Both codified and tacit knowledge exist in the financial industry. The combination of the development of the ICT sector and increasing regulatory requirements suggests that the magnitude of the codified knowledge – such as share prices, annual reports, quarterly reports, and other standardized financial statements – has increased tremendously over the last decades. With the help of the ICT sector, the codified information can be disseminated across the globe, almost in real time. Much of this knowledge is by itself not distance-sensitive; with only this type of knowledge, the financial industry would probably be much less concentrated in space. Instead, it is the existence of tacit knowledge that makes it crucial for firms in the financial industry to cluster in a small number of cities.

Tacit Knowledge and the Role of Face-to-Face Communication

Tacit knowledge is subjective and depends on the cognitive scheme of the recipient (Hayek, 1948). Thus the dissemination of tacit knowledge requires routines and interaction among individuals and firms. Firms and individuals in the same industry or in related industries for this reason develop a common culture as well as cognitive schemes that facilitate knowledge networks. Tacit knowledge is context-based and it is interpreted in the specific environment in which it takes place (Augier & Thanning Vendelø, 1999).

Codified knowledge and tacit knowledge are explicitly differentiated to highlight that it is the distribution of tacit or non-codified knowledge that is the most important explanatory factor for the high level of regional concentration in the financial industry (Audretsch, 1998; Cook et al., 2007). The nature of tacit knowledge means that it is disseminated between firms and individual via face-to-face contacts. The effective allocation of tacit knowledge is especially important in knowledge-intensive and innovative industries. In these types of industries, knowledge about the latest innovations and changes as well as specialized know-how from practice and mistakes is what really matters.

Storper and Venables (2004) model the importance of face-to-face communication in the urban economy. They argue that face-to-face contacts are highly efficient as "a means of overcoming coordination and incentive problems in uncertain environments; a key element of socialization that in turn allows people to be candidates for membership of 'in-groups' and to stay in such groups; and a direct source of psychological motivation" (Storper & Venables 2004, p. 365). Storper and Venables label these effects "*buzz*" and hypothesize that, in combination, they are super-additive and generate increasing returns for participating firms and individuals. In buzz environments, high-ability individuals interact and cooperate with one another, generating a platform for discussion of complex ideas and problems. To fully reap the benefit of the buzz environment, firms (individuals) need to be co-located; participating only occasionally does not generate the same advantages.[6] Storper and Venables (2004, p. 365) conclude by arguing that "people in buzz environment should be highly productive."

It is common for cities with this buzz environment to have many industry-specific networks that interact. Storper and Venables highlight, for example, the cross-interaction between higher education, finance, and government. Individuals working in these industries form powerful networks that enable both informal and formal meeting platforms for social and business purposes. The notion that cities provide platforms for interaction across various networks is in line with Jacobs's theory of cities, in which diversity plays a central role for economic growth. The buzz environment is also effective for spreading knowledge, both within specific industries and across networks that connect different industries. Hence face-to-face communication and buzz environments are directly related to Hayek's notion of knowledge and knowledge dispersion (see above).

The agglomeration effects in buzz cities are generated by classical agglomeration sources, such as (i) specialized labor, (ii) specialized suppliers, and (iii) knowledge dispersion (Marshall, 1920), as well as by interactive knowledge and information-based activities. These may include the following:

> (a) creative and cultural functions (including industries linked to this, such as fashion, design and the arts); (b) finance and business services; (c) science, technology and high technology and research; and (d) power and influence (government, headquarters, trade associations, and international agencies). (Storper & Venables, 2004, pp. 365–366)

The combination of professional and social networks makes it possible for buzz cities to attract skilled and specialized labor and to generate an environment in which "critical problems of coordination in the modern economy are resolved through F2F contact" (Storper & Venables, 2004, p. 366).

Table 2 presents an overview of how different types of knowledge are used in the coordination of various industries and milieus. The table relates the type of knowledge to the requirement for spatial proximity. Starting from the left, we see that in markets where knowledge is "ubiquitous and transparent" (e.g., trade in basic manufactured goods and commodities) there is a low (or zero) requirement for spatial proximity. To the left, we find industries where knowledge is "specialized and private," and this includes both tacit and codified knowledge. Industries that are dependent on private

Table 2. Modes of Coordination.

Coordination Environment	Knowledge Used in Coordination		
	Specialized/Private		Ubiquitous/ Transparent
	Tacit	Codified	
Stable	*Bureaucracy/firms* Specialized networks for search/matching (**HIGH**) *Financial services*	Bureaucracy/firms (**LOW**) *Car industry (mass production)*	Markets (**LOW**) *Basic manufactured inputs or services*
Fluid	Buzz (**HIGH**)	Organized networks for search/matching (**MEDIUM**)	Markets (**LOW**)
	Politics; arts; entertainment; science; high tech; advanced finance	*Aerospace; pharmaceuticals*	*Commodities (e.g., oil)*

Source: Adapted from Storper and Venables (2004, Table 3).
Note: **HIGH, MEDIUM,** and **LOW** indicate the relative importance of spatial proximity.

and specialized but codified knowledge, such as cars and chemicals, usually have a low requirement for proximity. These industries often operate in stable environments. The requirement for co-location increases for industries in which knowledge is codified but the environment is more fluid or flexible. Within these industries organized networks usually exist to match partners on a project-by-project basis. Face-to-face contact in these environments is more important; one can in this case lower transaction cost by implementing effective monitoring of both market and contractual relations within specific projects. For industries where tacit knowledge determines coordination, geographical proximity is of crucial importance for both stable and flexible environments. Knowledge-intensive and innovative industries are most often found in these categories.

Centrifugal and Centripetal Forces in the Financial Industry

There seems to be wide agreement that the spatial location of the financial industry is affected by both centrifugal and centripetal forces. Kindleberger (1974) contends that it is mainly scale economies arising from the organization of financial markets that generate centripetal forces in the industry. Conversely, localized information, different time zones, and regulations represent major centrifugal forces. The vital point here is the role and characteristics of knowledge and information. Gehrig (2000, p. 417) suggests that "[t]rade in informationally sensitive securities is likely to be geographically concentrated at those locations where information about those securities is aggregated and communicated." Trade in more standardized securities tends to be less spatially concentrated.

Given that complex information about investments is produced, communicated, and aggregated in financial centers, adjacent industries will also be attracted to these locations. Consequently, technological development and increased international trade support the expansion of GFCs in a longer time perspective. Firms that depend on distance-sensitive information benefit disproportionately from agglomeration economies and will therefore tend to locate in the same regions as financial centers. In contrast, firms that trade in goods or services that are associated with distance-insensitive information tend to locate in low-cost cities.

NEG theories assume a continuing clustering and higher levels of concentration in the financial industry due to ever-increasing, distance-sensitive transaction costs (Engelen & Grote, 2009). Despite the rapid development of the ICT sector, proximity continues to be of value and facilitates rapid dissemination of knowledge among traders, analysts, and other actors. The explanation is the existence of substantial knowledge spillovers, which play an increasing role in explaining the co-location of knowledge-based activities (Audretsch, 1998). Engelen and Grote (2009) use the NEG approach to analyze the changing role of second-tier financial centers, such as Amsterdam and Frankfurt. They argue that the financial industry will continue to be pulled in by GFCs at the expense of second-tier centers.

CONCLUDING REMARKS

Over the past several decades, the global financial industry, like other industries, has experienced both globalization and the development of sophisticated and complex ICT systems. This situation has improved the ability to spread codified knowledge and information to distant locations. Despite this development, the financial industry has seen an increase in geographical concentration over the same time period. GFCs such as London and New York have attained increasingly dominant positions in the industry at the expense of second-tier centers such as Amsterdam and Frankfurt. Following the rapid growth of Asia's economies, Shanghai, Hong Kong, and Seoul have however become increasingly competitive.

The explanation for the paradox of increasing access to knowledge and, in parallel, increasing geographical concentration can be found in the role of tacit knowledge and face-to-face communication. When tacit knowledge flows promote industry coordination, the consequence is that geographical proximity becomes extraordinarily beneficial. Thus, the financial industry is becoming more concentrated, as is implied by theories ranging from Hayek (1945) and Jacobs (1969) to recent contributions in regional economics and economic geography.

NOTES

1. The 10 most important financial centers according to the GFCI index are London (795), New York (786), Hong Kong (695), Singapore (675), Zurich (665), Frankfurt (642), Geneva (640), Chicago (637), Tokyo (628), and Sydney (621) (GFCI ratings within brackets).
2. See, for example, King and Levine (1993) and Levine (2004) for discussions and empirical evidence on the importance of financial development to economic growth.

3. The GFCI is based on two sources: (i) external indices and (ii) financial center assessment. The financial center assessment is based on an ongoing survey directed to "international financial services professionals." The respondents answer questions and assess centers that they are familiar with. There are many different factors that affect the competitiveness of a financial center. The GFCI focuses on five areas that are of special interest: people, business environment, infrastructure, market access, and general competitiveness. See Yeandle (2011, p. 332) for a detailed description of the survey.

4. See Saxenian (1990) and Kiriakos (2011) for excellent analyses of the importance of "being there." Saxenian analyzes the knowledge effects of labor turnover among Silicon Valley firms, while Kiriakos discusses the importance of serendipitous discoveries in Silicon Valley.

5. Technological externalities occur when "innovations and improvements occurring in one firm increase the productivity of the other firms without full compensation" (Glaeser et al., 1992, p. 1127).

6. Kiriakos (2011) documents this for Finnish executives in Silicon Valley.

REFERENCES

Agnes, P. (2000). The "end of geography" in financial services? Local embeddedness and territorialization in the interest rate swap industry. *Economic Geography*, *76*(4), 347–366.

Amel, D., Barnes, C., Panetta, F., & Salleo, C. (2004). Consolidation and efficiency in the financial sector: A review of the international evidence. *Journal of Banking and Finance*, *28*(10), 2493–2519.

Andersson, Å. E. (1985). *Kreativitet—Storstadens framtid*. Stockholm: Prisma.

Andersson, D. E. (2005). The spatial nature of entrepreneurship. *Quarterly Journal of Austrian Economics*, *8*(2), 21–34.

Audretsch, D. B. (1998). Agglomeration and the location of innovative activity. *Oxford Review of Economic Policy*, *14*(2), 18–29.

Augier, M., & Thanning Vendelø, M. (1999). Networks, cognition and management of tacit knowledge. *Journal of Knowledge Management*, *3*(4), 252–261.

Beck, T., & Levine, R. (2002). Industry growth and capital allocation: Does having a market- or bank-based system matter? *Journal of Financial Economics*, *64*, 147–180.

Cook, G. A. S., Pandit, N. R., Beaverstock, J., Taylor, P., & Pain, K. (2007). The role of location in knowledge creation and diffusion: Evidence of centripetal and centrifugal forces in the city of London financial services agglomeration. *Environment and Planning A*, *39*, 1325–1345.

Cooper, M. (2011). *The great game: Clustering in wholesale financial services*. London: Z/Yen Ltd.

Engelen, E., & Grote, M. H. (2009). Stock exchange virtualisation and the decline of second-tier financial centres—The cases of Amsterdam and Frankfurt. *Journal of Economic Geography*, *9*(5), 679–696.

Florida, R. (2002). *The rise of the creative class*. New York, NY: Basic Books.

Fujita, M. (1993). Monopolistic competition and urban system. *European Economic Review*, *37*(2-3), 308–315.

Fujita, M., Krugman, P. R., & Venables, A. J. (1999). *Spatial economics: Cities, regions and international trade*. Cambridge, MA: MIT Press.

Fujita, M., & Thisse, J. F. (2000). The formation of economic agglomerations. In J.-M. Huriot & J. F. Thisse (Eds.), *Economics of cities*. Cambridge, UK: Cambridge University Press.

Gehrig, T. (2000). Cities and the geography of financial centers. In J.-M. Huriot & J.-F. Thisse (Eds.), *Economics of cities: Theoretical perspectives*. Cambridge, UK: Cambridge University Press.

Gertler, M. S. (2003). Tacit knowledge and the economic geography of context, or the undefinable tacitness of being (there). *Journal of Economic Geography*, *3*, 75–99.

Glaeser, E. L., Kallal, H. D., & Scheinkman, J. A. (1992). Growth in cities. *Journal of Political Economy*, *100*(6), 1126–1152.

Glaeser, E. L., Kolko, J., & Saiz, A. (2001). Consumer city. *Journal of Economic Geography*, *1*(1), 27–50.

Goldberg, M. A., Helsley, R. W., & Levi, M. (1988). On the development of international financial centers. *Annals of Regional Science*, *22*, 81–94.

Hayek, F. A. (1937). Economics and knowledge. *Economica*, *4*(February), 33–54.

Hayek, F. A. (1945). The use of knowledge in society. *American Economic Review*, *35*(4), 519–530.

Hayek, F. A. (1948). The meaning of competition. In F. A. Hayek (Ed.), *Individualism and economic order*. Chicago, IL: University of Chicago Press.

Huriot, J. M., & Thisse, J. F. (2000). Introduction. In J.-M. Huriot & J.-F. Thisse (Eds.), *Economics of cities*. Cambridge, UK: Cambridge University Press.

Ikeda, S. (2004). Urban interventionism and local knowledge. *Review of Austrian Economics*, *17*(2-3), 247–260.

Jacobs, J. (1961). *The death and life of great American cities*. New York, NY: Random House.

Jacobs, J. (1969). *The economy of cities*. New York, NY: Random House.

Jacobs, J. (1984). *Cities and the wealth of nations*. New York, NY: Random House.

Kindleberger, C. P. (1974). *The formation of financial centers: A study in comparative economic history*. Princeton Studies in International Finance No. 36. International Finance Section, Princeton University, NJ.

King, R. G., & Levine, R. (1993). Finance and growth: Schumpeter might be right. *Quarterly Journal of Economics*, *108*(3), 717–737.

Kiriakos, C. M. (2011). Why being there matters: Finnish professionals in Silicon Valley. In D.E. Andersson, Å. E. Andersson & C. Mellander (Eds.), *Handbook of creative cities*. Cheltenham, UK: Edward Elgar.

Kirzner, I. M. (1973). *Competition and entrepreneurship*. Chicago, IL: University of Chicago Press.

Krugman, P. R. (1991). Increasing returns and economic geography. *Journal of Political Economy*, *99*(3), 7–17.

Krugman, P. R. (1998a). What's new about the new economic geography? *Oxford Review of Economic Policy*, *14*(2), 7–17.

Krugman, P. R. (1998b). Space: The final frontier. *Journal of Economic Perspectives*, *12*(2), 161–174.

Lachmann, L. (1978). *Capital and its structure*. San Francisco, CA: Institute of Humane Studies.

Latter, T. (2001). *Just another financial center—or is Hong Kong special*? Address by Mr. Tony Latter, Deputy Chief of the Hong Kong Monetary Authority, at the Foreign Correspondents Club, Hong Kong, April 25, 2011.

Lee, H. L. (2001). *Financial Centers today and tomorrow: A Singapore perspective*. Address by Mr. Lee Hsien Loong, Deputy Prime Minister of Singapore and Chairman of the Monetary Authority of Singapore, International Monetary Conference, Singapore, June 4, 2001.

Levine, R. (1997). Financial development and economic growth: Views and agenda. *Journal of Economic Literature*, *35*(June), 688–726.

Levine, R. (2004). *The corporate governance of banks: A concise discussion of concepts and evidence*. World Bank Policy Research Working Paper No. 3404. World Bank, Washington, DC.

Lucas, R. E. (1988). On the mechanics of economic development. *Journal of Monetary Economics*, *22*(1), 3–42.

Malmberg, A., & Maskell, P. (2002). The elusive concept of localization economies: towards a knowledge-based theory of spatial clustering. *Environment and Planning A*, *34*(3), 429–449.

Marshall, A. (1920). *Principles of economics*. London, UK: Macmillan.

Mises, L. von. (1922). *Socialism: An economic and sociological critique*. Indianapolis, IN: Liberty Fund.

Mishkin, F. S. (2007). Is financial globalization beneficial? *Journal of Money, Credit and Banking*, *39*(2-3), 259–294.

Polanyi, M. (1966). *The tacit dimension*. London, UK: Routledge.

Poon, J. P.-H. (2003). Hierarchical tendencies of capital markets among international financial centers. *Growth and Change*, *34*(2), 135–156.

Porter, M. E. (1990). *The competitive advantage of nations*. New York, NY: Free Press.

Reed, H. (1981). *The international finance system and economic development*. New York, NY: Praeger Publishers.

Romer, P. M. (1986). Increasing returns and long-run growth. *Journal of Political Economy*, *94*(October), 1002–1037.

Sautet, F. (2000). *An entrepreneurial theory of the firm*. London, UK: Routledge.

Saxenian, A. (1990). The origins and dynamics of production networks in Silicon Valley. *California Management Review*, *33*(1), 89–112.

Schumpeter, J. A. (1934). *The theory of economic development*. Cambridge, MA: Harvard University Press.

Schumpeter, J. A. (1942). *Capitalism, socialism and democracy*. New York: Harper and Row.

Storper, M., & Venables, A. J. (2004). Buzz: Face-to-face contact and the urban economy. *Journal of Economic Geography*, *4*(4), 351–370.

Venables, A. (1996). Equilibrium locations of vertically linked industries. *International Economic Review*, *37*(2), 341–359.

Yeandle, M. (2011). *The Global Financial Centres Index 9*. Financial Centre Futures Z.Y. Group, London, UK: Long Finance.

THE USE OF KNOWLEDGE IN INVESTMENT THEORY

Johan E. Eklund and Johan P. Larsson

Austrian economics has contributed a great deal to the development of capital theory and business cycle theory. Starting with Eugen von Böhm-Bawerk (1884, 1889) and later developed by Knut Wicksell (1893, 1901), economists belonging to the Austrian school have contributed to the development of capital theory. Böhm-Bawerk, for example, established the link between time and capital. Less effort has been devoted to understanding the implications that the Austrian tradition has for the theory of investment and its development. This is despite the fact that no theory of capital can be logically complete without a theoretical understanding of the investment process: the *stock* of capital is determined by the *flow* of investments.

The distinction between information and knowledge assumes such a central position in Austrian economics that it has been argued that it is one of its key distinguishing features (Boettke, 2002). Information in the strict sense is any sequence of ordered symbols, while knowledge is contextual and can be thought of as the interpretation of information by the human mind (or as judgment; see McCloskey & Klamer, 1995 for a discussion). While the distance decay involved in the communication of information is negligible, knowledge is not always as easily communicated across time and space. We therefore analyze the possible implications that this distinction between information and knowledge has for the theory of investment.

Recognizing that some types of knowledge are more difficult to transmit between individuals, we argue that investments in assets that are intangible

The Spatial Market Process
Advances in Austrian Economics, Volume 16, 335–351

ISSN: 1529-2134/doi:10.1108/S1529-2134(2012)0000016016

or require more local or tacit knowledge will be relatively more sensitive to the spatial proximity of financial services. Even in the case of tangible assets, similar spatial effects apply if the investment is part of a knowledge-intensive learning process.

In mainstream economics, the notion of information plays a crucial role and one of the key functions of the financial system is to overcome information asymmetries (e.g., Levine & Beck, 2004). Recognizing that there is a fundamental difference between information and knowledge, we argue that the Austrian tradition may shed light on the investment process, and in particular on how entrepreneurs need to transmit knowledge to financiers.

RATIONAL INVESTMENTS

The neoclassical theory of investments, as formulated by Dale Jorgenson (1963, 1967), can be expressed in a fairly straightforward way.[1] Neoclassical formulations such as Jorgenson's were preceded by contributions by many influential economists. Both John Maynard Keynes and Irving Fisher, for example, argued that investments are made until the present value of expected future revenues, at the margin, equals the opportunity cost of capital. This means that investments are made until the net present value is equal to zero.

Fisher referred to the discount rate as the *rate of return over costs* or the *internal rate of return*. Keynes, on the other hand, referred to it as the *marginal efficiency of capital* (Alchian, 1955; Baddeley, 2003). Keynes (1936) argues that investments are made until "there is no longer any class of capital assets of which the marginal efficiency exceeds the current rate of interest" (as quoted in Baddeley, 2003, p. 34). The fundamental difference between the "Keynesian view" and the "Hayekian view" lies in the perception of risk and uncertainty as well as in the formation of expectations about the future.

Keynes did not regard investment as an adjustment process toward equilibrium. Hayek (1941) and Fisher (1930), on the other hand, view investment as an optimal adjustment path toward an optimal capital stock. In the Keynesian theory, investments are not determined by some underlying optimal capital stock.[2] Instead, genuine or *radical* uncertainty takes a central position. Keynes believed that humans were "animal-spirited" and that this nuisance, combined with irrational and volatile expectations, made the notion of investment as an adjustment process toward equilibrium futile.

From Keynes and Fisher modern investment theories have emerged, incorporating various aspects of the earlier work. The net present value rule has become a standard component of corporate finance. Jorgenson's (1963) neoclassical theory of investment basically formalizes ideas put forward by Fisher. Keynes's work on subjective probabilities foreshadowed modern probabilistic approaches, such as Markowitz (1952), which has led to the emergence of a very large literature on portfolio choice.

Arguably, Keynes has also influenced the so-called accelerator theory of investment, known for its applications to business cycles by Samuelson (1939a, 1939b). Clearly, Keynes also inspired Tobin and Brainard in their development of Tobin's Q (Brainard & Tobin, 1968; Tobin, 1969) to incorporate expectations. The methodology to measure marginal q that was developed by Mueller and Reardon (1993) also belongs to this line of thought. However, these theories can also be said to be influenced by the Hayekian view, in the sense that investments represent an adjustment toward an optimal stock of capital.[3]

But these theories do not deal with the importance of agents' knowledge of investment opportunities. In a world with no information asymmetries and perfect knowledge, investments can indeed be expected to be made until the expected return equals the opportunity cost of capital. In addition to the differences in perception with regard to risk, uncertainty, and the formation of expectations between the Keynesian and the Hayekian view, there is also a fundamental difference between how mainstream financial economics and Austrian economics treat information and knowledge.

In mainstream economics information is mostly treated in a technical manner, as if it were some sort of homogenous matter. The primary concern for financial markets is thereby reduced to a technical question of how to overcome information asymmetries. When investors and entrepreneurs (lenders and borrowers) have different information (asymmetric information), this leads to a rise in the cost of capital and a subsequent reduction in investments. An example is Myers's and Majluf's (1984) demonstration of what happens when investors have different information sets from those of the firms that they invest in.

Most of the mainstream finance literature follows a probabilistic or Bayesian approach. Despite the fact that one of the fundamental functions of the financial system is to bridge information asymmetries, little attention has been devoted to defining the nature of the information that is needed, and no distinction is made between information and knowledge.

Recognizing that profitable investment opportunities arise for various reasons, it may mostly be profitable to invest in an incumbent firm although other investment opportunities arise due to an entrepreneurial discovery process. There is an important difference between these two types of investment opportunities in terms of the required transfer of knowledge between investors and entrepreneurs. In this respect, the Austrian tradition can contribute to our understanding of investment behavior. Boettke (2002) argues that the uniqueness of the Austrian economics lies in the distinction between information and knowledge. He notes that one of the major advances in economics was made when time and information was incorporated in the analysis of the market economy and further argues that the "successful entrepreneur perceives the imperfection in the current arrangement of affairs more accurately than others, and he acts upon that information to earn a profit and in so acting brings new knowledge into existence." This has implications for investments, since entrepreneurs must convey this new knowledge to investors and persuade them to invest.

KNOWLEDGE AND PLANNING

It is no secret that Hayek resented rigid economic modeling for, to some extent, the same reason that he resented central planning (even setting ideologies aside); he contended that the necessary knowledge is not available in tangible form to anyone, and this "knowledge problem" applied to both researchers and central planners. Hayek (1937, p. 35) complains that economic modeling all too often reduces to tautology, "subject to no other test but internal consistency." Thus such approaches can never be applicable to social relations.

The part of this critique that deals explicitly with central planning, but that lies at the heart of the information and knowledge distinction, is famously voiced in Hayek's (1945) article "The Use of Knowledge in Society." The following passage contrasts the view, not uncommon at the time, that a planner can make use of available "data" and, in part or wholly, renders the market economy inefficient or even superfluous:

> The particular character of the problem of a rational economic order is determined precisely by the fact that the knowledge of circumstances of which we must make use never exists in concentrated or integrated form, but solely as the dispersed bits of incomplete and frequently contradictory knowledge which all the separate individuals possess. The economic problem of society is thus not merely a problem of how to allocate "given" resources – if "given" is taken to mean given to a single mind which deliberately solves the problem set by these "data." It is rather a problem of how to secure the best use of resources known to any of the members of society, for ends whose relative importance only these individuals know. Or, to put it briefly, it is a problem of the utilization of knowledge not given to anyone in its totality. (Hayek, 1945, pp. 519–520)

The knowledge needed to run an economy under the supervision of a centrally planned authority is subject to a constraint that is inherent in the knowledge formation process: Knowledge in the hands of agents close to the everyday operations has to be exchanged for "data" in the hands of the authorities. Hayek referred to this trade-off as *replacing planning by the many* with *planning by the few*. In this view, central planning is not only burdened by practical difficulties such as collecting a vast array of "data"; it is more or less destined to inefficiency for metaphysical reasons, such as the difficulties that are intrinsic in the transformation of knowledge into "data." More explicitly,

> central planning based on statistical information by its nature cannot take direct account of these circumstances of time and place, and the central planner will have to find some way or the other in which the decisions depending on them can be left to the "man on the spot." (Hayek, 1945, p. 524)

This line of thought is – whether deliberately or not – to a large extent incorporated into modern theories of agglomeration economies: the study of how and why actors in the economy benefit from proximity to each other. In this chapter, we argue that, for example, a venture capitalist cannot possess the relevant "data" any more than a central planner can. Like the central planner, the provider of capital for new ventures must rely on "the man on the spot," that is, the entrepreneur, and this is the path that investment must therefore take. Just as centrally planned societies turned out to be driven by grandiose delusions, venture capitalism cannot function without local knowledge, since the absence of such knowledge would make the investment process mimic a centrally planned venture.

LOCATION DECISIONS AND KNOWLEDGE DIFFUSION

David Emanuel Andersson (2005) augments the framework of Israel Kirzner by incorporating a spatial perspective on entrepreneurship. He argues that the entrepreneurs themselves use their *spatial positioning* as profit-seeking actions; he further argues that profit opportunities are not equally discoverable in all locations, but that some locations are more suitable for transfers of tacit knowledge. Pierre Desrochers (2001) argues that direct contacts between producers, users, and other parties are essential for the diffusion of such knowledge, providing numerous examples from Silicon Valley and other places.

Israel Kirzner (1973) views the entrepreneur as someone who takes advantage of price discrepancies – someone who buys something at a certain price at one point in time and sells it at a higher price later; the entrepreneur is someone who economizes on knowledge. Hayek (1945) likewise makes remarks about the *arbitrageur* who uses superior knowledge of time and place to make profits, while noting that these types of activities are often referred to with contempt (cf. "cut out the middleman"). In a work strongly influenced by Austrian thought, Thomas Sowell writes:

> Observers' disdain and/or moral condemnation for practices which utilize the cost advantages of informal relationships often proceed on the implicit assumption that knowledge is either economically free or theoretically "given" in some cohesive block equally accessible to all. In reality, knowledge can be enormously costly, and is often widely scattered in uneven fragments, too small to be individually usable in decision making. (Sowell, 1980, p. 26)

Sowell (1980) notes that banks seldom provide direct funding of ventures. Instead, they lend money to individuals with personal confidence in specific business opportunities. What necessitates the middleman is the fact that banks do not have the relevant local knowledge of time and place. This brings to mind Hayek's (1945) note on the near metaphysical impossibility for a central planner to continuously acquire the relevant local knowledge; the most effective system will be that which to the fullest extent manages to make use of available knowledge. Moreover, this knowledge is by its very nature of such a kind that it cannot be rendered into statistics.

Sowell (1980) further remarks that this proposition is strengthened by the fact that economic activity has proven harder to centrally plan the more acute is the need for local feedback. Certain types of manufactured goods have been produced with some success under centrally planned systems, while agriculture has failed miserably under what appears to have been the same type of institutional constraints. Part of the answer has to do with the fact that agriculture must more effectively economize on local knowledge (e.g., of soils and grains) in order to be successful.

Local knowledge is essential for most types of business ventures. If not acquired already, such knowledge must be obtained by employing the right people, consultants, or via other available means. Either way, any approach to investment strategy that treats entrepreneurial opportunities as evenly spread out across space must also perceive of knowledge in the same way; a view that an Austrian perception of knowledge would refute. The view of the firm as an entity that can handle knowledge and information more efficiently than the market has also been an important building block in research on firm formation (see, e.g., Kogut & Zander, 1992).

An Austrian view of knowledge and its diffusion is central for making this point. Hayek (1945) postulates that knowledge of where to put an individual's skill to better use is socially equivalent to knowledge of alternative and better production techniques, indicating that he was no stranger to discussions about location decisions. In *The Constitution of Liberty*, he goes so far as to define "civilization" as a situation where actors in the economy may benefit from more knowledge than that of their own (Hayek, 1960).

INFORMATION, KNOWLEDGE, AND SPATIAL FRICTION

More than a century of literature on agglomeration economics supports the tendency for knowledge to be partially non-excludable, which is to say that it "spills over" from one actor to another in space (e.g., Marshall, 1920; Rauch, 1993).

The spillover phenomenon is thought about as occurring in a confined environment, though its size varies greatly between different approaches. The size of the area is by no means unimportant. Åke E. Andersson and Martin Beckmann (2009) point to the fact that search costs are likely to increase quickly as the area is increased, since its size is equal to the square of the distance to the point of origin.

The important distinction between information and knowledge should yet again be emphasized at this point. Information thus "consists of the irreducible modules or primitive building blocks that are combined and recombined in the pursuit of new knowledge" (Andersson & Beckmann, 2009, p. 7). While information is almost costless to transport via different forms of communication, knowledge is subject to significant spatial friction. Information should be thought of as an input into the knowledge formation process, while knowledge can be crudely defined as the ability to transform old into new information. (Andersson & Beckmann, 2009)

One important difference between knowledge and other related concepts (which are sometimes confused with knowledge) is that the diffusion of knowledge is often inseparable from its creation (Jovanovic & Rob, 1989). Established forms of knowledge are naturally easier to communicate by the written word, while new forms of knowledge (such as a newly postulated scientific model) require learning, person-to-person interaction, and perhaps even persuasion (Andersson & Beckmann, 2009).

Taken together, the above paragraphs allow us to make a few predictions. First, since knowledge is not easy to transfer, the knowledge-formation process is most effective in a confined environment. Second, since activities differ in the extent to which they deal with knowledge, those actors that deal most exclusively with knowledge have the most to gain from close proximity to one another. Third, since the investment process must deal at least to some extent with knowledge, successful investors must obtain relevant knowledge of local circumstances,[4] which can be expected to flow more easily in economically dense environments.

The empirical literature is no stranger to the first and second propositions. First, an increasing body of evidence now supports the notion that human capital externalities attenuate with distance. One strand of the literature goes straight to the core of explicit knowledge production; Jaffe (1989), for example, concludes that proximity to university education positively affects spending on research and development as well as local innovativeness. Other approaches deal with knowledge and learning more implicitly. There is some evidence regarding localized human capital spillovers around ordinary workplaces; by drawing circles (the smallest of which extend five miles from the workplace) around each individual in their dataset, Rosenthal and Strange (2008) found that individual workers are significantly and positively affected by human capital spillovers from other workers surrounding them, but that this effect is subject to significant distance decay.

Second, the relationship between worker heterogeneity and density is an increasingly well-researched phenomenon. Jovanovic and Rob (1989) argue that meetings involving people of diverse human capital sets result in especially large productivity spillovers. Bacolod, Blum, and Strange (2009) find that individuals with occupations requiring knowledge-intensive skill sets boost their productivity more than others when locating in close proximity to other workers. Workers in cognitive and management-intensive industries are found to benefit significantly more from agglomerating as compared with workers in industries that emphasize motor skills, such as manufacturing workers.

The remainder of this essay deals in greater detail with the third proposition. Certain aspects of the agglomeration economics literature deal explicitly with the diffusion and communication of knowledge in urban as compared with nonurban areas. The tendency for urban workers to earn higher wages is referred to as the urban wage premium. When alternative explanations are controlled for, the remaining wage differential is viewed as the productivity spillovers associated with working in cities, part of which is simply learning from other workers. In conjunction with the statements made about the spatial friction of knowledge, part of the differential seems to be explained by human capital spillovers, diversity in the industrial composition, and the pairing of specialized individuals with more suitable employers (Glaeser & Maré, 2001; Helsley & Strange, 1990; Jacobs, 1969; Wheeler, 2001; Yankow, 2006).

These spillover effects are appropriately thought of as public-good attributes of economically dense environments. Romer (1990) notes that non-excludable inputs in the production process implies increasing returns to scale, since inputs can be replicated without additional cost, invalidating the "homogeneous of degree one" type production function. This line of thought dates back to Marshall (1920), who described how individuals in cities learn from each other and famously stated that "the mysteries of the trade become no mysteries; but are, as it were, in the air." Generally, a doubling of city size increases productivity by between three and eight percent, controlling for observable characteristics (Rosenthal & Strange, 2004). The relevant question is to what extent investors can tap into public goods such as matching and human capital spillovers.

Fig. 1 provides a schematic illustration of the link between various combinations of information/knowledge, means of communication and the time–distance sensitivity of information/knowledge.

The figure illustrates how combinations of information and knowledge become increasingly difficult to transfer efficiently between agents as the nature of the information becomes more complex. The simplest form of

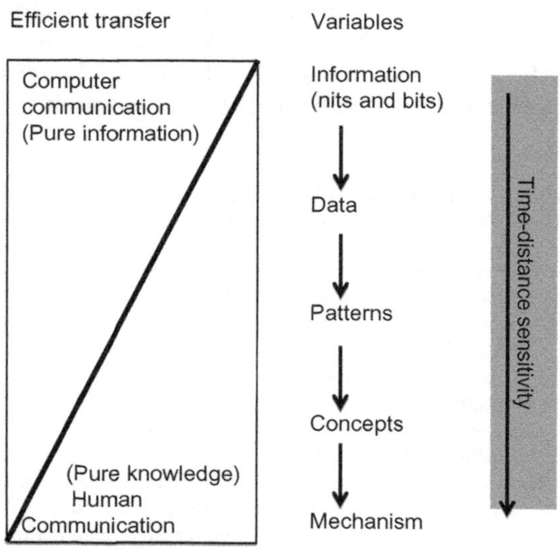

Fig. 1. Combinations of Information/Knowledge and Time–Distance Sensitivity. *Source*: Adapted from Andersson and Beckmann (2009).

information, a bit, is simply a binary variable with two possible values, such as 1 indicating true and 0 indicating false. Pure information can easily be transferred electronically across time and space with no consequences for the message sent, whereas tacit knowledge becomes difficult to transfer without direct human communication.

In their take on the importance of "talk" in the economy, McCloskey and Klamer (1995) argue for the importance of persuasion in economic activity and show how the concept itself seems to assume that knowledge is being communicated, that is, they note that there is no persuasion involved in making a computer process certain information. We argue that since access to finance in part is a process driven by persuasion, entrepreneurs seeking finance are bound by constraints imposed on them because of the local nature of knowledge.

THE KNOWLEDGE DIFFUSION CHAIN

An early observer of the knowledge diffusion process, Fritz Machlup (1962), categorizes different agents according to the degree that the message received by an agent is different from the message subsequently delivered (sent) by the same agent. Pure information can easily be transmitted without any change or loss of content or meaning, whereas some knowledge is difficult to transfer from one individual to another. The classifications are summarized in Table 1. As we shall see, these classifications have important

Table 1. Knowledge Conveyors in Machlup (1962).

Conveyor	Action
Transporter	A forwarder of a message. Delivers the exact same information as is received initially.
Transformer	Changes the form of the message received, but leaves the content intact.
Processor	Changes both form and content of the message received, though only by routine procedures.
Interpreter	Changes both form and content of the message received by use of own faculties and imagination.
Analyzer	Uses so much own judgment and intuition that the communicated message bears little resemblance to the message received.
Original creator	Uses so much "inventive genius and creative imagination" that only weak links can be found between what was received from different sources and what is communicated.

implications, both for our conceptions of knowledge and information, and for our understanding of the geographical constraints on the diffusion of knowledge.

It is clear that the further up the list in Table 1 we go, the more the material the agent deals with resembles pure information. Conversely, an original creator comes very close to dealing with the previously suggested definition of knowledge: the ability to transform old information into new information – in other words, the ability to engage in the process of recombining pieces of information into new knowledge. Machlup (1962) even remarks that we do not even think about something as knowledge in any real sense of the word if it is only available in the mind of one individual – that is, before its diffusion.

These classifications may be compared to the division in Polanyi (1967), who argues that certain forms of knowledge can be easier codified into information, while other forms are bound to be tacit, contextual, and embedded into its human carrier. Polanyi notes that knowledge of a theory can be internalized only after rigorous scrutiny and after it has been "extensively used to interpret experience."

Note how this observation is also well in line with the assertion in Andersson and Beckmann (2009); one of the reasons why the spread of knowledge is hampered by spatial friction is that it may require to be personally conveyed as knowledge *qua* knowledge, perhaps even "sold" on a face-to-face basis, starting from the original creator and further up the chain.

When an idea or a piece of knowledge – for example, the earth revolves around the sun – is sufficiently accepted, it may perhaps be repackaged as a piece of information and swiftly transferred by a transporter from point A to point B. All that the transporter would have to do would be to write that "the universe is heliocentric" on a piece of paper (or in an email) and send it to the relevant authority, but this was not the proper way for Copernicus, an original creator, to convey that knowledge.

Paraphrasing Machlup (1962), it might be the case that the transporter of information possesses an observation of a price and a quantity at a given point in time, and as we move further toward the original creator, we find individuals who analyze information in order to ascertain how to act in the face of such information.

Machlup's hierarchy harmonizes well with the remarks made above, regarding the spatial friction of knowledge. While the knowledge embodied in an original creator is subject to substantial distance decay, as we move up the chain the peculiarity of knowledge becomes less conspicuous.

The implication is that knowledge is communicated in very different ways, depending on where the knowledge is located between the original creator and the transporter. The previously noted need for face-to-face interaction is completely absent for the form of action optimally undertaken by a transporter.

Kirzner (1997) views the equilibrating process of entrepreneurial discovery essentially as independent actors improving their knowledge, or "pushing back the boundaries of sheer ignorance," sheer ignorance meaning that which was previously unknowable in the sense discussed above. The main conclusion is that an entrepreneurial opportunity must be viewed as strictly subjective; this point is where persuasion must necessarily enter the analysis. The next section relates this process to finance and the time–distance sensitivities involved in conveying knowledge of an opportunity that is inherently subjective.

KNOWLEDGE, GEOGRAPHY, AND INVESTMENTS

The Austrian view of the market as an equilibrating process in an out-of-equilibrium world has vastly enriched our understanding of entrepreneurship. The key point is that individuals perceive opportunities differently. Consequently, Shane and Venkataraman (2000) draw on Hayek and Kirzner in outlining "the promise of entrepreneurship as a field of research." They conclude from previous research that entrepreneurs may differ both in their access to information and in their cognitive profiles, meaning that different entrepreneurs will evaluate entrepreneurial opportunities differently. A useful way of assessing the relationship between entrepreneurship and investments lies in the role of the entrepreneur as a persuader (see, e.g., McCloskey & Klamer, 1995).

Translating the above analysis to the context of investments, it is reasonable to assume that one's access to finance depends on the nature of the asset that is being considered as an investment. As pointed out above, there is evidence that the knowledge formation process is most effective in geographically confined areas. Moreover, agents that act in a knowledge-intensive environment and with knowledge transfers stand to gain more from agglomeration economies than others. This has important implications for investment behavior.

The communication problem illustrates the need for information exchange between borrowers and entrepreneurs, and the need for knowledge about specific capital investments. How complex the knowledge exchange is will depend on the nature of the investment in a capital asset. We know from conventional investment theory that investments in physical assets that are easier to observe and value and are therefore less complicated to finance as compared with investments in intangible assets such as human capital. By implication this is all the more important for investors, entrepreneurs, and inventors in those parts of the economy that deal intensively with tacit knowledge, or where such knowledge is an essential part of the product being sold.[5]

Entrepreneurs seeking to finance their investments need to communicate their knowledge about the venture to potential investors. McCloskey and Klamer (1995) remark that persuasion lies at the core of what entrepreneurs do: the ability to convince others that it is in *their* interest to support *your* particular venture.

The entrepreneurial process brings new knowledge into existence (see Boettke, 2002). For the entrepreneur to be able to exploit this new knowledge it is often necessary for him or her to find someone willing and able to provide the necessary financial capital. In incumbent firms, the need to communicate knowledge about the product or service that it provides is presumably less problematic. Recalling that new knowledge is likely to be more tacit, and hence more distance-sensitive than knowledge that can be codified into information, we would argue that the knowledge that is needed in order to start a firm is more distance-sensitive than the knowledge of how to continue the current operations of an incumbent firm.

This difference in the type of "information-knowledge asymmetries" that agents that seek funding face may provide an expatiation as to why venture capital investments have been found to require spatial proximity. Monitoring investments in new firms in the early stages of their development may be associated with unusually high monitoring and other transaction costs (Fritsch & Schilder, 2008). This would imply that spatial proximity is more important in the early stages of firms' lifecycles than later on (Sorensen & Stuart, 2001).

This reasoning is also consistent with the observation that small firms face greater liquidity constraints than large firms (Gomes, 2001). One explanation for this is that large firms have overcome their initial difficulties in communicating with investors. Studies have also found that corporate investments are sensitive to the spatial proximity of their owners (see Carlin, Charlton, & Mayer, 2006).

CONCLUSION

This article assesses investment theory from the perspective of the Austrian school of economics. We argue that Hayek's insights regarding the importance of local knowledge have important implications for spatial economics and for investment theory. Hayek argued that local knowledge could not be rendered into statistics and therefore it could not be conveyed to a planning authority. We argue that a similar constraint applies to the financier of an investment. We further argue that a distinction between information and knowledge is necessary for the analysis; an implication is that the diffusion of knowledge is hampered by spatial friction, unlike the sharing of information. Emphasizing the geographical implications of viewing knowledge as distinct from information, we explore the role of the spatial proximity of finance. In the entrepreneurial discovery process new knowledge is brought into existence. If the entrepreneur lacks the necessary funds, this new knowledge must somehow be conveyed to potential investors. In contrast to pure information this knowledge cannot be easily transmitted; instead, it becomes necessary for the entrepreneur to persuade potential investors.

This view has three implications for our analysis:

1. The knowledge formation process is most effective in a confined geographic area.
2. Agents that deal intensively with knowledge exchange stand to gain most from agglomeration economies.
3. Since the investment process must include persuasion and transmission of knowledge from the entrepreneur to the investor and since entrepreneurial opportunities are not evenly spread out across space, knowledge flows that potentially benefit investors flow more intensively in economically dense areas.

We conclude that points 1 and 2 are well-researched phenomena in the agglomeration economics literature and that a growing body of evidence already supports both propositions. Point 3 is, on the other hand, rarely addressed in the literature.

Inspired by Machlup (1962), we view investment as a process where different combinations of information and knowledge are communicated at different stages. A novel idea is more effectively transmitted to entrepreneurs in areas where knowledge spillovers are frequent, and those same ideas are more easily communicated to a greater number of investors in the same type of geographical areas.

An intriguing implication is that start-ups that are trying to exploit a new market niche with a product that is unusually rich in tacit knowledge should benefit much more from dense environments than start-ups that produce more traditional manufactured goods (even though such goods may also be characterized by substantial tacit knowledge flows). Such environments will provide proximity to consumers, labor, and investors; proximity is needed for persuading the relevant actors. Our analysis thus supports the view that entrepreneurship research cannot be complete without the recognition of a spatial – as well as an Austrian – perspective.

NOTES

1. An investment is expected to generate a stream of future cash flows, $C(t)$. Since investment, I, represents an outlay at time 0, the relation can be expressed as the negative cash flow $-C_0$. The net present value (NPV) can then be written as: $\text{NPV} = -C_0 + \int_0^\infty C(t)e^{(g-r)t}dt$, where g denotes the growth rate and r denotes the opportunity cost of capital (the discount rate). As long as the expected return on investment, i, is greater than the opportunity cost of capital, r, the investment will be worthwhile. When $r = I$, the $\text{NPV} = 0$. The return on investment, i, is equivalent to Keynes's *marginal efficiency of capital* and Fisher's *internal rate of return*. From the PV of an investment, I, can be written as $C_1/(r-g)$, implying that $\text{PV}/I = 1$.

2. Keynes (1936) and many economists after him argue that the crucial issue is how individuals form expectations. In a world of "Knightian" uncertainty probabilities of alternative outcomes cannot be calculated. According to some economists, this leads to erratic shifts in expectations, which render the notion of an optimal capital stock meaningless.

3. It should be noted that the notion of investments as an adjustment process toward an optimal capital stock does not require or imply that equilibrium is ever reached.

4. Of course, a venture capitalist might outsource the acquisition of such knowledge to an entrepreneur.

5. Williamson's (1979) discussion about idiosyncratic knowledge may, at this point, enlighten us as to why markets not traditionally thought of as driven by tacit knowledge may still be characterized by such transactions.

REFERENCES

Alchian, A. A. (1955). The rate of interest, Fisher's rate of return over cost, and Keynes' internal rate of return. *American Economic Review*, *45*(5), 938–943.

Andersson, Å. E., & Beckmann, M. J. (2009). *Economics of knowledge: Theory, models and measurements*. Chelterham, UK: Edward Elgar.

Andersson, D. E. (2005). The spatial nature of entrepreneurship. *Quarterly Journal of Austrian Economics*, *8*(2), 21–34.

Bacolod, M., Blum, B. S., & Strange, W. C. (2009). Skills in the city. *Journal of Urban Economics*, *65*(2), 136–153.

Baddeley, M. C. (2003). *Investment theory and analysis*. New York, NY: Palgrave Macmillan.

Boettke, P. J. (2002). Information and knowledge: Austrian economics in search of its uniqueness. *Review of Austrian Economics*, *15*(4), 263–274.

Böhm-Bawerk, E. von (1890). *Capital and interest*. London, UK: Macmillan.

Böhm-Bawerk, E. von (1891). *The positive theory of capital*. London, UK: Macmillan.

Brainard, W. W., & Tobin, J. (1968). Pitfalls in financial model building. *American Economic Review*, *58*(2), 99–122.

Carlin, W., Charlton, A., & Mayer, C. (2006). *Capital markets, ownership and distance*. Discussion Paper No. 5764. Center for Economic Policy Research, London, UK.

Desrochers, P. (2001). Geographical proximity and the transmission of tacit knowledge. *Review of Austrian Economics*, *14*(1), 25–46.

Fisher, I. (1930). *The theory of interest*. New York, NY: Macmillan.

Fritsch, M., & Schilder, D. (2008). Does venture capital investment really require spatial proximity? An empirical investigation. *Environment and Planning*, *40*, 2114–2131.

Glaeser, E. L., & Maré, D. C. (2001). Cities and skills. *Journal of Labor Economics*, *19*(2), 316–342.

Gomes, J. F. (2001). Financing investment. *American Economic Review*, *91*(5), 1263–1285.

Hayek, F. A. (1937). Economics and knowledge. *Economica*, *4*(13), 33–54.

Hayek, F. A. (1941). *The pure theory of capital*. London, UK: Routledge.

Hayek, F. A. (1945). The use of knowledge in society. *American Economic Review*, *35*(4), 519–530.

Hayek, F. A. (1960). *The constitution of liberty*. Chicago, IL: University of Chicago Press.

Helsley, R. W., & Strange, W. C. (1990). Matching and agglomeration economies in a system of cities. *Regional Science and Urban Economics*, *20*(2), 189–212.

Jacobs, J. (1969). *The economy of cities*. New York, NY: Random House/Vintage Books.

Jaffe, A. B. (1989). Real effects of academic research. *American Economic Review*, *79*(5), 957–970.

Jorgenson, D. (1963). Capital theory and investment behavior. *American Economic Review*, *53*(2), 247–259.

Jorgenson, D. (1967). The theory of investment behavior. In R. Ferber (Ed.), *Determinants of investment behavior*. New York, NY: Colombia University Press.

Jovanovic, B., & Rob, R. (1989). The growth and diffusion of knowledge. *Review of Economic Studies*, *56*(4), 569–582.

Keynes, J. M. (1936). *The genreal theory of employment, interest and money*. London: Macmillan.

Kirzner, I. M. (1973). *Competition and entrepreneurship*. Chicago, IL: The University of Chicago Press.

Kirzner, I. M. (1997). Entrepreneurial discovery and the competitive market process: An Austrian approach. *Journal of Economic Literature*, *35*(1), 60–85.

Kogut, B., & Zander, U. (1992). Knowledge of the firm, combinative capabilities, and the replication of technology. *Organization Science*, *3*(3), 383–397.

Levine, R., & Beck, T. (2004). Stock markets, banks and growth. *Journal of Banking and Finance*, *28*, 423–442.

Machlup, F. (1962). *The production and distribution of knowledge in the United States*. Princeton, NJ: Princeton University Press.

Markowitz, H. M. (1952). Portfolio selection. *Journal of Finance*, *7*(1), 77–91.

Marshall, A. (1920). *Principles of economics* (8th ed). London, UK: Macmillan.

McCloskey, D., & Klamer, A. (1995). One quarter of GDP is persuasion. *American Economic Review*, *85*(2), 191–195.

Mueller, D. C., & Reardon, E. (1993). Rates of return on corporate investments. *Southern Economic Review*, *60*(2), 430–453.

Myers, S. C., & Majluf, N. S. (1984). Corporate financing and investment decisions when firms have information that investors do not have. *Journal of Financial Economics*, *13*, 187–221.

Polanyi, M. (1967). *The tacit dimension*. London, UK: Routledge.

Rauch, J. E. (1993). Productivity gains from geographic concentration of human capital: Evidence from the cities. *Journal of Urban Economics*, *34*(3), 380–400.

Romer, P. M. (1990). Endogenous technological change. *Journal of Political Economy*, *98*(5), S71–S102.

Rosenthal, S. S., & Strange, W. C. (2004). Evidence on the nature and sources of agglomeration economies. In J.-F. Thisse (Ed.), *Handbook of regional and urban economics* (Vol. 4, pp. 2119–2171). Amsterdam: Elsevier.

Rosenthal, S. S., & Strange, W. C. (2008). The attenuation of human capital spillovers. *Journal of Urban Economics*, *64*(2), 373–389.

Samuelson, P. (1939a). Interaction between multiplier analysis and the principle of acceleration. *Review of Economics and Statistics*, *21*(2), 75–78.

Samuelson, P. (1939b). A synthesis of the principle of acceleration and the multiplier. *Journal of Political Economy*, *47*(6), 786–797.

Shane, S., & Venkataraman, S. (2000). The Promise of entrepreneurship as a field of research. *Academy of Management Review*, *25*(1), 217–226.

Sorensen, O., & Stuart, T. E. (2001). Syndication networks and the spatial distribution of venture capital investments. *American Journal of Sociology*, *106*, 1546–1588.

Sowell, T. (1980). *Knowledge and decisions*. New York, NY: Basic Books.

Tobin, J. (1969). A general equilibrium approach to monetary theory. *Journal of Money, Credit and Banking*, *1*(1), 15–29.

Wheeler, C. H. (2001). Search, sorting, and urban agglomeration. *Journal of Labor Economics*, *19*(4), 879–899.

Wicksell, K. (1934). *Lectures on political economy* (Vol. 1). London, UK: Routledge and Kegan Paul.

Wicksell, K. (1954). *Value, capital and rent*. London, UK: Allen and Unwin.

Williamson, O. E. (1979). Transaction-cost economics: The governance of contractual relations. *Journal of Law and Economics*, *22*, 233–261.

Yankow, J. J. (2006). Why do cities pay more? An empirical examination of some competing theories of the urban wage premium. *Journal of Urban Economics*, *60*(2), 139–161.